'PRINCELINGS, PRI

THE TIVYSIDE GENTRY IN THEIR COMMUNITY

'Princelings, Privilege and Power . . .'

The Tivyside Gentry in their Community

Leslie Baker-Jones

First impression—1999

ISBN 1 85902 381 9

Printed in Wales by
Gomer Press, Llandysul, Ceredigion

I aelodau dosbarthiadau
addysg barhaus Prifysgol Cymru,
ac i ddiolch am a ddysgais ganddynt

Acknowledgements

This book is based on a thesis submitted for the degree of PhD of the University of Wales. I owe a great debt of gratitude to Dr D. W. Howell of the University of Wales, Swansea, for suggesting 'The Tivyside Gentry' as a subject of research, for his advice and unfailing concern in supervising the work, and especially, for devoting so much of his valuable time in reading the typescript of this book and making valuable recommendations.

I wish to record the encouragement and support I received from the late Professor D. J. V. Jones, and my indebtedness to the late Major Francis Jones, Wales Herald Extraordinary, for information relating to the background and origin of some west-Wales families. I was greatly helped by many elderly inhabitants of 'Tivyside' who spoke of their recollections of the old gentry families, of the jollification and grand occasions celebrated in the mansions, as well as the tensions and constraints of life in the vicinity of the 'Plas'.

The staff of the National Library of Wales, the Dyfed Archives and Libraries' Service, the Public Record Office, the Society of Antiquaries and the Dr Williams' Library, London, deserve my thanks for their assistance and courtesy. The staff of the Royal Commission on Ancient and Historic Monuments, Aberystwyth, helped me greatly by allowing me to make use of their information files on 'Tivyside' houses.

My thanks are also due to those who kindly gave permission for the publication of photographs in this book, and to Mrs Valerie Pelter, of Drefach, Felindre for the drawing of Castell Hywel. There are instances where it has been impossible to trace or contact the copyright holder. The publishers apologise foe this and, if notified, will be pleased to rectify any errors or omissions at the earliest opportunity.

I wish to record my appreciation of the work of Mr Brynmor Jones, Aberystwuth, in compiling the Index. Above all thanks are due to the staff of the Gomer Press for their skilled workmanship, and to Dr Dyfed Elis-Gruffydd for his advice and guidance in bringing this volume through the press.

For any faults the author must bear sole responsibility.

L. B-J

Contents

Preface

The aim of this study is to examine the nature of gentry dominance, its rise and decline, in 'Tivyside', a remote region of south-west Wales, from the period around 1700 until the 1930s. An attempt will be made to analyse the 'gentry' as a social class, their concepts of gentility, and to see how this class changed in its composition and structure over the years through marriage, land purchase and wider social and cultural horizons. As the foundation stone of 'gentility' was primarily the possession of land, one has to look at the means by which land was acquired, and how it devolved over many years. The administration of the landed estate, by the squire himself as farmer, by agents and stewards, will be examined to determine how far the squire was an 'improving' landlord, using his land to the best advantage in terms of its profitability to himself and the well-being of his tenants. Moreover, how far the economy of the estate was supported by other sources of income from commerce, trade and industry will be an important line of enquiry. The relationship between landlord and tenant, the nature of tenancies, rent and conditions in leases, will together show whether the estate was run selfishly to provide, merely, for the display and consumption of the squire, or wisely to benefit both landowner and tenant. The cumulative effect of dissatisfaction and hardship, as will be seen in some cases, came to the fore in evidence before the Welsh Land Commission in the 1890s.

The lifestyle of the squire in his *plas* (small manor house) and mansion, his aesthetic and cultural pursuits, his use of leisure in a variety of indoor and outdoor activities, his morality and defence of religious commitment, need to be examined against the background of native Welsh culture.

Lastly, as the squire was the natural leader in the community, holding important public offices such as that of magistrate, and, in a few cases, as a member of parliament, his record in this public domain will come under scrutiny. Above all, the 'character' of gentry dominance has to be assessed in terms of concern for the public good in the level of their patronage of schools and religious causes, the degree of their consideration for the welfare of the poor, conscientious regard for the community, or blatant selfishness, personal ambition and overweening *hauteur* towards their inferiors. These are difficult matters and no absolutely certain verdict for or against the gentry class as a whole can be given. Members of this class were, like those of every other class in society, the products of their age and of causes over which they had no control.

List of Illustrations

Abbreviations

Aber RO	Aberystwyth Record Office
Arch Camb	Archaeologica Cambrensis
BBCS	Bulletin of the Board of Celtic Studies
BIHR	Bulletin of the Institute of Historical Research
Cd Ad	Cardigan and Tivyside Advertiser
Camb LR	Cambrian Law Review
Cm Jnl	Carmarthen Journal
Carms Antiq	Carmarthenshire Antiquary
Carms Hist	Carmarthenshire Historian
CRO	Carmarthen Record Office
DWB	Dictionary of Welsh Biography
EcHR	Economic History Review
ER	Enumerators' (Census) Returns
FG	Francis Green Papers
FL	Folklife, A Journal of Ethnological Studies
HRO	Haverfordwest Record Office
Hist Jnl	Historical Journal
JHSChW	Journal of the Historical Society of the Church in Wales
JMH	Journal of Modern History
JWBS	Journal of the Welsh Bibliographical Society
NLW	National Library of Wales
NLWJ	National Library of Wales Journal
P and P	Past and Present
Pembs Hist	Pembrokeshire Historian
Proc Wes Hist Socy	Proceedings of the Wesley Historical Society
PRO	Public Record Office
R.C.A.H.M.	Royal Commission on Ancient and Historic Monuments
R.C.A.P.L.	Royal Commission on the Administration of the Poor Law
R.C.I.S.W.	Report of Commissioners of Inquiry for South Wales, 1844
R.C.C.I.	Report of Committee on Commons' Inclosure, 1844
R.C.I.S.Ed.W.	Report of Committee of Inquiry into the State of Education in Wales, 1847.
R.O.L.	Return of Owners of Land, 1873.

R.C.L.W.M.	Evidence and Report of the Royal Commission on Land in Wales and Monmouthshire, 1894-96
Tr Caerns Hist Soc	Transactions of the Caernarfonshire Historical Society
THSC	Transactions of the Honourable Society of Cymmrodorion
WHR	Welsh History Review
Wms. Lib	Dr Williams' Library
WWHR	West Wales Historical Records

Note—The traditional spelling of the names of gentry houses has been retained, e.g. Clynfyw, Coedmore, Ffynone, Manereifed, Plas Llangoedmore, etc. Rhosygilwen was also known as Morgeneu in the early years of this century. Any variation in the spelling, e.g. Blaenbulan, Blaenbylan, Ffosybleiddied, Ffosybleiddiaid, etc., follows the original mss. The families of Cwmawen, Cwmyar, Gellydywyll, Gernos, Llysnewydd, Penybenglog, etc., variously spelt their surname as Lewis or Lewes up to the end of the eighteenth century. The one-time occupants of Llwynduris were known as Birt or Byrtt.

Conversion Table

12 pennies (d.)	= 1 shilling (s.)
20 shillings	= 1 pound (£1)
21 shillings	= 1 guinea

Section 1

The Gentry:
the Structure and Values of their Class

Introduction

The sight of a ruined mansion and its bramble-covered walks still arouse nostalgia amongst certain people, and sentimental memories survive of the benevolent, paternalistic squire who held sway as landowner and patriarch of the community.[1] The disappearance of the country gentleman has meant, to some at least, that an honourable, picturesque, humane and protective influence and a disinterested personal relationship has disappeared which no modern experiments in government and public welfare can replace.[2] Not only was the squire the heir to flocks and herds and broad acres, but also to the goodwill of the community who responded with special regard towards him.[3] In exchange for the squire's patronage, protection and concern towards his 'homagers', the latter responded with deference, respect, loyalty and even awe towards him.

The question is whether rosy-hued recollections of elegant mansions, tea parties, croquet on velvet lawns, largesse for the poor and the glamour of hunt balls, horses and hounds cloud the reality of underlying tensions and the forced subservience of an underprivileged servile *gwerin* (common people) towards a parasite upper class.[4] H. M. Vaughan's apologia for gentry dominance, its Englishness, its unwavering support for Tory politics and Church of England dogma,[5] revived the bitter tensions of an earlier generation and failed, on the whole, in its attempt to protect the good name of the gentry.

Radical, nonconformist and nationalistic reaction to Vaughan's special pleading was immediate, and reaffirmed that the Welsh gentry were Tory, anti-Welsh churchmen, caring only for sport, and inimical to the claims of Wales as a nation. They had held aloof from nonconformity and had been content to see the demise of the Welsh language. They had cared little for the renaissance of Welsh culture. They had lived in their mansions as a pampered class reaping what they had not sown.[6] A modern politician has repeated such charges— the gentry's lack of identification with Welsh Wales; their lack of leadership and responsibility as Anglicised exploiters of Wales and its people, without giving anything in return.[7]

Professor Glanmor Williams summarizes the character and contribution of the Welsh gentry with more detachment and objectivity. As a class they were pedigree-conscious and proud of their ancient lineage with the insignia of arms and mottoes. They accepted the praise of native poets and lavished patronage and hospitality in return. Over the centuries they were an everchanging class, socially mobile, deriving new blood and new wealth from families in trade, industry and the professions. As landowners they held paternalistic sway over their tenantry and the local community. As pillars of society they supported the constitution, the common law and the established church. But as Welsh nonconformist Wales became more radical there followed a clash of religious allegiance between Anglican landowners and the mass of the populace. The conflict was between a privileged élite and 'y werin' with widely different bases to their respective cultures. The gentry's 'limited concept of Welshness' could not protect them against the rising tide of Welsh linguistic and democratic claims.[8]

The aim of this study is to examine the emergence of a powerful élite in that area of south-west Wales known as 'Tivyside'; to identify a social class and assess its composition and character. Evidence will be examined to reveal how this élite attained, held and lost its power. The nature and quality of their rule and the extent and duration of the deference of social inferiors have to be looked into. One has to question the indictment that the gentry governed by 'a sort of divine right [believing] that the land . . . was made for their convenience and pleasure . . .'[9]

Macaulay's caricature of the seventeenth-century squire—uncouth, gross and ignorant,[10] has to be weighed against the 'gentil, parfit knight' of Victorian romanticism. The metamorphosis of the gentry class in the lower Teifi valley will be examined, stage by stage, against the backcloth of continuity and change, consensus and conflict, disaffection and dissent, from around 1700 up to the 1930s.

NOTES AND SOURCES

[1]Reminiscences of the late Mr Esau Evans, Alderman Mrs M. Brynmor Williams, BEM and Mrs N. Young, Felindre.

[2]G. L. Lampson: *Life in the Country*, 1948. Ch. 1, 'The extinction of the country squire', pp. 7-9.

[3]P. H. Ditchfield: *The Old English Country Squire*, 1912, pp. 3-6.

[4]D. Parry-Jones: *Welsh Country Upbringing*, 2nd ed., 1949, p. 76.

[5]H. M. Vaughan: *The South Wales Squires*, 1926. Herbert Millingchamp Vaughan (1870-1948), the squire of Plas Llangoedmore, author and historian. 'Who's Who in Wales' 1920.

[6]Anon: *The Welsh Outlook*, August 1926.

[7]J. G. Evans: *Aros Mae*, 1971, p. 220.

[8]Glanmor Williams: *Religion, Language and Nationality in Wales*, 1979, pp. 148-70; R. Warner: *A Walk through Wales in August 1797*, 1798. p. 95.

[9]RCLWM, 1896, iii [Qu. 44, 312].

[10]T. B. Macaulay: *History of England*, 1861 vol. i, pp. 320-22.

The Emergence of a Ruling Class

Wales

With the disruption of tribal society in pre-Tudor times, the letting of the lord's demesne to tenants and the commutation of dues and services into payments, the rise of a gentry class had already begun.[1] The sale of crown lands, the enclosure of wastes and commons, the beginning of colonial enterprise and foreign trade in the sixteenth century, were factors which provided the economic climate suitable for the acquisition of new wealth by those who had the enterprise and acumen to grasp the opportunity. The replacement of *gavelkind* by the English legal devices of primogeniture and entail helped to consolidate land in fewer hands. The complexities of changing laws and a fluid society, and the civil commotions of the seventeenth century gave full scope for bullying, intrigue and sharp practice in the consequent scramble for land.[2] Within the new shires the key position of power, namely that of member of parliament, high sheriff, lord lieutenant and magistrate, could only be held by those who owned land. Side by side with landed wealth came power and prestige within the 'shire state'. Socially, the involvement of this powerful group with county business, led to an aristocracy of 'county' gentry displaying a cohesive and exclusive class outlook. Gradually, contact with other Wesh landowners in the Council of Wales and the Marches, as well as at Westminster and other centres, led to wider relationships and the intermarriage of families, not only within Wales but also with those beyond Offa's Dyke.

As a result, this aristocratic landowning class was to rule Wales for over three centuries—a 'rentier caste' who lived mainly on rents paid by those who actually cultivated the land.[3] In addition to the accumulation of large tracts of land through inheritance, auspicious marriage and judicious purchase, the pride of the gentry class in patrician sentiment, concepts of gentility and ancient genealogy further accentuated class distinction. But as wealth in terms of land-ownership became more and more the mainstay of status, power and influence, the glamour of ancient ancestry and the glow of heraldry survived as the embellishment of power rather than its reality. As the ownership of land became concentrated in fewer hands, there emerged a dispossessed class of 'genteel poor', the Welsh 'shentilman' of English satire,[4] proud of his descent, but, fading in importance into the social obscurity of impoverished yeoman and labourer.

Increased wealth from land allowed the gentry greater leisure and the means to move in wider social and cultural circles—the ancient universities and the Inns of Court. They were able to hold government and political office and to enjoy foreign travel. As a result the Welsh language became less vital in their lives. It was no longer the medium of legal argument, intellectual discourse and literary expression through *cywydd* and *awdl*.[5]

Nationalist historians and politicians have blamed Tudor legislation and the 'traitorous' defection of the gentry away from their native language and heritage as the prime cause of the decline of the Welsh language. A closer scrutiny of contemporary movements suggests that the clause in the Act of Union making English the official language of Wales did not anglicise the ruling classes overnight.[6] Patronage of bards and 'literati' continued, although on a diminished scale. There was no contempt of things Welsh, save that in a polite, urbane society canons of 'civilitie' demanded that a cultured man had to possess knowledge of English.[7] As a result there developed a sad social dichotomy in Welsh life as between the Welsh-speaking 'gwerin' on the one hand and the anglicised gentry, the supposedly natural leaders of the people, on the other.

Polemicists for Welsh culture have regarded the 'language clause' in the Act of 1536 as a Pandora's box which released all the plagues and perversions in subsequent Welsh history.[8] However, it can be argued that the progressive and gradual use of English as a language of 'curtisie, humanite and civillite', the hallmark of gentryhood, had come to be regarded as the basis of English and Renaissance ideas of a gentleman, and an important ingredient in his social evaluation over the next few centuries.[9]

In other ways, too, perspectives were changing rapidly. Colonial expansion attracted gentlemen adventurers to the Americas or to the East Indies. The fortunes of trading companies, such as the Hudson's Bay and the East India, lured many with stories of fabulous riches and of lands that could be acquired by conquest. In 1617, for example, an adventurous west Wales squire, Sir William Vaughan of Golden Grove, founded a north American colony of 'Cambriol',[10] and 'Tivyside' gentry in time also sought adventure and wealth beyond the seas.

The challenge to the energetic and ambitious was irresistible, especially to the younger sons of the gentry who were barred from any patrimony on account of legal arrangements. Wars against the Spaniards and the Dutch in the mid-seventeenth century demanded an efficient and strong army and navy. A professional class of soldier and sailor could be drawn from the educated gentry families, who were attracted by adventure and material gain. In this country, London, the centre of political, economic and social life, was a magnet to younger sons wishing to make a fortune in commerce or industry. In some instances they succeeded so well as to be able to found new estates in their native localities.[11]

Up to the mid-eighteenth century the typical stay-at-home squire held patriarchal sway over his own demesne; and although he could afford pastimes such as hunting and fishing, his lifestyle was similar to that of the larger freeholder.[12] The designations 'esquire', 'gentleman' and 'yeoman' are often blurred and indistinguishable. His *plas* was modest, simply furnished and situated amongst byres and barns, hay lofts and pig cots, unlike the larger mansion of a later period.[13]

As the political masters of the shire, the gentry were drawn to the county town for the transaction of county business and social diversion until gradually, however, increased wealth and extending horizons prompted them to look towards London and metropolitan values as the models to imitate.

In general, the gentry class in Wales was poorer than its English counterpart, and the economic and social climate was to erode the status of many in the years from about 1680 to 1740.[14] In economic terms some of the Welsh gentry belonged properly to the ranks of the yeoman-freeholders. The income of many estates in the seventeenth century could be as low as £100 a year.[15] Of the original 200 baronets created by James I in 1612 (with the basic requirement of an estate worth £1000 a year) only 12 were Welsh, and only 37 Welsh baronets were created out of a total of 866 in 1682.[16] Not one squire from 'Tivyside' was able to qualify.

Some of the inferior or lesser gentry became mere ordinary farmers, often having to sell or mortgage their land to more substantial neighbours with the result that the ancestral *plas* declined in status to that of a farm house.[17] Correspondingly, the more prosperous gentry, conscious of their position and influence in the county, acquired the prejudices and notions of a superior caste at the top of a hierarchical pyramid working downwards to the labourer and farm worker. The structure of society was thereby changing in a flux of upward and downward mobility. The upper classes absorbed from below, and because of changing circumstances some of them were reduced to a lower order.[18] Among the middling folk were the clergy, many of gentry stock, whose livings were often in the gift of the squire. Both parson and squire were essential pillars of the church and the constitution.

By the late seventeenth and eighteenth centuries, powerful gentry with substantial rent rolls, coveted seats in parliament which would give them influence on a national scale. County elections were to become struggles between rival clans and families, in which the animosity of the less wealthy was, at times, concentrated against the great.[19] Gentry and county magnates formed alliances to 'preserve the interest' by means of a chain of deference and support to the leader. As in the days of the feudal due of *cymorth* or *cymhortha*,[20] a candidate standing for parliament led his supporters to the polls to vote for him by means of threats, promises or bribes in exchange for patronage, favours, places and pensions for relations and dependants.[21]

Party politics were still in embryo and in the eighteenth century there was no clear cut political significance in the labels 'Whig' and 'Tory'. The protection and improvement of property were the main considerations. Tories supported church and king, while the Whigs favoured religious tolerance, and the interests of trade and commerce; but it was kinship, group and personal loyalty which really mattered in contests for the representation of the shire at Westminster.[22]

'Tivyside'

'Tivyside', according to H. M. Vaughan, meant 'the broad valley of the lower Teifi stretching from Llandysul to the river's mouth below Cardigan Town'. But, for the purposes of this book, the area extends as far as Llanybydder and even Lampeter, on account of blood and family relationships, social and cultural ties, political alignment, landownership, and the rights connected therewith which formed a bond between the gentry as a class apart from the rest of the community.

The river Teifi has over the centuries been the force unifying the inhabitants of the riparian administrative divisions of south Cardiganshire, north Carmarthenshire and north Pembrokeshire.[23] Without too distinct cultural divisions, save variations of dialect within the broad Demetian form, the area of 'Tivyside' embraced a typical Welsh community with its market towns of Cardigan, Newcastle-Emlyn, Llandysul, Llanybydder and Lampeter. It extended westward to the coastal parishes of Llandysilio-gogo and Llangrannog, continuing in a south-westerly direction towards the ancient town of Newport, enclosed by the ramparts of the Preseli range and the uplands of north-west Carmarthenshire and south Cardiganshire.

This diversity of landscape, with sea-faring occupations along the coastal strip, agriculture, flannel-weaving and ancillary crafts in the valleys and hillsides (not to mention the short-lived industrial activity in the form of tin-works and slate quarrying in Llechryd and Cilgerran) were never divisive forces.

'Tivyside' is not so much a geographical expression as an area of close social, religious, economic and human relationships. A proliferation of gentry houses existed along the valleys of the Teifi and its tributaries, and these were for centuries the homes of a ruling class.

From Tudor times a distinct gentry presence and pattern of landownership can be traced and of privileged people dwelling in family mansions which singled them out from the rest of society[24] Allowing for the 'mythology' of genealogical claims, a concentration of families connected by ties of common descent survived for centuries in the Teifi valley as in the rest of Wales.[25] They were the descendants of tribal chiefs and princelings like Cadifor ap Dinawal, Elystan Glodrydd, Gwynfardd Dyfed or Ednywain ap Bradwen (amongst others), who survived because they possessed the 'wit and enterprise to seize the economic basis of their dominion over a long period'.[26] On the other hand some families disappeared because of economic or biological factors, political or civil strife.

Shrievalty lists between 1540 and 1701 reflect the rise of families such as the owners of the estates of Blaenpant, Bronwydd, Noyadd Trefawr, Abernant-bychan, Gernos, Cilgwyn and Llwyngwair.[27] Amongst the families in decline were Vaughan of Cilgerran, Gwynne of St Dogmaels, Gwyon of Llanfechan and Phillips of Dolhaidd, who no longer possessed their former economic strength to hold power in the governance of the counties.

Parliamentary representation from 1545 to 1701 was partly in the control of only a few 'Tivyside' families. Thus, Dafydd ap Llwyd of Castell Hywel was M.P. for Cardiganshire in 1545; Thomas Revell of Forest, Cilgerran, was M.P. for Pembrokeshire from 1584 to1588 and Sir John Lewis, Knt. of Abernant-bychan was M.P. for Cardiganshire from 1603 to 1614. The Lewis clan of Abernant-bychan held the seat in about eight parliaments against the more powerful non-Tivyside houses of Gogerddan and Crosswood.[28] Although three of the four Cardigan Boroughs (Cardigan, Atpar and Lampeter) were situated in the Teifi valley, it was only for a short period, from 1689 to 1701, that the seat was held by Hector Phillips of The Priory, Cardigan and John Lewis of Coedmore.[29]

Participation in the Civil War reflects considerably upon the status and importance of the gentry involved. Traditional loyalty to the Tudors and their Stuart descendants prompted the Welsh gentry to rally to the king's side. Griffith Evans of Penwenallt in 'Tivyside' known as 'Captain Tory' . . . 'fought and bled' for his king.[30] Conscious of diminishing hopes of royal favour, sinecures and positions of profit, the gentry of 'Tivyside' vacillated in their loyalty to the contestants according to the strength of the prevailing wind. Constitutional issues were of secondary importance.[31] As the fortunes of the parliamentarians prospered, George Bowen of Llwyngwair, Thomas Warren of Trewern, John Lewis of Coedmore, to name but a few, supported them. James Phillips of The Priory, in Cardigan, was singled out for his sense of public duty rather than private gain, and although a strong parliamentarian was '. . . one that had the fortune to be in with the tymes yet thrived by none . . .' David Lloyd of Alltyrodyn was a royalist who had to pay a 'composition fee' of £17 for the recovery of his estate.[32] As circumstances changed and there was hope of a restored monarchy, some of the 'Tivyside' gentry shouted with the current noise, but, political loyalties apart, what is significant is the existence of a strong and established gentry class.[33] Genealogical collections point to the existence of a large number of 'plasau' in the area, the homes of minor squires proud of their ancient lineage. From the evidence of map makers like Blome (1677) and Adams (1700) the Hearth Tax Returns (1670) as well as the names of the Land Tax Commissioners (1702) there existed between twenty and thirty houses of well-established and important gentry.[34]

From the Hearth Tax Returns of 1670[35] (see table opposite) some broad indication of relative gentry status is possible. Allowing for a natural reluctance to give information about the size of respective houses, to the assessors or 'chimney men', as they were called, it is reasonable to assume that they were larger than the returns suggest. Less than three hearths would show an economic level which would provide only minimum comfort, although 'esquires' and 'gentlemen' are found within this category. A total of 10 hearths and upwards would point to considerable affluence. At a lower level the squirearchy merged into an almost illimitable group of persons described as 'gentlemen'.[36]

Hearth Tax Returns 1670

Householder	Parish	Number of hearths	Possible identification
Cardiganshire			
David Lloyd, esq.	Llandysul uwch Cerdin	3	Castell Hywel
John Lewis, esq.	Llangrannog	5	Cwmawen
John Williams, esq.	Penbryn	7	Abernant bychan
John Lloyd, esq.	Llandyfriog	5	Cilgwyn
Magdalen Lloyd, widow	Llangunllo	8	Bronwydd
John Lewis, gent.	Llangunllo	7	Gernos
Reignal Jenkins, esq.	Llandugwydd	7	Blaenpant
Gwenllian Morgan, widow	Aberporth	4	Plas Aberporth
James Phillips, esq.	Cardigan town	11	The Priory
Carmarthenshire			
Thomas Lewis, gent.	Llangeler	4	Llysnewydd
James Lewis, gent.	Cenarth	5	Gellydowyll
John Phillips, gent.	Penboyr	7 in 2 houses	Dôlhaidd-isaf Cryngae
Evan Jones, gent.	Llanfihangel Yorath	3	Llether-neuadd
Pembrokeshire			
James Lloyd, esq.	Llanfihangel Penbedw and Llangolman	8	Cilrhiwe
David Morgans, esq.	Clydai	4	Coedllwyd
William Owen, esq.	Nevern	10	Henllys or Penpedwast
James Bowen, esq.	Nevern	6	Llwyngwair
Thomas Parry, esq.	St Dogmaels	6	?

Members of the major landowning houses were appointed as Land Tax Commissioners in 1702;[37] and those lists partly coincide with the Hearth Tax survey and show that Bronwydd, Gernos, Blaenpant and Llwyngwair ranked amongst the most important. However, owing to the over-liberal ascription of the title 'esquire' (as in Montgomeryshire) and the minimum income qualification of £100 a year, names occur of lesser gentry, who, possibly, could only just meet the financial requirement.[38]

Land Tax Commissioners 1702

Cardiganshire
John Lewis, Coedmore, esq.
John Lewis, Gernos, esq.
Thomas Lloyd, Bronwydd, esq.
David Lloyd, Llanfechan, esq.
Jenkin Lloyd, Llanfechan, esq.
Oliver Howells, Wernmacwydd, esq.
Samuel Hughes, Alltgoch, esq.
Nathan Griffiths, Mountain Hall
Morgan Howells, Peny-beili
David Parry, esq. [?Noyadd Trefawr]
Stephen Parry, esq. [?Noyadd Trefawr]
Samuel Hughes, Crigmore, esq.
John Parry, Cwmsilltin

Carmarthenshire
Nathan Griffiths, Mountain Hall, esq.
David Lewis, Llysnewydd, esq.
Oliver Howells, Wernmacwydd, gent.
Richard Phillips, Pencarreg, gent.
John Williams, Dolgwm, gent.

Pembrokeshire
Morris Bowen [?Cwmgloyn] esq.
George Bowen [?Llwyngwair] esq.
George Warren [?Trewern] gent.
John Warren [?Trewern] gent.
Thomas Lloyd, Penpedwast, esq.

Sheriffs 1700-1750

	House/family	County	Cards	Carms	Pembs[39]
	Aberdwylan	Cms		1	
	Abernant bychan	Cds	1		
	Alltyrodyn	Cds	1		
	Blaendyffryn	Cds	2		
	Blaenpant	Cds	1		
	Bronwydd	Cds	1		
	Cilgwyn	Cds	1		
	Cilgynydd	Cms		1	
	Cilrhiwe	Pembs	1		1
	Coedmore	Cds	1		
	Coedstre	Cms		1	
	Cringae	Cms	1		
	Cwmawen	Cds	1		
	Dolau Cletwr	Cds	1		
	Dyffryn Cilgerran	Pembs			1
	Gernos	Cds	1		
	Llanfechan	Cds	1		
	Lletherneuadd	Cms		1	
	Llwyngrawys	Cds	1		
	Llysnewydd	Cms			
Total no. of houses 28	Mountain Hall	Cms	1	1	
	Morgan, Cardigan	Cds	1		
	Morris, Manordeifi	Pembs			1
	Noyadd Trefawr	Cds	1		
	Penybeili	Cds	1		
	Penyrallt	Cds	2		
	Vardre fach	Cds	1		
	Waunifor	Cds	1		
Total no. of High Sheriffs			23	5	3

Sheriffs 1751-1800

House/Family	County	Cards	Carms	Pembs
Aberdwylan	Cms		1	
Alltyrodyn	Cds	1	1	
Blaenpant	Cds	1		
Bronwydd	Cds	1		
Cilgwyn	Cds	1		
Cilrhiwe	Pembs			1
Cilwendeg	Pembs			1
Cwmgloyne	Pembs			1
Coedmore	Cds	2		
Dolau Cletwr	Cds	1		
Dolgwm	Cms		1	
Dolhaidd [uchaf]	Cds	1		
Gernos	Cds	2		
Lancych	Pembs		1	
Lowmead	Cds	1		
Llysnewydd	Cms		1	
Pantybetws	Cds	1		
Pigeonsford	Cds	1		
Rhosygilwen	Pembs	1		1
Stradmore	Cds	1		
Trefach	Pembs	1		
Trewinsor	Cds	1		
Troedyraur	Cds	1		
Waunifor	Cds	1		
Total no. of High Sheriffs		19	5	4

Total no. of houses 24

In the lists of sheriffs for the period 1700-1750 it is recorded that many members of Tivyside families had held the office mainly for Cardiganshire, with only a few from those families for Carmarthenshire and Pembrokeshire.

The sheriffs' lists for the years 1751 to 1800 indirectly point to the decline of the lesser gentry and their estates, and to the consolidation of wealth and power in the hands of an increasingly fewer landowners. It is significant that the names of many houses and their owners disappear, namely, Abernant-bychan, Cilgynydd, Coedstre, Cringae, Cwmawen, Dyffryn, Lletherneuadd, Llwyngrawys, Mountain Hall, Penybeili, Penyrallt and Faerdre fach. During this period slightly fewer families in the area produced sheriffs, but, as in the previous half century, the majority served in Cardiganshire where their position and authority weighed more strongly than in the neighbouring counties of

Carmarthen and Pembroke. Moreover, they were of sufficient consequence to fill the office, whether on account of personal ambition to assert themselves in the county, or because family pride and dignity prevented their avoiding what was often regarded as the irksome expense of the obligation.

By the early nineteenth century landownership with its concomitants of commodious mansion house (replacing the small Welsh 'plas'), timbered park and pleasure grounds, as well as a large estate, had reached a stage in its development in 'Tivyside' which survived almost unchanged for another century. Cary's map of 1803 along with the observations of topographical writers such as Meyrick, Fenton and Lewis all point to the many substantial gentry seats as the most prominent feature of the landscape. The Land Tax Returns towards the turn of the nineteenth century provide further evidence of the relative economic strength of the major houses.[40]

NOTES AND SOURCES

[1]Dd. Williams: *Modern Wales*, 2nd ed., 1957, pp. 77-90.

[2]Penry Williams: *The Council in the Marches of Wales under Elizabeth I*, 1958, p. 41; A. H. Dodd: *Studies in Stuart Wales*, 1952, pp. 1-3; '*gavelkind*'—land tenure involving equal division of property among all the sons; '*primogeniture*'—right of succession of the eldest son; '*entail*'—to cut off an estate from the heirs general, and settle it on a particular heir or series of heirs.

[3]RCLWM Report, 1896, p. 234, para 182.

[4]F. Jones: 'An Approach to Welsh Genealogy', *THSC*, 1948, pp. 381, 386.

[5]Welsh verse forms in the strict metres.

[6]J. I. Bowen: *The Statutes of Wales*, 1908, p. 87.

[7]Dd Williams: *op cit.*, p. 89.

[8]P. R. Roberts: 'The Act of Union in Welsh History', *THSC*, 1972-73, pp. 49-72.

[9]W. O. Williams: 'The Social Order in Tudor Wales', *THSC*, 1967, p. 178.

[10]DWB.

[11]P. Jenkins: *The Making of a Ruling Class—The Glamorgan Gentry 1640-1790*, 1983, pp. 239-41.

[12]A. H. Dodd: *op cit.*, pp. 11-12.

[13]P. Smith: *Houses of the Welsh Countryside*, 1975, pp. 11, 23, 279-280.

[14]D. W. Howell: 'Landlords and Estate Management' in Wales in *Cambridge Agrarian History of England and Wales*, Vol. 2 (ed. J. Thirsk), 1984, p. 252.

[15]J. Rhys and D. B. Jones: *The Welsh People*, 1906, pp. 449-52.

[16]Roll of the Baronets, 1960, pp. 15-21; T. Nicholas: *Annals and Antiquities . . .*, 1872, vol. i, p. 185.

[17]J. Rhys and D. B. Jones: *op cit.*, p. 451.

[18]A Wagner: *English Genealogy*, 1983, pp. 205 seq., and J. F. C. Stone: *An Open Elite? England 1540-1880*, 1986, pp. 3, 9, 132.

[19]J. H. Plumb: *England in the Eighteenth Century*, 1961, p. 37.

[20]A. H. Dodd: *op cit.*, p. 177, '*cymorth, cymhortha*'—assistance, support given to a leader by his inferiors.

[21]J. H. Plumb: *op cit.*, p. 38.

[22]P. D. G. Thomas: 'Society, Government and Politics' in *Wales in the Eighteenth Century*, 1976 (ed. D. Moore), pp. 9-26.

[23]W. Rees: *An Historical Atlas of Wales*, 1951, Plates 28, 56; H. M. Vaughan: *op cit.*, p. 32.

[24]F. Jones: 'The Old Families of South West Wales', *Ceredigion*, IV, 1960, No. 1, pp. 1-18.

[25]*id:* . . . Genealogy, pp. 303-05; P. C. Bartrum: Pedigrees of the Welsh Tribal Patriarchs, *NLWJ*, XIII, 2. 1963. pp. 126-43.

[26]G. Williams: *op cit.*, p. 153.

[27]T. Nicholas: *Annals and Antiquities* . . ., 1872, vol. i, pp. 180-84, 273-77; vol ii, pp. 882-86.

[28]*loc cit.*

[29]W. R. Williams: *The Parliamentary History of the Principality of South Wales, 1545-1895*, 1898.

[30]NLW Ms 116143.

[31]D. Williams: *op cit.*, p. 97.

[32]'A True Character of the Deportment . . . Gentry', c 1661, *Cambrian Register* i, 1795; NLW Ms 8716D.

[33]J. R. Phillips: *Memoirs of the Civil War in Wales and the Marches 1642-1649*, ii, 1874, pp. 4, 119-21, 163-68, 337-38, 418-19.

[34]F. Jones, *loc cit;* *WWHR* ii, 1913. pp. 97-193; T. Nicholas: *op cit.* R. Blome: *Brittanica or Geographical Description of the Kingdoms of England, Scotland and Ireland* . . ., 1677 (Preface). Adams: *Index Villaris or an Exact Register*, 1700. E. Bowen: *An Accurate Map* . . . 1763. Information from the late Major Francis Jones.

[35]PRO/E179/219/94; E/179/220/128, 130; *WWHR*, IX, 1920, pp. 217-40; X, 1924, pp. 177-216. 1924.

[36]T. M. Humphreys: Rural Society in Montgomeryshire in the Eighteenth Century (unpublished PhD thesis, Wales, 1982), p. 44.

[37]The Statutes of the Realm . . . viii, 1821, 1963 (ed). pp. 132-35; Land Tax imposed in 1692 @ 4 s in the £; information from PRO.

[38]Humphreys: *loc cit.*

[39]T. Nicholas: *loc cit.*

[40]J. Singer: *A New Map of Cardiganshire . . . Gentlemen's Seats etc.* Printed for J. Cary, 1803; S. R. Meyrick: *History and Antiquities of the County of Cardigan*, 1808; R. Fenton: *A Historical Tour through Pembrokeshire*, 1811; S. Lewis: *A Topographical History of Wales*, 1833.

Gentility, Old and New Gentry

According to Edward Chamberlayne the nobility and gentry had to possess the attributes of prudence, wisdom and valour. They were expected to act as loving parents and as gentle masters; their 'innate good nature' together with a liberal education, it was thought, rendered them 'exceeding civil'.[1] Their paternalism and benevolence was expected to be reciprocated by their inferiors with deference and respect. Nobility of birth and descent from ancestors who had never been servants, the bearing of coats of arms, education and the possession of wealth to lead a leisured life were some of the hallmarks of gentility.[2] A gentleman had to possess high ideals and a sense of duty, not least to 'open his purse wider and augment his position above others' and conduct himself so as to earn the goodwill of the community.[3] Moreover, the continuing power and the survival of the influence of the gentry into modern times had to be based on the consensus of the remainder of the community.[4]

Possession of land was another essential prerequisite of a gentleman, giving him the right to hunt and the means to support a large mansion sufficiently staffed, furnished and adorned to display the opulence of its owner. Theoretically, the acquisition of land by tradesmen, industrialists and professional people could not bestow the status of a gentleman, although, as will be demonstrated later, some 'Tivyside' gentry, as in the rest of the country, had such roots. Along with the possession of an ancient house and estate, the continuity and stability of the family were equally important. According to the old Welsh concept of gentility, noble descent mattered more than wealth—a poor farmer might have purer gentry blood than many a well-endowed landowner. Genealogical compilations by Lewys Dwnn, and the compilers of Peniarth 156, the Golden Grove Books, the Dale Castle Mss, and others, illustrate Welsh preoccupation with noble descent and kindred. Apart from placing an individual firmly in his historical context, family bonds and potential alliances contributed to real political and economic power.[5]

The wealth and leisure of a gentleman were expected to be employed in the patronage of poets and men of letters; in the succour of the poor and in good works (justifying what the gentry had inherited) rather than in rapacious greed, according to the Tory Anglican cleric and author, Ellis Wynne.[6] Gentry pre-eminence made them the 'natural leaders' of the community—sitting as JPs in their local and Quarter Sessions, acting as crown and government agents, and as lords of the manor adjudicating in domanial matters. All life revolved around the big house—fashion, culture, politics, the business of the locality, benevolence and charity towards dependants, and the continuing oversight of morals and behaviour.[7]

No opportunity was lost to acquire property through marriage, inheritance and purchase. Even the profits of an honourable profession and of trade could not ultimately deprive a man of the status of a gentleman as long as he could acquire land, the education, the manners and life-style of a squire. The extent of the squire's patronage and its manipulation to obtain court and government posts, church livings, county and parish office, was an important yardstick in assessing status.[8] Patronage was the other face of property—the *raison d'être* of government and of civil society itself.[9]

The notion of the leisured gentleman was not of a man who had the right to be idle, to follow hounds and the bottle, but one with the freedom to indulge in tastes, activities and pleasures consonant with the 'honour' of a gentleman. While some were content with the jollities of the hunting field or the table, gambling, irreligion or 'manly vices', the enlightened squire was expected to study agricultural improvement, architecture and the fine arts, science and philosophy, literature and religious 'enthusiasm', and above all, to participate in government.

The traditional concepts of gentility were to be challenged from at least two directions. The open nature of English society resulted in social mobility and the injection of new blood into the upper classes— from trade, the law and government service. The upward flow of new blood into the landed élite was matched by a downward flow into the middle ranks of society. Daughters of tradesmen brought new wealth into gentry families, while daughters of gentry (endowed with little cash) married down the social scale. Younger sons of poor gentry often had to take up a craft or a trade.[10] Social mobility replenished the aristocracy and landed gentry with heirs and new wealth, to replace loss and wastage through failure of heirs, bankruptcies, lavish display, and the drain caused by family jointures, portions and dowries.

In addition to this easy mobility, the writings of political and economic theorists along with new forces (in the form of industrial entrepreneurs and a rising radical and even revolutionary brand of propagandist) were to challenge the leisured gentleman and the idle unproductive rich. And yet, many of those who attacked the aristocracy and its privilege avidly sought to acquire the very basis of aristocracy in the form of land tenure. In the aftermath of the French Revolution, the landed classes responded by asserting traditional values. As each man had his station and particular responsibilities in the social order, it was essential to re-assert status through philanthropic activities towards the poor, the sick and the lower orders. Attacks against wealth, luxury, patronage and corruption, were answered by a quickened sense of their public and social obligations on the part of the gentry. The corresponding duty of the poor was to be content with their lot. That poverty inculcated virtue, and that it was hazardous to abolish distinctions of rank, were the themes of pro-gentry apologists. Welsh pamphleteers like Jac Glan y Gors and Tomos Glyn Cothi disseminated republican and 'levelling' ideas amongst the Welsh *gwerin*.[11] The gentry realised that, as the age of chivalry had disappeared in France, ancient opinions, manners and civilisation itself were in danger, and asserted that these values, which had their origin in ancient chivalry, depended on two principles—the spirit of a gentleman and the spirit of religion.[12]

The antiquarian movement, the gospel of chivalry, 'Gothick' culture— even what might only have been an aesthetic and refined interest—were to have important social and political dimensions. The defence of the crown and constitution, the maintenace of the rights of the established church and of landed property, were fused with the ideals of French Romanticism, and the currently fashionable Augustan studies. The *bon chevalier de Bayard* became the paragon to emulate—*sans peur et sans reproche* [without fear and without reproach].[13] In the early decades of the nineteenth century the social Victorian virtues of the landed gentry were in the process of being moulded—bravery, chivalry, honesty, compassion, generosity and magnanimity. The effects of a public school education, which emphasised the cultivation of the classical Roman *gravitas* and indoctrination in imperialism and élitism equipped the squire-class to rule at home and abroad. The Victorian squire adopted *chevalerie et courtoisie* in defending further the status which his family had attained over many centuries against the 'newly rich', the entrepreneurs of industry and the urban bourgeoisie who were invading the countryside, buying land and holding public office in the county. Sensitivity to personal insult led to feuds lasting for years, or sometimes to a duel, with its complicated code of etiquette, in order to resolve political, social and personal attacks on a gentleman's honour.[14] Col. John James, the squire of Pantsaison, killed a man in a duel and fled the country to escape the vendetta of the deceased's clan. Charles

Hassall fought a duel with General Picton concerning a point of honour, and Major Evans of Highmead and Colonel Powell of Nanteos similarly settled an argument on a 'public matter'. The Jenkins family of Cilbronne boasted as their motto *Da yw ffon amddiffyniad*[15] [A stout stave is a good defence]. *Nemo me impune lacessit* [No one provokes me with impunity] expressed a squire's pride in his honour.

The fealty of common people was secured by giving copious draughts of *cwrw da* [strong ale], through their participation in the young squire's coming of age and in their celebrating his military exploits or foreign adventure. The *werin* drew the squire's carriage, sang doggerel verses in praise of the lord's generosity, 'Welshness' and lineage. No longer enticed away to a distant crusade (as in medieval times), squire and retainer chased the fox and celebrated the day's exploits in panelled halls and well-stocked cellars. Common folk rationalised their dull and harsh lives in the glow of the squire's pleasure, and thanked God that they were, at least, allowed to witness the proceedings.[16]

In spite of the challenge from radicalism and nonconformity, disaffection on account of game laws, tithes, landlord and tenant relations and the like, the traditional concepts of gentility were never wholly abandoned. The squire's benevolence and patronage, albeit limited, still stretched out to deserving causes in spite of his reduced income, diminishing acres and the erosion of his political power.[17] Not until the 1914-18 War was the mortal wound dealt to 'knight errantry' and the *pax Brittanica*, resulting in socialist and nationalist politics. A new order rejected the squire as the *pater familias*, the model Christian gentleman, magistrate, and paragon of virtue. The dignity attached to land and family descent was discarded for values and concepts which were derived from the will of the people. The prestige which the gentry had once acquired through wealth and position, had to be weighed against the esteem which their behaviour deserved.

Strict dogmatic concepts of gentility were constantly broken in practice, and the fences dividing social ranks were in theory and in practice, surmountable. A dynamic society absorbed new blood, and the families of many noblemen and gentlemen had emerged from stock which had originally supported itself through toil on farm, trade in the market place or the practice of law and medicine.[18] Social 'consequence' could be gained through the purchase of land, and there were no legal restrictions on the right to acquire it. Honour and dignity were open to '. . . all who have the energy to pursue them . . . raising themselves from the most humble to the most elevated stations, by means honourable to themselves and useful to the community'.[19] In practice, few owners of estates could claim no knowledge of business or no connections with trading circles. The continuity and flexibility of English institutions owed much to the lasting marriage of mercantile and landed wealth.[20]

From the 1700s onwards the emergence of new families who acquired land in the Teifi valley is clear. Minor gentry to compare with the great clans of Williams-Wynn, Mansel-Talbot, Vaughan, Pryse and others in Wales, they ultimately acquired success and power, albeit on a local level. They sprang from yeoman, merchant and professional stock whose star was in the ascendant when they married into the old gentry families like Lewes of Llysnewydd and Lloyd of Coedmore in 'Tivyside' or Vaughan of Golden Grove in the Tywi valley. Thereby, in some cases, they threw off the garb of the illiterate and vulgar circles of their distant forebears. A 'status hierarchy', ranging from the nobility down to esquires and gentlemen, could be infiltrated by an 'occupational hierarchy'[21] motivated by ambition and the money to realise it.

A yeoman like William Colby, who in 1689 had little more than a sheep and a cow to bequeath, was one of the forebears of the Colbys of Ffynone who by 1873 had an estate of over 9,000 acres.[22] Through a diplomatic marriage with a distant relation of the Vaughan family of Golden Grove (and later a handsome legacy from a West Indies profiteer) John Walters of Perthgereint in south Cardiganshire and his descendants ultimately founded the Walters-Phillips family of Aberglasney in the Tywi valley.[23] Illegitimacy was no bar to gentry status, thus, Hector Jones of Coedstre-isaf in Llangeler parish was the putative son of a Cardigan exciseman, and held the office of High Sheriff in 1748.[24] Money originally derived from commerce, could be used to acquire a profession or commission in the army as in the case of members of the Ferrier family of Pembrokeshire. While one of them was a 'corvisor' or shoemaker, two others became a surgeon and a lieutenant of foot respectively. Anne Ferrier did well when she married the attorney, Thomas Howells. They were the ancestors of the Howell family who lived at Glaspant for some one hundred and fifty years. David Davies, M.D., the grandson of a Llandovery ironmonger, married Susannah Saunders, daughter and heiress of Erasmus Saunders, Pentre, and this event illustrates a typical instance of a cash injection without too much sensitivity as to its source.[25]

A move sideways and downwards resulted when the inheritance was divided or only possessed by the eldest son; disadvantaged other children now found themselves heading for social decline.[26] In such circumstances testamentary bequests, however, small were appreciated. Certainly, in the eighteenth century, heads of families, such as those of Pantyderi, Aberdwylan and Llysnewydd amongst others, tried to make provision for a dependant or relation whose calling might be that of corvisor, linendraper, cheese merchant, apothecary, milliner or shopkeeper.[27] Younger daughters within large families often lost in the county marital stakes. Their circumstances demanded some provision 'to set themselves up', although further down the social scale. Thus, a daughter of Jenkins, Cilbronne, married a Cardigan mariner, and a niece of Saunders of Clunfelin was reduced to marrying a saddler.[28]

A progressive social upgrading over many generations can be traced in the fortunes of families like Lewis of Llwyngrawys and Clynfyw, Brigstocke of Blaenpant and the Harfords of Falcondale, their forebears being respectively tanners, brewers, Bristol traders and bankers.[29] The meteoric quantum jump of John Lloyd Davies of Blaendyffryn and Sir Benjamin Hammett illustrates how drive, energy, with a combination of good fortune, auspicious marriages and the acumen to grasp opportunities, led in one generation from poverty to riches, a seat in parliament and a title.[30]

The acceptance of *advenae* or newcomers, as a ruling class, had been an age-long process. The Birts of Llwynduris, Mortimers of Coedmore and Revell of Forest had arrived in pre-Tudor times, but generations later disappeared or merged with other families. The process continued throughout the eighteenth century and gained momentum in the late nineteenth and early twentieth centuries. The Gowers of Castle Malgwyn, Miles of the Priory, Cardigan, and Lascelles of Pencraig were continental merchants, city bankers and lawyers, who, along with the executive clerk from a London railway station, John Francis Jones, later known as Francis Jones-Lloyd of Lancych, were mostly financially established before setting foot in 'Tivyside'. Eminence in a profession was also a key to limited social acceptance, as in the case of Sir John Lynn Thomas, an orthopaedic surgeon.[31] In the early decades of this century, native gentry could not resist the economic pressures forcing them to sell; for example, the descendants of William Frederick Lloyd James of Pantsaison sold out to a Breconshire family.[32] Daniel Daniel, a Glamorgan coalowner, sold his mining interests to Sir Alfred Mond in the 1920s and purchased the Ffynone estate from Spence-Colby.[33] The test of acceptance of these *advenae* by the older gentry was, by now, money, coupled with the readiness to continue the patronage and support of the local hunt, hospital and worthy causes.

Genealogical collections suggest that marriages of gentry families outside their regional peer group were fairly infrequent up to about 1700.[34] Later there was a marked acceleration, especially in the nineteenth century. Some families continued to make alliances largely within the regional boundaries, such as those of Lloyd of Bronwydd, Colby of Ffynone and Saunders Davies of Pentre, amongst others. The Brigstockes over three centuries chose English and Welsh brides, while the Harfords married mainly within their English peer group, save once, when a German lady by the name of Bunsen entered the family. The prospect of substantial dowries, possibly prompted the Lewes clan of Llysnewydd, and Lloyd-Williams of Gwernant, to seek English and Irish wives in the nineteenth century.[35] Wider social contacts made in London and Bath, foreign travel and government posts occasionally led to alliances with British and foreign aristocracy, leading to wealth and rank. Thus Jane Warren of Langridge married in 1773 Sir Basil Keith, Bt, a governor of Jamaica, whose income was £12,000 a year.[36] Social pre-eminence in the county resulted from marriage alliances made by the houses of Highmead, Pigeonsford and Noyadd Trefawr with the descendants of the Marquis of Hertford, the Earl of Hopetown and foreign nobility like the Baron von Hofrath of Frankfurt and the Count de Palatino of Corfu.[37] But at the other end of the social scale, daughters of gentry families, such as those of Bowen of Llwyngwair and of Waunifor, were content to throw in their lot with highminded and devoted clerics and 'Methodistical' divines, like the Reverend David Jones of Llangan and David Griffiths of Nevern.[38]

Social mobility often worked in a horizontal direction with the marriage of gentry with occupational groups—merchants, lawyers, medical men, clergy and administrators. But it has to be remembered that many established squires had very near relations (many of whom were left bequests in wills) who followed the occupation of—'cheese monger', 'peruke maker', 'saddler', 'corvisor' and so on. This is especially true in the eighteenth and early nineteenth century.[39] Many of those who derived their wealth from sources other than land were, however, equal to the minor gentry in terms of education, culture and leisure pursuits. Having acquired land, they gradually assimilated themselves into the gentry class. The respectable professions, as late as 1870, were those of cleric, barrister, soldier, sailor; only grudgingly was the profession of medicine regarded on the same social level, according to one observer.[40] In practice, however, Welsh squires, and those of 'Tivyside' in particular, often combined a profession with the rank of landowner.

'Tivyside' gentry had long realised that to be a lawyer brought with it social, material and perhaps political advancement. The courts of Ludlow and the Great Sessions constantly demanded the skill of lawyers. In the early 1600s Thomas Lloyd of Cilgwyn was a 'Ludlow clerk'.[41] Other estate owners such as Morgan of Plas, Aberporth, Lloyd of Plas Llangoedmore and Evan Pryce of Rhydybenne appeared in the courts, drafted documents and also carried on the administration of their estates. They are typical of the eighteenth-cetnury squire lawyers.[42] Some of these, however, indulged in sharp practices and were the terror of ordinary folk, like John Colby of Ffynone in the 1790s and John Beynon of Newcastle Emlyn who died in1857.[43]

The nineteenth century was particularly advantageous to many squire lawyers. In addition to estate administration, the introduction of new legislation dealing with tithe commutation, enclosure awards and the like, made the professional services of a lawyer essential and in some cases, provided a golden opportunity for malpractices and self-aggrandisement. Not without reason was it said that, '. . . attornies had to be restricted or they swallow up the commons, and attornies in disputed cases would only increase the dispute . . .'[44] Evidently, as eldest sons in legal practice until they inherited the family estate, or as younger sons who had to make a living for themselves, the times were propitious for them to feather their nests, and use their influence and patronage in politics as well. Griffith Jenkins of Cilbronne acted as agent for the Highmead and Peterwell estates. As clerk to the Lampeter burgesses, he compiled electoral lists and adjudicated in disputed elections.[45] With increased legislation relating to municipal and public matters, younger sons were able to obtain salaried posts under various government departments. In effect, they were continuing a centuries-old tradition of landowners being appointed by their peers in Quarter Sessions to act as coroners, 'scavengers', overseers of public works and county treasurers.[46] In the 1860s and '70s Edmund Lloyd of Coedmore and Barrett Price Jordan of Pigeonsford held such posts.[47] Education at the Inns of Court had attracted the gentry for centuries as a means of gaining part of their general education along with, or as an alternative to, study at Oxford or Cambridge. The utilitarian values of such training equipped a budding squire with useful knowledge in running his estate as well as dispensing public office. In the early 1700s

Lloyd of Foelallt and Peterwell held the offices of equity judge for north and south Wales, mayor of Cardigan and MP for Cardiganshire from 1734-42.[48] Leading 'Tivyside' squires continued to practise at the Bar throughout the period 1700-1900. Edward Crompton Lloyd Hall (1807-80), assumed the surname Fitzwilliams on inheriting the Cilgwyn estate in 1849, and, henceforth will be referred to as E. Crompton Ll. Fitzwilliams. He practised on the south Wales circuit and was a dedicated, albeit severe administrator of his estate.[49] James Bowen of Plas-y-Bridell and Marshall Griffith of Llwynduris both took silk and were chairmen of Quarter Sessions, while Lascelles of Pencraig, a kinsman of Lascelles of Harewood House, Yorkshire, acted as a Commissioner of Education in Ireland.[50] After a distinguished legal career in India, Sir Lawrence Hugh Jenkins of Cilbronne (1857-1928) returned to his native heath as squire of the parish of Llangoedmor.[51] Some members of the gentry class chose the calm waters of ecclesiastical administration, such as Owen Davies of Clynfyw, who in 1750 was receiver of rents for the Dean and Chapter of Westminster Abbey, and Dr Stephens of Dôl-Llan, who in the early 1800s was a Fellow of Doctors' Commons.[52]

Foreign wars, as well as service in the local militia during times of national danger, provided an attractive career to many sons of country squires. Family portions, or a timely bequest, made it possible to purchase a commission in the army which gave status, and was as well a secure career and a reliable source of income. The superior education and upbringing of the gentry suited them to take command in war. War itself was a sport like any other, only rougher and more dangerous, providing a challenge and adventure. With few exceptions the 'Tivyside' gentry were spurred on by the prospect of a soldier's profession. The Lloyds of Coedmore, the Lewes family of Gellydywyll and practically every landed family encouraged their sons to embark on a military or naval career and to recruit others. The influence of the gentry in their localities could help to fill the ranks. Ensign Brigstocke of Blaenpant, joining the navy in 1746, was allowed £3-13-6 for every extra recruit who volunteered for the East Indies.[53]

A military career sometimes combined a posting which had lucrative trading possibilities. This was the good fortune of Captain Lloyd Williams of Gwernant in the early 1800s, when he was serving with the 15th Regiment of North India and with the East India Company.[54] Some were port officials and collectors of customs; Col. Griffith Jenkins of Trefigin spent some 50 years in the Madras Army.[55] Consequently, these and other gentry could retire with a pension and, if lucky, with the fortunes of minor nabobs. Others were not so fortunate. Promotion and military honours, dangerous pursuits like tiger hunting or fighting warrior tribesmen, did enhance the prestige of squires like the young Capt. Charles Colby of Ffynone (if in some instances they led to an untimely end), making them cult figures and folk-heroes amongst their own people.[56]

The brutality and carnage of war did not deter the gentry. Most 'Tivyside' houses contributed their share in the 'sacrifices' of war, and, to quote two examples, the heirs of Bronwydd and Ffynone lost their lives in the 1914-18 war.[57]

As in the army, entry into the navy as an officer was governed by social background; promotion was 'tedious and uncertain unless seconded by a powerful interest . . .'[58] Apart from fixed emoluments, naval officers might make a fortune in a day if they happened to fall upon a foreign vessel with gold or precious cargo. Honours followed from the government for distinguished service. The opportunities and incentives were therefore high for men of good family, and yet the highest distinctions were not beyond those who had started their career with very modest means. Such good fortune fell to Admiral Thomas, son of a Llandysul vicar, who through his daring and enterprise gained much prize money during the Napoleonic Wars. Marrying a daughter of Lloyd of Mabws, he purchased the estate and mansion of Llanfechan, where he died in 1810.[59] Thomas Lewes of Gellydywyll was promoted captain of *HMS Sampson* in the West Indian service. Erasmus Gower (1742-1810) rose to be Vice-Admiral of the White and Governor of Newfoundland, and was awarded a knighthood.[60] The 'powerful interest' behind the brilliant career of Turnor of Crugmawr was John Colby of Ffynone; Turnor rose from the rank of midshipman to a position of prominence and favour with the Duke of Clarence.[61] Family tradition provided strong motivation in some families to join the navy. Thus the Jenkins family of Cilbronne and Penyrallt, the Webley-Parrys of Noyadd Trefawr, and the Hopes of Pigeonsford produced several admirals and high-ranking officers from about 1800 to the 1900s.[62]

Colonial expansion, with its promise of extensive trade, administrative posts and the lure of private enterprise, became a vast system of outdoor relief for the younger sons of the gentry, who otherwise would have been without sufficient provision for their maintenance. Trading companies like the Hudson's Bay and East India companies provided a link with the army and navy, especially in the West Indies, Canada, the Cape and India. Thomas Lloyd, son of the squire of Llanfechan and Castell Hywel, was governor of St George in Jamaica,[63] and by 1705, captain of HM Independent Company in Newfoundland, leaving at his death a small fortune of £2,500.[64]

A pension and a lump sum after long years of service, with all the opportunities for trade, gain and even loot, could be the financial basis for one like Thomas Jenkins to enable him to set himself up as squire in his new mansion of Penyrallt in Aberporth parish about 1814.[65] The reduction in the number of army commissions after 1815 temporarily put a brake on career opportunities in the army, but they were later to improve with the Crimean War and the Indian Mutiny, where the opportunity for gain was also a temptation to the astute and daring.[66] The Lloyd-Williams squires of Gwernant were involved for generations (from 1800 onwards) with colonial and commercial enterprises. The last of them was a tea-planter in Assam in the first half of this century.[67]

While it was the great aim of the gentry to acquire seats in parliament, most of them had to concede such an honour to the greater county magnates. At local levels, heads of families held the important offices of sheriff, lord and deputy-lieutenant and justice of the peace. Lower down the social scale, younger sons, had to resort to the often humble and low-paid government or county posts which were at the disposal of the county hierarchy. Some gentry were placed so low down in the economic scale that some of them acted as constables in their respective hundreds.[68] One of the Lloyds of Cwmgloyn in 1765 held the post of salt officer, and later his son became officer of customs in Cardigan.[69]

When a local post was not obtained, London was a magnet to some gentry, as for instance Maurice Morgan of Blaenbylan who held a position at the Mint Office in 1766.[70] Within the counties, a class of professional gentry emerged—treasurers of the county stock, coroners, 'scavengers' (a term which today would correspond to people with the functions of environmental officer), as well as tide-waiters and surveyors of roads and bridges. Aspiring candidates for such posts had no qualms in soliciting through family connections, the press and personal canvass. Thus, Owen Lloyd of Abertrinant (albeit outside the 'Tivyside' area), advertised his suitability for the post of coroner in Cardiganshire in 1826.[71] County treasurers' expense claims and other minutiae amply illustrate the opportunity to add a penny here or a shilling there![72]

The growth of bureaucracy in the nineteenth century, in relation to poor law unions, highway, burial and sanitary boards, provision of general education and the like, created incidental posts within the new legislation, which were largely in the gift or patronage of the gentry. These posts were not necessarily in their own area and near their estate. In the 1870s a solicitor-son of Taubman James of Pantsaison was appointed town clerk of Beaumaris, Anglesey.[73] Gentry with a notable record of military or naval service retired to salaried posts, such as Rear Admiral Hope who in 1879 became superintendent of Devonport dockyard.[74]

The impact of enclosure awards, tithe commutation and the arrival of the railway to west Wales prompted the gentry to seek professional qualifications which would in turn help them to manage and improve their estates. Owen Lloyd of Bronwydd set himself up as a land surveyor in Cardigan in 1839,[75] and was in later years 'extensively employed under the Tithe Commutation Act and with the projected Welsh and Midland Railway'.[76] Progressive farmer gentry like James Jenkins of Cilbronne studied at the Royal Agricultural College, Cirencester, and lectured on the 'new learning' amongst the ignorant farmers of Llangoedmor.[77]

At a period of brisk estate-selling, Bowen of Stradmore (later Sir George Bowen of Llwyngwair) in 1894 joined a Carmarthen firm of estate agents.[78] On the other hand, sons of the gentry with artistic temperaments and without any desire to take up farming or other calling related to the land, turned to the arts. One such, Gower of Glandovan, studied music at Oxford and became a professional organist. Other impecunious gentry abandoned their family homes and resorted to school teaching, such as Charles Bowen Lloyd of Waunifor, an MA (Oxon) in *Literae Humaniores*. In some cases, younger sons of gentry distinguished themselves in the civil service and in political circles, like Sir Patrick Gower, K.B.E., C.B., C.V.O., of Castle Malgwyn who died in 1964.[79]

As the practice of medicine gradually emerged into a scientific profession, gentry were attracted to it by their curiosity and enquiring minds, by the advantage of the practical application of medical knowledge for military and civilian purposes and by the appeal of new scientific attitudes. For generations, young men from 'Tivyside' gentry families had been drawn by the practice of 'physick', like Alban Thomas (1686-1771) who had gained the patronage of Sir Hans Sloane and the Royal Society.[80] Dr Lloyd or Llwyd of Cryngae, practised traditional lore and was regarded as a polymath. In the same mould were other squires such as Evan Jones of Llangoedmor, who through an auspicious marriage changed his surname and became Evan Protheroe, squire of Dolwilym.[81] Other instances of squire land-owning medicos were Dr John Jones of Haverfordwest, 'equal to any physician this day in Britain'.[82] Owner of considerable land, father-in-law of Thomas Lloyd of Bronwydd and *persona grata* in west Wales mansions, he was guaranteed gentry patronage and support. Especially was this essential in the case of younger sons of lesser houses; thus, Jeremiah Jenkins of Cilbronne, who was admitted M.R.C.S. in 1800— 'it cost over £11-7-6d . . .' was advised to go to Scotland for experience and education before settling in west Wales as surgeon and apothecary: '. . . the present surgeons there are well established in Business or protected by the Great Folk. These will thwart, envy and hunt [him] down . . .'[83] Dr Davies of Pentre, supported by private wealth, a large estate and family connections, may be cited as the squire physician *par excellence* with a widely scattered clientele in west Wales. A medical practice in fashionable centres like Bath attracted Bowen, youngest son of Squire Bowen of Troedyraur,[84] where social connections might lead to considerable financial rewards. Some of the squire doctors supported themselves largely from estate income, while their medical practice gave them a position of influence in the many houses they visited. Such a one was Walter David Jones of Lancych, owner of one of the smaller estates, who, with John Bowen of Cardigan and Richard Gower, practised locally.[85] As with other public offices, the gentry saw the advantages of salaried posts and, in the second half of the nineteenth century, squires such as Augustus Brigstocke of Blaenpant held the office of coroner and medical officer of health.[86] In this century Duncan Campbell Lloyd Fitzwilliams (1878-1954) of Cilgwyn, had a distinguished medical and military career and was the author of numerous medical publications.

As an occupational class, the clergy have never been a homogeneous group but rather a cross-section of society— 'deriving members of all classes and mingling with all'.[87] As the parson was rising in the social scale towards the end of the seventeenth century, many sons of gentry families sought ordination. Orthodoxy, loyalty to the sovereign and the constitution, sobriety, and 'sufficiency in learning manners and Conformitie', were the prerequisites to ordination. Thus John Lewes, who '. . . demeaned himself civilly and unblamely' and was sound in doctrine; James Price, 'proficient in learning and every aspect in the

British [sc. Welsh] tongue'; Maurice Vaughan and Edwardus Vaughan, incumbents of Clydai and Penboyr, and Johannes Parry, AM of Trefdroier i.e. Troedyraur, were all typical restoration clergy vouched for by squires, magistrates and public officials.[88] They belonged to the squire class and often, as younger sons without private means or married to moderately rich heiresses, used family and social influence to obtain livings in the gift of landed lay impropriators, perhaps a parent or older brother. Contrary to the aspersions of Erasmus Saunders and others,[89] the eighteenth-century clergy were not, as an entire class, ignorant, indolent, degenerate and rapacious. Many clergy were well-educated and devoted shepherds of souls, and from the 1680s it was becoming more common for men from good families to enter the church, a calling too, which depended on a basic amount of learning rather than social connections only.[90]

The squire clerics, in no small measure, contributed to the vitality of the church at this time and provided themselves with an honourable calling, which, in spite of often limited and meagre pecuniary reward, allowed them as a class to keep up some semblance of gentility and also to pursue ancillary interests like schoolmastering or letters. Some were, later on, 'methodistical' divines, 'slum' parsons in large cities or missionaries in distant lands, finding a vocation in spreading the Gospel, in charitable works and the care of the underdog—concepts basic to the ideals of gentility.

Some of these gentry clerics represent families ascending the social ladder like Price of Pigeonsford, founded by a cleric and schoolmaster who in 1675 lived in Dublin.[91] On the other hand, Griffith Jones of Llanddowror (1683-1761), evangelist and educationist, born in Penboyr parish, belonged to a family of freeholders in reduced circumstances, but his lineage (like that of Dafydd ap Gwilym) could be traced to Gwynfardd Dyfed.[92] Similarly, Theophilus Evans (1693-1767), grandson of Griffith Evans the 'Captain Tory' of Charles I's army, belonged to a declining family. Nevertheless, his contribution to Welsh letters was immense and he is rightly described as '*y llenor disgleiriaf a fagwyd ar lannau Teifi yn ystod y cyfnod hwn*' (the most brilliant man of letters brought up on the banks of the Teifi during this period).[93] Along with William Gambold the lexicographer, these clerics represent the minor gentry who were still able to survive in fairly comfortable, albeit, reduced circumstances. By the late eighteenth century the Rev. Watkin Lewes of Penybenglog represents the squire cleric, owner of an estate and rector of Meline. Descended from Ednowain ap Bradwen he could, as well, boast a DCL from Merton College, Oxford. A classicist and former chaplain to Lord Worthington, he stands out as a Welsh-speaking eighteenth-century squarson.[94]

A private chaplaincy and tutorship attracted Dr James Phillips to serve the Brigstocke family at Blaenpant, a situation which gave him the time and leisure to enjoy the splendid library and correspond with the leading Augustans of the day.[95] The Rev. John Jenkins (Ifor Ceri) (1770-1829), patron of bards and the eisteddfod, served in the navy before settling down in a quiet Montgomeryshire living.[96] Service in far-off lands, like India, could yield, after many years, a pension of about £300 a year, as well as the opportunity to acquire wealth and possessions, as happened in the case of the Rev. Benjamin Millingchamp of Plas Llangoedmore (1756-1829).[97] Amongst the colourful 'Tivyside' squarsons of the last century, Archdeacon North of Treforgan, sometime professor of Latin at Lampeter, was a 'scholar, wit and gentleman of the old school'.[98] The Tractarian, the Rev. Richard Bowen Jenkins of Llangoedmor introduced Puseyite practices into the church life of 'Tivyside'.[99] Motivated by an evangelical brand of Anglicanism, arduous and dangerous missions in China were undertaken[100] or a lifetime's ministry in the harsh poverty of a London working-class parish as was the fate of the Rev. James Colby of Pantyderi.[101] A less sensitive conscience was satisfied with the leisurely comfort of a college living; members of the Colby, Griffith, Brigstocke, Lewes and other families, with Oxford or Cambridge connections, happily settled down as patriarchs of English rural parishes.[102]

In the early 1700s strict Puritan views had waned among the wealthy ruling classes. The numbers of gentry of a dissenting persuasion had markedly diminished by the early decades of the eighteenth century.[103] The 'Tivyside' gentry, ambitious and far-seeing, quickly realised that conformity and loyalty led to public office and prestige. There is scant reference to 'Tivyside' dissenting gentry or to committed recusants, although some gentry had Jacobite leanings. While wealthy dissenters, promoters of trade and manufacturing, had 'estates fit for justices of ye peace', religious susceptibilities barred them from public office. It is only later in the eighteenth century that landowning dissenting ministers in the area could hold their own with landowners of the established church. The Baptist William Williams of Trefach boasted family arms and was a magistrate.[104] The Unitarian Lloyds of Brynllefrith were descended from Cadifor ap Dinawal, like the Lloyds of Alltyrodyn and Ffosybleiddied.

David Lloyd (1724-79) was regarded as a religious leader and champion of religious freedom. Erudite in ancient as well as in modern languages, he, along with other Lloyds, represents a unique type of lesser squire, possessing a concentration of intellect and an independent religious and political outlook.[105] Forward-looking, and with aims beyond the possession of acres, they achieved high academic distinction and made a notable contribution to Unitarianism and to the work of educational centres, such as the Carmarthen Academy.[106]

Perhaps tired of the arid and spiritless intellectualism of the time, or the prudential morality of latitudinarianism, a few gentry families were drawn into the 'Methodist Way': a new evangelism of self-discipline and an active faith. The Rev. David Griffiths of Nevern (1756-1834), son-in-law of George Bowen of Llwyngwair, was a squire and land-owning cleric.[107] Urged on by a fervent zeal, he preached damnation and doom upon his unrepentant flock and made periodic sorties to evangelise in London and Bath. In the same religious mould, the Rev. Daniel Bowen of Waunifor, although an unashamed pluralist, supported the Methodist Chapel of Waunifor, which had been built and endowed by his father.[108]

A survey of the categories within the 'Tivyside' gentry and land-owning class cannot ignore the comic, the quaint, crotchety and eccentric characters. A rustic disposition, lacking in urbane manners, characterised James Bowen of Llwyngwair and Morgan Jones of Cilwendeg. It was noted in 1761, '. . . *Digrif iawn y James Bowen a Morgan Jones*' (. . . very amusing . . . [are] both JB and MJ). The latter was regarded by some as a very strange man.[109]

Similarly, over a century later, Thomas Colby, squire of Pantyderi, presided over his odd ménage dressed like a farm labourer. Ante-diluvian in many ways, he campaigned against innovations like vaccination and women's suffrage.[110] It is said that satiety and surfeit sometimes lead to eccentricity. 'Ford Hughes' of Aberceri (christened Thomas Hughes Ford Davies) was eccentric to the point of mental affliction. After a rakish youth spent in London and abroad, he ended his life as a recluse in squalor and filth.[111] The Rev. Benjamin Lewis of Cilrhedyn, with an annual income of £1000 in the 1840s, believed he was in dire poverty and was always armed with a gun against bailiffs and marauders. In the early 1900s Charles Hope of Pigeonsford suffered from religious mania and constant visions of hellfire and eternal damnation.[112] The rector of Troedyraur, the Rev. Rhys Jones Lloyd, was another colourful character whose theatrical mannerisms, idiosyncratic intonation of the liturgy and quaint garb attracted large crowds.[113] An untutored zeal for archaeology led Sir John Lynn Thomas (a retired orthopaedic surgeon who bought a mansion and a small estate near Llechryd) to collect spurious artefacts and promote bizarre theories about the early history of the Teifi valley.[114] With generous gifts of money, unlimited zeal and a crusading spirit, the Celtophile 'Dame' Mallt Williams of Pantsaison gave much support to the Welsh Nationalist party and unemployed miners in the early days. She was an ardent member of the Celtic League and campaigned for odd causes, like—the abolition of the currency, trade by barter, and the end of formal government. Curious in dress and behaviour, she ranked as a kind and harmless, if eccentric, gentlewoman of 'Tivyside'.[115]

NOTES AND SOURCES

[1]E. Chamberlayne: 'Angliae Notitiae', 8th ed. in *English Historical Documents, 1660-1714* (ed. A. Browing), 1966, pp. 467-68.

[2]R. Allestree: *The Gentleman's Calling*, 1659 (preface).

[3]P. H. Ditchfield: *loc cit.*

[4]T. M. Humphreys: *op cit.*, pp. 33-4.

[5]P. Jenkins: *op cit.*, pp. 197, 201-03; F. Jones: 'The Old Families of Wales' in D. Moore, *op cit.*, pp. 27-8.

[6]Ellis Wynne: *Gweledigeutheu y Bardd Cwsc*, 1703 (1948 ed), p. 21; DWB.

[7]W. Marshall: *On the Landed Property of England*, 1804, p. 12.

[8]Sir L. Namier: *The Structure of Politics at the Accession of George III*, 1929, vol. i, pp. 164-82.

[9]H. Perkin: *The Origins of Modern English Society, 1780-1888*, 1969, pp. 24-5, 34, 38, 49-51.

[10]*ibid*: pp. 60-2; A. Wagner: *op cit.*, pp. 205-45.

[11]A. Briggs: *The Age of Improvement*, 1979, p. 13; Wm Paley: *Reasons for Contentment*, 1781; J. Miller: *The Origins of Distinctions of Rank in Society*, 1771. Thomas Evans (Tomos Glyn Cothi 1764-1833) unitarian minister; b. at Gwernogle, Carms., admirer of the radical thinkers of the day; his anti-royalist and political pamphlets in support of the French Revolution led to a period of imprisonment in Carmarthen gaol. John Jones (Jac Glanygors 1766-1821) left his native Denbighshire and settled in London; pamphleteer and radical propagandist. *DWB: sub* John Jones, Thomas Evans; T. O. Williams: *Hanes Cynulleidfaoedd Undodaidd Sir Aberteifi*, 1930.

[12]Edmund Burke: *Selections from his Political Writings and Speeches* (n.d.), pp. 283-86.

[13]M. Girourard: *The Return to Camelot*, 1981, pp. 20-22; S. Lewis: *A School of Welsh Augustans*, 1924; *Enc. Britt.* 1937.

[14]P. Jenkins: *op cit.*, pp. 199-201.

[15]NLW Ms 11091E (margin note by F. Jones); *DWB sub* Hassall; NLW/Cilgwyn/Ms LB/44/20/6/1872. Heraldic window at Cilbronne, parish of Llangoedmor.

[16]NLW/Howell (Glaspant)/Confessions Book 19c; the late Mr Enoch Davies, Dre-fach Felindre.

[17]J. Hd. Davies: The Social Structure and Economy of South West Wales in the Late Nineteenth Century (unpublished MA thesis, University of Wales 1967), pp. 178-9.

[18]H. J. Habakkuk: *The European Nobility in the Eighteenth Century* (ed. A. Goodwin), 1953, pp. 15-16; R. Porter: *English Society in the Eighteenth Century* (Penguin Social History of Britain), 1990, p. 50.

[19]Address of Chairman of Gloucester Quarter Sessions quoted in E. Moir: *The Justice of the Peace*, 1969, p. 77.

[20]C. Wilson: *England's Apprenticeship 1603-1765, 1965*, p. 10; A. Wagner: *English Genealogy*, 1983, pp. 154-73.

[21]L. Stone: 'Social Mobility in England, 1500-1700', *Past and Present*, 33, 23-24.

[22]FG/15/288; Return of Owners of Land 1873. ii Wales 1875; for the families of Williams-Wynn of Wynnstay, Mansel-Talbot of Margam, Vaughan of Crosswood [Trawsgoed], Pryse of Gogerddan, see Burke: *Peerage, Baronetage and Knightage* . . . 1893. For non titled gentry: id. *Landed Gentry*, 1906.

[23]F. Jones: 'Walters of Perthgereint', *Ceredigion*, vi. 2, 1969, pp. 168-200.

[24]NLW/Ms 12381.

[25]FG/15/298; HRO/SMB/HC/c95, 184; NLW/Owen Colby/ 1080, 1083-4; HRO/Lewis, Henllan/1/88; HRO/D/Pen/26/1.

[26]A. Wagner: *op cit.*, p. 217.

[27]FG/18/393-94; 20/82-3; 21/163; 22/50; NLW/Lancych/30; NLW/Eaton Evans and Williams/619.

[28]FG/21/155; HRO/D/Pen/1/31/

[29]Information concerning Llwyngrawys from the late Major Francis Jones; Burke: *Landed Gentry 1906*; A. Harford: *Annals of the Harford Family*, 1909, p. 157.

[30]DWB; W. Davies: *Hanes Plwyf Llandysul*, 1896, pp. 112-13; J. R. Phillips: *History of Cilgerran*, 1867, pp. 139, 163.

[31]DWB;. T. Nicholas: *op cit.*, Cd. Ad. 21/6/1895. NLW/Lancych/58; Ms. 8716D; J. R. Phillips: *History of Cilgerran*, 1867, pp. 102-03; information from the late Major Francis Jones; The Priory estate Cardigan had been mortgaged by Thomas Johnes of Havod, Cards, to Philip John Miles of Miles, Savil, Harford and Miles, Bankers and W. Indian Bankers of Bristol; C.R.O./EG/Box 9.

[32]HRO/D/RW/81.

[33]Information from the late Captain Fitzwilliams of Old Cilgwyn, 1983; *Who's Who in Wales*, 1920.

[34]Burke: *op cit.* WWHR, i, 1910-11, pp. 1-96; ii, 1911-12, pp. 1-103; NLW/Dale Castle Mss; CRO/Golden Grove Books.

[35]*loc cit.*

[36]*Gentleman's Magazine*, 1773, p. 156.

[37]Burke: *op cit.*, 1906, *sub* Davies-Evans; *id*: *Peerage, Baronetage and Knightage*, 1893, *sub* Earl of Hopetown; Walford: *County Families*, 1907.

[38]*Cylchgrawn Cymdeithas Hanes y Methodistiaid Calfinaidd*, LIII, 1968, pp. 66-77; DWB.

[39]L. Stone: *op cit.*, pp. 23-24, evidence from Wills in NLW and those noted in Francis Green: *op cit.*

[40]A. Trollope: *The Vicar of Bullhampton*, p. 55-6 quoted in A. Wagner: *op. cit.*, pp. 253-55.

[41]*ibid*: p. 191; *Cambrian Register*, 3, p. 352.

[42]CRO/JF/209-10; NLW/Clynfyw/Box 1; F. Jones: Report of Welsh Mss in the College of Arms, 1957. p. 8. (unpublished typescript in CRO).

[43]D. L. Baker-Jones: 'The Orielton Chancery Proceedings', *NLWJ*, XV, 3-4, 1968, pp. 344-422; NLW/D. Pryse Williams/15625 B.

[44]*Report of Select Committee on Commons' Inclosure*, 1844 [Qus. 909, 2184-85, 2190].

[45]NLW/Highmead/Box P. File 5.

[46]CRO/Carms/QS/OB; NLW/Cards/QS/OB; 'scavenger' would nowadays correspond to an official responsible for 'environmental health'.

[47]*Slater's Directory*, 1868. Cd Ad: 28/11/1878.

[48]J. Foster: *Alumni Oxonienses 1500-1714*; FG/viii/192 seq; W. R. Williams: *op cit.*, *sub* Cards.

[49]Evidence from the voluminous Cilgwyn Letter Books, 1855-1934 in *NLW*.

[50]*Cd Ad*: 10/2/1888, 19/10/1894, 21/6/1895.

[51]W. R. O. Jones: 'The Contribution of Welshmen to the Administration of India', *THSC*, 1970, ii, pp. 250-62; D. L. Baker-Jones: 'Sir Lawrence Hugh Jenkins of Cilbronne', *THSC*, 1968, ii, pp. 122-32; NLW/11, 111 E.

[52]NLW/Clynfyw/Box/1; *Cm Jnl*: 6/5/1842.

[53]NLW/Evans George/1391-93.

[54]NLW/Noyadd Trefawr/1676-77.

[55]NLW/Clynfyw/Box/13.

[56]NLW/Owen Colby/2008; Memorial in Old Maenordeifi Church.

[57]D. Cannadine: *op cit.*, p. 87; *Who's Who in Wales*, 1920; local knowledge.

[58]NLW/Add Ms 1896E. iv.

[59]W. J. Davies: *op cit.*, pp. 199-200.

[60]NLW/Llwynduris/1, 46, 74; DWB.

[61]NLW/Ms 6753 B.

[62]*Cd Ad*: 14/3/1890; *Who's Who in Wales*, 1920.

[63]NLW/Ms/8710 E.

[64]FG/25/70-71.

[65]NLW/Add Ms/1897 E. iii. iv; DWB.

[66]FG/442.

[67]NLW/Ticehurst Wyatt (Gwernant) Boxes I, II.

[68]HRO/Pemb/QS/OB 1738-48.

[69]FG/21/168.

[70]NLW/Llwynduris/4,5.

[71]*Cm Jnl*: 17/3/1826.

[72]NLW/Cards/QS/OB; CRO/Carms/QS/OB.

[73]*Cd Ad*: 24/5/1872.

[74]*ibid*: 3/1/1879.

[75]*Cm Jnl*: 11/1/1839.

[76]*ibid*: 17/1/1859. *The Welshman*: 5/10/1849.

[77]*Cd Ad*: 14/12/1894.

[78]CRO/Trant/Box 189.

[79]*ibid*: 23/4/1880; *The Times*, 1/9/64.

[80]NLW/Add Ms/4706D; NLW/Ms/19B (Sir John Williams 223 p. 101).

[81]FG/23/22.

[82]J. H. Davies: *op cit.*, ii, p. 345.

[83]NLW/Ms/1896 E. i; Jenkins studied at the London Hospital, Whitechapel Road, London.

[84]FG/10/447.

[85]G. Phillips: *Llofruddiaeth Shadrach Lewis*, 1986, pp. 10-14.

[86]*Cm Jnl*: 28/6/1878; 10/5/1895; *Who's Who in Wales*, 1920; information from the late Capt C. Fitzwilliams.

[87]A. Wagner; *op cit.*, p. 94.

[88]NLW/SD/0/-.

[89]E. Saunders: *A View of the State of Religion in the Diocese of St David's*, 1721; J. Brown: *An Estimate of the Manners and Principles of the Times*, 1757-58, pp. 52-6.

[90]S. R. Thomas: The Diocese of St David's in the Eighteenth Century (unpublished MA thesis, Wales, 1983), p. 276.

[91]FG/26/9-10.

[92]G. T. Thomas: 'A Short Study in Welsh Genealogy. The Lineage of Griffith Jones of Llanddowror', *Arch Camb.*, 1923, 2, pp. 269-78.

[93]*DWB*; G. H. Jenkins: 'Bywiogrwydd Crefyddol a Llenyddol Dyffryn Teifi, 1689-1740', *Ceredigion*, viii, 4, 1979, p. 444; *DWB*.

[94]*DWB*; NLW/Ms 15774B.

[95]*loc cit.*

[96]*DWB*; R. T. Jenkins: *Cymru yn y Bedwaredd Ganrif ar Bymtheg*, 1933, pp. 115-16; NLW/Ms/1897E. ii, iii.

[97]*DWB*; H. M. Vaughan: *op cit.*, pp. 119-22.

[98]*ibid.*, pp. 123-24.

[99]*ibid.*, pp. 125-27.

[100]*Cd Ad*: 21/8/1896.

[101]*The Welshman*: 10/7/1874.

[102]*Gent. Mag.*, 1816; *Cm Jnl*: 9/3/1832, 13/4/1832; the Rev. Robert Colby, Ll.B., educated at Clare College, Cambridge; rector of Ansford, Somerset, 1874-88; the Rev. Thomas Lewes, M.A. (1792-1874) of Llysnewydd, Carms, rector of Taynton and Great Barrington in the diocese of Gloucester.

[103]A Wagner: *op cit.*, pp. 200-21.

[104]Information from the late Major Francis Jones.

[105]*DWB*.

[106]W. J. Davies: *op cit.*, pp. 67-9, 204-05.

[107]*DWB*; NLW/Llwyngwair/16987-1701; NLW/Ms/6345C.

[108]W. J. Davies: *op cit.*, pp. 67-9; J. M. Jones a W. Morgan: *Y Tadau Methodistaidd*, 1895, i, pp. 330-35, 347, 467.

[109]J. H. Davies: *op cit.*, ii, p. 316; information from Francis Jones.

[110]H. M. Vaughan: *op cit.*, pp. 89-90, 91-93.

[111]*loc cit.*

[112]CRO/Beckingsale/52/2744.

[113]H. M. Vaughan: *op cit.*, pp. 123-25.

[114]*DWB*; Sir J. Lynn Thomas: *The Key to All Wales*, 1932.

[115]HRO/RW/101-02; J. Graham Jones: 'Forming Plaid Cymru, Laying the Foundations 1923-26', *NLWJ*, xxii, 4, 1982, p. 445; local knowledge.

Status and Wealth

The status, wealth and culture of landowners varied greatly and ranged from the splendour of the nobility (whose lifestyle outdid in magnificence the courts of foreign monarchs) to the humdrum existence of the small squire, reckoned to be worth a few hundred pounds a year and farming part of his own land. Only slightly distinguished from yeomen (among whom he mingled on almost equal terms), the squire received special deference on account of traditional attributes and respect paid to him as a 'gentleman'.

In the eighteenth century Welsh landowners were generally poor by English standards, and in the 'Tivyside' they were poorer than in some other Welsh counties. Recent studies of Glamorgan and Montgomeryshire suggest that the annual income of the landed classes in those counties was roughly as follows:

Great landlords or great gentry	£2,000—£3,500	Peers, baronets, knights
Wealthy gentry	£1000—£2,000	and wealthy commoners.
Squires	£400—£1,000	Lesser baronets, knights, etc.
Lesser gentry	£100/150—£400[1]	

The highest income of £3,500 fell considerably short of £5,000-£6,000 a year estimated for the great landlords of England and Wales in 1690. While it is held that the Glamorgan gentry were very wealthy by Welsh standards, in the years 1700-1750 the annual income of 'Tivyside' gentry was low, ranging from about £150 to £650 and over, while in the second half of the century there were a few estates which brought in annually quite exceptional sums like £2,500 (Coedmore), £1,678 (Noyadd Trefawr) and £1,575 (Blaenpant).[2]

Throughout Wales a large proportion of the land-owning families and estates, already established at the end of the eighteenth century were also to be listed in the returns of owners of land of 1872-73 (see Table A). The buoyant landowners, named in the Land Tax Returns for 1786 and 1798, survived almost without exception for a century and more. The long history of Welsh estates as economic entities, and owned by the same families, was remarkable enough to be commented on by the Welsh Land Commission of 1896.[3]

From the evidence of estate records which are unfortunately incomplete and diverse in content and quality through loss, destruction and, in some cases, the reluctance of landowners to collaborate with those who compiled the 'Domesday' Return of 1873 and with Bateman's attempt to produce a more accurate survey in 1876, it is difficult to arrive at exact figures. In some instances the rental from land held in more than one county was given, while the income from one county only was sometimes recorded.

TABLE A—Approximate annual rental of 'Tivyside' Estates in the 1870s.[4]

- £1,000	£1,000-£2,000	£2,000-£3,000	£3,000-£4,000	£4,000-£5,000	£5,000-£6,000	£6,000 +
Bridell	Cilgwyn	Aberceri	Alltyrodyn	Blaenpant	Ffynone	Bronwydd
Castle Malgwyn	Glanarberth	Castle Green	Highmead	Falcondale	Pentre	Penylan
Cilbronne	Gwernant	Clynfyw		Llwyngwair		
Cwmhyar	Lancych	Coedmore		Llysnewydd		
Dolhaidd	Llanfair + Dôl Llan	Cwmgloyn				
Gernos						
Gilfachwen	Maesycrugiau					
Glaspant	Thomas Morgan, Cardigan					
Llwynduris	Noyadd Trefawr					
Manereifed	Pigeonsford					
Pantyderi						
Rhosygilwen						
Troedyraur						
Tŷ Llwyd						
Waunifor						

In comparison with the great Welsh landowners of the end of the nineteenth century, the squires of 'Tivyside' ranked as lesser gentry and as small landowners with estates ranging from 1000-10,000 acres and a rental of £1,000-£7,000 a year. For the whole of Wales the names and income per annum of landowners like Lord Penrhyn (£63,375), Lord Tredegar (£124,598) and the Marquess of Bute (£203,613) stand out as the very great landowners whose rents from land were greatly increased by industrial profit and who could compete in status with the English nobility. Within the three south-west Wales counties the acreage and rents of the major landowners were as follows:

TABLE B

County	Estate	Acreage	Rent per annum
Cardigan	Crosswood (Lord Lisburne)	42,706	£10,619
	Nanteos (Powell)	30,582	£ 9,372
	Gogerddan (Pryse)	32,359	£11,325
Carmarthen	Golden Grove (Lord Cawdor)	51,538	£35,043
	Dynevor (Lord Dynevor)	10,509	£18,552
	Derwydd (Gulston)	6,744	£10,976
Pembroke	Bush (Meyrick)	4,253	£21,737
	Picton Castle (Phillips)	21,455	£23,696
	Williamston (Scourfield)	13,439	£10,087

In terms of social status, acreages and estate income, the 'Tivyside' gentry could not compete with the families of Vaughan of Crosswood, Vaughan and Campbell of Golden Grove, Rice of Dynevor and the baronets of Gogerddan, Bush and Picton Castle. It was only after social and political manoeuvring that Thomas Davies Lloyd of Bronwydd acquired a baronetcy in 1863. During the nineteenth century, Blaendyffryn, Bronwydd, Pentre, Coedmore and Llwyngwair each produced an MP but (with the exception of Lloyd Davies of Blaendyffryn) they were largely undistinguished. While Col. Herbert Davies Evans of Highmead held the most important 'county' office of lord lieutenant, typical gentry families, such as those of Llysnewydd, Maesycrugiau, Alltyrodyn and Pigeonsford, were further down the social rank. All in all, they were far below the status of the few families of wealth in Wales (and the social power commensurate with it) whose influence was paramount.[5]

Within their own group, changes had taken place, rendering families like Gernos and Noyadd Trefawr far less important at the end of the period than they were in the early eighteenth century. In some cases the paper value of estates, such as Bronwydd, in no wise reflected their true solvency. The changing fortunes of the landed estate—its growth and decline—were due to factors constantly present in the structure of families, relationships and attitudes, and especially the political, social and economic forces of the time.

The evidence of wills, especially down to the 1750s, provides further indication of the degree of personal wealth, domestic comfort and lifestyle of the gentry. Once again, it is clear that standards of comfort, and associated levels of status, varied considerably between one gentry family and another. Although the inventories of items in houses and on the farmyard have the disadvantage of not showing clearly the differences between real market prices and the values given, and appraisors had no fixed scale of the exact worth of the deceased's effects, they are valuable in placing an individual in his general peer group, showing how his material prosperity can be compared with other members of that group whose names have survived.[6]

Before the days of banking, considerable sums of money were kept in the squire's mansion house, reflecting not only any propensity on his part to hoard, but also to provide for the personal needs of his establishment and the various transactions for which he had to provide ready cash (as can be seen from Table C).

TABLE C

	Date	Name	Residence	Cash Amount
£300+	1683	David Lloyd, esq	Alltyrodyn	£344-4-0
	1719	John Lewis	Gernos	£398-15-0
	1752	John Lloyd	Alltyrodyn	£383-9-0¾
£200-300	1709	Thomas Lloyd, esq	Penpedwast	£207-11-6
£100-200	1692	Thomas Lloyd, esq	Bronwydd	£190-7-0
	1697	John Morris	Cardigan	£156-0-2
	1702	Theophilus Jones, gent	Rhosygilwen	£144-11-0
	1731	Griffith Jenkins	Cilbronne	£140-5-0
		George Lloyd	Cwmgloyn	£118-9-6
	1735	Robert Griffiths	Penbenglog	£149-9-6
	1745	John Parry	Cwmcynon	£126-17-0
	1748	Daniel Bowen	Waunifor	£132-6-8
- £100	1703	Morris Morgan	Blaenbulan	£77-5-8
	1716	John Lewis, gent	Cwmhyar	£16-17-6
	1719	Thomas Saunders	Clunfelin	£48-15-0
	1728	David Lloyd, gent	Alltyrodyn	£57-0-0
	1743	John Williams, gent	Henllan Deifi	£27-4-0
	1748	David Saunders	Pentre	£19-18-0[7]

Many well-to-do yeomen, bordering on the lower levels of the gentry, also had money in their houses, and were able to bequeath sums ranging from £40-£100, but were never included within the gentry ranks on account of lineage or inferior social standing.[8]

In Wales, as in outlying areas of England, eighteenth-century gentry families lived in old and unfashionable houses. This seems to have been the case in a number of Teifi valley *plasau*, which could boast only modest comforts and few items of luxury. From the end of the seventeenth century to about 1760, only kitchen and household effects are usually mentioned in probate inventories. In 1694, John Lloyd of Cwmgloyn's possessions were valued at about £79 and comprised '8 plater dishes, 3 pewter dishes, 6 spoons, 3 candlesticks, 2 sause celers, 2 salt selers, a pewter plate, a pewter plate print and 1 chamber pott'.[9] Household furniture seems to have been ignored in this instance, although doubtless there would have been the essential tables, chairs and beds at least. Maybe, the appraisors turned a blind eye to many items of value.

In addition to furniture and other household goods, items not infrequently mentioned are 'a horse saddle, bridle, sword and pistol'— important requisites for comfortable and safe travel and listed in a Llysnewydd inventory of 1706. In this mansion, household goods were mainly of pewter, brass and iron with wooden coffers, chests, beds and 'usuall silver tumbler and 5 old silver spoons'.[10] The acquisition of items of silver and gold seems to have taken place slowly, as taste and family fortunes improved. Thus the household contents of Pantyderi and Rhosygilwen later in the century included such items and were valued, in all, at over £200. Occasionally, the appraisors made quick work of their valuation by lumping everything in the house as 'household stuff' or 'trumpery', and farm items were generally regarded as being of more importance in the contemporary range of priorities. In terms of status, early eighteenth-century 'Tivyside' gentry houses lacked style and sophistication, and were poor relations compared to the big houses of Wales, like Chirk, Erddig, Powis Castle, Tredegar, Dynevor and Picton Castle. They were run on very simple lines, and were self-supporting; bread-making, butter and cheese-making and brewing of ale were prominent activities. Most items of consumption and usefulness were derived from the squire's farm and his immediate dependants such as country craftsmen, artisans and farm labourers.[11]

Given that many of the squires were actual working farmers, their way of life was both economically and 'culturally' based on the soil, and intermarriage between the families of the poorer gentry and richer yeomen meant that they often lived on terms of social equality.[12] David Rees, gent., of Camnant in Llandysul parish, in 1693 left 2 yoke of oxen, 5 cows, 2 steers, 2 heifers, 3 yearling beasts, 1 calf, 1 horse, 1 mare, 1 colt, 39 sheep, 18 lambs, a sow and 4 suckling pigs, together with a plough and four harrows valued at over £35.[13] Ten years later the larger and more important establishment of Gellydywyll had stock worth twice as much,[14] while Gernos in 1719 could boast of farm stock worth £143-15-0, comprising 50 head of cattle, 40 sheep, 7 horses, to mention only a few items. Along with John Lewes of Gernos, William Lewes of Llwynderw at his death in 1722 possessed a well stocked home farm with sheep predominating and which grazed on the upland reaches of Llangeler parish. Typical of the impoverished gentry class of the time, David Havard of Penboyr, gent, in 1747 left ony a few cows, a stack of hay and effects in the house and barn amounting in value to a trifling £3-15-0. Contrasting strongly with this general run of impoverished gentry were those adventurous gentry like Captain Lloyd of Llanfechan who sought foreign service, a government or trading commission and sometimes acquired relatively large fortunes.

Clergy, even of gentry stock, were usually at the lowest strata in terms of money, such as the Rev. Owen Rice of Maenordeifi whose worldly goods were worth about £20. On the other hand, personalty reckoned to be of little value was not always a true indicator of wealth; for instance, the incumbent of Clydai in 1730 left goods worth £13 but owned land on which he made a charge of £100 a year for the benefit of his children, and which would rate him almost with the lower gentry. Very rarely, there were instances of rich clergy such as William Laugharne of Maenordeifi, who in 1756 left cash bequests of £1,000.

From about 1750 inventory valuations decrease in respect of the property of the smaller gentry, who were being ousted by the greater landowners as they enlarged their estates. Sums of £200-£300 were recorded of cash in house or in total bequests. In 1750, the incumbent of Cilrhedyn bequeathed £200 in cash, and in addition had personalty valued at £75 and realty comprising six farms. The squires of Crugmawr, Pengelly uchaf, Penywenallt and the squire parson the Rev. Watkin Lewes of Meline, were each approximately in the same category.[15]

Towards the last decades of the century a prosperous tradesman such as Thomas Makeig of Penylan in Llechryd parish, like others of his kind, was investing in land, and was in a position to leave £660 to his children. A few of the larger freeholders and minor gentry such as John Parry of Llwyncadfor and William Harries of Nevern each left several hundred pounds, but these represent a class of landowner which was disappearing.[16]

With enlarged estates and increasing rent rolls over the course of the eighteenth century the major gentry were rebuilding their houses and adopting a more cosmopolitan lifestyle, so that there was a widening gulf between them and the lesser squirearchy. The value of jewels, plate and household furniture, together with the cash, in the mansion of Coedmore in the 1770s was estimated at between £4,000 and £6,000. Its rental of £2,500 was then the highest in 'Tivyside'.[17] By the end of the eighteenth century, as the Land Tax Returns for 1786 and 1798 illustrate, the major landowning families—through the resilience of the old and the acquisitiveness of the new—had reached a peak in landownership for the area, and this was to survive for another century. Allowing for the inherent problems in the returns—carelessness in identifying individual owners, maladministration, double-counting, as well as local politics, rivalry and even corruption of some commissioners—the names of long-established families and estates appear like Llwyngwair, Bronwydd, Cilgwyn, Llysnewydd, Blaenpant and Noyadd Trefawr together with the newer estates of Ffynone, Gwernant and Highmead.[18]

The eighteenth century had witnessed the extension and consolidation of estates in England through marriage, inheritance and piecemeal purchase, and although in Wales it was on a smaller scale, accumulation was unmistakably present.[19] Greater wealth from land, buttressed by income from a profession and trade, is very clear from the wills and probate valuations in the period after 1815. Thomas Davies of Castle Green, Cardigan—whose family had risen socially by marrying into county families like Bowen of Llwyngwair—was a landowner with trading and shipping interests as well, and left personalty of about £14,000.[20] But, conspicuously large sums have to be cautiously considered against the background of family liabilities and arrangements, for example, John Colby of Ffynone in 1823 left personalty of £55,747, but four-fifths of it was a residuary legacy from his sister Lady Owen of Orielton. While his own fortune was about £9,000, it would barely cover the debts on his estate which had later to be cleared by his heir.[21] The profits of public office, a thrifty lifestyle and careful investment of portions could sometimes lead to fair-sized personal fortunes of between £4,000-£5,000, like those left, for instance, by the two younger Bowen brothers of Llwyngwair.[22]

Many years of service in India or British dependencies again sometimes led to considerable personal wealth. Relatively speaking, Archdeacon Millingchamp of Llangoedmor's personal estate of £8,000 in 1829 (although his landed property amounted to only a few hundred acres) made him a fairly rich man in the area, undisturbed as he was by all the problems connected with land-holding on a large scale.[23] A broad view of personalty in the years up to 1850 would suggest that the 'Tivyside' gentry could boast of cash, bonds, plate, furniture, pictures and other effects worth sums ranging from a couple of thousand pounds to about £9,000-£10,000.[24] Davies of Castle Green, Cardigan, mentioned already, seems to have been an exception.

From the 1850s onwards, considerably larger sums are recorded. As will also be seen later, a few of the more resilient gentry, deriving income from sources other than land and through the careful 'husbandry' of surplus cash, could leave sums ranging from £18,000-£20,000.[25] Thus Saunders Davies of Pentre's fortune was reckoned at £18,000, while Thomas Lloyd of Coedmore who died in 1857 and Griffiths of Llwynduris in 1869 (owner of a very small estate) had, respectively, personalty worth about £20,000.[26] At the very summit, in terms of personal wealth, Morgan Jones of Penylan and Llanmiloe, Carms. left, in the early 1900s, £45,000.[27] At the other extreme, a younger son of an impoverished family, such as Gernos, might have less than £100 to his name.[28] An illustrious pedigree, a notable record of public service, 'county' influence—all the *indicia* of gentility—were no substitute for the vital means of survival.

NOTES AND SOURCES

[1]T. M. Humphreys: *op cit.*, pp. 40-7; J. O. Martin: The Landed Estate in Glamorgan, c1660-1760 (unpublished PhD thesis Cambridge 1978), p. 23.

[2]D. W. Howell: *Patriarchs and Parasites: The Gentry of South West Wales in the Eighteenth Century*, 1986, pp. 7-11; CRO/Trant (Yelverton) 177; NLW S.D./Arches 8 (a-y); Noyadd Trefawr/732, 742; Evans George/519.

[3]RCLWM Report 1896.

[4]Return of Owners of Land in England and Wales, 187, ii, Wales, 1875; J. Bateman: *The Great Landowners of Great Britain and Ireland*, 1876 (reprinted 1971); for a *critique* of the 1873 Domesday see J. Bateman: *op cit.* preface, p. vi and B. Ll. James: 'The Great Landowners of Wales in 1873', *NLWJ*, XIV, 3, 1966, pp. 301-320.

[5]I. G. Jones: 'Cardiganshire Politics in Mid Nineteenth Century Cardiganshire', *Ceredigion*, V, 1, 1964, pp. 18-20.

[6]G. H. Williams: 'Probate Records. A Source for Folk Life Studies', *Folk Life*, XX, 1981-82, pp. 8-11.

[7]NLW/St D/CC Cd(P); FG/20/139; 16/32; 25/335; 16/106; 16/60; 9/10; 8/94; 17/5; 20/165; 20/27-8; 16/33; 5/81; 18/358; 20/46-7; 20/195; NLW/Ms 12, 381B.

[8]For an analysis of comparative gentry status and wealth, see D. W. Howell: *op cit.*, pp. 11-14.

[9]FG/8/96.

[10]NLW/St Davids/Wills. FG/18/393-94; 19/191-92.

[11]CRO/Dyn/201-02.

[12]A. Wagner: *op cit.*, p. 124.

[13]NLW/Ms 8732E.

[14]NLW/Noyadd Trefawr/457.

[15]NLW/St D/Arch Carm Probate Records 1720. *ibid*: 1723, 1743, 1747, 18/384, 21/51, 23/78.

[16]NLW/SD/Arch Carm/Wills/1753, 1764; FG/21/170, 260; 25/43. *Ibid*: 22/85; 1/196-97.

[17]NLW/SD/Arches 8 (a-y/1/50).

[18]W. R. Ward: *The English Land Tax in the Eighteenth Century*, 1953, p. 22, 54. F. Jones: The Pembrokeshire Land Tax 1786 [HRO/unpublished typed transcript and introduction]; PRO/IR/113, 114.

[19]D. W. Howell: *Land and People*, 1976, p. 23.

[20]NLW/T. I. Ellis/188-91.

[21]NLW/Owen Colby/887.

[22]NLW/Llwyngwair/692, 2146.

[23]NLW/Llangoedmore/1522.

[24]NLW/Morgan Richardson/2168; NLW/Evans George/859; NLW/St Davids/Wills 1828; NLW/Morgan Richardson/189.

[25]NLW/Llwyngwair/965; NLW/Morgan Richardson/1054.

[26]NLW/Llwyndyrus/123; F. Jones: 'Lloyd of Gilfachwen, Cilgwyn and Coedmore', *Ceredigion*, Vol. VIII, No. 1, 1976, p. 95.

[27]Cd Ad: 18/8/1895.

[28]NLW/Morgan Richardson/974.

Estates—Their Growth and Devolution

With the replacement of *gavelkind* by primogeniture, English land law led to the consolidation and holding of land by one central proprietor who usually, as the eldest son, added to his property, and through '. . . opulence, prudence or cunning . . . swallowed into one mass the surrounding petty freeholders'.[1] The law was geared to the maintenance and survival intact of great landed estates, so that it was impossible to subdivide or transfer land. Through the process of entail, real estate could be tied up in the possession of a line of descendants, with each succeeding generation only having a life interest, subject to the strict control of trustees. The obvious dangers to an estate (which could have been built up carefully over many generations) were the whims and extravagances of a spendthrift who would waste resources on lavish display: houses, the racecourse, foolhardy elections, or the wild pastimes of drink, women and the gaming table. Estates were organised to secure the survival of a caste. Life tenants had a duty to leave their estates intact to their successors. It was the estate which mattered, and not the holder or life tenant; and the law went to considerable lengths to prevent the holder from alienating or wasting the capital.[2] Hence, it was difficult to mortgage or sell land to acquire capital for estate enterprises, agricultural improvement or industrial investment. The 'accidents' of hereditary ownership were burdens on the estate—jointures, portions for dowagers, for younger sons and daughters, which might continue over more than one generation—and only an act of parliament could bar an entail.[3]

In acquiring and extending an estate, three important factors at least were in operation—marriage, inheritance and purchase. A 'good' marriage could be the vital means of extending landowners' estates or of rescuing their faltering finances. Marriage was a commercial arrangement and romantic notions were unimportant.[4] Through the failure of male heirs, and the estate's devolving on an heiress, the property often passed through marriage into another line. With the intermarriage of small neighbouring gentry, the owners of the amalgamated estates were raised to the level of squires. A large established estate might include widely-scattered properties in three or even four counties—leading consequently to the extension of the sway and influence of the owner—as in the case of the Bronwydd, Ffynone and Pentre estates by the 1870s. Throughout the period 1700-1900 instances can be cited of the merger of the lesser estate with that of the larger. The Waun estate,

Henllan, was merged with the Carmarthenshire properties of Ystrad Corrwg in 1711.[5] The Brigstockes of Llechdwnni in Cydweli, Carmarthenshire, 'absorbed' by marriage the Llwynduris and Vaynor estate of Robert Byrtt around 1674, and the Blaenpant and Carrog, Cardiganshire estates belonging to William Jenkins a generation later, thus founding the new Brigstocke dynasty at Blaenpant who were to be influential in the 'Tivyside' area for two hundred years.[6] Small estates such as those of Griffiths of Mountain Hall, Phillips of Lletherneuadd, Lloyd of Pantcilgan and Howells of Wernmacwydd became merged by marriage, only to be fragmented later among co-heiresses.[7] And in the 1750s a similar fate befell the estate of Clynfyw and Duffryn, Llanwnda. Such estates were often sold[8] and in the case of the former, it was bought by Lewis of Llwyngrawys, a prosperous entrepreneur. Inheritance by co-heiresses might result in the sale of an old estate, the proceeds of which might provide valuable dowry to assist in purchasing a new estate for the husband, as, for example, when Captain Stephen Colby acquired Ffynone in the 1750s.[9]

The decline of the Castell Hywel estate largely coincides with the marriage of the heiress of David Lloyd of Brynllefrith and Castell Hywel to Thomas Thomas of Llanfair, in 1779, adding greatly to the latter's estate.[10] When an estate had to be partitioned in order to settle realty on an heiress, a special act of parliament was necessary. This happened when the Neeston estate in south Pembrokeshire was sold on the occasion of the marriage of the heiress into the Pigeonsford family.[11]

'Tivyside' estates which had passed to heiresses sometimes became the property of outsiders. For example, the small 400-acre estate of Tŷ Newydd in Bangor Teifi parish passed in the year 1850 (by the marriage of the heiress) to a London wine merchant.[12] Similarly, Treforgan, near Cardigan, and Cwmhyar in Llandysul parish became part of the Nantgwillt (Radnorshire) and Glangwili (Carmarthenshire) estates.[13]

Side by side with the disappearance of estates and family names in 'Tivyside', one must notice the almost phenomenal rise in the fortunes of some houses in the area over a period of several generations. Notwithstanding the arguments, for and against, the degree by which the landed classes gained or lost through marriage and inheritance,[14] it appears without question that some of the larger 'Tivyside' estates increased considerably through marriage. The Lloyds of Bronwydd married heiresses over a period of 250 years, and acquired the estates of George Bruyne of Pantdafydd at the end of the sixteenth century;

those of Wogan of Wiston and Cilrhiwiau in 1704 and Lloyd of Penpedwast and Henllys in 1737. The estate of Dr John Jones of Haverfordwest was added late in the eighteenth century and that of John Thomas of Llwydcoed, Carmarthenshire, in the early 1800s. The latter union brought in a cash legacy of £7,000, as well as lands in east Carmarthenshire with valuable industrial potential.[15]

The estates of George Bowen of Llwyngwair and Walter Lloyd of Coedmore were enhanced when marriages were made with Anna Posthuma and Easter or Hesther, the co-heiresses of William Thomas of Pentowyn, in Mydrim parish, Carmarthenshire, in 1758. Their uncle William Thomas of Castell Gorfod further added to their good fortune by leaving his valuable estate between them.[16] The Lewes family of Llanllyr and Llysnewydd were able to absorb the Dyffryn estate in Llandybïe (adding mining revenues to their income) in the early eighteenth century, as well as the broad acres of Llanayron (Llannerchaeron) estate in the Aeron valley in 1812.[17]

Not always were auspicious marriages able to sustain estates indefinitely. The Parrys of Noyadd Trefawr had made advantageous marriage alliances since the sixteenth century, resulting in the acquisition of considerable realty in Cardiganshire and north Pembrokeshire. Stephen Parry of Noyadd Trefawr was wealthy and influential enough to sit as MP for Cardigan Boroughs from 1714 until his death in 1724, and at that time the estate's rents surpassed all others in the county. More than a century later the estate was in decline through an unfortunate match between Frances Parry, the heiress of Noyadd Trefawr, and the spendthrift Marmaduke Gwynne of Garth, Breconshire. The merger of Cwmcynon with Gernos augured well in 1711 (when the heiress and daughter of John Lewis married Thomas Parry of Cwmcynon) but this estate, like Noyadd Trefawr, declined owing to mismanagement, recklessness and misfortune.[18]

The failure of male heirs and inheritance by heiresses wiped out the names of Lewis of Cwmawen and Phillips of Moelifor and Dôlhaidd-isaf, when the estates were merged with those of Saunders of Clunfelin and Pentre. Erasmus Saunders' heiress married Dr David Davies of Llandovery, a man of wealth derived from trade, land and his medical profession. He virtually founded the new family of Saunders Davies of Pentre about 1800, whose estate survived for more than a century.[19]

Sometimes, a condition of inheritance, when an heiress married an outsider, was that the husband should adopt the family name and arms—a means whereby the family name could be saved from extinction, albeit by artificial means.[20] It was an exception in the area when Davies of Pentre and Tyler of Gernos did not acquire the family names of Saunders and Parry. The procedure was rigidly followed when inheritance by will imposed such conditions. For example, David Edward Lewes of Dolhaidd took up the additional surname of Lloyd on inheriting the Wern Newydd estate near New Quay and again Capt. William Henry Webley acquired the Parry surname as heir to the Noyadd Trefawr estate in 1816.[21] From the early nineteenth century to the end of our period the convention survived, as, for example, in the families of Lewis-Bowen of Clynfyw, Webley-Parry-Pryse of Noyadd Trefawr and Spence-Colby of Ffynone.[22]

In the devolution of property, family ties remained strong, even when there were no direct male or female heirs. Younger generations, distant cousins—with no exception of succeeding to a patrimony—were fortunate to inherit the estates of wealthier relations. Parcels of the Lloyd estates of Bronwydd and Cilrhiwe were transferred (by means of various settlements) to great nephews and cousins from 1730 to 1870, when they again were merged with the main estate. Lands in Llangeler, Llangoedmor and Penboyr expanded the Cilbronne estate by devise from relatives. The consolidation and preservation of estates such as Ffynone, Rhosygilwen and Atpar Hill meant (over many generations) the devise of property to kinsmen, near and distant. Family feuds were not a bar to ties of blood, as in the case of the Wervil Brook and Atpar Hill estate of John Beynon, which was inherited by a nephew, David Pugh of Manoravon, Carmarthenshire, who in turn left it to the Protheroe-Beynon family of Trewern, Whitland.[23]

Bonds of friendship and obligation were reasons for the transfer of property to outsiders. In 1787 Thomas Lloyd of Cwmgloyn left his estate to his godson, Morris Williams of Trellyffant, provided he resided at Cwmgloyn and maintained the testator's aged uncle.[24] For his work as receiver of the Orielton estate John Colby of Ffynone was amply rewarded with 2,000 acres in east Carmarthenshire.[25] Cilgwyn diminished considerably when the old family of Lloyd had (according to the will of Thomas Lloyd, dated 29 October 1790) to part with two-thirds of their patrimony to Admiral Braithwaite, father-in-law of Benjamin Edward Hall, ancestor of the Fitzwilliams family.[26] Similarly, for some inexplicable reason, John Vaughan of Golden Grove disinherited his numerous kinsfolk, leaving some 50,000 acres in Carmarthenshire to John Campbell of Stackpole Court, who was created Lord Cawdor in 1796.[27] Personal grief for near relations and the loyalty of a young assistant were rewarded when Charles Evans Davis Richardson inherited the Plas, Aberporth, estate from Thomas Morgan, the Cardigan solicitor. Morgan-Richardson, after this fortuitous windfall, further rose socially by marrying the daughter of a West Country baronet and settling at Rhosygilwen.[28]

Failing the acquisition of an estate through marriage to an heiress, an important factor, stemming from marriage which could buttress an estate's finances was the procurement of a substantial dowry. As income from land was precarious owing to the vagaries of weather, crops and the market, the financial stability of the estate was paramount. Each injection of cash was vital for the continuity of the family and its acres. Diplomacy was required in wooing a suitable bride. David Lloyd of Alltyrodyn in 1744 could boast of £200 a year and a fortune of £4,000. He also boasted that he was a 'man of parts' equal to the delicate charms of his would-be-bride.[29] Commonsense and brains were not essential according to David Havard of Goitre-uchaf:

> *Cerais ferch â gwaddol ganddi*
> *Aur ac arian ar eu rhifo—*
> *Ond synnwyr hon oedd fach i'w handlo!*[30]

[I wooed a maiden with a dowry, gold and silver, just for their counting; but common sense she had little of.]

Only very rarely did other factors like religious commitment, discreet conduct and thrifty habits outweigh financial considerations.[31] Blatant fortune hunting as practised by such families as Lloyd of Alltyrodyn roused the scorn of satirists.[32] Marriage portions generally reflect the status of respective families; the better the marriage the greater the portion, which became a vested interest in the bridegroom or his father from the day of the wedding. The young woman's marriage prospects depended on the size of her portion, the greater landlords providing larger portions than lesser folk, often by raising a mortgage or charge on the estate.[33] Generally the large landowners must have attracted the wealthiest heiresses.[34]

This seems to have been the case in 'Tivyside' although on a lower financial scale than in some other parts of Wales. In the early decades of the eighteenth century, small Welsh landowners in decline towards yeoman status could only provide meagre portions of £40 to £80.[35] More well-to-do squires like the owners of estates such as Rhosygilwen, Plas Llangoedmore, and Llanina could afford sums ranging from £300 to £800, the latter being the portion which Lucy Jones of Llanina had on the occasion of her marriage to Squire Lewes of Gernos.[36] However, the £1,500 which the daughter of Lloyd of Mabws had on her marriage to Philip Jones of Lletherneuadd in 1725 was by no means typical.[37]

From about 1750 onwards, such sums were common. For example, Phillips, a doctor in Haverfordwest, provided each of his daughters with £1,750 on their marriage into county gentry families.[38] In 1787, George Bowen of Llwyngwair gave £1,500 to his eldest daughter on her marriage to the Rev. David Griffiths, the 'Methodistical' vicar of Nevern.[39] The exception for this period was the portion of £3,000 which a Miss Fisher of 'Laningel', i.e. Llanfihangel Yeroth (Llanfihangel-ar-Arth) parish, had when she married Phillip Jones of Wernmacwydd in 1757. On the other hand a modest cash sum could be compensated for, when the bride would inherit an estate of a few thousand acres, as, for example, when the Rev. Thomas Thomas of Llanfair married the Lloyd heiress of Brynllefrith and Castell Hywel.[40]

From 1800 onwards families such as those of Bronwydd, Blaenpant, Clynfyw and Pigeonsford on the whole gained through marriage alliances with other south-west Wales families, such matches bringing in sums ranging from £4,000 to £14,000.[41] In the case of some estates, however, it was realised that successive portions could prove to be a burden; for example, when, in 1826 the heir of Pentre, David Arthur Saunders Davies, married the only daughter of Col. Owen Philipps of Williamston, Pembrokeshire, her portion was £4,000. But a similar sum had to be raised by means of a mortgage on the Pentre estate, to provide a dowry for Catherine Angharad Saunders Davies on her marriage to William Webley-Parry of Noyadd Trefawr. In 1851 a further £6,000 had to be raised through another mortgage on the Pentre estate for a similar purpose. Small wonder that Saunders-Davies of Pentre stipulated in his will of 1856, that, after his death, portions were not to exceed £500, and that no further excessive charges were to encumber the estate.[42]

As marriage was, perhaps, the most important single factor in the successful accumulation of estates,[43] some gentry families sought brides with substantial dowries from outside their local shires. Perhaps, as elsewhere, they did so because there was a lack of wealthy heiresses at home.[44] Portions acquired by 'Tivyside' squires through marriage with English heiresses seems to support this view. In the eighteenth century sums ranging from £1,000 to 'several thousand pounds' were not uncommon. The Rev. Alban Thomas, a chaplain at Portsmouth, married a Miss Acton with a portion of £1,000 and a further large unspecified sum. Again the marriages of Jones of Wernmacwydd and Thomas Lewis of Llwyngrawys seem to have greatly profited their estates.[45] A family with heavy debts had to struggle hard to acquire an heiress with sufficient money to rescue the estate, as in the case of David Parry of Noyadd Trefawr, who in 1744 married a Londoner with £4,000 to 'discharge legacies encumbering the Noyadd estate'. This stratagem was to be repeated later in 1800 and 1854, when brides were procured with dowries of £4,000 and £25,000 respectively to underpin the estate's precarious finances.[46] Doubtless the injection of money in order to support younger children, to provide dower in the event of widowhood, and to pay off estate debts prompted the heirs of Blaenpant, Gwernant and Llysnewydd and Cilgwyn to seek brides from outside Wales. In 1905 William Lewes, heir to the Llysnewydd estate, with an annuity of £500, married Daisy Franzeska Wylie of Blaendyffryn, Cardiganshire, and Westcliffe Hall, Hampshire. Her annual income from trusts was about £5,000, a sum which exceeded the rental of many a 'Tivyside' estate. It is significant that there still survived considerable sensitivity concerning marriages which linked the gentry with those involved in trade. In 1899 Edward Crawford Lloyd Fitzwilliams of Cilgwyn married Maud, daughter of Hawtrey Collinssplatt of Brixton House, Devonshire. At the time, the Cilgwyn estate was burdened with a mortgage of £24,000. The marriage settlement meant raising some £30,000 '. . . for the benefit of the young people', according to Charles Home Lloyd Fitzwilliams, the bridegroom's father. Moreover, he (Fitzwilliams) informed Hawtrey Collinssplatt, '. . . I shall I think do more, viz, give your daughter *a safe position and rank which you in trade, being partly dependent on business, cannot.'*[47]

In addition to marriage and inheritance as significant factors in the build-up of estates, sales and purchase were also decisive. Throughout the eighteenth century, land was 'gravitating towards the more substantial gentry, the behemoths of property'. By 1760, in Cardiganshire, nothing is more striking than the changes which had taken place in land ownership.[48]

Many an estate was to disappear, while new ones came into being belonging to families hitherto unknown. Growing indebtedness, depressed agricultural prices and sluggish rentals, and the difficulty in procuring new mortgages, affected the small landowners especially. In the Teifi valley the lesser gentry of Blaenbylan, Cilgynydd, Llwynderw, amongst many others, had disappeared from the scene by the second half of the eighteenth century. The disappearance of the small landowner who could style himself as 'gent', could also be attributed to the precarious proceeds of farming his own land, with little or no rent from other property. The financial plight of the lesser gentry is well demonstrated by the following examples: from 1663 onwards the Llewelyn family of Plas Gilast had to raise several successive mortgages, and Philip Harryes of Clydai parish morgaged six properties to the affluent Warren family of Trewern. Charles Mason 'gent' of Cilgerran in 1711 sold his properties to the *then* prosperous Morgan of Ffynone.[49] The frequency of such transactions provoked the wrath of socially conscious moralists like the *literati* Ifan Gruffydd and Samuel Williams.[50] By the 1740s the Colby family of Bletherston and Bangeston were taking over properties in 'Tivyside' when the estates of Morgan of Pengwern and Blaenbylan were facing increasing debts.[51] Typical of the indebtedness of the lesser gentry were the incumbrances amounting to £4,000 on the estate of Gwynne of St Dogmael's during the years 1726 to 1762.[52]

The theory that the great estates of well established gentry swallowed the smaller ones is not totally applicable for this region. Occasionally, an industrialist and entrepreneur like John Morgan of Carmarthen would underpin debts (and become owner of an estate if the debts were not repaid), such as the £1,800 borrowed by Price of Coedstre in Llangeler parish in 1755.[53] Sometimes, it was not only the landed magnate or wealthy man of commerce who profited from such transactions, but also well-to-do freeholders like Christmas Evan of Henfryn, Llangeler, who acquired farms in the distant parish of Abergwili through mortgages of over £500.[54] The surrender of the family home was a galling experience for bereaved widows and orphans, as when Thomas Owen of Glogue, 'gent', in 1767 mortgaged his home to Stephen Colby of Ffynone for £400, which sadly led to fore-closure against Owen's widow two years later.[55] A decline in social status naturally followed the compulsory surrender of one's property. Thus in 1774 a descendant of the Morgan squires of Pengwern Fawr had to resort to trading as an 'apothecary' in Cardigan following the sale of his property to the wealthy Dr Jones of Haverfordwest.[56]

The impression of a grasping landowning class, only motivated by greed and avarice and intent on annexing vast tracts of land, does less than justice to the situation, when investment in land was the only means possible for absorbing surplus capital. Before the full development of commerce and manufactures had its impact on a modern economic system, land was not simply the most desirable and safest investment; it was the only readily available investment for any capital beyond what could be prudently used in actual farming. The provident and fortunate freeholder, or man who had made money in trade, invested in more broad acres. As has been seen already in 'Tivyside', and as in other parts of Wales, the improvident and unfortunate were compelled to face irredeemable mortgages, unpaid debts and family ruin. Not only was the prosperous landowner constantly enlarging his estate as an economic investment but also for the social standing which was measured by the extent of his property. Along with tithes, advowsons and manorial rights, such landowners were buying up the perquisites of a social class, the undisturbed control of the life of a neighbourhood.[57]

In 'Tivyside' the process continued apace, and may be illustrated as follows: the Lewes family of Gellydywyll and Lewis of Llwyngrawys both enlarged their estates, the latter buying Clynfyw from Davies of Little Cloister, Westminster, for £800 in the 1750s.[58] One means of acquiring land indirectly was by wholesale mortgage. The Morgan family of Plas, Aberporth, did this over scattered properties within their own parish and farther afield. Foreclosure often followed, along with more purchases, so that from 1742 to 1802 the estate had expanded to some 1,300 acres, with mortgages on lands in the Carmarthenshire parishes of Abergwili, Cydweli and Llanpumsaint.[59] The nucleus of the Pantsaison estate had a long history since the time when John Devonald, gent, had mortgaged his holding in the early 1600s to James ap Evan ap Rees.[60] The James family continued purchasing land, especially from 1710 onwards, and in the same way other small estates, such as Cilbronne, continued to expand.[61] The prosperous merchant, too, was constantly making inroads into landownership. The Nugents and Makeigs, eager to acquire the social cachet associated with landownership, bought and leased more and more land in Llandygwydd and Cardigan.[62]

An example of a new estate coming into being is Gwernant, originally the home of medieval *uchelwyr* and later absorbed by the Parrys of Noyadd Trefawr.[63] In 1795, when the latter were in dire financial trouble, Gwernant was bought from Frances Gwynne of Noyadd Trefawr and Garth, Breconshire. The new 'dynasty' of Lloyd Williams of Gwernant came about with the marriage of Thomas Williams and Mary Lloyd, heiress of the Llwynrheol estate in mid-Cardiganshire.[64] The Lloyd Williams family had trading links with the Orient which lasted for over a century. Through purchase and mortgage (some £10,000 in all and no compunction in foreclosing) Gwernant became a significant estate.[65] Profits from eastern enterprises and a handsome dowry made it possible for the Rev. Benjamin Millingchamp to buy Plas Llangoedmore from David Edward Lewes Lloyd of Dolhaidd for £3,500.[66]

Of the large estates, Bronwydd, Llwyngwair and Ffynone expanded through a deliberate policy of purchase, in addition to the more fortuitous incidence of prosperous marriages and fortunate inheritance. Bronwydd, described in 1562 as 'Tyddyn y Bronwydd' (the homestead of Bronwydd) developed into a major 'Tivyside' property.[67] In the many stages of land purchase, the most important was that of a moiety of the barony of Kemes (Cemaes) in 1762 from the insolvent John Laugharne of Llanrheithan for £2,000.[68] In addition, parts of the Henllys estate in Pembrokeshire and lands in mid-Cardiganshire were added to the Bronwydd acreage.[69] The voracious acquisition of land by Dr Jones of Haverfordwest (an investment of about £30,000) at the end of the eighteenth century in widely scattered areas further added to the Bronwydd estate through the marriage of Thomas Lloyd to Jones' daughter.[70]

Possibly to gain parity of social prestige which Thomas Lloyd of Bronwydd had in the Newport area, and to create a compact estate in close proximity to his demesne lands, George Bowen of Llwyngwair purchased property in neighbouring parishes—part of the Haroldston estate of Sir John Packington for £4,462.[71] Some twenty years later, in 1774, part of the Wenallt estate was acquired for £4,727, and later Bury or Berry Hill was bought from Thomas Lloyd of Bronwydd comprising some 456 acres of 'arable . . . meadow . . . and pasture lands . . . an extensive warren . . . a good salmon weir . . . with all those slangs of Thomas Lloyd intermixed.'[72]

Through their tenacity of purpose the Colby family of Ffynone and Rhosygilwen developed over two centuries from minor squires to one of the principal families in 'Tivyside'. In addition to extreme good luck, they carefully used their resources to build up an estate in Clydai and Cilgerran, starting in 1716 with a purchase of lands worth £117.[73] After a series of small gains the major prize in the family's history was Ffynone acquired for £1,748 in 1742.[74] Captain Colby continued to invest in land to the extent of some £10,000 at least, of which about £3,000 was paid for the Skyrme estate of Vaynor in Llawhaden parish following Chancery proceedings in 1787. Of the three hundred acres involved, two lots—Amroth and Rhydlangoig—were of particular

value because of the 'good veins of coal and mines'.[75] From the year
1800 transactions amounting to at least £25,000 can be traced to
acquire land as a 'ring fence' around Ffynone, purchases being made
of outlying parts of the estates of Bronwydd, Cilwendeg and Pentre.[76]
Thereby, an eagle-eyed landlord could keep his tenants under close
surveillance, not to mention the convenience to estate carpenters and
masons with workshops near the big house, the availability of casual
labour for the squire's home farm, and such incidentals as the keep of
hounds for the squire's sporting pursuits. Lands at the other end of the
county were acquired with a view to quarrying and commercial development, such as parts of the Corston estate in south Pembrokeshire.[77]

From 1875 onwards, when investment in agriculture land was not
attractive, Colby of Rhosygilwen invested some £5,000 for parcels of
land in the industrial areas of east Carmarthenshire in order to have a
profitable stake in leasehold development, tin works and mines.[78]

The families of Jones of Cilwendeg and Penylan followed a policy of
estate expansion. Enriched by the revenues and sale of the Skerries
lighthouse for about £300,000 in 1844,[79] they bought up the lands of
impoverished yeomen and minor squires like Evans of Treffgarne
Hall, Pembrokeshire. Thus, some £13,000 was expended on lands in
Clydai and Penrhydd parishes which bordered on the Cilwendeg
demesne lands, and provided sporting facilities as well. Above all, they
were extending their sway and prestige within easy radius of the big
house.[80]

NOTES AND SOURCES

[1]Walter Davies: *A General View of the Agriculture . . . of South Wales*, i, 1814, p. 119; see p. 17, n. 2.

[2]G. Kitson Clark: *The Making of Victorian England*, 1962, p. 218.

[3]H.J. Habakkuk: 'English Landownership 1680-1740', *EcHR*, X, i, 1940, p. 7.

[4]D. W. Howell: *op cit.*, pp. 14-15.

[5]NLW/*Evans George*/443-44, 452.

[6]NLW/*Ms 12374C*; Burke: *op cit.*

[7]NLW/Cwrtmawr/1640.

[8]CRO/JF/219; NLW/Owen Colby/865.

[9]*loc cit.*

[10]NLW/Ms 8716 B.

[11]T. I. Jeffreys Jones: *Acts of Parliament Concerning Wales, 1714-1901*, 1966, pp. 1-24.

[12]CRO/JF/SC/1894.

[13]J. Francis: Sale Catalogue 1896—Tŷ Newydd Estate; CRO/Trant (Yelverton) 1350; the Cwmyar estate was valued £5,000 in 1845; in 1873 its acreage was 1,000 acres.

[14]C. Clay: 'Marriage, Inheritance and the Rise of Large Estates in England, 1660-1815', *EcHR*, 2 ser, 21 (1968), pp. 509-10.

[15]NLW/Bronwydd/1567, 2008, 2011, 2803, 6054.

[16]F. Jones: 'Bowen of Pentre Ifan and Llwyngwair', *Pembs Historian*, 6, 1979, p. 49; FG/20/169; id: Lloyd of Gilfachwen, Cilgwyn and Coedmore, *Ceredigion*, vol. viii, no 1, p. 92.

[17]Burke: *op cit.*

[18]D. Huws: 'Noyadd Trefawr Deeds and Documents', *NLWJ*, X, 4, 1962, pp. 381-83; NLW/Morgan Richardson/862; Walford: *op cit.*

[19]D. E. Jones: *Hanes Plwyfi Llangeler a Phenboyr*, 1899, pp. 408-10.

[20]C. Clay: *op cit.*, p. 504.

[21]FG/22/180; NLW/Noyadd trefawr/1296-98.

[22]NLW/Owen Colby/827; *Who's Who in Wales* 1920.

[23]FG/22/187-88; CRO/EG/Box 75, 87; FG/23/140; *The Welshman*: 31/7/1874; NLW/Owen Colby/735.

[24]FG/5/79.

[25]NLW/Owen Colby/267-68; *ibid*: (Spence Colby) 1134.

[26]CRO/Coedmore/10/29; F. Jones: *op cit.*, pp. 90-1.

[27]*id*: 'The Vaughans of Golden Grove', *THSC*, i, 1960, pp. 210-14.

[28]D. L. Baker-Jones: 'C.E.D. Morgan-Richardson', *Ceredigion*, iii, 2, 1977, pp. 147-80.

[29]NLW/Ms 8742 B.

[30]NLW/Penboyr Vestry Book 1748-80.

[31]NLW/MS 8742B.

[32]J. H. Davies: *op cit.*, i, p. 157; NLW/Cwrtmawr/111-13.

[33]C. Clay: *op cit.*, pp. 503-18.

[34]D. W. Howell: *op cit.*, p. 23.

[35]NLW/Morgan Richardson/1941; FG/20/182-83.

[36]CRO/JF/642; FG/26/89; NLW/Morgan Richardson/720-21.

[37]NLW/Highmead/447.

[38]FG/15/550-53.

[39]NLW/Llwyngwair/825; NLW/Morgan Richardson/1863; *Gent. Mag.*, 1757, p. 531.

[40]NLW/MS 8761B.

[41]HRO/Pen/10/3; NLW/Evans George/81112; NLW/Morgan Richardson/1048; FG/17/556; NLW/Bronwydd/3727-30; NLW/Owen Colby/349.

[42]NLW/Bronwydd/3727-30; NLW/Morgan Richardson/1054.

[43]Dr Hoskins believes it was so—see W. G. Hoskins and H. P. R. Finberg: *Devonshire Studies*, 1952, pp. 217-28.

[44]J. O. Martin: *op cit.*, pp. 228, 276; D. W. Howell: *op cit.*, p. 21.

[45]NLW/Ms/4706D; *Gent Mag.*, 1759, p. 531; NLW/Clynfyw/Box 1.

[46]NLW/Noyadd Trefawr/485, 503.

[47]NLW/Llysnewydd/Bundle 64; NLW/Ticehurst Wyatt (Gwernant) Box I; NLW/Cilgwyn Ms LB/50/23 Dec 1897; CRO/Beckingsale/DD/-. In 1817 Edward Lloyd Williams of Gwernant married Dorothea de Pipe Bell of Uttoxeter whose portion was £3,000.

[48]P. R. Roberts: 'The Decline of the Welsh Squires in the Eighteenth Century', *NLWJ*, XIII, 2, 1963, pp. 159-61; J H. Davies: 'Cardiganshire Freeholders in 1760', *WWHR*, III, pp. 73-8.

[49]NLW/Owen Colby/229-32; 242.

[50]G. H. Jenkins: *op cit.*, p. 463; Ifan Gruffydd (1656-1734), poet, b. at Twrgwyn, Troedyraur parish, Cards; wrote carols in the 'halsingod' form as well as religious 'cywyddau' [odes] ; the Rev. Samuel Williams (1660-1722), vicar of Llandyfrïog, author of religious poems and 'halsingod', copier of mss. and antiquary, father of the Rev. Moses Williams. *DWB*.

[51]NLW/Owen Colby/242, 1003, 2324.

[52]CRO/JF/70-1, 73-4, 77-8.

[53]CRO/Trant (Yelverton) 183; J. E. Lloyd (ed), *History of Carmarthenshire*, 1939, ii, p. 323 seq; H. J. Habakkuk: *op cit.*

[54]CRP/Trant, Yelverton/1375.

[55]CRO/JF/335-38.

[56]*ibid*: 616-17.

[57]J. Rhys and D. B. Jones: *op cit.*, pp. 440-42; H. J. Habakkuk: *op cit.*, p. 12.

[58]NLW/Evans George/355; CRO Coedmore/1/116-18.

[59]NLW/Morgan Richardson/1644, 1661, 1663, 1709.

[60]FG/25/128.

[61]NLW/Llangoedmore/1465.

[62]CRO/Beckingsale/30/1275; NLW/Llwyndyrus/46, 131.

[63]NLW/Noyadd Trefawr/10, 11.

[64]*loc cit*; Burke: *op cit.*, 1906; information from Dr. Evan L. James.

[65]NLW/Ticehurst Wyatt (Gwernant) Box I.

[66]NLW/Morgan Richardson/1469-70.

[67]NLW/Bronwydd/679.

[68]*ibid*: 1951-54.

[69]*ibid*: 1460, 2303, 2873, 3382.

[70]*ibid*: 1762-63, 2632-39, 2666-67, 2692-95, 3078-79.

[71]NLW/Llwyngwair/796, 858, 1163.

[72]NLW/Morgan Richardson/1968; Bronwydd/3468.

[73]CRO/JF/588.

[74]*ibid*: 192, 220.

[75]NLW/Owen Colby/254, 1011.

[76]CRO/JF/22, 238, 240, 254, 287, 290-92, 404, 440, 541, 652-53.

[77]*loc cit.*, S. Lewis: *op cit.*, i, *sub* Castlemartin.

[78]NLW/Owen Colby/98, 114, 118, 120.

[79]NLW/Penally/43, 47.

[80]NLW/Morgan Richardson/2173; CRO/JF/379-80.

Trewern

Penybenglog

Pantsaison

Castle Green, Cardigan

(Illus. from *Annals and Antiquities*, T. Nicholas, 1872.)

The Priory, Cardigan
(Illus. from *Cardigan Priory in Olden Days*, E.M. Prichard, 1904.)

A gentry town house, Cardigan

Glaspant

Llwyngrawys

Cilbronne

Coedmore

Pant-gwyn

Noyadd Trefawr

Penylan

Penylan: garden front

Plas Penwenallt

Blaenpant

Illus.: National Monuments Record Wales – H.R. Lloyd (Thomas Lloyd Collection)

Section 2

The Squire and his Estate

Landed Wealth

According to H. M. Vaughan three qualifications were necessary for a person to rank as a squire—the possession of a mansion, a home farm or demesne, and an estate, no matter how large or small, farmed by tenants of the owner of the mansion.[1] Other components might be added—pleasure grounds around the mansion; cottages and gardens let to labourers by the landowner for rents or services; lands let for building purposes for a ground or rack rent (especially in developing urban sites in the second half of the nineteenth century); unenclosed land or wastes with tenants' rights of common, the landlord exercising control over commons, rivers, lakes, fisheries, mills, markets, sporting rights and other franchises. The pecuniary gain and prestige considerations attached thereto were factors in assessing the status of the squire and the economy of his estate.[2]

The traditional close psychological and social bonds between the squire and tenant, their mutual well-being and the economic success of the estate, deemed by the elite to be impregnable bastions of the *status quo* against radical attack, were expressed in 1882 by Mrs Saunders Davies of Pentre, thus: 'The union of landlord, tenant and labourer is the chief strength and support of our country and her institutions; I cannot conceive of a happier picture than that of the owner of land, who by prudence and care, improves his estate and watches over the interests of his tenants and labourers.'[3] This ideal relationship was part of the 'mythology' that many of the gentry believed in sincerely, and tried to foster. How far it existed is difficult to assess, and there is considerable evidence which strongly suggests the contrary.

The marked ecological change which took place in Wales over the centuries had meant the clearance of dense forests to allow settlement and the heavy grazing of livestock. In the nineteenth century Cardiganshire was 'very bare country' with 'barren and champion land', i.e. land open and unenclosed. Travellers described uncomfortable and dangerous journeys over desolate hills and moorlands, and the happy relief of reaching cultivated valleys. B. H. Malkin in 1805 drew attention to enclosed parcels of land where corn such as wheat, oats, a good deal of barley and some rye were cultivated.[4] Of the Teifi valley, other topographical writers such as Richard Fenton and Samuel Rush Meyrick commented on the new mansion houses and plantations which dotted the landscape, reflecting the affluence of the local gentry whose wealth largely came from their landed estates.[5]

The activities and mode of living of the 'Tivyside' farmers—tenant farmers, small freeholders and lesser gentry—were inevitably conditioned by prevailing geographical and climatic factors. A narrow valley, hemmed in by steep slopes, resulted in shallow soil on the hillside and relatively deep soil on the valley floor, ranging in quality from light sandy loam to fairly heavy clay. The Teifi valley peasant community was largely made up of agriculturalists, with a sprinkling of fishermen in the coastal hamlets. Apart from country crafts, there was virtually no heavy industrial development, with the exception of short-lived tin works near Llechryd, slate quarrying in Cilgerran, and, by the end of the nineteenth century, a flourishing woollen industry on factory lines along the Teifi and its tributaries from Newcastle Emlyn to Llanybydder.[6] Towns like Cardigan, and the villages along the coast had, for centuries, been involved in 'ship building' in terms of fishing boats and small craft.[7]

From the observations of Lloyd and Turnor in 1794, one gleans that a largely pastoral region produced mainly store livestock, butter and cheese, with surplus quantities of such dairy produce exported to Bristol and West Country towns. Owing to enclosure, sheep rearing had declined, and the concentration of cereal crops on the same ground, year in and year out, had led to diminishing returns. The growth of peas intermixed with oats and barley also caused soil impoverishment. Turnips and root crops were grown by only a few. The main fertilisers were lime and marl, decayed manure, and seaweed in the barley growing areas along the coast. Composts were rarely made, draining was neglected and the burning and paring of soil had debilitated the land. Farm implements were poor, methods backward, and accommodation for man and beast deplorable. Lloyd's view of Cardiganshire is corroborated by others, especially Walter Davies who considered the farmer and his holding very unfavourably in relation to his counterpart in similar areas in England.[8] The same situation prevailed in the geographically similar north Pembrokeshire and Carmarthenshire areas of 'Tivyside'.[9]

During the nineteenth century the character of farming was mixed, with emphasis on livestock and dairying, the breeding and rearing of store animals and the making of butter and cheese. In cereal production, oats and barley predominated over wheat in the years 1801-1870, with pasture acreage significantly increasing afterwards. Rotation husbandry, though included in leases, could not be followed always, on account of the soil and humid climate. For the most part, farming in Wales throughout the century was backward apart from a few large and progressive farms. The small tenant farmer lacked sufficient capital; and the education and enterprise to farm skilfully and scientifically was lacking. Artificial manures were but little used, although the application of lime had increased since the eighteenth century. Farmyard manure was universally in use although methods of storage deprived it of much of its efficiency. Animal feeding stuffs—hay, oats and barley—were home-grown, with a little linseed oil and cattle cake purchased. The insufficient cultivaton of root crops, use of cheap grass seed and outmoded tools and implements, along with an antiquated bias against mechanisation, were the marks of most Welsh husbandry even in the last decades of the nineteenth century.[10]

Communications had remained restricted because of geographical features. Not until the nineteenth-century turnpikes and railways was it possible to open up a distant and remote region like 'Tivyside' for greater travel and trade. Over the centuries surplus farm crops, such as cereals and dairy produce, had been exported from places like Cardigan to Bristol and the west of England (as Lewis Morris observed in 1748).[11] Local markets and fairs provided an outlet for the sale of farm produce and stock, the latter purchased by the drovers ending up in the fattening pastures of the English midlands and south-eastern counties.[12]

A marked feature of the rural economy (as in Cumberland and Westmorland) was the number of small farms of the peasant or family type. A natural instinct to live by the land, the pastoral character of farming and the hereditary instincts and traditions of landlord and tenant all contributed to 'customary relations' which survived for centuries.[13] The process of amalgamation which George Owen of Henllys had observed in the early 1600s in south Pembrokeshire had not affected the size of holdings in the Teifi valley.[14] Greater parcels of land were rented in south Pembrokeshire, in 'Little England beyond Wales', in the seventeenth century,[15] and to a certain extent in parts of Carmarthenshire a hundred years later.[16] In our area, farms averaged 50-60 acres, and a Cardiganshire farm of 200-300 acres was exceptional.[17] On the whole, holdings varied from a *tyddyn* (homestead) of a few acres to an average farm of about 50 acres and a large unit of between 100-150 acres. These small farms were worked by the family, with the help of extra casual labourers during the hay and corn harvest, the latter often living in a *cott* on the main holding and enjoying the benefit of a little land to support a cow or two and a few sheep. It is probably correct to say that, as these holdings were hardly viable economically, their tenants would be linked with ancillary occupations carried out in shops, smithies, inns and taverns. A degree of self-support would be provided by a cow, pigs and poultry. Even larger acreages sometimes had to complement income from a trade or craft. For example, Thomas Jones of Danygribin in Penboyr parish, a stonemason and weaver, had a holding of 25 acres. Again, the innkeeper at Llechryd was also a carpenter, who farmed some 30 acres of land.[18] In fact, this was the pattern in 'Tivyside' up to the war years 1939-45.[19]

Of particular significance to any study of the 'Tivyside' area are the recollections of two remarkable parish historians at the end of the nineteenth century.[20] They reiterate what observers like Walter Davies and others had said of an earlier period—the stagnant state of agriculture in equipment, methods, hidebound customs and attitudes.[21] The farmers' and labourers' diet was basic in the extreme—*cawl*, porridge, barley bread, cheese and buttermilk—with a little meat upon occasion. Farmhouses and cottages were generally poor in every respect—overcrowded and insanitary, with fevers and diseases rampant. The much vaunted Agrarian Revolution had passed them by, and such efforts as had been made by innovative improving landlords had changed little of the outlook and methods of the average farmer. A deep bond existed between farmer and labourer, the latter providing extra help during busy times in exchange for ground to plant a few rows of potatoes or turnips. Given that farmers were too poor to pay for this extra help, the system was vital for the farmer's success in operating his holding. The cottager, craftsman or artisan, who provided the casual labour, depended also on the farmer's help in ploughing and planting his couple of acres.

The fortunes of an agricultural community, with the squire's landed estate, tenants, farmers and labourers as its components, were very much at the mercy of economic movements—the vagaries of weather, fever and plague, as well as the outbreak of war, civil commotion and agricultural change. The increase in population, and the consequent need for more food, were strong market forces to challenge the methods of landholding and cultivation.

The effect of wars in the eighteenth century—the Seven Years' War ending in 1763, the War of American Independence, 1775-83, and the Napoleonic Wars with a continental blockade—led to the price of corn reaching an unprecedented scale. A sustained upward movement in prices from the mid-eighteenth century, reaching a high war level after 1790, lasted until 1815.[22]

The years of peace brought about a slump resulting in protective measures such as the Corn Laws. As has been seen, agriculture in Wales lagged behind that of England. The chill economic depression was keenly felt in the Teifi valley. John Vaughan of Tŷ Llwyd bemoaned in 1813, 'hard times for farmers, no sale of anything ye land produces —ye country gentlemen will be badly off excepting such rich ones as Mr Lloyd of Alltyrodyn and there are not many of his description I believe.' Two years later in 1815 he wrote that 'farmers [are] broken hearted'. Scarcity of money was severely felt, and although there was an ample supply of farm labourers there was no money to pay them. Again, only squires like David Lloyd of Alltyrodyn were financially buoyant having 'been hoarding all their lives'.[23]

Meetings were held to petition parliament for tax relief in respect of horses, malt, salt and other commodities.[24] The slump in prices was noticed by a Rhydlewis farmer: locally good wheat had fallen from 20s. a bushel to 5s., fine barley and oats had slumped to 2s. and 1s. respectively, while butter, cheese, pork, beef and mutton had fallen in price 'and everything in proportion'. As a result, many farmers could not pay their rents: 'in consequence of the high prices of the lands which rose with the high price of commodities—the landed proprietors in general are very cruel to their tenants.' Bailiffs, like carrion crows, were delivering distress warrants upon poor tenants and Cardigan gaol was full of debtors. The value of land was so low that the local estates of the bankrupt Sir Watkin Lewes could not be sold to clear his debts of £30,000.[25] Between 1830 and 1853 a continuing depressed agriculture, a slump in land values and restricted markets were the besetting evils facing the farmer. Protectionist measures like the Corn Laws failed the hopes of their promoters and were repealed in 1846. The social conditions and economic depression in west Wales have been carefully analysed by Professor David Williams in connection with the Rebecca riots.[26] Distress and semi-starvation befell many, with a wide gulf between gentry and peasantry.

Whereas the introduction of railway transport helped the agricultural economy indirectly, its effect was not fully felt in the lower Teifi valley for another half century. Nevertheless, rising prices from the 1850s to the mid 1870s changed farming fortunes. To some extent at least, butter, cheese, fat pigs and other agricultural produce could find its way easier to the 'pits' and 'works' of the Glamorgan industrial areas. Cattle, too, could be sold to dealers for further sale in northern industrial towns as well as in south Wales. But this short-term prosperity was not to last, a depression in agriculture setting in from 1873 onwards. A series of bad harvests culminating in the disaster of 1879 meant more and more imported corn and other goods which, since about 1860, had made a dent in home production. According to some estimates, 37% of British consumption of cereals, 50% of cheese and butter and about 20% of meat were being imported by the 1870s.[27] Uncontrolled free trade and cheap food from the New World led to an exodus from an agriculturally-based economy. In the face of foreign competition, capital invested in land, improvement of buildings and equipment gave a poor return. Government intervention to ameliorate the plight of the farmer led to the Agricultural Holdings Acts of 1875 and 1883 which recognised the principle of compensation to departing tenants for unexhausted improvements to their holdings. Reduced rates, through government grant aid, and the setting up of the Ministry of Agriculture in 1889 were mere palliatives which had no long-term effect. The switch from arable to dairy farming was another expedient, but with only short-term results.

In the decades after 1870 the main farm products in the Teifi valley were store cattle, dairy cows, sheep for breeding and slaughter, and pigs for the pork and bacon market, along with farm dairy produce.[28]

The spread of railways in the industrial areas of south Wales gradually extended westward. The railway reached Llandysul in the 1860s linking up the area with Carmarthen and eastwards, but it was only at the end of the century that it reached Cardigan via Whitland and north Pembrokeshire, while the Llandysul line was at this time extended to Henllan and Newcastle Emlyn. The advantages to the farmer were cheaper transport costs and speedier access to new and better markets other than local fairs, along with droving which inevitably declined to some extent at least.[29] The Welsh farmer had now the means of breaking away from the traditional pattern of semi-subsistent agriculture. But achievement, however, fell far short of opportunity, and the railways did not lead to any basic change in the traditional system of Welsh farming, as happened in many areas of Scotland and England. The outlook of Welsh farmers was not altered as a result of the opening of markets, a fact especially shown in their failure to take advantage of railways in the development of the dairying side of their industry.[30]

In a wider context, a relatively stable society, optimistic of economic progress and industrial expansion, was shaken to its foundations from the 1870s. Economic forces had struck at the base of agriculture;

landholding was no longer as safe as it had been, and political forces in Wales from 1868 onwards were inimical to the centuries-old power of the landlords and gentry rule. By 1890 a stake in land was no longer a valuable asset and had become too risky. As W. P. Ll. Lewes of Llysnewydd put it, '. . . the tenure of land is an uncertain quantity in these days of robbery and spoliation'. Another landowner said, '. . . I am not a believer in Welsh land mortgages just at these times of tithes, riots . . . anything to do with land in Wales now I do not at all fancy.' The landlord class and dependent tenantry were in deep financial trouble with the squires' estates heavily mortgaged.[31] What was happening to agriculture had more serious results than any setback which commerce or industry suffered. Politically, it had the ingredients of massive change which shook the aristocratic control of the parliamentary representation of the counties, as became evident in the general elections of 1880 and 1885.[32]

Landlord and tenant relations depended as much on the human element as upon the bonds of contract and capital.[33] When Mrs Saunders Davies of Pentre spoke of the union of landlord, tenant and labourer as the chief strength of the country and its institutions—the prudent landowner improving his estate and caring for his tenants and labourers—she was expressing the sacrosanct dogma of the ruling classes. This paternalistic benevolence was derived from a feudal and medieval view of the natural order, and of the relationship between lord and peasant.[34] A society of preordained ranks and orders with its necessary degrees of authority and subordination to the gentry as a class, was hardly called in question. Good order, politeness, peace, social relationships were moral as well as social terms, conceived by the architect of the universe who had distributed mankind into different ranks yet had united them under the superintendence and patronage of the rich. At a time when such a dogma had long been rejected H. M. Vaughan was still at pains to defend the system in his book *The South Wales Squires* which was published in 1926.[35]

The squire's paternalistic concern for his social inferiors might be termed the squire's prerogative, in as much as his income allowed him 'superior' activities and pursuits not shared by the rest of the community. His lifestyle—mansion, hounds, horses, carriages and equipage, books, pictures, literary and aesthetic pursuits—was part of the 'image' and 'conspicuous display' of the squire. All this had to rest on sure economic foundations, yet, more often than not, the landed estate was a unit of consumption rather than of agricultural production and profit and it is argued that profit was not of paramount concern to either landlord or tenant before 1900.

The squire's superintendence was of a 'general' nature, delegating duties to personnel with more specialist knowledge—agents, bailiffs, stewards and the like. Consequently, the squire had the freedom to pursue activities not dictated by economic necessity,[36] but the cost of his lifestyle had to be paid out of rent. A wise landlord managed and improved his estate judiciously—irrigating, draining, manuring, building suitable cottages for workmen, employing carpenters and masons to do maintenance work. Capital expenditure had to be weighed against possible return in terms of estate profit and the welfare of the squire and his dependants. 'A country gentleman has an immense power of usefulness and mischief at his disposal . . .,'[37] wrote one observer, and a good squire was motivated by the utilitarian ethic of the greatest good for the greatest number within his community.

From evidence already examined, it appears that many of the 'Tivyside' gentry in the eighteenth century were actual practising farmers. There existed a large number of small *plasau* with the farm buildings surrounding the main house—such as Dôlhaidd-isaf, Ffosesgob, Llwynderw, Tredefed, Aberdwylan, Pantcilgan, Pantyrlys and Perthgereint—which have survived to this day as farmhouses. A lesser number of houses were larger as the Hearth Tax Returns suggest. Inventories, as we have shown, certainly up to mid-century concentrated more on farm implements, live and dead stock than on 'household stuff'. Mansions such as Bronwydd, Alltyrodyn and Llwyngwair were to be rebuilt and enlarged as the fortunes of the squire determined, while the lesser houses declined in importance. Generally speaking, as the lifestyle and 'status' of the squire advanced, so his commitment to the task of farming decreased. In the middle decades of the eighteenth century William Brigstocke of Blaenpant and his 'mistress' worked the home farm, looked after poultry, made butter and cheese for household consumption and marketed the surplus.[38] From 1778 to 1797 Anne Evans, wife of the squire of Highmead and a sister of Sir Watkin Lewes, closely supervised dairy maids at the early hour of six in the morning, and made detailed notes in her diary.[39] The processes of butter- and cheese-making, washing utensils and the like fell under the eagle eye of this redoubtable and unrelenting gentlewoman. Few of the gentry, however, showed the assiduous concern for up-to-date estate management and agricultural practice as did Thomas Lloyd of Bronwydd. No doubt influenced by new ideas, as was Thomas Johnes of Hafod, Lloyd (from 1780 to 1795) kept a detailed journal of useful information on good husbandry.[40] Lime was brought to Bronwydd from kilns along the Cardiganshire coast, with Lloyd himself participating in farming tasks. In 1786 he recorded: 'I carried myself thirty-eight cart loads.'[41] In the nineteenth century it was only a few gentry who actually practised farming themselves. A Llandysul rustic, Daniel Josi (1809-95), recalled how in the early decades of the century John Lloyd of Gilfachwen did a lot of farm work himself—'. . . *fel y byddai boneddigion yr oes honno*' (. . . as gentlemen used to do in those days).[42] In the 1860s the Thomas brothers of Dôl-Llan and Llanfair—perhaps the 'booby' squires of the area—were working farmers.[43] No task was beneath some country gentlemen, as Howell of Glaspant recorded of himself in 1896. He drove cattle, mucked out cowsheds and performed the seasonal tasks of thinning and weeding turnips, hay making and corn binding.[44]

Although the impression is conveyed that the number of squires who got their hands dirty by working on their farms grew progressively smaller from the late eighteenth century onwards, nevertheless the home farm remained a significant feature of the lord's mansion and demesne. It provided food for the house, fodder for farm stock, horses and cattle, while surplus produce was sold in local fairs and markets. Thus, poultry, dairy produce, potatoes, apples, cattle and sheep were sold from Alltyrodyn and Highmead in the years 1820 to 1832 to local consumers in Llandysul and Llanybydder.[45] From the point of view of agricultural development, even if costly items in estate expenditure, the experiments with improved techniques and new breeds of stock were important. The gradual pace of change and advance in knowledge was achieved, no doubt here, as much as has been claimed for other parts of the country, partly by the lengthy work of trial and error carried on by little-known country gentlemen.[46]

For economic and social reasons, the involvement of the 'Tivyside' squires with the home farm varied considerably during the nineteenth century. Generally speaking, it would appear that the expense of maintaining a home farm was not justified in relation to the total estate income. Owing to incomplete records it is difficult to pronounce firmly about the profitability of the home farm. From July 1812 to April 1813, the large Falcondale estate's home farm accounts show only £100 or so in credit, while another farm on the estate run by the landowner showed no profit at all.[47] No doubt the importance and continuation of the home farm depended on a variety of considerations, such as the interest of the life tenant, the state of agriculture, domestic factors within the squire's family, as well as political issues. During the period 1829 to 1848 a spate of sales at home farms took place, such as those at Llysnewydd, Bronwydd, Glaspant, Troedyraur and Llwyngwair. The home farm at Gwernant was reduced gradually from 1845 to 1848, the land being let to tenants, at a time of acute depression and civil disturbance.[48] Moreover Lloyd Williams, the squire of Gwernant, was intensely disliked for his cavalier attitude towards the Rebecca rioters and for his threat to dismiss estate workmen.[49]

The decease of the squire, and the winding up of his personal estate or change of ownership, could lead to the sale of farming stock, as took place at Castle Malgwyn, Hafod Grove and Noyadd Trefawr. A life tenant interested in agriculture, and in providing work for the local community, might revive farming activity, as at Blaenpant, Llysnewydd and Pentre at the end of the nineteenth century.[50]

In 1909 a practical squire like Charles Home Lloyd Fitzwilliams of Cilgwyn, carrying out a drastic policy of retrenchment on his estate, realised that a diminishing market for surplus produce, owing to the shortage of workers now emigrating to the 'works', rendered it cheaper to buy corn, hay, stock feed as well as dairy produce for the mansion from local tenants.[51]

The live and dead stock, implements and machinery of the home farm varied considerably. From sale lists, it can be seen that Castle Malgwyn in 1812 demanded a large number of draught and riding horses, brood mares, colts, cows and poultry, along with items of pleasure and ornament like dogs and peacocks.[52] A pioneering farmer squire like the Rev. Lewis Turnor of Wervil Brook in the early 1800s had a large number of horses—possibly to supply wartime demands— as well as 50 head of Castlemartin cattle, in addition to the usual stock and crops.[53] William Lewes of Llysnewydd in 1825-29 concentrated on sheep rearing with breeds such as Ryeland, Leicester and South Down.[54] Certain gentry were prepared to experiment with different and new breeds of cattle: 50 head of cattle at Gwernant comprised Durham, Hereford, Guernsey, Ayrshire and Shorthorn. Lloyd Williams' progressive outlook is also shown in the cultivation of 6 acres of beans with 24 for turnips, mangolds and swedes, essential ground clearing and winter fodder crops.[55] New machinery included Gardner's Patent Turnip Cutter, a bone bruiser, a threshing machine, a chaff cutter and oil cake crusher.[56]

A 'high point' in home farm practice was reached by Mark Anthony Saurin of Cilwendeg in the years up to 1871. A wide-ranging variety of animal breeds of exclusive pedigree stock and patent machinery to meet with every farming need by modern manufacturers such as Murton and Turner, Ransom and Sims display an advanced degree of interest and sophistication.[57] On the other hand, an extravagant sporting squire like Sir Edward Webley-Parry-Pryse Bt., of Noyadd Trefawr, in the early 1900s, had a relatively small number of heads of usual farm stock and only two carthorses, but about thirty hunters and thoroughbreds.[58]

Details are scant of the numbers employed on home farms. The large acreage farmed by Thomas Lloyd himself at Bronwydd—some 231 acres[59]—at the end of the eighteenth century does point to the need for a fairly large workforce of skilled and unskilled labour. Years of training would be necessary to learn skills relating to the care and feeding of cattle and horses and the supervision of sheep at lambing time. The carter and waggoner would have to know how to load his vehicle so that it did not topple over on uneven tracks. Much of this country lore would be handed down and gradually learnt by inexperienced and often ignorant farm-hands. Animal diseases would be cured by traditional country remedies and what had been picked up orally from a local farrier. The squire, too, had his *Gentleman's Magazine* and the occasional book in his library dealing with useful veterinary knowledge. In addition, casual labour was in demand at seed time and harvest, and for ditching and draining, clearing woodland and coppices, stone gathering on leys, weeding the garden and the like. At Gellydywyll in 1772 four men and three women were regularly employed around the house and farmyard, and were paid, according to their degree of responsibility and skill, an annual wage of:

Men	£7-7-0	£4-15-0	£4-5-0	£3-2-0
Women	£4-0-0	£2-8-0	£2-10-0	

This constituted a total of £28-7-0 out of estate income of about £333.[60] In the larger establishment of Blaenpant, additional casual labour amounted to between 15 and 17 men. Women and boys engaged during haymaking peak periods in the 1790s were paid 4d to 6d per day—a higher wage than the permanent workers at Gellydywyll.[61]

A nineteenth-century mansion and its home farm evolved into a complex social organism. As the house became more elaborate with its distinct occupational hierarchy of butler, housekeeper, cook and

numerous maids, so the home farm, stables and coach house became
separately placed from the main house, with a staff comprising a bailiff,
coachman, grooms, gamekeeper, cowman and shepherd as well as
workmen under the general description of servants or labourers, male
and female. In addition to farming tasks, ornamental gardens, flower
borders and hothouses provided work for 'weeding women' who would
also attend to the feeding of calves and pigs, pick wool and hair for
mattresses and clean out saddle rooms. The total permanent workforce
at large establishments like Blaenpant, Coedmore and Cilgwyn varied
from about 13 to 20 or more in the 1870s and '80s.[62] In spite of new
labour-saving farm machinery on some home farms, the numbers of
harvest-time casual workers seem to have remained the same. Casual
work on the squire's demesne was a welcome opportunity for local
artisans and craftsmen to add a shilling or two to what they would
otherwise earn, as was the case with the cobbler who lived in one of the
lodges at Cilwendeg.[63] Slight variations occur in wages computed on a
weekly basis: male workers at Coedmore and Cilgwyn received
something like 9s to10s a week with women receiving half as much At
harvest time, a few shillings extra were paid to guarantee enough
available 'hands' to gather in before the weather changed.[64] Wages are in
many ways deceptive on account of the traditional tendency of the
'lower orders' to depend on the big house for all sorts of 'vails', i.e
gratuities and largesse from the kitchen and dairy—basins of dripping
and lard, surplus food from the squire's banquet, cheese and butter, and
vegetables from the garden.

Open discontent was rare between squire and employee. Only one
instance can be traced of unrest, namely, a casual female worker at
Cilgwyn who 'struck for increase'.[65] Owing to the economic difficulties
from the 1880s Blaenpant, Cilgwyn and Llysnewydd cut down
markedly on their workforce. Whereas at Cilgwyn in 1881 there were
20 full-time outside workers, they were reduced to 9 by 1900.[66] A poor
house like Tŷ Llwyd never boasted of more than two or three male
workers—and in those circumstances the carter and stable lad had to
don the livery of butler and footman on special occasions.[67]

NOTES AND SOURCES

[1]H. M. Vaughan: *op cit.*, p. 2.

[2]A. W. Jones: Agriculture and the Rural Community of Glamorgan, circa 1830-1896 (unpublished PhD thesis, Wales, 1980), p. 93.

[3]*The Welshman*: 25/8/1882; F. O'Gorman: *Electoral Deference in 'Unreformed' England 1760-1832*, J.M.H., no 56, 1984, pp. 392-394.

[4]B. Howells: 'Social and Agrarian Change in Early Modern Cardiganshire', *Ceredigion*, VIII, 3, 4, 1974/75, pp. 256-57.

[5]R. Fenton: *op cit.*, pp. 271-76; S. R. Meyrick: *op cit.*, pp. 162 seq.

[6]J. G. Jenkins: *The Welsh Woollen Industry*, 1969, pp. 247-52, 257-59, 262.

[7]*id*: 'The Maritime Heritage of Some Southern Ceredigion Villages', *Ceredigion*, X, 2, 1981, pp. 111-127.

[8]T. Lloyd and the Rev. Mr Turnor: *A General View of Agriculture in the Counties of Cardigan*, 1794, pp. 8-17; W. Davies: *General View of the Agriculture of South Wales*, 1814.

[9]C. Hassall: *A General View of the Agriculture of the County of Carmarthen*, 1794, . . . *Pembroke*, 1794; 'marl'—a mixture of calcium carbonate, clay and sand.

[10]D. W. Howell: *Land and People in Nineteenth Century Wales*, 1977, pp. 3, 39, 75-6, 129-39; R. J. Colyer: 'Crop Husbandry in Wales before the Onset of Mechanisation', *Folk Life*, 21, 1982-83, pp. 49-70.

[11]Lewis Morris: *Plans of Harbours . . .*, 1748, p. 12.

[12]NLW/Highmead/5, 22; R. J. Colyer: *The Welsh Cattle Drovers*, 1976, pp. 83-4, 92-102.

[13]J. Rhys and D. B. Jones: *op cit.*, p. 434-36.

[14]George Owen: *Owen's Pembrokeshire* (ed H. Owen), 1897, pp. 59-63; *DWB*.

[15]T. Dineley (ed); *Official Progress of the First Duke of Beaufort . . .* Wales, 1684 (1888 ed), p. 276.

[16]RCLWM Report, 1896, pp. 328-30.

[17]C. Hassall: *op cit.*, (Pembs), p. 10; *op cit.*, (Carms), p. 11; T. Lloyd and Turner: *op cit.*, p. 8.

[18]ER/1851; C. Thomas: 'Rural Society in Nineteenth Century Wales', *Ceredigion*, VI, 4, 1971, p. 330.

[19]Personal recollection.

[20]D. E. Jones: *op cit.*, p. 330; E. Davies: *Hanes Plwyf Llangunllo*, 1906, pp. 31-44.

[21]W. Davies: *op cit.*, pp. 31-4, 44-6; RCLWM 1896, Appendix, p. 29.

[22]C. W. Crawley: *Economic Change in England and Europe* (New Cambridge Modern History), 1965, IX, pp. 30 seq.

[23]NLW/Highmead/Box P/File 18.

[24]*Cm Jnl*: 29/3/1816, 25/2/1817.

[25]NLW/D. Pryse Williams/MS 15638A.

[26]Dd Williams: *The Rebecca Riots, A Study in Agrarian Discontent*, 1955, pp. 90-117;

[27]P. Deane and W. A. Cole: *British Econmic Growth, 1688-1959*, 1969, p. 32.

[28]J. Ll. Davies: 'The Diary of a Cardiganshire Farmer, 1870-1900', *W. J. Ag.*, X, 1934, pp. 5-7.

[29]D. W. Howell: *op cit.*, pp. 121-27.

[30]*id*: 'The Impact of Railways on Agricultural Development in Nineteenth Century Wales', *W.H.R.* 7, 1, 1974, pp. 60-61.

[31]NLW/Llysnewydd/Bundle 38; RCLWM, ii, pp. 735, 740; iii, p. 586; *The Welshman*: 14/10/1892.

[32]G. K. Clark: *op cit.*, p. 51; K. O. Morgan: *Wales in British Politics*, 1970, pp. 84-90; D. Cannadine: *op cit.*, p. 27.

[33]A. W. Jones: *op cit.*, p. 400.

[34]J. Rhys and D. B. Jones: *op cit.*, p. 481.

[35]A. Briggs: *op cit.*, pp. 9-10; H. M. Vaughan: *op cit.*

[36]D. W. Howell: *Patriarchs and Parasites . . .*, pp. 52-62; F. M. L. Thompson: *Landed Society in the Nineteenth Century*, 1969, p. 151; M. Cragoe: *An Anglican Aristocracy, the Moral Economy of the Landed Estate in Carmarthenshire, 1832-1895*, 1996, pp. 69-70.

[37]'Maxims on the political, social and domestic economy of the English Country Gentleman . . .' NLW/Ms 9319C.

[38]NLW/Evans George/1322-50.

[39]B. G. Charles: 'The Highmead Dairy, 1778-1797', *Ceredigion*, V, 1, 1964, pp. 76-83; *DWB*.

[40]Cardiff Public Library/4.4669.

[41]*loc cit.*

[42]J. Thomas: 'Gyda'r Camera', *Cymru*, 1895.

[43]HRO/WIL/226.

[44]NLW/Glaspant/Diary 1896.

[45]NLW/Highmead/5, 22.

[46]D. W. Howell: *op cit.*, p. 219; G. E. Mingay: *The Gentry* . . ., p. 97; *id*: *The Agricultural Revolution, Changes in Agriculture, 1650-1850*, 1977, pp. 1-5, 59.

[47]NLW/Falcondale/Gp V/138/xii, xvi.

[48]*Cm Jnl*: 20/5/1829, 16/4/1842, 25/9/1846, 16/7/1847, 11/8/1848, 22/9/1848.

[49]Dd. Williams: *op cit.*, pp. 218, 273.

[50]*Cm Jnl*: 2/3/1812; NLW/Noyadd Trefawr/1516-17; NLW/Owen Colby/823-24; *The Welshman*: 28/4/1882; NLW/Evans George/1916.

[51]NLW/Cilgwyn/LB53/2 Mch. 1909.

[52]*Cm Jnl*: 21/3/1812.

[53]*ibid*: 4/8/1810; the Rev. David Turnor (1751-99) cleric and agriculturalist of Crugmawr, Llangoedmor, along with Thomas Lloyd of Bronwydd, author of a *General View of Agriculture of the county of Cardigan 1794*; his brother the Rev. Lewis Turnor (1757-1834) lived at Wervilbrook, and continued his brothers' agricultural interests; *DWB*.

[54]*ibid*: 4/4/1828; 20/5/1829.

[55]*ibid*: 16/7/1847.

[56]*ibid*: 22/9/1848.

[57]*ibid*: 25/8/1871.

[58]*Cd Ad*: 6/5/1904.

[59]NLW/Bronwydd/6804.

[60]NLW/Noyadd Trefawr/1684.

[61]*ibid*: 1587-88.

[62]NLW/Cilgwyn/LB27-29; CRO/EG/Box 23.

[63]ER/1861.

[64]CRO/Coedmore/5/1.

[65]NLW Cilgwyn: *loc cit*; R. Porter: *op cit.*, pp. 89-90.

[66]NLW/Evans George/1916; Llysnewydd Farm Account Book 1895-1910 (photocopy in the Carmarthen Record Office).

[67]NLW (Tŷ Llwyd) Journal of Mrs E. B. Wood.

The Administration of the Landed Estate

Most of the acreage of the landed estates, especially the larger ones, was let to tenant farmers and in order to function efficiently, a large estate had to be organised and administered by an almost professional class of agents, stewards and bailiffs. The absence of the squire through public business, pleasure and foreign travel meant that the responsibility for the smooth running of the estate fell upon such officials. Moreover, the 'enlightenment' of the eighteenth century which influenced agricultural methods, land use and the highest standard in good husbandry demanded a considerable degree of professionalism. In 1815, Walter Davies observed that estates were managed by agents, professional land stewards 'well versed in the several departments of rural economy', and others who received rents and drew up leases.[1] The ideal person had multifarious responsibilities, whether the squire was resident or absent, above all to keep his master's confidence without indulging in tittle tattle. Diligence, competence with accounts, business acumen and probity were essential virtues.[2] Richard Morris claimed that he had succeeded in making great improvements in the estate rentals of his employers,[3] in contrast to estates which were in financial trouble. Morris claimed that the problems of Mr Vaughan of Nannau in Merionethshire (doubtless like many in 'Tivyside') were due to '. . . ye deficiency of Mr Vaughan's education and his being unacquainted with ye common Rules of Arithmetick'.[4]

On a small compact estate the squire was able to keep an eye on his tenants, but properties like Bronwydd, Ffynone and Pentre, spread over three or even four counties, rendered the services of an agent essential. Estate officials, over-zealous and perhaps acting beyond their powers, could be symbols of oppression, enforcing harsh leases, watching over commons' encroachments, acting parsimoniously with regard to monies for estate improvements, unconscionable in dealing with rent arrears and urging distraint of goods and evictions. The Welsh agent in the eighteenth century was certainly depicted as unscrupulous by satirists like Twm o'r Nant, but not all agents, by any means, were of this description. In addition to organising farm repairs and the renovation of the mansion house, deploying woodwards, cowmen, farm hands as well as indoor staff, a steward occasionally attended to important ceremonial functions in the annals of the big house, such as manorial perambulations, birthdays, funerals and processions.[5] More than anything, the official concerned had to develop the estate and advise the landlord of the 'most profitable way of utilising the estate in regard to the present and its welfare for the future'.[6]

Having become a recognisable profession in England and Wales by the late eighteenth century,[7] land stewardship attracted persons from all over the British Isles to west Wales. Settling in towns like Cardigan, Haverfordwest and Carmarthen, they quoted the patronage of noblemen like Lord Dynevor or Lord Cawdor in the local press. They advertised their skills in accounting, keeping journals, and double-entry ledgers, as well as in advising on draining land, mineral exploitation, caring for woodlands and plantations and other forms of capital outlay.[8]

On account of more widely spread estates, 'county' business, travel and absence from home, especially from the mid-eighteenth century onwards, 'Tivyside' squires of standing and consequence could no longer administer their estates personally. A type of lesser squire, often a county attorney, acted on behalf of his more substantial neighbour, such as Thomas Howell(s) of Glaspant who was employed by John Colby of Ffynone from the 1790s—supervising the building of the new mansion, plantations and mining enterprises. Owing to constant disputes and Colby's shady dealings, he resigned.[9] A lawyer-agent of a widely different complexion, and a considerable landowner in his own right, John Beynon, was appointed by Thomas Lloyd of Bronwydd as steward of the barony of Cemaes in 1817. His ill-repute was aggravated because he was remunerated '. . . from the profits arising out of Chief Rents, Estrays, Mortuaries, Alienations derivable from the barony',[10] at a time when these feudal dues had in many instances fallen into abeyance.[11] A harsh exacting steward like Beynon, when in the employ of Benjamin Edward Hall of Cilgwyn in the 1820s, insisting as he did on 'rent days as fixed and steadily kept', could at least strain the relationship between landlord and tenant, especially at a time when the Cilgwyn estate was being partitioned, revalued and relet.[12]

Animosity within a rural community could result from the efforts of a conscientious and capable agent, like George Goode of Carmarthen, who worked for George Bowen of Llwyngwair, not only in adminis-trating his estate but in asserting the latter's claims against Thomas Lloyd of Bronwydd's hegemony in Newport and neighbouring parishes.[13] Members of the Jenkins family of Cilbronne were landowners and agents born and bred in the locality, and fortunately had personal knowledge of tentants and their needs. Thomas George of Cardigan was appointed in 1837 by Lloyd of Bronwydd to look after estates and mining operations in the three south-west Wales counties.[14] This policy was followed by the Bronwydd estate for generations with the agent being paid an annual retainer 'free from tax and deductions', and other cash burdens imposed on the tenants, thereby helping to create harmony between tenant and landlord.[15] It was essential for a wise landlord to have not only a competent agent skilled in his profession, but a wise man who could distinguish between feckless and indolent tenants, the thrifty and industrious, and who could also be the arbiter between jealous tenants. Such a one was David Thomas of Gelliorlas, Lord Cawdor's agent in Cenarth, at the end of the nineteenth century, a local farmer who was acclaimed as 'the most reliable and capable man of business . . . with a mental capacity far beyond the average'.[16]

But, however efficient and conscientious individual agents were, as a class they were, as already indicated, not popular, especially if they participated in measures to enclose commons. Charles Hassall and Richard Jones of Pantirion aroused bitter passions in north Cardigan-shire,[17] especially when they acted for Brackenbury in enclosing land which resulted in violent law breaking during *Rhyfel y Sais Bach* (The Little Englishman's War).[18] In January 1831 a Cilgerran land surveyor was attacked and robbed by a gang 'dressed as sailors'. Although the situation in 'Tivyside' was on the whole fairly peaceful, a deep sense of injury continued over many generations after Thomas Saunders of Perthyberllan and others enclosed parts of Llangeler common.[19]

Ignorance of the Welsh language, suspicion of the non-native informer, and an authoritarian disregard for Welsh folk and their sensitivities often exacerbated an already bad relationship.[20] The local lawyer, auctioneer, squire-agent, even of Welsh extraction, was often suspect as the landowner's lackey. He might also lack the necessary knowledge and expertise relating to good husbandry. Agents of Gogerddan lands in south Cardiganshire in 1744 were incompetent, according to Lewes of Gellydywyll,[21] a situation unsatisfactory to both landlord and tenant. In 1875 Edward Crompton Lloyd Fitzwilliams of Cilgwyn, exasperated by his lawyer-agent's incompetence in drafting legal documents, dismissed him as '. . . a round man in a square hole'.[22] The most serious objection to the land agent was that he was a petty tyrant, partial, unjust, one who accepted bribes, and often, as an outsider, biased against nonconformists.[23] The Llwynrhydowen chapel furore highlighted the iniquities perpetrated against a Welsh dissenting community. Although not typical of the state of affairs in the Teifi valley generally, it was sufficient to stir latent ill-feeling into a blazing conflagration, especially when the agent concerned was totally without principle in the way he manipulated a young landowner, who was an absentee rake and imbecile to boot.[24] On the other hand, some prudent and wise landowners administered their estates themselves without going to the expense of employing an 'English or Scottish Agent'. In the 1870s James Bevan Bowen of Llwyngwair won admiration and praise for his sympathy and practical help to tenants of every denomination.[25] The Blaenpant and Pentre estates were administered at the end of the nineteenth century, mainly, by the widows Maria Brigstocke and Fanny Saunders Davies. Both were considered with some regard on account of their concern for the welfare of their tenants and families, provided the latter supported them in religion and politics, and showed the usual deference expected from the lower orders towards their betters.[26]

The compilation of map books, charts and surveys were important features in estate management. A large landed estate was constantly changing, with the sale, exchange or consolidation of otherwise scattered properties into compact farms or blocks of property, not intermixed with the lands of other owners. It was essential, therefore, to have properly delineated plans of estates and farms.[27] The profession of a land surveyor became more important from the 1750s, with Welsh landowners imitating their counterparts in England. Often in the eighteenth century land surveyors combined their special skill with other activities, such as farming. They had intimate knowledge of climate and soil, and of the whole spectrum of society from squire to peasant.[28] In 'Tivyside' the names of John Butcher and Samuel Bartley suggest that they were 'professionals' from outside Wales, although there were local surveyors, too, like Richard Jones of Pantirion, Thomas Lewis, William Couling and the well-known Charles Hassall. In order to use land to the best advantage, estates like Llwynduris and Rhosygilwen were surveyed in the 1750s and larger properties like Bronwydd and Pentre at the end of the century. Fear of one landowner's encroaching upon his neighbour's land was ever present. To protect his interests Thomas Lloyd of Bronwydd, in 1795, had Newport marsh surveyed 'to show boundaries', and thereby asserted his manorial rights which included fishing and shooting.[29]

A fairly new owner of an estate might wish to have a valuation and advice on future development or sale, as did David Lewis of Llwyn-grawys in 1776.[30] Because of family arrangements such as settlements or mortgages, sound reliable valuations were essential before money could be raised. Railway and industrial development, in the last century, made the landowner aware of the opportunities for utilising his land for other sources of profit as well as farming. The services of established firms like Davies of Ffrwdfâl and John Francis of Carmarthen were indispensable.[31]

By virtue of letting their land, British landowners became partners with their tenants in the business of agriculture. Owners provided the land and the fixed capital—farmhouses, buildings, roads and fences. Tenants, for their part, provided the working capital—stock, plough teams, implements, seeds and manure, as well as the labour, skill and enterprise in husbandry.[32] Leases were regarded by some commentators as the essential instruments towards an improved system of agriculture, and security of tenure motivated tenants to embark on long-term improvements such as liming, manuring, planting trees and cash outlay on farm buildings.[33] According to Hassall, however, farm buildings were often in a state of wretched dilapidation through the apathy and poverty of tenants, who felt wholly secure in their holdings.[34] This attitude towards the whole running of the farm, was possibly engendered by the lease for three lives which gave security of tenure. On the other hand, insecurity of tenure was the reason given for the neglected and dilapidated condition of the Peterwell estate in 1811: '. . . the tenants dread of any expense in improving their lands, repairing their houses, or building new ones, lest they not be permitted to occupy them'. Generally, clauses in leases were seldom used to impose new methods but to prevent the tenant from misusing property, with detailed clauses aimed to improve soil fertility.[35] Up to the mid-eighteenth century, 'Tivyside' leases specified merely duration, annual rent and feudal dues. A Blaenpant lease of 1716 seems exceptional for its restrictive covenants concerning timber, woodlands and enclosure to keep out cattle.[36] From the 1760s, however, a more progressive attitude is discernible on the part of landowners in our area, who tried to encourage tenants to lime and manure ploughed land,[37] and to stamp out the pernicious custom of cutting 'matts', i.e. blocks of turf for fuel and burning the ground surface, a custom which impoverished the soil.[38] Moreover, penalty clauses came into operation—'not to lop or cut down or uproot timber . . . break up any lay ground or plough etc., under penalty of £4 per acre', as in a Ffynone lease.[39] Landlords like Thomas Lloyd of Bronwydd and James Bowen of Llwyngwair stipulated the quantities of lime and other fertilisers to be spread, the reseeding with clover and rye grass, while straw and manure were not to be sold or removed from the farm.[40] Some landlords such as Hart Davis imposed stiff penalties for tree lopping or ploughing up of meadow land; for example, in 1807 a Peterwell lease imposed a penalty of £20 per acre for the latter.[41]

Good husbandry clauses appear to have been increasingly the pattern in the nineteenth century, not only relating to fertilising the soil and preventing 'matting' but also with regard to the maintenance of farm buildings. Disregard of these clauses could lead to penalties and possibly surrender of the lease.[42] Unrestricted freedom of cropping, the sale of straw and manure, and other bad practices had led to soil exhaustion and had impoverished farmers before the days of more enlightened agricultural practice. Such a sorry state of affairs had been largely due to loose terms in leases, according to one English observer.[43] But instances occur in 'Tivyside' of harsh terms resulting in inequitable burdens falling upon the tenant, e.g. a Ffynone tenant in 1815 had to build a suitable farmhouse within one year, keep and repair outbuildings, and observe strict husbandry conditions on pain of being given notice to quit in three months.[44] Again in 1865 a 21-year lease of Blaenbylan Fawr in Clydai parish (at an annual rent of £100) laid the entire burden of maintaining and repairing buildings on the tenant.[45] It was this type of lease which was so obnoxious to radical politicians like Samuel Roberts (S. R. of Llanbryn-mair) and Tom Ellis, who alleged that the overwhelming mass of farm improvements had been carried out solely by the Welsh tenant farmer. From estate rentals, correspondence and evidence before the Land Commission it is manifest that (to a certain extent at least) some landlords had devoted part of their income to estate improvement.[46] James Lewes of Gelly-dywyll had in the mid-eighteenth century remitted rent of £23 a year on Pontgarreg, a holding of 90 acres, for a period of four years on condition that the tenant built a new house.[47] Likewise, on the Ffynone estate a tenant paying £75 a year in 1788 was allowed £20 from the first year's rent, 'such a sum to be laid out for repair of hedges' and 'a boundary wall about the Fold'.[48]

By the middle decades of the nineteenth century a few efficient landlords were active in estate improvements. Thus Cilgwyn farms were equipped with water pumps at the landlord's expense, so long as tenants undertook their haulage from Carmarthen.[49] Aware of the backwardness of some farmers, E. Crompton Ll. Fitzwilliams in 1869 lamented 'ye lack of modern methods and pattern of farming'. He inaugurated a rebuilding project on his estate, such as the model farm of Blaenpant and dairies, cheese room, and other farm buildings at Cafan along with cottages, hedges and roads, costing in all about £5,000 capital outlay.[50] Frequently a young squire inheriting his patrimony initiated a programme of reassessment and improvement, as did Thomas Thomas of Dôl-Llan who in 1865 inherited an estate 'in dilapidated condition',[51] or Thomas Davies Lloyd of Bronwydd who embarked in 1845 on a programme of repairs which, for example, amounted to £500 in 1860 and £1,250 in 1861-62.[52]

In the absence of detailed estate accounts for the area, it is difficult to assess the percentage of estate income spent on repairs and improvements. A few isolated examples may indicate the attitude of a few landlords. Thus over a four-year period in the 1850s £330 was spent on the 300+ acre farm of Trefaes Fawr on the Noyadd Trefawr estate, the rent per annum rising from £214 to £228 as a result.[53] On the same estate, Hirwaun Mill and house, let at £30 per annum on a 21-year lease, was rebuilt for £120.[54] During the years 1872-78 a programme of repairs and renovation was undertaken on the Blaendyffryn and Alltyrodyn estates of the young John Davies Lloyd, amounting to an outlay of £1,115 followed by intensive planting of 189,000 trees, a project costing £318.[55] One-third of the Blaenpant estate rents of £4,500 was spent on 'estate outgoings and repairs' in 1898-99, but this figure also included remission of tithe, and management costs.[56]

As in the rest of Wales, improvement in 'Tivyside' was limited because of the amount of capital made available by the landowner, while the tenant had little surplus cash to invest. Burdens such as tithes, feudal dues and services, the backward attitude on the part of tenants, and, above all, the fear of increased rents were forces inimical to a buoyant agriculture. A survey of the Llanaeron estate in the Teifi valley in 1863 is typical in showing the problems facing landowners in the area, however enlightened and eager some at least may have been to improve their estates and the living conditions of their tenants. It mentions '. . . buildings generally very much in the ordinary condition of buildings in the district—except in some of the farms where they are new and good and can be renewed without *any great drain on the rental of each current year*'.[57]

With so many areas of conspicuous consumption proving a constant drain on the financial resources of the gentry, it is hardly surprising that expenditure on their estates to bring about lasting improvements should have been inadequate. Very few estates could claim, like

Clynfyw, to be in '. . . a state of repair considerably above average of estates in this county [Pembrokeshire] and many of the farm houses and buildings are magnificent . . .', according to Davies of Ffrwdfâl's survey in 1888.[58] As far as can be ascertained, this property, unlike most estates in the area, bore little or no heavy incumbrances and, above all, the landowner had the will to do what was best for his estate and tenants.

It goes without saying that a prudent landowner desired as much profit as possible from his land and, to secure this, improved methods of agriculture were paramount. Walter Davies had observed in 1814 that there existed in south Wales a number of landowners eager to promote 'improved culture', and who in their respective localities experimented on their home farms with the latest husbandry techniques.[59] Although new ideas about agriculture had been put abroad in Britain since the end of the seventeenth century, and a 'gradual pace of change' had taken place rather than a dramatic agrarian revolution following the experiments of Tull, Townshend and Coke of Holkham,[60] it was towards the end of the eighteenth century that marked strides were made in our district. Thomas Johnes of Hafod in north Cardiganshire, and to a lesser extent Thomas Lloyd of Bronwydd in the south of the county, stand out as farsighted pioneers who realised the importance of soil fertility, crop rotation, the intro-duction of new breeds of cattle and sheep and the like. A rapidly increasing population, the threat of famine in 1793, the possibility of a long war with France made agriculture a cause of concern for the government, and the improving and spirited landlord became an important feature of the period.[61] Reports on a county basis, prepared for the new Board of Agriculture, were aimed at assessing the existing state of agriculture and the means for its improvement. County agriculture societies had come into existence since the 1780s in the south-west Wales shires, fostered by leading public men, and to a certain extent by gentry eager to apply new knowledge to farming. The initial enthusiasm of these societies, however, was not sustained. Walter Davies and Thomas Johnes of Hafod complained of the apathy of some gentry, noticeable in their absence from meetings and failure to keep up subscriptions.[62] Moreover, the tenant farmer was conservative and backward-looking, lacking the means to adopt new methods. He was, possibly, reluctant to embrace agricultural change and improvement because of the burden of tithes which swallowed up any profit before he had recouped the cost of improvement.[63]

In varying degrees, however, some gentry continued their patronage of county societies and local agricultural shows up to the end of the nineteenth century. It took the form of money subscriptions, prizes for agricultural crops, ploughing, hedging and ditching and other farming skills, as well as incentives to local labourers and artisans to keep their cottages and gardens tidy and to be industrious in local crafts such as knitting, spinning and weaving. John Vaughan of Golden Grove (with lands in Cenarth and Penboyr parishes) subscribed twenty guineas to the Carmarthenshire Society in the 1780s.[64] Gold medals and money prizes figure prominently as incentives. It must not be forgotten that the gentry regarded support and attendance at agricultural gatherings in the 1840s as an essential facet of their social status, and an exercise in the good relations supposed to exist between squire and tenant, gentleman and yokel, such as in the 'merry making . . . of the bonnie lasses and merrie laddies . . . on premium Friday'.[65] The gentry themselves competed in certain classes, but not against tenants; individual landowners sponsored ploughing matches on their own land as, for example, at Pantgwyn in 1864 and at Cwmcynon in 1877. Mrs Brigstocke of Blaenpant annually awarded prizes for the best root and green crops grown on her estate in the 1880s.[66]

A few 'Tivyside' squires, like Thomas Lloyd of Bronwydd in the early 1800s, were actual innovators on their own holdings. Edward Lloyd Williams of Gwernant had some six different breeds of cattle on his 446-acre demesne farm;[67] likewise, Mark Anthony Saurin of Cilwendeg could boast of pedigree livestock and the very latest in agricultural machinery. Towards the end of the nineteenth century Col. Jones-Parry of Tŷ Llwyd and John Vaughan Colby of Ffynone introduced 'ensilage' as a new method of hay harvesting, while Augustus Brigstocke at Blaenpant won national awards for poultry in the early 1900s. Prize bulls and boars, as well as fertiliser-spreading machines, were kept at Ffynone for the benefit of tenants.[68] C. E. D. Morgan-Richardson raised pedigree shorthorns which were exhibited throughout the land.[69] Local critics of the gentry in the nineteenth century regarded many of them as a 'good set of fellows . . . but they are not distinguished for depth of thought or business qualifications, and as passive spectators . . . landlords of such character deserve to have the ignorant and unimproving clowns they are likely to get as tenants . . . the *adscripti glebae* of olden time . . .'[70] E. Crompton Ll. Fitzwilliams of Cilgwyn in the 1870s refused to support agricultural societies and ancillary activities.

He was equally caustic about the backward state of the Welsh farmer, which could only be cured by landlords's demanding full economic rents for their farms and 'taking care that tenants had sufficient capital'.[71] Whilst it is true that, in too many instances, the gentry were passive onlookers exercising genteel patronage in social diversions—dinners, concerts and such gatherings held under the agricultural improvement banner—nevertheless, some of them were eager for change and the betterment of their estates and tenantry.[72]

In 1846 David Arthur Saunders Davies of Pentre advocated not only agricultural improvement but also 'religion and morality'—no doubt with the Rebecca troubles in mind—as part of general education so that 'every extension of agriculture added to the social comforts of all men'.[73] In August 1854 John Battersby Harford of Falcondale added an altruistic and moral dimension to the utilitarian argument for better farming, improved cottages, and the education of the 'ignorant and degraded', in stating that it was a duty 'to God and my neighbour, to lay out from any superfluity as much as I can spare for the good of the people and the estate'.[74] Capt. S. H. Jones-Parry, the squire of Tŷ Llwyd, advocated caution against bringing politics into education in agricultural improvement at a time when the land question was seething in the 1880s and 1890s.[75]

Apart from experimenting in the actual practice of agriculture, some 'Tivyside' squires took steps to enlighten the farming community in their localities. According to W. O. Brigstocke of Blaenpant, Welsh farmers were not a go-ahead class; living in an isolated neighbourhood 'they naturally cling to old customs and old ways'.[76] Lord Cawdor's encouragement had led to publications on drainage and rotation of crops,[77] but as these were in English they would hardly have made an impact on the average Welsh-speaking farmer. Apart from the occasional publication, books in Welsh dealing with the day-to-day practice of farming were rare.[78] Morgan Richardson, Jones-Parry, as well as a few clergymen, undertook the education of the Tivyside farmer through public lectures and demonstrations. The invention of 'butterine' and the importation of foreign butter led to a campaign for better quality home-produced butter and improved hygiene in dairying methods, such as the 'Laval' separator, milk analysis and a central creamery. The most advanced factories in this country and abroad were visited, and their methods recommended in and around Cardigan and Newcastle Emlyn.[79] Brigstocke campaigned for agricultural co-operatives (so that middle men did not pocket the profits) and a measure of protection in respect of the price of dairy produce. The Welsh yeoman class would be saved, and landlords would be involved in the organisation 'for them to have something to do'.[80] As a persistent propagandist for better farming Morgan Richardson circulated information on continental model farms and urged the need for state loans to smallholders as well as the setting up of local creameries and bacon factories.[81]

In addition to their involvement in agriculture, British landowners were frequently engaged in exploiting the mineral resources of their estates, and (contrary to their theories of gentility) saw no disgrace in industrial and commercial enterprise. Landowners were keenly aware of the additional revenues that could be derived from industry and trade to meet any pressing financial demands facing them.[82]

But, in some gentry circles in 'Tivyside', trade was frowned upon even as late as the end of the nineteenth century. With an air of exasperation Gwinnett Tyler of Gernos complained that '. . . a gentleman is the last person to have anything like business to do with', a comment concerning lack of gentry support for bringing the railway to the area.[83] Inglis Jones of Derry Ormond and Davies of Castle Green were frowned upon because their wealth originated in trade[84]—although they had family connections on account of marriage with the Vaughan (Crosswood) and Bowen (Llwyngwair) families.[85] In the 1890s Hawtrey Collinssplatt of Devon (whose daughter was to marry Edward Crawford Lloyd Fitzwilliams, the heir to the Cilgwyn estate) was regarded disparagingly because, although he was a wealthy businessman, he was unable to provide the status and station in life for her as the future *grande dame* of Cilgwyn (see above p. 51).

The sparse mineral resources capable of profitable exploitation in the area, and the social attitudes and financial constraints of the 'Tivyside' squires, account for the very limited commercial and industrial developments of estates. Unlike the estates of Cawdor, Dynevor, Gogerddan and Nanteos, few 'Tivyside' landowners had lands over rich coal and lead deposits, apart from the comparatively limited resources of Bronwydd, Ffynone and Llysnewydd in the south-west Wales coal belt and in the lead producing areas of Llanfyrnach, Pembrokeshire. Hassall had observed in 1794 that it was the ingenuity and perseverance of entrepreneurs from outside that had exploited the extraordinary wealth and resources of south Wales.[86] While, in view of recent research, this is only partially true of Wales generally, it is nevertheless fairly near the mark with regard to the 'Tivyside' squires. Capital from outside sources through small partnerships, whose business could only be expanded by ploughing back profits, seem to have been the usual arrangement in this area. 'Tivyside' landowners found it easier to make arrangements with local miners, outside operators or larger south-west Wales landowners with surplus capital, to work their mines. An agreement of 7 July 1752 between James Lloyd of Cilrhiwe with local miners is typical of the 1750s, wherein they were to 'sink, digg and cutt' for 50s. a fathom, for 45s. per 'ton of oer' and 4s. per week for subsistence. The landowner provided fixed capital for draining, processing and pumping equipment, while the miners paid for their own candles, powder and sundries. Strict provisos were included for the ore to be 'clean, washed, merchanteable and fitt for market', with all implements left in good workmanlike order. By 1759 the venture had proved to be a failure and 'capitalist gentlemen' from Walsall, prepared to sink capital, erect engines and smithies together with smelting and processing sheds, were granted the lease.[87] In the following decades various speculators tried to operate the mines but failed.[88] In the 1840s Benjamin Edward Hall, owner of the Cilgwyn estate was attracted to the idea of forming a joint stock company of south-west Wales gentry to work the Llanfyrnach mines. As in past efforts to work the mines, the enterprise was a failure and Hall, the largest shareholder, lost about £650 of the total invested capital of £1,000.[89] During the 1860s and '70s the fortunes of the mines improved and the lessor, Thomas Davies Lloyd of Bronwydd, received revenues ranging from £100 to £260 a year; but these sums were only a very small proportion of his total estate income.[90]

The north Pembrokeshire slate quarries had existed for centuries. George Owen in 1603 had described well-established and extensive slate quarrying around Newport and Nevern. At Cilgerran and Glogue it revived in the eighteenth century, but its main development was later.[91] The rebuilding of mansions required roofing slate, ornamental stonework on park walls and garden features. In the 1790s slates from Glogue were procured for Colby's new mansion at Ffynone;[92] and at a time of considerable building, George Bowen of Llwyngwair in the early 1800s owned the quarries of Broden, Three Steps and Garth.[93] As in other mining ventures, rarely did the landowner himself assume the function of entrepreneur, working the quarries directly, but granted a lease for an annual rent and/or royalty for what was sold. In 1827, Thomas Lloyd of Coedmore leased Cilgerran quarries 'to sink and draw slate stones', which had to be surrendered in 1836 on account of disputes. He paid £60 for 'tools', £160 consideration for surrender and £8 for 'the horse in the quarry'.[94] Royalties, rent arrears and liabilities were a constant worry to landowners involved in such ventures.

Further attempts were made in the 1870s with enterprising Cilgerran quarrymen undertaking the whole expense of working the quarries, Lloyd being allowed stones and slates for the mansion of Coedmore and an annual rent of £60, which was to be raised when the railway reached Cilgerran.[95] But it was only at the end of the century that slate quarrying in this area could hope to be successful when Erasmus Gower of Castle Malgwyn formed a syndicate of London businessmen with £20,000 capital. Because of employment prospects there was general jubilation and gratitude for the enterprise and patronage of the squire.[96]

Landowners fortunate to possess coal deposits under their land were quick to realise that there was an expanding market for coal at the end of the eighteenth century. John Colby of Ffynone had got his hands on Orielton properties in Carmarthenshire[97] and a stake in mines at Landshipping and Hook in south Pembrokeshire, worked by the Owens of Orielton since the 1780s.[98] London contacts, like coal and corn factors, were useful to advise on the market for good coals,[99] and easy transport was afforded by sea from Milford Haven and Landshipping Quay. Colby put capital in the south Pembrokeshire enterprise, Thomas George acted as manager to advise on technical problems, and the most advanced plant was installed similar to that at the new works at Llanelli, Landore and Swansea. A singular recommendation was Trevithick's four-horsepower engine which could work non-stop and do the work of six horses![100]

As with an agricultural estate, mining ventures demanded a reliable agent, and Colby's man at Rhydlangoig, Amroth, was dismissed for mismanagement.[101] A squire like Colby, living away from the 'works', might have to face untold problems with regard to wayleave rights and trouble from neighbours, the advent of the new railway, and jealous entrepreneurs who could hamper any enterprise.[102] From the 1820s, Colby, realising the extent and importance of industrial developments —mines, railways, 'works' and urban leases—made further purchases of parcels of land in the area near Cydweli, St Ishmael's and Pembrey.[103]

But squires such as Colby were usually content with granting leases on their estates to entrepreneurs, and were rarely active participants in industrial ventures. A typical hard-headed businessman, Colby granted leases to prospectors from Spalding, Lincolnshire, to mine for coal and stone and culm near Pembrey at £500 a year rent plus one-sixth of any profits over £500. Moreover, a punitive clause was added, namely, that the rent would be doubled if these prospectors worked mines other than Colby's within ten miles.[104] To safeguard further the industrial value of their estates, landowners like Colby were reluctant to grant too many leases (to the chagrin of entrepreneurs like George Bowser, a pioneer of mining, railway and shipping development in Burry Port and Pembrey).[105] In some cases, it was the excessive protection of their monopoly on the part of squires which led to legal action, such as that in 1840, when Bowser castigated landowners as those who '. . . in lieu of laying out capital themselves for the improvement of their estates offer every impediment in their power to those who come into the county to do so.'[106]

It is difficult to ascertain the actual income landowners derived from any investments or leases. In 1853 David Griffith Davies of Castle Green, Cardigan, received about £630 from his share in Neath collieries;[107] the Moreton mine, Saundersfoot (south Pembrokeshire), yielded Caulfield Tynte Lloyd Williams of Gwernant royalties of 1s. a ton for coal and 6d on culm but the total annual royalties are not known.[108] Other landowners profited to the following extent:

1875	Lewes, Llysnewydd	— £500 + royalties	— Llanon,	Carms
1884	" "	— £900 royalties	— "	"
1889	" "	— £440 royalties	— "	"
1900	" "	— £500 rent + royalties	— "	"
1909-14	Lloyd, Bronwydd	— £500-£600 royalties	— Llangennech,	"
	Colby, Ffynone	— £300-£400 royalties	— Llanelli	"[109]

The income from industrial sources of the Brigstocke estate of Blaen-pant in 1898-99 amounted to only £99—a mere fraction of the rent from land, which at the time was about £4,500 a year.[110] It can be said, therefore, that to the 'Tivyside' gentry, coal mines, slate quarries and industrial activity were only peripheral to the basic agricultural economy of their estates.

Before the days of road networks and railways, and even for some considerable time afterwards, the small ports and creeks along the Welsh coastline were focal points in the commerce and trade of the people. Their importance over the centuries has been noticed by several historians,[111] and the landed gentry whose estates bordered on the coast participated in maritime commerce and shipping investment. As in mining, there was a strong element of personal risk, shared out by companies of local people. A vessel was divided into 64 shares and the unit of ownership was four shares or one-sixteenth—'an ounce of a ship'. Such shares were held as personalty, and could be bequeathed by will as was done, for example, by Philip Jones of Cardigan in 1729 who left his son 'one-third share in the Dispatch Brigantine'.[112] The wealthy squire of Cwmgloyn was himself an owner of ships, and when two of them were sunk by storm and tempest and a French attack, a local bard composed an ode of condolence.[113] Such an example of complete ownership was rare, the gentry feeling safer in only owning a part share, like Essex Gwynne of Pantirion in 1754,[114] and spreading the risk over several craft as in the case of George Bowen of Llwyngwair in the dangerous years 1804-11.[115] Even with the decline in shipping because of the easier transport on the turnpike roads and later the railways, shipping shares continued to be valuable personalty. Davies of Castle Green owned shares in 23 craft—one being £150 invested in a Newport-built schooner, *The Economy*.[116]

A private vessel or a stake in shipping conveniently and usefully provided cheap transport of commodities such as coal, culm and lime to houses and estates like Llwyngwair. In addition, the hope of further profit was always present; for example, John Lloyd Williams of Gwernant in 1830 obtained shares in a vessel trading from Gloucester, Bristol and Carmarthen to Liverpool, capable of carrying 2,500 bushels of corn and able to make a profit of £240 a year.[117] It was rare, however, to find landowners investing in large ocean-going vessels, as happened in the case of Capt. Thomas Jenkins of Penrallt, Aberporth, who with another bought *The City of London* for a large sum of money —£14,500. He confessed that it was '. . . a great serious undertaking for a person with small funds like myself . . . this speculation is the means of making some competences [sc. provision] for my family'. During the first voyage he expected to make a clear profit of £7,000.[118]

When shares in ships were bought, as happened when James of Pantsaison joined others in purchasing the sloop *Denis* of Cardigan for over £393,[119] major shareholders insured both the captain's life and the ship. A premium of £118 a year was a costly burden which fell solely upon Thomas Lloyd of Coedmore in 1821.[120] Investment in shippping continued well into the nineteenth century, and many of the 'Tivyside' gentry sank a little capital in numerous small craft, built and plying their limited but important trade along the south Cardiganshire coast.[121]

Increasing trade with industrial south Wales and the Lancashire coast, as well as with Ireland, stimulated the gentry to support new harbours. Thus, for example, Brigstocke of Blaenpant gave £500 to improve Cydweli harbour near his Carmarthenshire estates,[122] and a dozen other prominent 'Tivyside' gentry, like Thomas Lloyd of Bronwydd and David Edward Lewes Lloyd of Dolhaidd, were members of the New Quay Harbour Board which had, among its other aims, the construction of a coastal railway.[123] Likewise, the 'material importance' of Newport and Fishguard was fully understood by north Pembrokeshire landowners. Bowen of Llwyngwair and Lloyd of Bronwydd had an obvious vested interest to develop Newport in order to facilitate transport and trade to Ireland.[124] E. Crompton Ll. Fitzwilliams, the owner of the Cilgwyn estate, saw the advantage of a railway from Carmarthen to Cardigan and thence to New Quay; improved port facilities at Cardigan and the formation of a company with £1 million capital, were some other ideas put forward. Some immediate support came from the gentry, and from the rising professional middle classes and well-to-do farmers, but its original aims did not materialise. Nevertheless, a few gentry had a nominal financial interest in the New Quay Harbour Company until the 1920s.[125]

Equally, gentry support for any other new schemes never led to any big investment of capital, and when Fitzwilliams and John Lloyd Davies of Blaendyffryn had advocated a 'harbour of refuge and defence' in Cardigan bay, the response from landowners was lukewarm.[126]

During the eighteenth century a limited development of heavy industry took place along the banks of the Teifi near Cilgerran in the form of 'iron and tinned plate' manufacture.[127] The advantages of the area were a navigable river and a plentiful supply of local timber, with raw materials like tin and pig iron brought in large open boats up river from Cardigan. Forges were set up in the vicinity of Llechryd and Castell Malgwyn, with landowners granting leases and selling timber from their estates for conversion into charcoal. William Brigstocke of Blaenpant and John Lloyd of Coedmore made agreements with entrepreneurs like Thomas Lewis of Llwyngrawys from the 1720s onwards, but did not operate 'the works' themselves.[128] The development of the Cilgerran-Llechryd 'works' was due to Sir Benjamin Hammett, who had settled in the area, had built the grand mansion of Castle Malgwyn and employed several hundred persons. Diminishing profits, and the death of Hammett in 1806, led to the decline of these works; and the dismantling of the buildings and plant led to unemployment in the area. Although both Lewis and Hammett had become landowners and squires, it is significant that they were the new gentry with wealth originally acquired from trade. As has been emphasised, long-established families did not for social or financial reasons operate 'works' themselves. Other factors, too, have to be taken into account, such as the long distances to the 'works' from the squire's principal residence. For this reason, Owen Brigstocke of Blaenpant in 1766 sold his Cydweli (Carmarthenshire) forge—some 40 miles away—to John Morgan, the Carmarthen entrepreneur.[129]

The reluctance of the gentry to participate in business enterprises did not prevent some of them from supporting the commercial and employment prospects in their locality. In the 1860s Col. Davies Evans of Highmead and others promoted the Llandysul Market Company to encourage the sale of livestock and farm produce. For cheaper house building and increased employment in developing urban areas, the Cardigan and Llandysul Brick Company was set up in 1864 by the Rev. Robert Henry William Miles of Cardigan Priory and E. Crompton Ll. Fitzwilliams, the latter stating the need '. . . to supply bricks for ye Corners (a great cause of expense in Welsh masonry) as then no time will be wasted in hacking Corner Stones'.[130]

Rural depopulation and a depressed countryside in the last decades of the nineteenth century led the Lloyds of Bronwydd, in conjunction with south Wales notables like Windham-Quin of Dunraven who had estates in Glamorgan and Ireland, to support the Welsh Industries' Association towards developing an arts and crafts market based on rural industries. The buoyant woollen industry in the lower Teifi valley (as well as the tottering financial state of their landed estates) led the Tylers of Mount Gernos to set up a weaving and dyeing mill at Maesllyn in the 1890s. In spite of its initial success and the international acclaim won by their products, a change in the economic climate eventually resulted in the mill being leased to a local flannel weaver.[131]

While surplus capital which the gentry possessed was often invested in land, smaller cash sums were borrowed by the gentry themselves either from their equals or from the farming community. Before the days of a modern banking system, bonds were a means of raising money for short-term needs at a rate of interest favourable to the lender. In the first half of the eighteenth century there is little evidence of investment in government stock, and the growth of borrowing by the government to stem crises, caused by wars from time to time, seem to have made little impact on the 'Tivyside' gentry. The opening up of trading on a worldwide scale did not stimulate investment by the squirearchy of the backwaters of the Teifi valley, except for those adventurers who were themselves participants in such developments. By the early nineteenth century, however, the large-scale manipulation of capital and industry, creating a shareholder class, was to have its repercussions even in 'Tivyside'. As the century advanced, the local gentry were to have a share in the 'irresponsible wealth' detached from the land and the duties of the landowner. This is particularly true of gentry whose wealth was largely in landed estates and had successfully with skill and good management survived the ups and downs of a precarious agriculture.

As in the case of cash in the house, bonds in the early eighteenth century were relatively small and could range from £10 to £50 or £100. These could be redeemed or, failing that, were bequeathed as personalty along with household items like tankards, plate and the like.[132] The onus of recovering these money debts fell upon the legatee. Sometimes the bequest was of very doubtful benefit, as it might be linked to a disparate transaction such as a straightforward loan, unpaid debt or part of a marriage settlement, all to be resolved after the testator's death whether amicably between claimants or by decree of a probate court.[133] A borrower or beneficiary usually held himself liable to pay double the sum named in the transaction. This could be a heavy burden, as in the case of William Lloyd of Penpedwast, who borrowed in the early 1700s the large sum of £800 from his father.[134] Ephemeral needs caused by a farming disaster, the loss of a ship at sea or a dispute between neighbours, depended on the preparedness of an obliging friend to lend money at short notice. John Lloyd of Cryngae in Penboyr parish bound himself in the sum of £1,000 to abide by a legal verdict.[135] By the early 1800s much larger sums were prevalent, and Thomas Davies of Castle Green had lent about £6,500 to local persons like Sir Benjamin Hammett of Castle Malgwyn, George Bowen of Llwyngwair, and to gentry outside the area such as Gwynne of Monachty and W. E. Powell of Nanteos—in sums of £100 to £2,000.[136] Davies' investment in other ways such as government 3½% stock, mortgage interest and other sources made him a rich man who left in 1836 over £14,000 in cash funds, not to mention real estate.[137] At a time of depressed land values, Colby of Ffynone, with an eye to the future, spread the word in 1823 that he had up to £50,000 to invest in real property.[138]

Perhaps dim memories of the South Sea Bubble and other government fiascos led to a certain reluctance on the part of the gentry to risk any surplus money in such dangerous adventures. Nonetheless, Consols, i.e. Consolidated Annuities, paying 3-5% interest, attracted investment by many 'Tivyside' squires; for example, Griffith of Llwynduris in 1812 left in all about £18,000 held in various government funds.[139] Later on in the century Saunders Davies of Pentre and Colby of Rhosygilwen, to mention just two, had considerable sums in such funds.[140] An expanding empire and flourishing trading posts led gentry like Abel Gower of Castle Malgwyn and Lloyd Williams of Gwernant to have extensive holdings in East India stock. When he died in India in 1852 Capt. Charles Colby of Ffynone had a large portion of his £25,000 fortune invested in the Calcutta 5% Loan.[141]

At home, large city corporations with expensive projects of public works and facilities attracted money from the purses of the gentry. Diversifying his risks in the last decades of the nineteenth century, W. O. Brigstocke of Blaenpant invested over £20,000 in the corporation funds of Hull, Bradford and Cardiff.[142] Industrial railway and mining ventures in the Americas, Europe and the Far East also absorbed investments. By the 1890s, as already stated, land was no longer the profitable, attractive and safe basis of wealth.[143]

A significant aspect of landownership was the squire's interest in advowsons, a form of real property which granted to its owner the perpetual right of presentation to an ecclesiastical living.[144] It grew out of a world where the squire was the virtual owner of the parish; perhaps he had built the church, needed a clergyman of whom he approved, and therefore retained the advowson as the right to appoint.[145] Advowsons were assets which could be bought, sold, leased or left by will. Thus Ann Lloyd of Bronwydd in 1785 sold the 'next presentation to the rectory of Meline' to a Cardigan mercer for £300.[146] Such a transaction included rights over glebe land, tithes and 'oblations', i.e. any offerings related to the living. William Lewes of Llysnewydd in 1826 devised the advowson of Llanfihangel-ar-Arth to his eldest son.[147] Rich outsiders seem to have acquired advowsons so as to have a stake in a particular locality through the exercise of patronage and influence, as, for example, Sandham of Horsham, Sussex, who bought the advowson of Meline in 1786.[148]

Cathedral dignities were also leased; for example, a Welsh absentee cleric residing in the parish of Glynde, Sussex, leased the prebend of Clydai in St David's Cathedral for three lives to Watkins of Defynnog, Brecs.[149] In order to obtain maximum revenue, landlords obtained periodic valuations from actuaries who could take into account the conditions of parsonage houses, the extent and nature of glebe land as well as their proximity to the sea and market towns.[150] Six Bronwydd 'livings' in north Pembrokeshire were reckoned to bring in £500 a year. If the advowsons of Dinas and Newport were sold, it was estimated that they could bring in about £2,000.[151] Evidently livings varied in value; for example, in the 1840s Llanglydwen (Carms), Maenclochog and Llandeilo (Pembs) were together worth annually £200, whereas Llangoedmor (Cards) on its own was worth about £450.[152]

Broadly speaking, while advowsons were an additional, although minor part of estate income (which could be traded during any contingency), their importance lay in the additional power given to the squire to provide for a younger son or relation, and to ward off a 'methodistical' or other 'enthusiastic' cleric from settling in the area and, perhaps, might disturb the *status quo* and the quietude of rural parishes.

Legally, tithes were a form of personalty which could be traded or bequeathed like advowsons. Stephen Parry of Noyadd in 1711 left in his will the tithes of several parishes to a cousin.[153] Tithes could be bequeathed as part of provision for younger children, or a means of discharging lesser debts without upsetting the essential structure of an estate.[154] Legal title to tithe often went back to a hoary and sometimes unsavoury antiquity, for example, Brigstocke of Blaenpant's claim to Cenarth tithes was derived from one John Lloyd, 'an unprincipled grabber' who had cheated the administrators of Queen Anne's Bounty.[155] Lay impropriators living some distance from their tithe parishes sometimes found it simpler to sell or lease to persons in the locality; for example, in 1741 Lloyd of Ffosybleiddiaid sold Cenarth tithes to a local landowner, Lloyd of Plas Llangoedmore, for £320.[156] These were later acquired in 1765 for £600 by Brigstocke of Blaenpant, the purchase price possibly reflecting a more buoyant agricultural economy at the time.

As collecting tithes was becoming more and more irksome and contentious, a few tithe owners, through leases to local farmers or gentry for a cash sum, saved themselves the trouble. To take two examples, the Rev. Benjamin Millingchamp of Plas Llangoedmore in 1820 leased his glebe lands in Wiltshire to a baronet residing in that county. John Colby of Ffynone let the Clydai tithes to local farmers.[157] In a few cases the cost of collection exceeded the value of the tithe.[158] Although investment in tithes occasionally yielded a good return,— 10% or more, as when Colby purchased Clydai tithes in 1796[159]—any income from tithes could fluctuate and was only incidental and a small proportion of estate income. William Brigstocke of Blaenpant received sums ranging from £23 to £60 in the years 1750-60.

Llangeler tithes in 1773 amounted to about £48.[160] Tithe revenues from any parish depended on the weather and the crops as well as the price of produce on the market. Other factors had to be taken into account—outgoings like the curate's stipend, and the repair of the church and the parsonage. By the end of the nineteenth century income from tithes had become an almost minor element in estate revenues; for example, the Llysnewydd tithes from Llanfihangel-ar-Arth parish amounted to £161 gross from which the parson's stipend of £92 had to be paid.[161] The unrest and dissension between landlord and tenant created by the 'contentious tithe' made it not only worthless, but a most troublesome element (particularly in nonconformist Wales) in estate administration.

NOTES AND SOURCES

[1]W. Davies: *op cit.*, i, p. 120.

[2]E. Hughes: 'The Eighteenth Century Estate Agent' in Cronne, Moody and Quinn (eds), *Essays in British and Irish History*, 1949.

[3]H. Owen: Additional Morris Letters, pt 2, 1949, no 391.

[4]NLW/Nannau/145 quoted in P. R. Roberts: 'The Decline of the Welsh Squires in the Eighteenth Century', *NLWJ*, XIII, 2, 1963, pp. 157-61; G. E. Mingay: 'The Eighteenth Century Land Steward' in *Land, Labour and Population* (eds. E. L. Jones and G. E. Mingay), 1967, p. 8.

[5]*loc cit. DWB.*

[6]RCLWM Report 1896, p. 249.

[7]D. W. Howell: *Patriarchs and Parasites*, p. 55; G. E. Mingay: *loc cit.*

[8]*Cm Jnl*: 12/1/1811; NLW/Falcondale/Gp vi/214; CRO/Dynevor/154; CRO/Cawdor/2/141, 145; F. M. L. Thompson: *op cit.*, pp. 151 seq.

[9]NLW/Owen Colby/1876.

[10]NLW/Bronwydd/609.

[11]NLW/Owen Colby/733.

[12]NLW/Cilgwyn Ms vol LB/32/27 Dec. 1825; *ibid.* correspondence 1828-30.

[13]NLW/Bronwydd/3822-61; *Yr Haul*: 1860, p. 192.

[14]NLW/Bronwydd/7041.

[15]*ibid*: 3243.

[16]NLW/D. Pryse Williams/15622E.

[17]*DWB*; NLW/Add Ms 1896E iv; Charles Hassall (1754-1814) land agent and surveyor active in west Wales; compiled reports on the state of agriculture in Carmarthenshire and Pembrokeshire. *DWB.*

[18]D. J. V. Jones: 'Rhyfel y Sais Bach', *Ceredigion*, V, 1, 1964, p. 84; *Cm Jnl*: 25/1/1831.

[19]CRO/AE/10/1853; D. E. Jones: *op cit.*, pp. 34-5.

[20]RCLWM Report 1896: pp. 249-260, paras 197-206.

[21]D. W. Howell: *op cit.*, p. 57.

[22]NLW/Cilgwyn Ms/LB/44/12 Oct. 1875.

[23]NLW/9871 C.

[24]RCLWM: iii [Qus 44 944-53]; NLW/Ms 906c: 'An Essay on the Advantages of a Resident Gentry' by Emyr Gwernabwy, 1850; the congregation of Llwynrhydowen Unitarian Chapel were evicted in Oct. 1876 because their minister, the Rev. Wm Thomas (Gwilym Marles) preached against the harshness of landlords in evicting their tenants because they failed to vote Tory. *DWB*.

[25]*Cd Ad*: 5/1/1877.

[26]CRO/Beckingsale/1092.

[27]M. C. S. Evans: 'Pioneers of Estate Mapping in Carmarthenshire', *Carms Antiq*, XXIII, 1977, pp. 52-3.

[28]C. Thomas: 'Land Surveyors in Wales 1750-1850. The Matthews Family', *BBCS*, 32, 1985, pp. 216-32.

[29]NLW/Bronwydd/3862.

[30]NLW/Ms Maps vol 10.

[31]NLW/Clynfyw/Box 13.

[32]D. W. Howell: *op cit.*, p. 60; G. E. Mingay: *The Gentry*, p. 84.

[33]W. Davies: *op cit.*, i, p. 169.

[34]C. Hassall: *op cit.* (Pembs), p. 33.

[35]H. J. Habakkuk: *op cit.*, pp. 92-3.

[36]NLW/Evans George/5.

[37]*ibid*: 693.

[38]NLW/Bronwydd/6804.

[39]CRO/JF/505.

[40]NLW/Llwyngwair/66; NLW/Bronwydd/1812.

[41]NLW/Falcondale/Gp v/138/1.

[42]CRO/Cawdor/Box 141-10 Jan, 1865; CRO/EG/5.

[43]C. S. Read: *op cit.*, see RCLWM Report 1896, pp. 88-90.

[44]NLW/OwenColby/675.

[45]CRO/JF/505.

[46]D. W. Howell: *Land and People*, pp. 46-7; *Hansard*: Parl. Debates, ii, 16/3/1892; *DWB*.

[47]CRO/EG/23/-.

[48]NLW/Owen Colby/272.

[49]NLW/Cilgwyn LB/32/5 July 1834.

[50]*ibid*: 22/7/1869.

[51]*The Welshman*: 17 Nov. 1865.

[52]Bronwydd Buildings Book in private hands.

[53]NLW/Morgan Richardson (Noyadd Trefawr Gp) 32.

[54]*ibid*: 51.

[55]NLW/Ms 9871 C.

[56]NLW/Evans George/2063.

[57]NLW/Lucas/61; my italics—D.L.B-J.

[58]NLW/Clynfyw/Box 1.

[59]Walter Davies: *op. cit.*

[60]*id: Patriarchs and Parasites*, 1986, p. 77; G. E. Mingay: *The Agricultural Revolution*, pp. 1-5, 19; Charles Townshend (1674-1738).

[61]E. W. Jones: 'The First Carmarthenshire Agricultural Society', *Carms. Antiq.*, VIII, pp. 152-57; R. Porter: *op cit.*, pp. 316-17.

[62]W. Davies: *op cit.*, ii, pp. 493-94; H. M. Vaughan: 'Some Letters of Thomas Johnes of Hafod 1794-1807', *Y Cymmrodor*, XXXV, 1925, p. 201.

[63]E. J. Evans: *The Contentious Tithe—The Tithe Problem and English Agriculture 1750-1850*, 1976, pp. 76-8.

[64]CRO/Cawdor (Vaughan) 26/2025.

[65]*Cm Jnl*: 20/5/1842; 3/5/1844.

[66]*Cd Ad*: 19/2/1864; 9/3/1877; 28/1/1881.

[67]NLW/Highmead/3065.

[68]*Cd Ad*: 14/1/1884; 21/2/1902; 18/11/1905.
[69]NLW/Morgan Richardson/2462, 2465.
[70]*The Welshman*: 21/6/1862; 'adscripti glebae'—serfs tied to the land.
[71]NLW/Cilgwyn/LB/44/16 May 1872.
[72]NLW/Bronwydd/7234; *Cd Ad*: 20/1/188; 9/1/1903.
[73]*The Welshman*: 11/9/1846.
[74]A. Harford: *op cit.*, p. 131; letter of John Battersby Harford to his uncle John Scandrett Harford, August 1854.
[75]*Cd Ad*: 15/9/1882.
[76]*ibid*: 3/12/1886; M. Cragoe: *op cit.*, pp. 33-34.
[77]T. Morgan: *An Essay in Draining*, 1846; *id. An Essay on the Systems of Agriculture and the Rotation of Crops*, 1852.
[78]J. R. James: *Yr Amaethydd Cymreig*, Cardigan, 1869.
[79]Cd Ad: 12/11/1886; 8/4/1887.
[80]loc cit.
[81]Cd Ad: 12/1/1890; 15/6/1894.
[82]D. W. Howell: *Patriarchs and Parasites*, p. 91; G. E. Mingay: *The Gentry*, p. 107.
[83]*Cd Ad*: 12/1/1877.
[84]NLW/Cilgwyn LB/34/3 May 1853.
[85]Walford: *County Families*, 1907.
[86]C. Hassall: *A General View of Agriculture*, Monmouth, 1812.
[87]NLW/Bronwydd/3738.
[88]*ibid*: 1985, 2003.
[89]CRO/Coedmore/10/8.
[90]NLW/Bronwydd/4340-75.
[91]G. M. Tucker: 'The Old Slate Industry of Pembrokeshire and other parts of South Wales', *NLWJ*, XXIII, 2, 1983, pp. 140-43.
[92]NLW/Owen Colby/1204.
[93]NLW/Llwyngwair/43.
[94]CRO/Coedmore/10/16.
[95]*ibid*: 1/171.
[96]Cd Ad 20/4/1894.
[97]NLW/Owen Colby/1136, 1138.
[98]D. W. Howell: *op cit.*, p. 94.
[99]NLW/Owen Colby/1951-52.
[100]*ibid*: 2105, 2154.
[101]*ibid*: 1880; Rhydlangoig was later known as Colby Lodge near Amroth, where the Colbys had built a small country house.
[102]*ibid*: 1978, 1995.96.
[103]CRO/JF/22, 37, 104-06.
[104]NLW/Owen Colby/873.
[105]Information kindly given by the late W. H. Morris, MA, of Cydweli.
[106]CRO/DD/Bowser/-.
[107]NLW/Add Ms 5538.
[108]NLW/Ticehurst Wyatt (Gwernant) Box ii.
[109]NLW/Llysnewydd/Bundle 66, 57; NLW/Bronwydd/7304; CRO/JF (Colby) 58.
[110]NLW/Evans George/2063.
[111]E. A. Lewis: *The Welsh Port Books (1550-1603)* 1927; M. I. Williams: 'The Port of Aberdyfi in the Eighteenth Century', *NLWJ*, XVIII, 1, 1973, p. 95.
[112]J. G. Jenkins: *The Maritime Heritage*, pp. 111-112; FG/18/395.
[113]NLW/Ms 196 (Sir John Williams 223).
[114]NLW/St Davids/Wills, 1754.
[115]NLW/Llwyngwair/2146.

[116]NLW/Ms 5538.

[117]NLW/Ticehurst Wyatt (Gwernant) Box II.

[118]NLW/Ms/1897E iii.

[119]NLW/Morgan Richardson/2102.

[120]CRO/Coedmore/2/22.

[121]Aber RO/HT/Ship/1/1, 3.

[122]*Cm Jnl*: 31/8/1811.

[123]5-6 Wm IV (1835); T. I. J. Jones: *op cit.*, p. 182.

[124]E. L. Stephens: *A Review of the National Advantages to be derived by the Improvement of Fishguard Harbour*, 1837; *Cm Jnl*: 9/9/1836; NLW/Bronwydd/3962-65.

[125]NLW/D. Pryse Williams/15625B; *Cm Jnl*: 18/4/1851; CRO/EG/Box/41/-.

[126]NLW/Cilgwyn LB/40/27 April 1860; *The Welshman* 17/8/1860; 21/9/1860.

[127]J. T. Barber: *A Tour Throughout South Wales*, 1803, p. 95; J. R. Phillips: *op cit.*, pp. 159-64.

[128]M. C. S. Evans: 'Coedmore Forge, Llechryd' in *Carmarthenshire Studies*, (eds) T. Barnes and N. Yates, 1974, pp. 186-95; J. R. Phillips: *op cit.*, pp. 159-67.

[129]CRO/Trant (Yelverton) 458-59; NLW/Noyadd Trefawr/672.

[130]NLW/Cilgwyn Ms LB/43/26 Feb. 1864.

[131]*Cm Jnl*: 12/8/1898; NLW/Morgan Richardson (Gernos)/927; *Cd Ad*: 22/6/1888; Burke: *op cit.*, sub. Wyndham-Quinn; *DWB*.

[132]FG/25/61; 16/103; 16/16.

[133]NLW/SD/CC Cd (P) 3.

[134]NLW/Bronwydd/1547.

[135]HRO/Pentre/Box 11/11.

[136]NLW/Mss/5537/C, 5538.

[137]NLW/T. I. Ellis/188-91.

[138]NLW/Owen Colby/1989.

[139]NLW/Llwynduris/123.

[140]NLW/Morgan Richardson/2346, 1054; NLW/Owen Colby/252, 602; NLW/Bronwydd/1867.

[141]NLW/Ticehurst Wyatt (Gwernant) Box II; NLW/Owen Colby/2004, 2006.

[142]NLW/Evans George/1991, 2136.

[143]CRO/EG/Box 10.

[144]R. E. Megarry: *Real Property*, 2nd. ed. 1951, pp. 431-32.

[145]O. Chadwick: *The Victorian Church*, i, 1970, p. 208 seq.

[146]NLW/Bronwydd/1627.

[147]NLW/Sir John Williams/119.

[148]NLW/Bronwydd/1615.

[149]CRO/JF/554.

[150]NLW/Bronwydd/608.

[151]*ibid*: 6954.

[152]*Cm Jnl*: 6/3/1840; *The Welshman*: 14/2/1845.

[153]NLW/Noyadd Trefawr/465.

[154]HRO/D/Pen/23/10; TCAS, 18, p. 81.

[155]NLW/Evans George/917-18.

[156]*ibid*: 911-12.

[157]NLW/Plas Llangoedmore/101; CRO/JF/562.

[158]NLW/Tŷ Llwyd/312.

[159]CRO/JF/563.

[160]NLW/Evans George/1382.

[161]CRO/EG/Box 7/-; NLW/SD/LET/-; NLW/Llysnewydd/Bundle 66.

The Gentry and Transport—
Roads and Railways

Improved roads and safe bridges were of primary concern to the gentry to provide access to their scattered properties, and more comfortable journeys to the fashionable centres of Bath and London. Moreover, the easy movement of livestock by drovers was also an important element in the estate's economy; a ready market for store cattle and sheep with ready cash in return, was welcome when the bulk of capital was sunk in land. The movement of lime, coal and culm also depended on a good network of roads to bring supplies to farm and mansion.

On account of the difficulties and hazards of travel, attempts were made (especially after the 1760s) to remedy the lack of roads by means of turnpike trusts to administer long stretches of road linked up by coaching services. The trusts were financed and controlled by wealthy men—usually the landed gentry. Following a series of acts of parliament, roads in south-west Wales were improved to help communications between the main towns. Thus the road from Carmarthen to Felindre Shinkin and Newcastle Emlyn opened up a route towards Cardigan and north Pembrokeshire. In 1786 Carmarthen was joined with Lampeter, and the latter with Llandovery thereby linking the valley of the Tywi with that of the Teifi. By 1791-92 the towns of Cardigan, Fishguard and Haverfordwest were joined as part of a wider network.[1] The building of bridges also helped what was becoming a wide system of transport and communications. The example of pioneer bridge-builders like the Edwards family of Pontypridd was followed elsewhere, and according to Walter Davies, Cardiganshire was better equipped than many Welsh counties, with 13 bridges over the Teifi from Strata Florida to Cardigan.[2] The advances made by Macadam, Metcalfe, Telford and others became the models to follow on a wider scale.

'Tivyside' gentry who were riparian owners along the river Teifi formed a local trust which was active from 1809 to 1845. Landowners like William Lewes of Llysnewydd, the Rev. Daniel Bowen of Waunifor and John Lloyd of Gilfachwen, amongst others, supported a scheme to develop a road from Henllan to Llandysul and Llanfihangel-ar-Arth. By 1825 the trust comprised the principal landowners and several substantial yeomen of the area.[3] Additional trusts were formed, such as the Carmarthen and Newcastle Emlyn Trust, to include a wider representation of landowners whose estates in the Teifi valley extended towards Cardigan and north Pembrokeshire. Money was raised for road extension and tollgates, and some gentry were singled out 'for their liberal grant of the Land necessary'. Some like Sir Benjamin Hammett of Castle Malgwyn, Webley Parry of Noyadd Trefawr, and Thomas Lloyd of Coedmore, from 1798 onwards, had even allowed road diversion through their estates in order to facilitate the construction of a good road system.[4]

Gentry subscriptions of cash, too, were not uncommon—ranging from a few guineas to £50.[5] When trustees invested money, the amounts varied from £25 to £300 for most gentry, while a major landowner like Lord Cawdor could afford £1,000 in the years 1806-08. In 1816 the total invested by 'Tivyside' gentry in Cardiganshire turnpike 'tallies' amounted to £700,[6] but individual sums of £25, £50, £100 or more bore no relation to the extent of their estates, as prominent farmers invested per head much more than their gentry superiors. For investors to receive their dividends, 'tolls' were farmed out to the highest bidder; for example, the tolls of the Carmarthen-Newcastle Emlyn trust were let in 1810 for the sum of £353.[7]

As hinted, the support and drive of the gentry in improving roads and communications were on the whole limited; and some landowners were niggardly in the amount of money they were prepared to invest. They failed to realise that a 'turnpike trust was a business concern, not a philanthropic institution, for hard-headed men who sank their money with the expectation of a reasonable return'.[8] John Lloyd Davies of Blaendyffryn, an enlightened and far-seeing landowner and a pioneer of road and bridge building, found to his cost (when promoting the road from Newcastle Emlyn to Llandysul, thence to Lampeter and Llandovery to join with roads to England) that 'Several gentlemen had promised to advance sums to complete the road, but after I had given employment to about one hundred and fifty men, I found each of those gentlemen refuse to advance a single penny'.[9]

The advent of the railways was another challenge to the gentry, a test of their business acumen and foresight with regard to the potential benefit to their estates and to the whole community. To many gentry throughout Britain, the railway was an 'intrusion' which would disturb their game preserves and their domestic privacy, diminish the amenities of their mansions and parks, and reduce the value of their property.[10] Railway promoters had to face long-drawn-out parliamentary proceedings to obtain legislative sanction, and costly technical surveys and estimates; and finally, land had to be bought from often recalcitrant and old-fashioned landowners who failed to see the benefits of a system of railways.

The expansion of railways in south Wales can be traced back to Trevithick's steam locomotive carrying freight and passengers in the Merthyr Tydfil area in 1824. A proper railway ran from Merthyr Tydfil to Cardiff in 1841, and extended to Swansea reaching Carmarthen by 1852 and Haverfordwest some two years later. From this period onwards about ten parliamentary acts were passed to extend the railway to connect with the south-west Wales towns.[11]

Generally, the opening of the south Wales railway was welcomed by such people as the Rev. David Rees, Llanelli in *Y Diwygiwr* [The Reformer] of the time, as providing a link with the outside world, encouraging tourism and trade, and bringing financial advantages such as rising land values. Prosperity outweighed the moral dangers of the 'socialistic and hellish ideas of England', while the danger to the Welsh language mattered not one whit as its death was in any case inevitable! Rees' outlook is typical of the commercial pragmatism of the day, as against the apathy of the landed gentry and the gloomy prophets of doom who feared the railway would not pay its way.[12] The response of some gentry in 'Tivyside' was initially encouraging, when in 1844 Lloyd Williams and Lord Emlyn (the latter, albeit an absentee landlord, who had considerable acreage in Cenarth and Penboyr parishes) amongst others decided to support Brunel's railway so long as 'mineral and agricultural interests' and the maritime trade of south Wales ports were safeguarded.[13] A main line to Fishguard was advocated which, with its natural harbour, would form an important link with Ireland.[14] During the next decade Lloyd Williams of Gwernant, John Lloyd Davies of Blaendyffryn and others tried to stir up local interest, pointing out the advantages of links with centres of trade in farm produce, such as Bristol, and the cheaper importation of Caernarfon slates and merchandise from Manchester, 'the greatest emporium of the manufacturing world'.[15]

It was argued that, apart from cheaper consumer goods, a great reduction could be made in the cost of lime and coal brought to the farms, as well as facilitating the 'quick despatch of troops', a matter of urgent topical interest in 1845 because of the recent Rebecca Riots.[16] E. Crompton Ll. Fitzwilliams was one of the few who saw the railway as a radical force to change life in the Teifi valley, where people never rubbed minds with the outside world and were 'encrusted with the rust of antiquity'. A landowner would be able to increase rents on account of new prosperity, and would have the political advantages of being returned to parliament if he were chairman of a railway board, so Fitzwilliams wrote to Sir John Mansel of Maesteilo in May 1853.[17]

Of all the 'Tivyside' gentry only Lewes-Lloyd of Dolhaidd, Lloyd Davies of Blaendyffryn, Brigstocke of Blaenpant and E. Crompton Ll. Fitzwilliams campaigned for extending the railway from Carmarthen to Newcastle Emlyn and Cardigan.[18] As in the case of turnpike trusts, promises of investment came easily from many gentry, but were never fulfilled. Fitzwilliams was the principal local shareholder after the bill bringing the railway to Newcastle Emlyn was passed in 1854, but the whole project failed on account of the dishonesty of London speculators, the intransigence of the Carmarthen burgesses concerning a diversion, and the general apathy of most of the gentry.[19] In the mismanagement of the enterprise, Fitzwilliams lost some £17,000 but his efforts were to result in partial satisfaction at least, when a section as far as Llandysul was completed in 1864. It had '. . . freshened up ye Llandysul folks wonderfully and put more life and animation into them then ye last fifty years of progress'.[20]

As with turnpikes, the negative response and failure to honour promises by the gentry, as well as disputes concerning technical points, for example, the width of gauge, inclines, diversions and where the terminus at Newcastle Emlyn was to be, caused unnecessary cost and delay. The value of cheap lime from east Carmarthenshire to fertilise large tracts of uncultivated land, an argument which had been emphasised by Lewes-Lloyd and Lloyd Davies, had fallen on deaf ears.[21] Although a few landowners like Brigstocke of Blaenpant and Saunders Davies of Pentre were prepared to grant land on fair and equitable terms,[22] others had made exorbitant demands upon the railway companies. Thus the 'grandee', Thomas Davies Lloyd of Bronwydd, had obtained £150 an acre plus £40 for agricultural disturbance on the land he owned in the parishes of Abergwili and Newchurch, Carmarthenshire, in 1860.[23]

From time to time criticism of the gentry was repeated, namely, their lack of business acumen; they were not so 'animated as the English', in commercial enterprise. They were also devious, according to *The Welshman*, 'sometimes spreading a doubt as to the character of the undertaking in order to shield themselves from merited reproach in not supporting it'.[24] As in other business ventures, expense and risk were paramount in their minds; their 'first idea was not to involve themselves in liability'.[25]

Fitzwilliams had diagnosed gentry mentality as indifference to mercantile enterprise, since 'spirit and cash do not go hand in hand in Wales . . . and there is no such thing as in England—a middle class'.[26] *The Welshman* newspaper was of the same opinion, adding that the current state of agriculture was also a contributory factor.[27] Furthermore, the obstinate attitude of even enthusiastic promoters like Fitzwilliams in his preventing the railway touching his own Cilgwyn land meant that the Tivyside Railway Bill was withdrawn in 1872.[28] The few miles from Llandysul to Newcastle Emlyn were not completed for almost 30 years mainly for the same reasons as those which had bedevilled earlier development. Gwinnett Tyler of Mount Gernos with a 'thorough and practical knowledge of railways' tried to get other landowners to put up £10,000 but failed.[29] Once more the old argument concerning disturbance and intrusion into 'rural quietude' raised its head.[30] One squire expressed satisfaction at the delay: 'I do not want a railway at all'.[31] Legal constraints on estates such as Llysnewydd, were used as arguments—often specious—to explain why land could not be granted.[32]

The failure of the line from Llandysul to Newcastle Emlyn and Cardigan gave impetus to extend the Whitland-Taf line from Crymych to Cardigan.[33] Support came from self-made capitalist, David Davies of Llandinam, MP for the Cardigan boroughs, with an investment of £1,000.[34] More gentry in north Pembrokeshire like William Henry Lewis of Clynfyw, Mark Anthony Saurin of Cilwendeg, and John Vaughan Colby of Ffynone, and leading businessmen, were drawn in, with the Great Western Railway Company backing the scheme with £10,000. Tradesmen and farmers in St Dogmael's and Ferwig injected a further £2,000,[35] in spite of local misgivings on the part of vested interests in Cardigan that the town's seaport trade would suffer. Brigstocke of Blaenpant put in his oar for the Crymych to Cardigan project, having argued *ad nauseam* against the prevailing idea that railway investment was a 'chapel collection' effort.[36] Further concentrated effort by Capt. W. Erasmus Gower of Glandovan and Castle Malgwyn resulted in the opening of the Cardigan line in 1886.[37] A new bill for the extension of the line to Newcastle Emlyn was passed in 1880-81, but it took another fifteen years for the project to be completed.[38] Muddleheadedness and prejudice, and the lack of invested capital on the part of most gentry (with notable exceptions), resulted in lost opportunities. Lacking a sense of priorities, they preferred to spend vast sums on new mansions, on expensive lifestyles and unbridled 'display'. In such a 'scandalous' situation the only remedy, it was argued by Jones-Parry of Tŷ Llwyd, was for the government to provide state aid for railways as in other countries.[39]

NOTES AND SOURCES

[1]T. I. J. Jones: *op cit.*, pp. 38, 45, 49, 51, 56, 62, 66-71; D. Williams: *op cit.*, pp. 158-70.

[2]W. Davies: *op cit.*, p. 366; *DWB.*

[3]CRO/TT/39.

[4]*ibid*: resolution of 11 Feb. 1836; HRO/PQ/AH/2/1.

[5]*Cm Jnl*: 9/6/1837.

[6]NLW/Highmead/Box p/File 15.

[7]*Cm Jnl*: 8/9/1810; 12/9/1812.

[8]A. H. Williams: *John Wesley in Wales 1739-90*, 1971, intro., p. xxxiv.

[9]RCISW (Turnpike Trusts) 1844, p. 21.

[10]F. M. L. Thompson: *op cit.*, pp. 238 seq.

[11]Dd Wiliams: *Modern Wales*, pp. 195, 214-15, 217-19; T. I. J. Jones: *op cit.*, pp. 87, 92, 107, 113, 123, 134, 136, 147, 161.

[12]E. T. Davies: *Religion and Society in Wales in the Nineteenth Century*, 1971, pp. 68-9; *DWB.*

[13]*Cm Jnl*: 26/4/1844.

[14]*ibid*: 26/4/1844, 26/7/1844, 30/8/1844.

[15]*ibid*: 17/10/1845; *DWB.*

[16]*The Welshman*: 14/11/1845.

[17]*Cm Jnl*: 10/9/1852; NLW/Cilgwyn/LB34/10 May 1853.

[18]*Cm Jnl*: 18/11/1853.

[19]*ibid*: 3/2/1854; 3/10/1854.

[20]NLW/Cilgwyn LB/36/24 Mch 1853, 18 Mch 1856, 22 Nov. 1857, 3 May 1856; *ibid*: LB/43/4 Sept. 1864; *ibid*: LB/44/15 Mch 1871.

[21]*loc cit.*

[22]*Cd Ad*: 15/3/1872.

[23]NLW/Bronwydd/5262.

[24]*The Welshman*: 21/5/1858; 1/11/1861.

[25]NLW/Add Ms 5532 E.

[26]NLW/Cilgwyn LB/34/21 April 1853.

[27]*The Welshman*: 20/8/1862.

[28]*Cd Ad*: 15/3/1872.

[29]*The Welshman*: 21/1/1870.

[30]*Cm Jnl* 10/1/1877.

[31]NLW/Cilgwyn/LB49/24 Aug. 1874.

[32]*Cm Jnl*: 27/10.1871.

[33]*Cd Ad*: 12/1/1877.

[34]*DWB*; Cd Ad: 31/8/1877.

[35]*ibid* 7/9/1877, 19/10/1877.

[36]*The Welshman*: 2/7/1880.

[37]*Cd Ad*: 3/9/1886.

[38]T. I. J. Jones: *op cit.*, p. 147; *Cd Ad*: 28/6//1895.

[39]RCLWM, iii, pp. 483-84 [Qus 44904, 44920] evidence of Jones-Parry, Tŷ Llwyd.

Arboriculture and Horticulture

Towards the end of the eighteenth century, progressive landowners in Britain planted trees extensively to enhance the value of their estates and to meet the country's growing and changing demand for wood. The needs of agriculture, shipbuilding and charcoal production for industry, had led to the destruction of much of Britain's native oak woodland. The protection of woodlands and 'timber trees'—oak, beech, ash, elm, sycamore and the like—had led to the unpopular Act for 'The Protection of Timber Trees . . .' in 1760.[1] But the aesthetic and utilitarian value of tree planting on estates was to be advocated more and more by progressive gentry, although in some quarters complaints were raised concerning the lack of encouragement to plant.[2]

Some 'Tivyside' squires, however, had earlier in the century been aware of the commercial value of timber as a cash crop; in 1743 William Brigstocke of Blaenpant obtained £135 for timber from his Cydweli estate, which was possibly sold to iron manufacturers in the area.[3] Periodic sales had taken place on the Gellydywyll estate from 1775 onwards, during which, the total sum of £2,649 was realised, and figures like '2000 ash trees sold' were quoted.[4] Ash was used to make carts, waggons and 'implements of husbandry', and the timber was possibly floated downstream to Cardigan, as was the practice followed by other landowners such as Vaughan of Golden Grove on the river Tywi.[5] Landowners like Colby of Ffynone and Dr John Jones, held periodic sales of timber for the use of forges and ironworks, bark for tanning, and for house-building, with 'straight oaks' for the latter, while 'very crooked' timber could be used for a 'colery or cordwood'.[6] From the 1790s there was, in addition, an increasing demand for timber from naval dockyards, and landowners adopted a more professional attitude to tree cultivation. Scotsmen with practical skills were employed as woodwards on Welsh estates, with a supporting force of woodmen and labourers for planting, weeding and bark stripping, but before 1800 instances of good management of estate woodlands were rare.[7] As in other areas of estate administration, details of the precise economy of forestry on the small 'Tivyside' estates are few. Clauses in leases laid down that tenants had to plant and maintain trees, as well as thorns and 'quick setts' on hedgerows, the landlord paying compensation for damage during felling and haulage. Nevertheless, many tenants regarded tree growing as unwanted extra burdens.[8] Walter Davies and topographical writers noticed the 'sylvan groves' around gentry houses. Brigstocke of Blaenpant was complimented upon his 'prudent economy in the management of woods'. There was praise for the skilled woodmen at Gellydywyll, while John Colby of Ffynone, Llywelyn Parry of Gernos, and Lewis Turnor at Wervil Brook were but a few of the 'spirited planters' of trees mentioned.[9] One random receipt shows that, in February 1796 alone, John Colby planted 40,000 trees on his estate, which suggests an extensive and vigorous plan of tree planting. Thomas Lloyd of Bronwydd, too, an indefatigable agriculturalist, also engaged in extensive tree planting.[10]

Hassall complained of the dearth of nurseries in the area for raising forest trees. Trees were brought in from Scotland and elsewhere, and sold by agents in Carmarthen and Cardigan.[11] But a few nurseries existed, like those at Llechryd and Felindre—the latter run by a Mr Hindes whose annual sales amounted to about 400,000 forest trees out of his stock of two and a half million.[12]

In the absence of comprehensive estate accounts, press advertisements of 'Tivyside' timber sales suggest that arboriculture was a continuing aspect of estate economy in the nineteenth century. 'Harvesting' estate timber and long-term planting for future generations was standard policy.[13] In 1812 timber sales at Falcondale and Highmead realised over £850. In March 1816, 160 'capital oak trees' were sold off the Gellydywyll estate, the best part of which were 'fit for ship-building'.[14] Large quantities of about 4,000 trees were sold off the Cawdor and Blaendyffryn estates in the years 1816 to 1820[15] and in the following decades Thomas Lewis of Clynfyw and Benjamin Edward Hall, amongst others, were active in tree planting, the latter setting apart nursery plots for 'acorns and ash "keyes"'.[16] In varying degrees other estate owners sold their timber at periodic intervals, realising such sums as £200 (Noyadd Trefawr) in 1856-59 and £400 (Blaenpant) in 1899.[17]

The incentive towards large-scale afforestation had been the commercial gain regulated by national needs, as well as the aesthetic improvement of the estate. From the mid-nineteenth century the trade in oak bark declined and the death blow for naval oak occurred in 1862 at the battle of the Hampton Roads.[18] On the other hand, timber acquired for industrial purposes partly made up for losses in shipping requirements.[19] In 1872 William Price Llewellyn Lewes of Llysnewydd made about £500 from timber on his Dyffryn, Llandybïe estate which lay over coal mines.[20] From 1879 to 1888 a vigorous afforestation plan was carried out on the Fitzwilliams' Cydweli property, again for use in an industrial area.[21] After the arrival of the railway at places like Llandysul and Crymych, timber from estates such as Llanfair, Dôl-Llan, Cilwendeg and Pentre could be sold for use ultimately in distant coal mines and other industries. On these estates one sale of timber for pit wood and poles fetched about £1,605, and over 13,000 trees were felled in the winter of 1887-1888.[22]

A factor which made a serious dent in commercial afforestation on private estates was the importation of foreign timber, which had gradually taken place since free trade measures were applied in the late 1840s. Dr Linnard argues that this accelerated so much by the end of the century that woodlands on estates were no longer profitable sources of income, but merely served as 'game covers'.[23] Fitzwilliams of Cilgwyn in March 1909 put the landowners' dilemma very clearly: '. . . landowners have ceased to plant because the business does not pay . . . the market is swamped by foreign goods'. Labour costs, rates, the shortage of skilled labour as well as agricultural depression, compelled the landlord to invest in '. . . the colonies and abroad', and not in local forestry enterprises.[24]

A necessary appendage to the squire's mansion and estate was his garden, and horticulture was prized as a means of providing the needs of the household with fruit and vegetables throughout the year, as well as flowers to adorn the main rooms of the house. The walled garden was conveniently placed between the kitchens and the home farm so that manure and compost could be easily carted to it. High walls of stone or brick enclosed several acres; for example, the enclosed garden at Ffynone was almost three acres in area while another outside the walls was just as large and used for less exotic items like brassicas and root vegetables. Other gardens like those of Llysnewydd, Dolhaidd and Highmead had devices in which fires could be lit to give warmth to tender trees, such as peach trees trained along the walls, and to prevent frost damage to early blossom.[25]

Ideas about horticulture spread into Wales like other fashions. The Morris brothers spoke of their connection with the Welsh gardener at Wanstead House, one of the great showplaces of England. Miller's *Dictionary of Gardening*, 1724, influenced opinions on cultivation, hot houses, cold frames and other aspects of garden technology, while popular journals like the *Gentleman's Magazine* had columns on horticulture.[26]

In 'Tivyside', squires like David Lloyd of Alltyrodyn in 1744 boasted of his 'delicious arbours', 'melonry' and 'wide canals' to irrigate his cauliflowers, cucumbers and beans.[27] John Campbell of Bangeston, in October 1783, sent cuttings of fruit shrubs to Dr Jones at Bronwydd.[28] Wealthier landowners like Lord Cawdor could afford to employ a highly trained professional gardener. Many of the gentry strove to educate their workers and tenants as to the best means of cultivating their gardens and allotments. Motivated by societies for improving the condition of the labouring classes, a taste for gardening was considered to be the best means 'to keep up that simplicity of character which is the boast of the English peasant'. John Scandrett Harford of Peterwell, with theological and moral imperatives foremost in his mind, founded the Lampeter Cottage Gardens Allotments Society in the 1830s, to reward industry through premiums of clothing, implements and furniture, and, significantly, any 'moral lapse' automatically disqualified the competitor. Likewise, fifty years later, Sir Marteine Lloyd promoted a garden society in the neighbourhood of Bronwydd.[29]

The horticultural knowledge and practice of the gentry spilled over to the local gardening societies they encouraged. While the squires themselves took pride in the cultivation of the exotic and *recherché* items for their dining rooms, the lower orders were encouraged to grow more useful produce—potatoes, carrots, onions, turnips and herbs—and skill in destroying pests counted also in their favour.[30]

The Great Exhibition of 1851 had given a tremendous stimulus to new technical and mechanical aids to the country-house gardener. The catalogues of specialised firms like Messenger and Co. of Loughborough and London circulated, carrying advertisements for every conceivable apparatus for heating, controlling light and air, humidity and so on. The horticultural interests of the gentry were in many ways part of the 'conspicuous display' of their lifestyle. The gardener at Castle Malgwyn had been trained at the Glasgow Botanical Gardens,[31] and the exotic flowers grown in the glasshouses at Blaenpant in 1889 included orchids and gardenias.[32] The cross-cultivation of fruit and the improvement of strains resulted in each country house competing against its neighbour. The influence of the big house and its garden is still traceable in the old-fashioned plants—bourbon and gallica roses, lavender and musk—that still survive in old cottage gardens near the sites of old mansions which in many cases have disappeared from the landscape.

NOTES AND SOURCES

[1]W. Linnard: 'Thomas Johnes of Hafod, Pioneer of Land Afforestation in Wales', *Ceredigion*, VI, 1970, p. 309; *Gent Mag*, 1766, pp. 319-20.

[2]*ibid*: 1784, pp. 267-69; 1797, pp. 212-15, 370-71; *The Seventh Report of the Commissioners . . . Woods, Forests etc*, 1792, App. ii, 87, 107.

[3]NLW/Evans George/1299-1309; J. E. Lloyd (ed) *op cit.*, ii. p. 326.

[4]NLW/Noyadd Trefawr/1689; NLW/Evans George/375.

[5]F. Jones: 'The Vaughans of Golden Grove', *THSC*, 1964, ii, p. 211.

[6]NLW/Owen Colby/650; NLW/Bronwydd/2261.

[7]W. Linnard: *Welsh Woods and Forests*, 1982, pp. 128-37.

[8]*ibid*: pp. 138-40.

[9]W. Davies: *op cit.*, i, pp. 37-8; ii, pp. 33-36, 51.

[10]NLW/Owen Colby/2248; Cardiff Public Library: 4/4669.

[11]W. Davies: *op cit.*, ii, p. 33; *Cm Jnl*: 12/1/1811; 6/10/1810; 24/10/1812.

[12]W. Davies: pp. 37-38; D. E. Jones: *op cit.*, p. 141; Phillip Hindes came to the Felindre area in 1794 from Irby, Lincs. In 1814 his nephew, William, joined him and developed nurseries at Goitre-isaf.

[13]NLW/Owen Colby/1875; NLW/Falcondale/Group V/138/xii.

[14]*Cm Jnl*: 8/3/1816.

[15]*ibid*: 15/2/1816, 24/3/1820.

[16]NLW/D. Roy Evans/123; NLW/Cilgwyn LB/32/6 Jan. 1834.

[17]NLW/Noyadd Trefawr/1571-74; NLW/Evans George/1909.

[18]W. Linnard; *op cit.*, p. 145; the battle of Hampton Roads, 9 Mch 1862, at the beginning of the American Civil War marked the introduction and superiority of iron-clad fighting ships.

[19]D. W. Howell: *op cit.*, p. 35.

[20]NLW/Llysnewydd/Bundle 74.

[21]NLW/Cilgwyn LB/46, 47/1879-1808.

[22]NLW/Morgan Richardson/1409; *Cd Ad*: 20/3/1888.

[23]*loc cit.*

[24]NLW/Cilgwyn LB/53/correspondence Oct. 1907-March 1909.

[25]Personal knowledge.

[26]J. H. Davies: *op cit.*, i, pp. 38, 48; *Gent Mag*: 1759, pp. 370-77; Wanstead House in Essex.

[27]NLW/Ms 8724B.

[28]NLW/Bronwydd/2263.

[29]*Cm Jnl*: 4/8/1810; NLW/Falcondale/Gp vi, 7, 187, 189, 195, 201-2; *Cd Ad* 29/8/1884.

[30]*ibid*: 3/3/1866.

[31]*ibid*: 14/1/1876.

[32]NLW/Evans George/1908.

Domanial and Manorial Jurisdiction

Up to the end of the nineteenth century landowners asserted rights which, they claimed, went back to medieval times. They regarded rent almost as a commutation of the dues and services which the medieval villeins had owed to their ancestors. As a governing élite over immense areas of property, they claimed the allegiance, loyalty and deference of tenants and inhabitants within their manors. Squires like the Lloyds of Bronwydd, especially, invoked the authority of early deeds to substantiate their claim to the homage and other feudal obligations of their dependants, and also to rents, tolls, rights, claims to wrecks and, in particular, to the mineral possibilities beneath the soil of the manor or barony.[1] Tudor legislation had done much to deprive the landed magnates of all semblance of their former feudal power save for a few vestigial rights, as mentioned above, along with courts leet and courts baron.[2] A recurring problem for the gentry, who claimed such rights, was to prove that they were *de jure* rather than *de facto*.[3] In most cases manorial rights were sought, like any other estate asset, as sources of influence and profit. The Lloyds of Bronwydd were besotted with the mythological and antiquarian glamour concerning the 'Barony of Kemes', forgetting that it was through marriage, inheritance and purchase that they had gained hegemony over vast tracts in north Pembrokeshire. A royal grant in Tudor times, it was supposed, had given the manor of St Dogmael's to the Parrys of Noyadd Trefawr, and of Emlyn uwch Cuch, to the forebears of the Vaughans of Golden Grove.[4]

· But proof of title was not always clear-cut: for example, the manor of Iscoed uwch Hirwen claimed by the Lloyd family of Coedmore, and inherited from Sir John Lewis of Abernantbychan, had a very dubious title. A survey of 1651 stated that, although the manor was in the tenure and occupation of Sir John Lewis, '. . . by what Right and Title he holds the same wee know not for that noe Evidence was produced to us'.[5]

A strong motive, too, in acquiring manors was the possibility of extending an estate by enclosing contiguous common land. Thomas Lloyd of Bronwydd asserted manorial claims along the sea front and in the vicinity of Newport, Pembrokeshire, in order to lease out 'the strand . . . for storehouses, keys [sic] etc not forgetting the thousand acres of commons . . . highly capable of improvement by an Enclosure Bill'.[6] In addition, small encroachments and the right to build a cottage on the common given to 'homagers', extended the social and political power of the lord of the manor over those occupants who had to pay chief rents ranging from 1d to a shilling or two. Likewise, 'tolls', 'standings and pitchings' and claims to wrecks were seized upon in the lord of the manor's name against the Admiralty or the Excise man.[7]

Manors were bought in order to develop the industrial potential of an area. Thus Lloyd of Bronwydd purchased Llanfyrnach manor with its lead mines.[8] Competition for profit and the struggle for prestige possibly motivated Thomas Lewis of Clynfyw in 1790 and W. O. Brigstocke of Blaenpant in 1878 to purchase the manors of Castellan and Gwynionydd-is-Coed respectively, the latter for £1,000 from the Commisioners of Woods and Forests.[9] In 1829 B. E. Hall was more concerned with political advantages in the immediate vicinity of his Cilgwyn estate, namely, the possible resuscitation of the political status of Atpar, one of the Cardigan boroughs which returned its own member of parliament.[10] In 1897 his grandson wished to buy the manor of Dyffryn Teifi in order to '. . . keep the tenants quiet on our Parish Councils, I cannot expect the acquisition to be a source of much pleasure or profit, but I hope it may lead to peace and quietness',[11] a diplomatic rearguard manoeuvre against victorious democratic forces.

Not only did the gentry rule their communities through the courts of Petty and Quarter Sessions in matters where the sovereignty of the Crown was paramount, but assumed for themselves as lords of the manor a hold on everything and everybody within the manor. The lord's sanction was enforced through manorial courts with judicial and administrative functions in matters relating to the 'custom of the manor'. The lord's steward acted as judge, with chosen and 'proven' jurymen of the lord's outlook and persuasion listening to the 'presentments' brought before them by the 'homagers'.[12] The exceptionally extensive extant archives of the barony of Kemes, and of the Vaughans of Golden Grove, illustrate well the place of the landowner as lord of the manor. On the Golden Grove manor of Emlyn uwch Cuch feudal dues were strictly enforced—'mortuaries', 'heriots', 'lederwite', fines and the like—even on neighbouring squirearchy. Thus William Lewes of Llysnewydd had to pay 5s. on acquiring property in Llangeler parish in 1815; a mortuary of 10s. was demanded on the death of Lewes-Lloyd of Dolhaidd and when his daughter was married a 'lederwite' of 5s. had to be paid.[13] These continued until the end of the century, and it was only when local government was reformed by legislation in the 1880s that the power of these squires—especially the Lloyds of Bronwydd—was removed.[14]

If the liberty of the individual was diminished by manorial custom, it was also protected by appeal to the lord of the manor. Trespass and misuse of hill pastures and rights of common by interlopers had been a problem since courts leet had been robbed of much of their powers by the Act of Union.[15] Encroachment had been facilitated, too, by the centuries-old Welsh custom of putting up a *tŷ-un-nos* (one-night-cottage)—an act which acquired freehold rights to the cottage and adjoining plot of land.[16] Small freeholders and tenants possessing customary rights were generally hostile to such 'squatters'; for example, riotous scenes took place in Llanfyrnach and Nevern during the years 1805 to 1811 when objectors appealed to Thomas Lloyd of Bronwydd.[17] The community also frowned upon excessive cutting of 'matts' (turves) for fuel; pigs roaming about 'unringed' on grazing land; and vessels taking foreshore sand for ballast.[18] Disputes about encroachments, and loss of rights by persons who were 'honest, sober and industrious', were fomented by the high-handed conduct of rough layabouts. On such occasions Lloyd of Bronwydd, Parry of Noyadd Trefawr, and other landlords were constantly asked to arbitrate between rival factions.[19] The cavalier attitude of stewards sometimes roused the indignation of 'commoners' who preferred to deal with the lord of the manor himself.[20]

Although the squire's protection was vital to the quiet enjoyment of their rights, some commoners had long displayed reluctance and even hostility to the payment of tolls and chief rents, an attitude which had plagued George Owen of Henllys, and his Bronwydd descendants since the seventeenth century. Even a squire like Lloyd of Cwmgloyne in 1773 owed £4-5s. in chief rents arrrears over many years. Such was the experience of other lords of the manor in the area. Chief rents payable to Brigstocke of Blaenpant had dropped to a trickle by 1858, a situation which reflected the rising tide of radicalism against the gentry.[21]

There was equal objection to the payment of tolls, usually farmed out to unscrupulous collectors, and a hindrance to just and free trading by vendors and buyers, who had no choice but to trade at a fair or market controlled by the lord of the manor.[22] Hostility to paying tolls at Meigan fair in 1843 led to a rival fair at Maenclochog, and in the years 1851-62 another rival fair at Eglwyswrw (free from pressure from the lord of the manor) successfully attracted dealers from as far as Swansea.[23] In some areas tolls continued to be paid, as at Cardigan where the right was invested in the mayor and corporation. Elsewhere, at Newcastle Emlyn, Llandysul and Lampeter, they fell into desuetude by the 1880s along with other vestiges of gentry power.[24]

To claim manorial rights and jurisdiction was one thing, but to sustain them was another matter, as envious neighbouring landowners would not tolerate the overweening claims of a squire who set himself above the rest. James Bowen of Llwyngwair in 1750 challenged the Lloyd of Bronwydd claim to appoint the mayor of Newport, questioning the validity of so-called traditional privilege, as well as the extent of Bronwydd lands in the area.[25] Thomas Lloyd, in the last decades of the eighteenth century, revived an ancient custom of perambulating the barony, recording landmarks, taking depositions from aged folk and checking encroachments—a 'spectacle' which continued (with retainers in uniform and led by the Bronwydd band) until the last decades of the nineteenth century—as a conscious assertion of family prestige.[26]

Over the years, other landowners like John Colby of Ffynone and Henry Scourfield of Moat were not slow to challenge Lloyd. In the 1830s and '40s supporters of Bowen of Llwyngwair were incited not to pay chief rents to Bronwydd; rival mobs comprising the 'Orange' and 'Blue' factions in Newport indulged in riotous behaviour, so that open warfare led Lloyd supporters to plead '. . . it is high time this Rebeccaite system should be put a stop to immediately'.[27] Thomas Lloyd of Bronwydd himself indulged in rough tactics and coercive behaviour in distraining the goods of abysmally poor people, while on the other hand, protecting the rights of commoners so long as they acknowledged his authority.[28] In the event of refusal to pay chief rents, a strong radically-minded *gwerinwr* like Thomas Rees of Brithdir (described by Lloyd as 'that impudent little cur') found himself on trial at Cardigan Assizes where the judgement went against Rees and in favour of the landowner.[29] Other landlords, too, such as Parry of Noyadd Trefawr, in 1815 and Mrs Brigstocke of Blaenpant, in the 1860s, took high-handed remedies to assert manorial rights with scant regard for anyone who challenged them.[30]

Thomas Lloyd's paranoia reached its climax when, with his connivance, the mayor of Newport usurped the functions of a JP. In 1849, Thomas Davies Lloyd attempted to revive baronial courts on equal terms with the new county courts,[31] and was only restrained by wise legal advice and considerable cost. From 1850 onwards Bronwydd suzerainty was sustained by more temperate methods— *rapprochement* with the rival house of Llwyngwair; a more equitable sharing of their respective revenues within the barony; and the appointment in 1870 of a Bowen of Llwyngwair, the first for a long time—a 'model landlord' and a 'highly respectable citizen'—as mayor of Newport.[32] Towards the rest of the community Lloyd's policy was to cajole rather than coerce. Prudent landlords more and more sensed that change was bound to take place. Radical dissent, parliamentary attitudes and rampant denominational issues had persuaded enlightened gentry like W. O. Brigstocke by the end of the nineteenth century that it was time to capitulate to the forces of change.[33] Thus the domanial and manorial power of the squire ceased. The descendants of the Lloyds of Bronwydd, have retained the semblance of manorial sway, by appointing annually the mayor of Newport.

NOTES AND SOURCES

[1]*Cd Ad*: 25/6/1875; FG/6/428.

[2]P. Williams: *op cit.*, p. 25; I. Bowen: *op cit.*, pp. 1421-48.

[3]NLW/Bronwydd/7271-72; FG/6/428.

[4]*ibid*: 6/428; NLW/Bronwydd/7022; NLW/Noyadd Trefawr/7022; F. Jones: 'The Vaughans', *THSC*, i, 1963, pp. 99-100; B. G. Charles: *George Owen a Welsh Elizabethan*, 1973, pp. 3, 16-18.

[5]T. Nicholas: *op cit.*, i, p. 204; M. Richards: 'Iscoed uwch Hirwen in 1651', *Ceredigion*, IV, 1963, p. 387.

[6]NLW/Bronwydd/6954.

[7]*ibid*: 537-40; 6949-53; 6902-46.

[8]F. Jones: 'Blaenbylan', *Ceredigion*, VII, 3, 4, 1974/75, p. 329.

[9]NLW/Clynfyw/Box 1/-; CRO/EG/Box 8.

[10]NLW/Cilgwyn/LB/32/20 April 1829.

[11]*ibid*: LB/50/1 June 1897.

[12]*Enc Britt*. 1937.

[13]CRO/Cawdor/2/258; '*mortuary*'—gift to an ecclesiastical dignitary on the death of a priest, or to a feudal lord on the death of a tenant; '*heriot*'—gift of best beast to the lord of the manor on the death of a tenant; '*lecherwite*' or '*lederwite*'—a penalty or tax payable to the lord on the marriage of a woman, e.g. daughter of a tenant.

[14]NLW/Bronwydd/6670-73.

[15]R. Flenley: *Calendar of the Register of the Council of the Marches of Wales 1569-71*, 1916, p. 105.

[16] D. W. Howell: *op cit.*, pp. 29-31.

[17]NLW/Bronwydd/3734-36; NLW/Owen Colby/612-13.

[18]NLW/Bronwydd/6776-80.

[19]*ibid*: 558; NLW/Noyadd Trefawr/734-36.

[20]*ibid*: 612-13.

[21]*ibid*: 505-08; 6665, 574, 6642-47, 6628; CRO/EG/Box 11.8, 88.

[22]*Yr Efangylydd*: 1833, p. 98 quoted in RCLWM, 1896, Appendix, pp. 187-88.

[23]NLW/Bronwydd/6690, 7003-08.

[24]Return of Markets and Tolls, 1886; NLW/Cilgwyn/LB/52/22 Sept. 1906.

[25]NLW/Bronwydd/6635.

[26]*ibid*: 6775-79, 3953-54, 3473-77; Cm Jnl: 17/7/1846.

[27]NLW/Bronwydd/64, 3804-20, 524-29, 4430-39, 7027-30.

[28]*ibid*: 3867, 4417, 7026, 4270-75.

[29]*Cm Jnl*: 16/3/1838.

[30]NLW/Noyadd Trefawr/1730; CRO/EG/Box/67.

[31]NLW/Bronwydd/4428-29, 6886; County Courts Act (9 and 10 Vict. c. 95).

[32]NLW/Bronwydd/6822-23; *Cd Ad*: 11/11/1870.

[33]NLW/Ms 3607 E.

Enclosure and the Landed Estate

By the end of the eighteenth century, much of the wasteland of Cardiganshire, Carmarthenshire and Pembrokeshire had been enclosed.[1] The Teifi valley reflected this process so that a traveller in 1805 could say that the area was 'full of enclosures, hedgerows, corn and grass fields and bounded by a various outline of naked hills, which strikingly contrast with the fertility below'.[2] Enclosure had been carried out piecemeal since the 1750s, but there still remained sizeable areas of commons to be enclosed which became the subject of parliamentary legislation. From 1811 to 1855 some eleven enclosure acts were passed which related to commons bordering on the river Teifi.[3] Hitherto, some enclosure had been sporadic, with or without the lord of the manor's acquiescence.[4]

Enclosure Acts were private acts of parliament promoted by landed proprietors, which resulted in the extinction of grazing rights and the consolidation of often scattered holdings—giving more pasture 'closes', especially in the years from 1790 to the 1830s. Walter Davies considered that enclosures were beneficial, with owners of property improving their land, increasing production and profit, and inducing tenants to be more industrious. On the other hand, he conceded that poor people would be deprived of their pasture rights and fields as well as an independent livelihood, while industries like rural woollen production might suffer[5]

Some historians have commented on the adverse effects, the deprivation and loss suffered by a pastoral folk as a result of enclosures,[6] forgetting that the agricultural production which followed created an increased demand for labour.[7] Moreover, the poverty of the period was due not so much to the ill effects of enclosure as to the rapid growth in population.[8] While there was loss of 'keep' for geese, cows and sheep, the value of the land doubled through improved drainage, irrigation, fencing and manuring. Protagonists of the deprived peasantry expressed their views in a much quoted jingle—

> It is a sin in man or woman
> To steal a Goose from off a Common,
> But who can plead that man's Excuse
> Who steals a Common from a Goose—

to which Hassall replied:

> He stands in need of no excuse,
> Who feeds an ox where fed a Goose . . .[9]

The advantages of enclosure appealed to the gentry as a whole, especially, as there was so much well-informed opinion in its favour.[10] It is argued that it represented the major areas of capital investment by landowners which would bring about agricultural improvement.[11] One discerns, however, rather mixed motives on the part of gentry in the Teifi valley which suggest that agricultural improvement was not always predominant in their minds. Such motives can be gleaned from the following instances. John Colby of Ffynone opposed the Cydweli enclosure bill in 1812-13 for fear of commercial competition. As has been noticed, Thomas Lloyd of Bronwydd allowed small enclosures on the barren hill behind Newport only in so far as his own authority was enhanced.[12] Evans of Pantycendy (only a few miles outside 'Tivyside') would gladly surrender any claim to his commons in order to benefit the poor, and to relieve the burden of the poor rate.[13] The unproductive wasteland comprising Cardigan common was deemed worth enclosing for the good of the town. Limited public enjoyment rights were to be preserved, and its cultivation would employ labourers to everybody's benefit.[14] In 1847 Lewes Lloyd of Dolhaidd opposed the enclosure of commons in Llangeler parish, as they were manorial commons with traditional rights, against the claims of B. E. Hall of Cilgwyn who supported enclosure in order to establish strictly legal landowners' rights and equitable division.[15] The latter's son, E. Crompton Ll. Fitzwilliams supported further enclosure in Llangeler to increase his estate with new farms and sheep walks, and in order to make new roads to link up with Llanpumsaint railway station, a step which he thought would be of benefit to farmers.[16] In 1877 Sir Thomas Davies Lloyd of Bronwydd granted encroachments, without limit on Newport common, in the hope that lessees could qualify as electors in returning a member of parliament for the county, especially someone favoured by him.[17]

There was little violence resulting from enclosure by act of parliament, because such acts were few and because of the difficulty in resisting constituted authority.[18] Disaffection within the barony of 'Kemes', for example, was on a limited scale where the participants were often the puppets manipulated by rival landowners. There was no dramatic outburst of disaffection comparable to the north Cardiganshire *Rhyfel y Sais Bach* (The Little Englishman's War).[19] Nevertheless, there was simmering discontent, and cottages, fences, banks and hedges were pulled down. Surveyors like Hassall and Couling were unpopular, and at the end of the nineteenth century bitter memories survived of the peremptory eviction and cavalier treatment of smallholders by local gentry. In the parish of Llangeler, for example, landlords like Lewes of Llysnewydd sold the enclosed smallholdings and '*tai-un-nos*' over the heads of their occupants.[20]

Only in relation to a few 'Tivyside' estates is it possible to estimate the amount of land and consequent gain the landowners obtained through enclosures. For example, Thomas Lloyd of Bronwydd acquired some 400 of the 2,500 acres of Llanfyrnach common following an act of 1809.[21] About 100 cottages and gardens on the steep and rocky Newport common yielded Lloyd of Bronwydd some £133 in rent in 1834. B. E. Hall was mainly concerned with the quarrying rights over the stone, lime and gravel[22] under some 350 acres of common bought in the parishes of Llangyndeyrn and Cydweli which, with the extension of the railway as a possibility, would provide lime for his Cilgwyn estate in 'Tivyside'.[23] It would appear that when common land was enclosed the lion's share went to the local landowners, approximately in proportion to their estate acreage in the parish; for example, the Llysnewydd estate gained 120 acres of the Llangeler (Grange) common in 1848 with other landowners each acquiring from 10 to 50 acres respectively.[24] Again in 1852, with the Waunmeiros (Llangeler) Enclosure Act, 97 acres out of 138 were absorbed into the adjacent Llysnewydd demesne.[25] The impression that only major land-owners benefited from enclosure requires qualification; the well-to-do yeoman farmer, wealthy professional or businessman and even ordinary folk all took advantage of the spoils. In the case of the enclosure of Cardigan commons, Miles of the Priory, Cardigan (with an estate of 1,000 acres), only acquired 29 acres, while Loveden Pryse of Gogerddan with 400 acres locally was awarded 5 acres. The remaining 164 acres of Cardigan common were divided into small plots, some only amounting to a fraction of an acre, and were taken up by local inhabitants.[26]

One undesirable social consequence of enclosure was the acquis-ition of land by landowners who were living in places some considerable distance outside the area. A pattern of absentee landlordism occurred leading to often tenuous and strained landlord and tenant relation-ships. Of the large tract extending over 6,300 acres of hilly moorland, forming the commons of Llanfihangel-ar-Arth, Llanybydder and

Pencarreg parishes, only about 168 acres were acquired by a local resident landlord, namely John Jones of Maesycrugiau.[27] The remainder was taken up by J. W. Gwynne-Hughes of Tregib in the Tywi valley, and by the well-to-do in parishes as far apart as Llangrannog in Cardiganshire, Llanelli in Carmarthenshire and Barry in Glamorgan, amongst others. Consequently, they showed little interest in the welfare of people in the areas where the enclosure took place. On the other hand, Lord Cawdor who lived outside the area and acquired 600 acres of the 2,230 acres which comprised the Cilrhedyn, Llangeler and Penboyr commons in the 1870s,[28] took a lively interest in the social and religious welfare of the area, and by employing wise and prudent agents was held in great esteem.

Although the large landowners were not the only members of the community to benefit from enclosure, the process helped to concentrate and consolidate gentry power in areas where it was already strong. Landowners acquired title to more acres on the basis of their existing wealth, while small folk who had only a limited but vital stake in the land were deprived of the slender means of livelihood, as well as their sense of possession and pride—the very backbone of the *gwerinwr*'s independent outlook. The enclosed commons in 'Tivyside' were largely upland tracts of heather and gorse. Apart from a few enclosed farms, the land was not improved agriculturally. Up to 1939 their function was to satisfy the sporting interests of the gentry. To some observers, the leisure pursuits of the landed classes had been given priority over traditional peasants' rights which were, more often than not, their only means of survival.

NOTES AND SOURCES

[1]D. W. Howell: *Patriarchs and Parasites*, pp. 66-7.

[2]Anon: 'A Tour in Wales, 1806', p. 52 quoted in A. E. Davies: 'Enclosures in Cardiganshire 1750-1850', *Ceredigion*, III, 1, 1976, pp. 101-2; Lloyd and Turnor: *loc cit.*; Hassall: *loc cit.*

[3]I. Bowen: *The Great Enclosures of Common Lands in Wales*, 1914, pp. 49-56. D. W. Howell: 'Landlords and Estate Managements in Wales', in the *Cambridge History of England and Wales*, V, pt. 2 (Ed. J. Thirsk), 1984, pp. 269 seq.

[4]M. Turner: *Enclosures in Britain 1750-1830*, 1984, p. 11.

[5]W. Davies: *op cit.*, p. 111.

[6]J. L. and B. Hammond: *The Village Labourer*, 1912, pp. 40-41; O. M. Edwards: *Gwilym Marles*, 1905, pp. 17-18.

[7]C. Hassall: *op cit.*, p. 21.

[8]G. E. Mingay: *op cit.*, p. 92.

[9]NLW/Poyston/342 (NLW/Ms 1444 F); RCLWM, v, p. 104.

[10]*The Cambrian Register*, i, 1795, p. 250; *Gent Mag*, 1819, pp. 522-23.

[11]G. E. Mingay: *English Landed Society in the Eighteenth Century*, 1963, pp. 179 seq.

[12]CRO/JF (Colby) 95-7.

[13]Evidence of RCCI 1844 quoted in RCLWM, App 1896, p. 37.

[14]RCCI, 1844 [Qus 1287-88); *The Welshman*: 26/12/1845.

[15]CRO/Cawdor/2/258.

[16]NLW/Cilgwyn/LB 34/8 Mch 1854; *ibid*: LB/44/1 Aug. 1873.

[17]NLW/Bronwydd/4402-14.

[18]Dd. Williams: *The Rebecca Riots*, p. 84.

[19]D. J. V. Jones: 'Rhyfel y Sais Bach', *Ceredigion*, V, 1966, no. 3, p. 84.

[20]RCLWM, iii, pp. 467-75; D. E. Jones: *op cit.*, 271-321, 339-40; *Cm Jnl*: 19/11/1813, 14/1/1814; *The Welshman*: 3/6/1853; 8/2/1856; 20/11/1874.

[21]I. Bowen: *op cit.*, p. 49; HRO/QRE/3.

[22]NLW/Bronwydd/6785.

[23]CRO/EG/Box/18/-.

[24]1848. 11-12 V c 27; CRO/AE/CC/1.

[25]1852. 15-16 V c 2; CRO/AE/11A.

[26]1854. 17-18 V c 9; ARO/cc/1.

[27]1868. 31-32 V c31; 1850 13-14 V c66; CRO/AE/5, 9, 21; 1885, 48-49 V c 58; I. Bowen: *op cit.*, p. 56.

[28]CRO/AE/19; 1865, 28-29 V c39; NLW/JCD/Map vol.

Landlord and Tenant Relationships

The 'Land Question' was a phrase which brought into sharp focus the relationship between the squire and his tenants. It became one of the most sensitive and acrimonious issues in the Welsh countryside in the last decades of the nineteenth century. Radical protest against the landowning classes had intensified since the days of S. R. of Llanbrynmair,[1] especially through the advocacy of new Liberal leaders, notably Henry Richard and Tom Ellis, in parliament.[2] The Welsh vernacular press and pulpit led by Thomas Gee and the populist preaching of E. Pan Jones added to existing disaffection and discontent.[3] The alleged grievances suffered by the *werin* were: arbitrary evictions, harassment for religious and political reasons, extortionate rent increases, insecurity of tenure, no compensation for improvements and the burden of paying tithes to support an alien church.[4]

In the lower Teifi valley the main radical propagandists were Dr Enoch Davies of Bangor Teifi, John Bowen of Llwyncynon and Alderman John Lewis, a Drefach woollen weaver. Evictions for political and religious reasons were alleged, especially after the decisive 1868 election. The squires of Alltyrodyn, Maesycrugiau, Blaenpant, Llysnewydd and Pigeonsford were accused of evicting tenants because they had not voted Tory along with their landlords. The 'exquisite cruelty' with which the tenant of Ffynnon Llewelyn and the Unitarian flock of Llwynrhydowen chapel were treated was highlighted as typical of gentry conduct and attitudes generally.[5] In addition, there was bitterness arising from clauses in leases which were considered unfair to the tenants, and also because of arbitrary eviction of squatters with time honoured claims to cottages and plots. Tension was high and Enoch Davies and John Lewis were described as '*twrneiod radicalaidd*' (radical attorneys); assaults took place between rival groups and court cases followed.

The evidence of Davies and Lewis was almost entirely condemnatory of the gentry, and was received, albeit with a degree of reservation, by the Liberal-minded Daniel Lleufer Thomas, secretary of the celebrated Welsh Land Commission of the 1890s. Even so, it was significant that only about half a dozen of the 'Tivyside' squires had the courage to come forward to challenge the allegations made against them by those who gave evidence before the Land Commission. Sir Marteine Lloyd of Bronwydd, alone, amongst his fellow gentry, went so far as to urge his tenants to give evidence.[6] At the time, J. E. Vincent, the landowners' legal representative, attempted to place the Welsh landlords in a more favourable light, and modern historians have sought to redress what they deem to be the over-balance of radical polemics.[7]

The eruption of the 'Land Question' was only part of a wider movement of disaffection and dissent which, as will be examined later, came about through latent grievances borne by the lower orders for many generations. In the narrower context of landlord and tenant, the contractual bond between them was the lease. Thomas Rees observed in 1815 that Welsh landlords had no uniform system in the letting of their estates.[8] It has been argued that in the eighteenth century the most common leases were for terms of lives; foe example, three lives or, to a lesser extent, for terms of years. Yearly agreements or varying terms of years seem to have been usual in the nineteenth century. The greater landowners were supposed to have granted leases for lives before the Reform Act of 1832 in order to acquire influence in county elections. The sanctity of the lease, and the benevolent paternalism of a rare type of squire were enshrined in a saying of a Lloyd of Bronwydd—'Cursed be the first Lloyd to evict a Bronwydd tenant' which was quoted in evidence before the Land Commission.[9] Views as to the suitability of long leases for good husbandry differed as we have already noted. Utilitarian minded landowners regarded long leases as leading to indolence and 'run down' farms, while short leases, it was thought, stimulated good management. On the other hand, a long lease, according to Walter Davies, could lead to improved agriculture and long-term improvement.[10] A perusal of 'Tivyside' leases over the period 1700 to 1900 displays a wide variety of terms; for example, leases for 1 year, 21 years, 99 years, as well as for one, two or three lives. Between 1770 and 1775 there was considerable variation in leases on the Gellydywyll estate, some for three lives and others from year to year.[11] A term of three lives was common on the Bronwydd estate in the eighteenth century. During a period of rising prices and agricultural prosperity, such as during the French Wars, Ffynone leases were granted for three or four lives on substantial farms, and a similar pattern is discernible in Coedmore leases.[12]

But as the nineteenth century wore on the tendency here, as elsewhere in south Wales, was for life leases to give ground increasingly to shorter terms of years and to year-to-year agreements. Nevertheless, on some estates like Blaenpant,[13] Cilgwyn[14] and Noyadd Trefawr[15] a diversity of terms applied from 1807 to 1893.

With the new annual agreements introduced in the nineteenth century, a whole series of restrictive clauses regulating husbandry practices were introduced, as, for example, restrictions on corn crops which could be taken in succession. The Land Commission Report of 1896 pointed out the opposition on the part of some tenant farmers to such restrictive clauses as suffocating their enterprise and methods of farming. That such clauses were only intended to keep in check the slovenly tenant and were, in fact, largely nugatory so far as the better tenants were concerned, may not have been appreciated by the tenant community.[16]

To assert their power status *vis-à-vis* their tenants, squires invoked medieval usage and custom in the form of dues and services. Feudal dues were levied as a contribution to the maintenance of the squire's mansion and family, and comprised wide-ranging and useful commodities, like bottles of cider and barrels of ale. The provision of cockles and flat fish were conditions in some Blaendyffryn leases of properties in Carmarthen in 1742.[17] Lobsters figured in a Rhosygilwen lease of 1773. Eggs and poultry at Easter and Christmas occur more frequently. The squire of Llwyngwair insisted that those of his tenants who supplemented their income by fishing had to fish for herrings from his boat, and he claimed part of the catch.[18]

Another burdensome clause in leases was the service rent, like grinding corn at the lord's mill or working a number of days on the lord's demesne farm, as took place at Blaendyffryn and other places in the years 1742 to 1745.[19] A greater aggravation was the lord's demand of coal, culm and lime which had to be transported long distances by pack-horse or cart, as, for example, in the period 1734 to 1744 to Noyadd Trefawr, and to Bronwydd until the last quarter of the nineteenth century.[20] Not only was the tenant responsible for the haulage, but also for the cost of these items, as well as paying turnpike tolls when demanded. When the tenants of the Blaendyffryn and Alltyrodyn estates had to bring building materials for the new church of St John's, Pont-siân (erected in an area of strong Unitarian dissent), a religious dimension was added to an existing economic grievance.[21]

Some historians hold the view that the continuance of feudal payments implied a deep resentment and a sense of servility on the part of tenants who, by the late nineteenth century, no longer possessed close emotional links with the gentry. Although Brigstocke of Blaenpant could, however, regard these customs as friendly and neighbourly acts, memories still survive of deep resentment towards having to carry out these duties on the Noyadd Trefawr and Pantgwyn estates.[22]

Landowners, for the most part, were concerned with letting their land to the best advantage, depending on the economic and other factors existing at the time. From the early decades of the eighteenth century, there was a gradual upward tendency in rents claimed by landowners who desired to make the most of their property.[23] While in the early 1700s livestock prices were low, and difficult periods for Welsh stock breeders occurred intermittently from 1722 to 1756, nevertheless increases in rent took place. Sometimes domestic matters within families led to rent increases, such as the life tenant coming into his estate, and revaluing it to increase its potential. The raising of mortgages for family portions, the building of a new mansion house, or retrenchment to make up for estate prodigality, were all to be considered as affecting estate rents and income. Although 'Tivyside' rentals are sparse and sporadic, the general upward trend is clear. Thus, on the Noyadd Trefawr estate, the total rent was raised from about £700 a year in 1723 to some £835 in 1758. From then on to 1777 it was further increased to over £1,200 a year.[24] By 1791 it had reached over £1,686, £2,894 in 1804 and rose to a peak of £3,723 in 1815. Even allowing for some increased acreage through informal enclosure, this increase on a substantial scale between 1791 and 1815 can be accounted for by improved land values during the Napoleonic wars. In addition, there may have been a desperate attempt in this particular example (as will be illustrated later) to underpin the parlous finances of the Garth estate in Breconshire whose owner, Marmaduke Gwynne, had married Frances Parry, the heiress of Noyadd Trefawr. Thomas Lloyd had claimed in 1794 that rents generally had at least doubled since 1763, and perhaps this was partly due also to enclosure.[25]

A similar trend of increased rents is observed on the Golden Grove estate in our area, which almost trebled from the 1750s to the end of the century. The expanding activity of drovers, as well as more trade in fairs and markets, may account for higher tolls at Newcastle Emlyn.[26] The estates of 'Tivyside' landowners which were partly in the prosperous industrial belt of east Carmarthenshire stood to gain. This may explain why the Blaenpant estate rental increased from about £1,500 a year in the 1750s to about £2,900 in 1807 and to some £5,000 by 1850. Likewise, the Ffynone estate which brought in £3,999 in 1820 could claim in the 1850s some £8,000 income per annum.[27]

While favourable economic stimuli and considerable increased acreages in respect of an estate like Ffynone, and commercial activity and urban development in the industrial areas, added to the value of an estate, general upward trends in rents were not reversed during periods of economic depression. Walter Davies acutely observed that the slump in prices after 1814 was not accompanied in Wales by a corresponding reduction in rents. The increasingly more affluent lifestyle, conspicuous display and sheer greed of some landlords made them reluctant to reduce rents on those many holdings which, in the early nineteenth century, had been let on long leases. Moreover, many a Welsh peasant farmer was so emotionally attached to his land that he was willing to pay a ridiculously high rent rather than give up a farm held by his forefathers.[28] A fast growing population, without any hope of other employment, resulted in intense competition for farms. It was the smaller landowner, often himself heavily committed with charges on his estate, who consciously exploited this 'land hunger'. Thus it was that farm rents were maintained at a high level during the difficult decades of the century. In spite of the agricultural depression from the late 1870s, rents increased in the south-west Wales shires by between 18 and 33 per cent, although, as will be seen, abatements were given in some instances.[29] The general high level of rents on 'Tivyside' estates notwithstanding, it would be wrong to conclude that all the gentry, without exception, were lacking in concern for their tenants' welfare in times of difficulty. Certainly some landowners showed sympathy, from time to time, towards tenants whose rents were in arrear.[30] Humanitarian and even sacrosanct attitudes on the part of squires like Thomas Lloyd of Bronwydd in the years 1775 to 1785, prevented rent increases either because a tenant was 'old and poor' or had 'pleaded poverty', or on account of the 'low price of corn and cattle'.[31] In the 1820s Maria Webley-Parry of Noyadd Trefawr, was very concerned that the cow of an old cottager had to be sold to clear debt. But such gestures were not indicative of maudlin sentimentality, for indolence on the part of tenants was not tolerated: 'The miller's family went out of Tavern y bigel yesterday. I have therefore got rid of that plague', she wrote concerning one of her feckless tenants.[32]

Arrears of rent were accepted as inevitable and landlords were resigned to the existence of 'insolvent debtors'. In 1815 rent arrears on the Noyadd Trefawr estate amounted to £430.[33] During periods of hardship and distress some landowners accepted rent payment in kind; a few Blaenpant tenants, for example, paid in 'hay' or 'cattle' in the period 1806-1820. Such arrangements continued off and on throughout the century on some estates such as Coedmore, and in the 1870s tenants on the Llysnewydd (Grange) estate paid in 'casks of butter'.[34]

Another means of alleviating distress was rent abatement, such as on the Cilgwyn estate in 1822;[35] and again, during the acute depression from the 1870s onwards, allowances ranging from 10 to 15 per cent were given to tenants on estates such as Blaenpant, Bronwydd and Castle Malgwyn.[36] Towards the end of the century, tenants on the Ffynone estate went so far as to organise a public tribute to their landlord for the '. . . kind way they had been dealt with during the depression'.[37] Such paternalistic concern occasionally prevailed until the twilight of gentry power as, for example, in the 1920s when Lady Lloyd of Bronwydd informed the agent: '. . . I expect we shall have to meet their wishes [sc. rent abatement] *as these days we must all help each other to exist*'.[38]

On an estate like Cilgwyn during the 1820s and 1830s, B. E. Hall regarded economic viability and profit foremost in dealing with tenants and resented any attempt to appear 'squeezable' to them. Nevertheless, his keen business approach did not preclude some degree of sympathy for those whom he deemed to be deserving: '. . . I am ready to help (as far as I can) those who I see are ready to work hard, and do their best to bring things round. I have no patience with those who sit down and do nothing extra to meet difficulties.'[39]

The evidence that emerges from estate correspondence and from what was said to the Welsh Land Commission suggests that, in spite of such acts of generosity on the part of certain landowners, the general atmosphere pervading landlord/tenant relationships was strained. Indeed, witnesses before the Land Commission spoke of the 'vindictive spirit' of landlords towards their tenants.[40] How far sound economic and prudent management caused bad feeling is difficult to measure. The ugly image of landlordism certainly repelled those who, through social underprivilege or political motivation, resented subservience to a 'superior' caste. In this sense, the Land Question was far wider than a matter of tenurial relationship between landlord and tenant. Indeed, at heart it was a social question arising from a fundamental clash of cultures and values, namely, those of an English Anglican Tory landed élite and a radical nonconformist Welsh-speaking peasantry.

Without doubt, the gentry as a class were prepared to invoke the full rigour of the law to deal with any recalcitrant stance on the part of their inferiors. The temperate attitude of Webley-Parry of Noyadd Trefawr in 1817 (as expressed to his agent)—'. . . as to distraining it is not my wish [that] you should proceed to such extremities as the total sale of all their effects . . . but there are some people who will never pay except but under such a proceeding'—in its concern to be fair,[41] is not entirely typical. For other landlords had no such scruples. B. E.

Hall encouraged good tenants, but arrears of rent or other debts were not tolerated notwithstanding any mitigating circumstances such as bad harvests, illness or dire misfortune.[42] In the 1840s Thomas Lloyd of Bronwydd treated his smallholders shabbily,[43] and in the 1870s Fitzwilliams of Cilgwyn demolished cottages which did not yield an economic rent, turning out the aged and infirm to the highways and byways.[44] Similar instances can be quoted concerning the Llysnewydd estate from 1865 to 1880.[45] And the traditional myth of Bronwydd benevolence was shattered when the aged tenant of Henllys in the parish of Nevern was given notice to quit, an event which led to public meetings in protest against Sir Marteine Lloyd (although in mitigation it must be said that he was young and inexperienced as a landlord, and the incident was not typical of his treatment of tenants in later years).[46]

The terms of the Agricultural Holdings Acts of 1875 and 1883, to protect tenants by compensating them for improvements and outlay on holdings, were flouted as a 'dead letter' by most gentry by means of exceptive clauses in new leases and 'private' arrangements forced upon the tenants.[47] Summary notices to quit and religious and political pressures, as clearly focused in the Llwynrhydowen affair, continued in the 1870s and '80s. In spite of a measure of political and denominational bias in the evidence before the Land Commission in the 1890s by witnesses like Dr Enoch Davies and Alderman John Lewis, the local gentry were far from able to exonerate themselves of all the charges levelled against them.

Apart from the eviction of tenants mentioned already during the 1868 election, gentry like Mrs Brigstocke of Blaenpant, the Rev. Thomas Lloyd of Gilfachwen and Capt. Thomas of Llanfair and others had brought pressure to bear on the way their tenants voted. The squire of Alltyrodyn, a fervent Tory supporter, compelled his tenants to go in a procession to the polling place, 'guarded' by his agent and steward in front and behind. To counteract such tactics E. M. Richards, the Swansea industrialist and Liberal candidate, brought to Cardiganshire a posse of navvies from his 'works' to protect those who wished to vote for him. Rents were raised out of spite on account of the independent resistance of tenants. Thomas of Llanfair forbade one of his tenants to send his son to William Thomas' (Gwilym Marles) school on account of the latter's radicalism. In Penboyr parish during the 1880s, the rector, the Rev. John Lloyd, tried to persuade his flock to vote Tory at the behest of Earl Cawdor, the patron of the living. Religious and political pressure by the landlord led tenants on the Llysnewydd estate to leave their nonconformist chapels and their support for the Liberal cause for church Toryism, in order to appease their landlord.[48] Loss of squatters' rights through enclosure such as that of the Llangeler common has already been mentioned. Uncertainty of tenure, no compensation for improvements, as well as the harsh game laws were some of the many combustible elements creating suffering to, and oppression of, the lower orders. J. E. Vincent's claim that the evidence and conclusions of the Land Commission pointed to the fact that Welsh landlords were not all the evil ogres they had been made out to be, cannot really serve to whitewash the squires of 'Tivyside' as a class. In evidence before the Land Commission the name of Sir Marteine Lloyd had been singled out as a landlord who could be trusted in spite of the Henllys furore mentioned above; and the benevolence of a few other houses was also remembered.[49] Dr D. W. Howell, amongst others, holds the view that many landowners in Wales were personally liked and respected after they had been rejected as political leaders.[50] In the Teifi valley, however, some had wielded their power as a privileged class for their own benefit, and only within those constraints which ensured that they did not utterly lose the goodwill of the community. There was no open revolt, but by the end of the nineteenth century the *werin* had at least opened its eyes to the truth of nonconformist and radical enlightenment. No longer could adherence to the conventions and customs of deference and the overlordship of one class over another be accepted. Even if a few individual landlords might continue to enjoy a measure of personal popularity in their communities, nevertheless, as a class they were regarded as having forfeited the loyalty and support of the community through selfishness. Hence it was, as we shall see, that they were voted out from office in local government elections from the 1880s.

NOTES AND SOURCES

[1]*DWB.* sub Samuel Roberts, Hy Richard, T. E. Ellis, Thos. Gee, E. Pan Jones.

[2]H. Richard: *Letters and Essays on Wales*, 1884, pp. 113-23; T. I. Ellis: *Cofiant Thomas Edward Ellis*, 1944, i, pp. 24-35; A. J. Ellis: *Speeches and Letters by the late T. E. Ellis*, 1912, pp. 243-47; p. 304, n. 33.

[3]E. Pan Jones: *Oes Gofion* [No date]; *DWB.*

[4]K. O. Morgan: *op cit.*, pp. 1-27; RCLWM Report 1896, pp. 440-48, 485-89, 510.

[5]*ibid*: p. 308; NLW/Llysnewydd/Bundle 73/Notices to quit, distraints, etc., 1868-80; W. J. Davies: *op cit.*, pp. 72-3; the eviction of a radical nonconformist family from their farm and the consequent tragedy because they voted Liberal against the wishes of their Tory landlord; anti-Tory feelings of Unitarians in that locality.

[6]*ibid:* pp. 84-5 [Qu. 44, 271]; p. 304, n. 22; *Cm. Jnl.* 17/4//1894; 24/4/1894.

[7]*DWB*; J. E. Vincent: *The Land Question in South Wales*, 1897; K. O. Morgan: *op cit.*, pp. 123-29, 174-77; D. W. Howell: *Land and People in Nineteenth Century Wales*, 1978, pp. 85-92, 150-55.

[8]T. Rees: *A Topographical . . . South Wales*, 1815, p. 276.

[9]RCLWM, iii [Qu. 44, 303].

[10]W. Davies: *op cit.*, i, p. 169.

[11]NLW/Noyadd Trefawr/214. 403, 1703.

[12]NLW/Bronwydd/5023; NLW/Owen Colby/675; CRO/Coedmore/8/43.

[13]CRO/EG/Box/11/-.

[14]NLW/Cilgwyn Rental/1833.

[15]NLW/Noyadd Trefawr/1604.

[16]RCLWM Report 1896, pp. 492-513, 519.

[17]NLW/Evans George/5; FG/15/526 seq; NLW/Ms/793 B.

[18]NLW/Morgan Richardson/1965; NLW/Bronwydd/1820, 1979; NLW/Llwyngwair/5.

[19]NLW/Evans George/5; NLW/Bronwydd/1967; NLW/Ms/7933.

[20]NLW/Noyadd Trefawr/742; RCLWM Report 1896, p. 473.

[21]*loc cit.*

[22]R. J. Colyer: 'Aspects of Land Occupation in Nineteenth Century Cardiganshire', *THSC*, 1981, p. 82; personal information.

[23]D. W. Howell: *Patriarchs and Parasites*, p. 83.

[24]NLW/Noyadd Trefawr/741-42, 753, 592; NLW/D. Pryse Williams/15963 B; NLW/ Noyadd Trefawr/775, 802, 816.

[25]Lloyd and Turnor: *op cit.*, p. 13.

[26]CRO/Cawdor (Vaughan)/41/5777, 22/682.

[27]NLW/Evans George/2443, 2519; CRO/EG/Box/11; NLW/Owen Colby/2312, 1131.

[28]Dd Williams: *Modern Wales*, pp. 105-06; D. W. Howell: *Land and People*, pp. 9-10.

[29]RCLWM Report 1896, p. 374.

[30]D. W. Howell: *op cit.*, pp. 54-5.

[31]NLW/Bronwydd/6804.

[32]NLW/Noyadd Trefawr/1375-65.

[33]*ibid*: 869.

[34]CRO/EG/Box/18; CRO/Coedmore Rental 1871; NLW/Amphlett Lewis and Evans/ Grange Estate Map Book 1796 with additions 1873.

[35]NLW/Cilgwyn Rental/1822.

[36]CRO/EG/Box 18; *Cd Ad*: 27/2/1880; 26/2/1886; *The Welshman*: 29/1/1885.

[37]NLW/Owen Colby/2160.

[38]NLW/Bronwydd/5995-99.

[39]NLW/Cilgwyn/LB/32/27 Dec. 1825; 3 Dec. 1833.

[40]*loc cit.*

[41]*loc cit.*

[42]*loc cit.*

[43]NLW/Bronwydd/7026.

[44]NLW/Cilgwyn/LB/44/18 Dec. 1875.

[45]NLW/Llysnewydd/Bundle 73.

[46]NLW/Bronwydd/3217-23.

[47]D. W. Howell: *op cit.*, pp. 74, 75, 89; RCLWM, iii [Qus 44, 427, 669-934].

[48]*loc cit*; J. Llewelyn (Borth): *Cofiant y Parch Thos. Jones, Cilcennin*, 1899, pp. 80-1; Y Parch J. E. Davies, Llandeilo: *Cyfrol Goffa y Parch Thomas James, M.A., Llandysul*, 1922, p. 77; E. M. Richards, a Swansea industrialist, Liberal Member for Cardiganshire, 1868-71.

[49]*ibid*: iii [Qus 44, 837-38.]

[50]D. W. Howell: *op cit.*, p. 152; M. Cragoe: *op cit.*, pp. 107-10.

Incumbrances, Indebtedness and Decline

Apart from current economic trends which could bring prosperity or the reverse, there had existed within the landholding system and in the outlook and temperament of the gentry, internal weaknesses which were the seeds of the eventual decline of landlordism. Legal constraints such as the strict settlement, trusts to preserve contingent remainders, marriage settlements and the raising of long-term mortgages to provide for dowries, annuities and jointures, weighed heavily on the often flimsy economy of an estate; and in the case of 'Tivyside' estates were a burden up to the early years of the twentieth century. Paradoxically, it was this system which was responsible for the survival of landlordism up to the nineteenth century, when its crippling restrictions prevented landlords from employing their fixed capital as efficiently as possible. Moreover, since the Tudor settlement of Wales, the gentry had been inclined to go to the courts on the slightest pretext and their litigious temper was a by-word.[1]

The prenuptial settlement was aimed at providing for the life tenant's widow and his legitimate issue. Sums like £2,000 and £6,000 were common on estates like Penrallt near Aberporth, Cilgwyn and Aberceri in the years 1763 to the 1840s.[2] But in the 1850s the very large sum of £40,000 was raised for the ultimate benefit of the widow and children of E. Crompton Ll. Fitzwilliams of Cilgwyn.[3] Optimistic reliance on future agricultural prosperity, or the social advancement of the family, were some of the reasons for placing such a burden on estates, and which could last for many years. Likewise, charges in a will could be a long-term burden, sometimes lasting for generations. In 1753, George Bowen of Llwyngwair left charges of £2,000 on his estate, while in the early 1760s, a 'confident profligacy' imposed a debt of £16,000 on Brigstocke property.[4] In the early decades of the nineteenth century, John Colby of Ffynone made a charge of £12,000 on his estate for the benefit of younger children, and this could be recouped on a prosperous estate. On the other hand, such financial arrangements could be a burden on a very small estate like Dolhaidduchaf, which was saddled with a charge of £2,000 in annuities paid to various relations in 1900.[5] Squires did not grieve unduly at the decease of such annuitants: 'I am going on Wed. to Manderdivy church to ye funeral of old Mrs Lewis of Clynfyw whose death relieves me of a payment of £50 a year', wrote Fitzwilliams in February 1864 with unashamed glee.[6]

The Welsh addiction to litigiousness was fomented by the very complicated nature of legal processes devised to safeguard the inheritance of large areas of land and other forms of wealth, as well as by problems relating to boundaries, rights over minerals, road and railway development, manorial claims and the like. A well-run estate depended greatly on the sagacity of the owner and his legal adviser. A hot-headed squire, acquisitive and unprincipled, could often be the prey of lawyers who waxed fat on the folly of those who engaged them. Wills were constantly challenged on grounds of a questionable signature or mark as, for example, that of Jenkin Jones of Llanfihangel Yeroth in 1748,[7] or senility, as in the case of the Cryngae widow, when, in a Chancery action the contestants were described as a '. . . very numerous and beggarly race ever rapacious of other men's property'.[8] William Brigstocke of Blaenpant in 1746 was regarded as being mentally incapable of knowing the meaning of a will purported to have been made by him, and this matter, like many others, was contested in the bishop's court.[9] Such actions continued until the end of the nineteenth century, and involved claims by fraudsters,[10] or the manipulation of the 'reckless and dissolute', like the young squire of Alltyrodyn by an unscrupulous agent.[11]

Bitter family feuds erupted amongst the gentry concerning the interpretation of wills, due possibly to ambiguous drafting or a multiplicity of terms and parties. The Lloyds of Cilrhiwe went to law concerning lands in Nevern, Monington and St Dogmael's in 1700-01.[12] The patrimony of Abel Griffiths of Pantybetws was the subject of an action before the House of Lords in the 1760s, and was fresh in the public mind a century later.[13] Disgruntled and disappointed relations had no qualms about challenging rival claims, so that Colby of Ffynone in 1775 inserted a clause in his will to the effect that any person challenging it would forfeit any share he might otherwise have.[14] Only rarely did country attorneys try to put a brake on the wilfulness of the squire; for example, a Cardigan lawyer urged Thomas Lloyd of Bronwydd in 1825: 'Will you have the goodness to countermand your instructions to Mr Beynon to save further expenses of law?'[15]

The laxity of executors, trustees and guardians could lead to the misappropriation of rights of dower or infants, as in 1752, when some 1,200 acres of Blaenpant land and revenues were in dispute. Trust funds from lands were lost to the Jones sisters of Lletherneuadd (some £2,000) when the lands were wrongly sold.[16] When a will demonstrated the immorality of the testator, thus bringing open disgrace on the family and disinheritance, every step was taken to make it void. For example, the heirs of Bowen Davies of Maesycrugiau in the 1840s challenged his will which included bequests to numerous named illegitimate children and their mothers.[17]

A covetous eye on other people's property led many gentry to enormous expense in pursuing foolish claims. The Lloyds of Bronwydd laid claim to a reversion of the Priory estate, Cardigan, in prolonged litigation from the 1790s to about 1813, which cost them some thousands of pounds.[18] Delusions of grandeur led the Lloyds to further waste of money in pursuing a phantom claim to a lost peerage from the 1870s to the 1920s.[19]

By its very nature, ownership of a large estate meant that a competent agent was required to administer it and the eagle eye of an attorney to protect its interests. A landowner had constantly to dig deep into his pocket to pay lawyers' fees for a variety of transactions. The formal act of taking possession of freehold land might require a sheriff's writ.[20] In a dispute between Griffiths of Pantybetws and Abel Gower of Glandovan in 1733 lawyers' fees came to more than £200, a third of the total sum in issue.[21] A fair portion of the proceeds of sale of property could mean substantial fees, like the £360 it cost William Lewes of Llysnewydd to sell part of his Dyffryn, Llandybïe, estate in 1819.[22] The assertion of the squire's position as landowner in the community cost Lloyd Williams of Gwernant about £560 in fees to the rapacious lawyer, John Beynon of Newcastle Emlyn, for taking legal action against recalcitrant tenants and poachers.[23] While details of lawyers' fees are often sporadic, one suspects that they were much more than the surviving documents suggest—thus Thomas Davies Lloyd of Bronwydd paid London and local lawyers during the year 1852 about £6,000 in pursuit of his political, antiquarian and genealogical interests, not to mention what he would normally spend on estate and other transactions.

Sources of revenue derived from commercial and industrial enterprises situated far from the squire's mansion caused further problems concerning boundary and other rights, damage and loss, and downright dishonesty. Thus, Colby of Ffynone had to issue injunctions against rival iron and coal companies in east Carmarthenshire to restrain them from taking coal to which they were not entitled, to the detriment of his estate.[24] Likewise, there was constant litigation concerning the Skerries lighthouse off the north Wales coast (a major source of revenue to the Cilwendeg estate) on account of Irish and other shipping which avoided paying dues.[25]

That the 'Tivyside' gentry, like other Welsh landowners, resorted to litigation on the flimsiest pretext was all too frequent, and without regard to the cost and consequences. Personal pride and a distorted sense of injury, pettiness and sometimes a spiteful nature were the chief motives rather than economic gain. Thus a dispute about tithes belonging to Noyadd Trefawr was bitterly contested in the years 1746 to 1751, the action costing £73 while the value of the tithes was only £48.[26] Attitudes basic to the gentry character did not change over the years. In 1899 Mrs Saunders Davies of Pentre, in a fit of pique against neighbouring gentry, obtained a court injunction restraining the 'Tivyside' hunt from trespass on Pentre land.[27] Only a few landlords saw the futility of wasting money on lawyers, as, for example, in 1819, when Thomas Thomas of Llanfair had a dispute with a tenant which was settled before 'respectable neighbours', namely Davies of Maesy-crugiau and Bowen of Waunifor.[28] But such instances were rare indeed.

As became their station and degree, the gentry were great spenders, and many a squire, like Webley-Parry of Noyadd Trefawr in 1824, maintained that whatever financial constraints burdened the estate he was determined '. . . to live comfortably according to rank and situation'.[29] While the eighteenth century can be singled out as an age of extravagance for the nobility, it can be said that since the sixteenth century Welsh country squires had converged on London; and to be 'in the mode', they had acquired fashions of dress, habits of idleness and love of pleasure.[30] There was no compulsion to exercise thrift, far less frugality. Sometimes the shifty companions and low intelligence of a squire like Thomas Jones of Faerdrefach, in the eighteenth century, led him to 'fool away' £5,000, as he was 'destitute of understanding and prudence' and the 'dupe of knavish and designing people'.[31] During the nineteenth century, an Epicurean lifestyle and the expense of public duties and offices could lead to a drain on estate finances, as occurred in a big way on the north Cardiganshire estate of Nanteos from 1800 onwards, and also, on the Bronwydd, Aberceri, Llanfair and other estates in 'Tivyside'.[32]

Sudden whims of spending were often satisfied by immediate borrowing through bonds and notes of hand—which could accumulate over the years to the dismay of descendants. Creditors pounced on the personalty of Morgan of Pengwern between the years 1735-39.[33] In mid-century Lloyd of Bronwydd borrowed heavily to meet increasing personal spending and in order to purchase more and more land: 'It was the ambition of the day to covet many acres not to cultivate the few'. His heir had to pay off debts of about £8,000 in 1787. Foreign travel and an expensive lifestyle led James Lewes of Gellydywyll into debts of £2,000 in one year only—far in excess of the estate's income; and the excesses of a young blood like 'Smash' Lewes of Llysnewydd led to debts of £6,000 and a £10,000 mortgage in the 1840s.[34] The necessary education for their station in life meant that the gentry faced expenses from boys' public schools and girls' boarding establishments. The employment of private tutors for the Colby, Ffynone and Lloyd Williams, Gwernant, families in the years 1823 to 1837 cost in all some £5,000.[35] But the best education might not produce a model landlord—Augustus Brigstocke, heir to Blaenpant at the end of the last century, 'wasted his substance' at Cambridge, and ended up in financial straits.[36] The expense of running a landed estate, the home farm, attending to parks and woodlands, rebuilding and refurbishing the mansion house, along with lavish hospitality, often left little in the estate coffers. The finances of Coedmore and Noyadd Trefawr showed that there was little left in the years 1859 to 1891,[37] while the ostentation of Sir Thomas Davies Lloyd of Bronwydd led to personal and estate debts of about £100,000, so that his heir was faced with a heavily encumbered estate which could not hope to recover.[38]

The demands of public office, such as high sheriff, constituted a burden often reluctantly undertaken but which could not easily be avoided lest the lustre of the family was tarnished. In 1828 John Griffith of Llwynduris was about £400 out of pocket in respect of sheriff's expenses.[39] The most prized public office of member of parliament, had been beyond the means of most 'Tivyside' gentry from the early 1700s. In the early and mid-nineteenth century Edward Lloyd Williams of Gwernant shuddered at the expense of standing for parliament, the status of M.P., he thought, would enhance his legal practice.[40] But squires like Saunders Davies of Pentre, and Thomas Davies Lloyd of Bronwydd, were in no wise deterred by expense; the former spent some £2,250 on canvassing, meetings and bringing supporters to the poll, while Davies Lloyd paid £4,000 to innkeepers to provide liquour for his supporters during one election campaign.[41]

The raising of mortgages had been the traditional means of relief for every landowner faced with the need for cash, and mortgage repayments caused the greatest single source of financial stress upon landowners. Unable or unwilling to sell land to raise capital, they were obliged to raise mortgages on their properties, often at high rates of interest, and sometimes out of all proportion to the income of their estates. A few wise and prudent landowners, such as the Lloyds of Cilgwyn in the years 1718-22 had in their day raised mortgages and had later repaid the loan.[42] The Brigstockes of Blaenpant indulged in 'confident profligacy' by raising £16,000 in the early 1760s,[43] and it turned out that this did not have any long-term damage. But it is questionable whether the 'Tivyside', like other Welsh estates, were, at any time, sufficiently economically viable to be anything other than units of heavy and excessive consumption, rather than of production and profit. Personal factors, rather than economic causes, could occasionally put an estate in jeopardy—like the calamitous marriage of the heiress of Noyadd Trefawr to the foolhardy spendthrift squire, Gwynne of Garth, Breconshire. The reckless 'facility for borrowing money' of the Webley-Parrys led to the sale of half the estate, and to mortgages of £20-30,000 in the 1830s and a further mortgage of £15,000 by 1855.[44] The rapid accumulation of economic and political pressures from the 1860s to the end of the century inevitably led to the collapse of landlordism here as elsewhere.

The years 1879 to 1900 brought an acute depression in the affairs of the landed estate, although a mixed farming pattern and the availability of local markets for farm stock and produce provided a cushion against the more devastating effects of market fluctuations.[45] Estate rentals generally show payments in arrear, and in 1878-79 even on the most efficiently run Cilgwyn estate, arrears had increased from £415 to £1,093.[46] While harvests and prices fluctuated towards the end of the century, agriculture was a pathetic and struggling spectacle. Landowners and employers of labour were also hit by the drain to 'the works', i.e. industrial areas, while those who remained in the countryside were able to press for higher wages.[47] But in spite of the agricultural depression in the countryside, and the possibility of work through migration to the industrial areas, large families and the traditional inward-looking character of the rural community meant that the demand for land did not abate. Although rent levels were maintained in the face of this land hunger, landowners nevertheless suffered from the inability of tenants to meet their rents with the consequent accumulation of arrears. Moreover, they had to make some allowances and abatements to help their tenants, while at the same time their estates were encumbered by mortgages without any reduction in the rate of interest levied. It is also true that the landowners made no real effort to retrench on their traditional, extravagant and wasteful lifestyle. Consequently, most of the 'Tivyside' estates were heavily in debt, and in addition to the type of incumbrances and indebtedness already examined, the following mortgages on estates are typical of the precarious plight of the area's squirearchy—Alltyrodyn, £22,500; Bronwydd, £94,000; Cilgwyn, £26,000; Gernos, £25,000; Gogerddan (S. Cards), £20,000; Pentre, £15,000; Pigeonsford, £8,000 and Wstrws, £4,000.[48]

By about the 1880s the landed gentry had surrendered the keys of power in politics and administrative essentials, and, whereas up to that period England (and to a lesser extent Wales) had been a country of landed aristocracy, it only remained for economic depression to make plain the extent of the accomplished fact. Respect for family tradition meant that the landlord class held on to land despite heavy encumbrances, and at a time when landownership was an expensive luxury. The possession of land was still the symbol of wealth and status[49] to which they clung, marking time as the wealth of the community from other sources surged forward. By the early years of this century the landlord system, so long in decay, finally began to disintegrate. Up to the 1914-18 war landlords had little or no trouble in selling their property. From 1908 to 1912 the *Estates' Gazette* commented that the large estates coming into the market appeared unending.[50] The process in 'Tivyside', however, had started much earlier. Landlords were advised to take advantage of the financial climate to shed their unprofitable estates and any sentiment attached to them. The boom in land sales, however, did not mean that mansions and parks were easy to sell and some squires like Sir Marteine Lloyd of Bronwydd, C. H. Ll. Fitzwilliams of Cilgwyn and a few others, clung tenaciously to their houses. During the 1920s gross rentals were considerably reduced; a deepening depression in agriculture led to falling rents and by 1936 they reached their lowest point since 1870, or even since 1800.[51] Throughout the inter-war years the position of landowners who had remained continued to weaken, with more and more of their land being sold and their mansions abandoned.

A few greatly diminished estates such as Cilgwyn, Llysnewydd, Lancych and Clynfyw still survive in private hands—their owners supporting themselves by farming, trade and commerce or through the professions. 'Tivyside' today is no longer dominated by an estate economy; many of the mansions are in ruin while a few have been adapted to the needs of tourism and leisure.[52] Descendants of the former ruling class have had to abandon the power and privilege of birth and lineage, status and wealth, and strive to earn their living like the rest of the community. Only a few remain in the mansions where they were born and bred; some live in a cottage rather than in a mansion. Others have gone to create a new life for themselves in business, politics industry, science and the arts—far away from their native heath.

NOTES AND SOURCES

[1] P. R. Roberts: *op cit.*, pp. 159-61; H. J. Habakkuk: 'English Landownership 1680-1740', *EcHR*, X, (1940), p. 2 seq; J. Howard Davies: *op cit.*, p. 176.

[2] FG/21/40; CRO/Coedmore/3/91, 93; CRO/EG/Box/61.

[3] CRO/Coedmore/3/17.

[4] FG/16/174. 20/58-9.

[5] CRO/JF/190, 386, 499-501; NLW/Evans George/2311.

[6] NLW/Cilgwyn/LB/43/1 Feb. 1864.

[7] NLW/DS/CC Cm (P) a-e.

[8] HRO/D/Pen/11/37.

[9] NLW/SD/Prerog/1 (c 1746).

[10] *ibid*: /CC Cm (P) 217.

[11] *Cm Jnl*: 11/7/1879; 18/7/1879.

[12] FG/9/418.

[13] *Y Genhinen*: 1889, p. 128.

[14] NLW/Owen Colby/182.

[15] NLW/Bronwydd/2921.

[16] NLW/Gt Sessions/Wales/25/366; FG/25/155-56.

[17] NLW/SD/CC Cm (P) 1530.

[18] NLW/Bronwydd/3923-52, 6254-69; FG/23/29 seq.

[19] NLW/Bronwydd/4391, 5027-58, 6520-39.

[20] FG/6/421.

[21] CRO/Coedmore/66-8.

[22] NLW/Llysnewydd/Bundle/59.

[23] NLW/Ticehurst Wyatt (Gwernant) Box/1; NLW/Bronwydd/4979-97.

[24] NLW/Owen Colby/867.

[25] NLW/Penally/43.

[26] NLW/Noyadd Trefawr/492A, 504-531.

[27] *Cd Ad*: 17/2/1899.

[28] NLW/Ms 122086.

[29] P. R. Roberts: *op cit.*, p. 164; NLW/Noyadd Trefawr/1366.

[30] J. H. Plumb: 'The Noble Houses of Eighteenth Century England' in *Men and Places*, 1963, pp. 67-79; J. Cresset of the Charterhouse—A Pamphlet . . . 1662, quoted in *Carm Jnl*: 24/2/1827, R. Fenton, *op cit.*, p. 264.

[31] NLW/Ms 12378 B.

[32] R. J. Colyer: 'A Landed Estate in Decline 1800-1903', *Ceredigion*, IX, 1, 1980, pp. 58-77.

[33] NLW/Owen Colby/2284.

[34] NLW/Bronwydd/541-50, 2329, 5016, 6504; NLW/Evans George/3115; NLW/Highmead/Box P/File 6; NLW/Sir John Williams/119.

[35]NLW/Owen Colby/1103-1115; NLW/Ticehurst Wyatt (Gwernant) Box/6.
[36]CRO/EG/49/-.
[37]CRO/Coedmore/2/125-26; NLW/Noyadd Trefawr/867.
[38]NLW/Bronwydd/6050.
[39]NLW/Ms 5539 C.
[40]NLW/Ticehurst Wyatt (Gwernant) Boxes/1, 11.
[41]CRO/Coedmore/2652; *Hansard*: 188/4 July 1857.
[42]NLW/Cilgwyn/196-200.
[43]NLW/Evans George/2767-95.
[44]NLW/Noyadd Trefawr/660-61, 1079, 1119, 1345-46.
[45]J. Hd. Davies: *op cit.*, p. 36 seq.
[46]NLW/Cilgwyn Rent Book/8.
[47]RCLWM, ii [Qus 28, 985-86], iii [qu 45474].
[48]Aber   RO/BRA/a;   CRO/JF/SC/642;   NLW/Bronwydd/595:   CRO/EG/Box/9.11;
CRO/ Beckingsale/12/1610; NLW/Morgan Richardson/976, 1056; *The Welshman*: 24/7/1882;
NLW/ D. Roy Evans/138.
[49]F. M. L. Thompson: *op cit.*, pp. 1 seq, 264-91; D. L. Baker-Jones: 'Local Government in
Pembrokeshire 1815-1974' in D. Howell (ed.), *Pembrokeshire County History*, vol. iv, 1993, pp. 272-
304.
[50]J. Howard Davies: *op cit.*, pp. 152 seq; *Estates' Gazette*, xii, 1912, p. 72; for the break up of the
large Welsh estates, see D. Cannadine: *op cit.*, pp. 106-07, 704-05; CRO/JF/SC/-.
[51]F. M. L. Thompson: *op cit.*, p. 338.
[52]T. Lloyd: *The Lost Houses of Wales*, 1986.

Stradmore House or Stradmore Vale

(Illus. from *Beauties of South Wales*, T. Rees, 1815.)

Rhos-y-gilwen

(Illus. from *Tom Mathias: Ffotograffydd Bro*, Gomer 1995.)

Pentre

Cilwendeg

Ffynone

Plas, Aberporth

Tŷ Llwyd

Old Tŷ Llwyd

Aberceri

Wstrws

(Photo: J. Jenkins, Llangeler.)

Bronwydd

Dolhaidd

Llysnewydd: architect's drawing for rebuilding, 1890s

Ffosesgob

Castell Hywel

Bwlchbychan

Section 3

Social Life

The Squire's Home

The eighteenth-century squire in Wales, as in some outlying parts of England, lived in old and unfashionable houses.[1] Travellers, like Warner, noticed that frequently their mansions were no more than large farmhouses.[2] These houses were strongly built; plain in style with heavy oak timbers; large, tall, square chimneys; high pitched roofs covered with heavy stone tiling, and comprising two stories and an attic. This Welsh *plas* was the nearest equivalent to an English manor house.[3]

The concentration of landownership into fewer hands, resulting in larger estates and richer rent rolls, meant that, by the beginning of the nineteenth century many of the older *plasau* had been deserted by their owners and allowed to fall into ruin or to be rented out to tenants. Fenton in 1815 bemoaned this process pointing to the decline of old families of fortune and the advent of the new through the 'vicissitudes of human affairs and the precariousness of human possessions'.[4] Meyrick and Lewis cite Cwmcynon and Castell Hywel as typical examples of the ancient family homes of the clans of Parry and Lloyd which had been reduced to ordinary farmhouses.[5] The process had gone on very gradually since the early 1700s. For example, Gilfachwen-uchaf, the home of the Lloyds, was let to a tenant in 1712;[6] again, Lletherneuadd which had provided two sheriffs had declined by mid-century leaving only a faint trace of its former glory;[7] and such was the fate of at least a dozen other *plasau* from the upper 'Tivyside' to the region around Cardigan town. In their place new houses had sprung up at an accelerating speed by the end of the eighteenth century.

The period 1715 to 1815 was throughout Britain a period of good taste in the design and proportion of houses, many of which were built in the style of classical Palladian models. The Georgian houses in the Teifi valley were modest imitations of very grand mansions in the rest of the country.[8] The country squire, if not possessing the means to travel widely and employ the leading architects of the day, had recourse to design and pattern books, such as Crunden's *Book of Designs 1767*, '. . . to provide convenient and ornamental architecture . . . designs, plans, elevations and sections . . . beginning with the farm house and regularly ascending to the more grand and magnificent villa'.[9] Aesthetic judgement and practical advice could be gleaned from Isaac Ware's *Complete Body of Architecture 1755* and from Sir John

Soanes' *Plans, Elevations and Sections of Buildings . . . 1788*, while in west Wales William Thomas of Pembroke, had published his *Original Designs in Architecture* in 1783. By the early nineteenth century, the characteristic dwellings of the gentry were square, box-like houses, with windows symmetrically placed around a central doorway. In many instances a pedimented elevation crowned with a lunette above a prestige portico, delicate glazing bars to the windows, fanlights, architraves, ingenious corner and quarter rounded doors, pilasters and all the other Georgian features had become fashionable.[10]

As mentioned earlier, the ascription 'classical' or 'Georgian' has to be qualified in discussing 'Tivyside' houses. They were watered-down versions, limited by the squire's means and, in most cases, erected by the local master mason and estate workmen, often adapting to their own skill and needs the drawings and specifications of the standard pattern books. 'Tivyside' gentry houses possessed a modest classical elegance. Blaenpant, Ffynone, Cilwendeg, Plas Llangoedmore, Glaspant, Gwernant and others were functional and restrained, as were the smaller ones like Gilfachwen-isaf, Manereifed and the old rectory at Maenordeifi.

The name of the architect is known only in a few instances, like that of John Nash who designed Ffynone, Emlyn Cottage, the Priory, Cardigan, Llanfechan and Llysnewydd in the 1780s and 1790s.[11] The lesser known John Calvert had designed the very plain yet commodious house of Highmead in 1777,[12] and Ambrose Poynter was responsible for the large house of Castle Malgwyn in a heavy and unexciting style.[13] The wealth of David Lloyd of Alltyrodyn, in the years after 1815, is reflected in his new house at Alltyrodyn built in 1827, comprising a three-storeyed residential block and lower service courtyard, a good example—according to Peter Smith—of axial planning with symmetrical rooms.[14]

In the early decades of the nineteenth century movements in architectural taste were gaining ground throughout Britain, wherein the styles of earlier centuries were going to be repeated. While the 'classical' modes of the Georgian era were percolating downwards in diluted form, and clearly seen in farmhouses and nonconformist chapels, the world of fashion had become weary of classical taste and sought inspiration in medieval architecture.[15] Thomas Johnes of Hafod had been infected with notions of the 'curious', the 'medieval' and the 'antique'.[16] The Gothic style was felt to be essentially English, and its adoption marked a patron's link with the manorial past and the world of old landed families.[17]

In the Teifi valley a series of houses in that style started with the rebuilding of Cardigan Priory by Thomas Johnes of Hafod, followed by Lloyd Hall's Emlyn Cottage as a *bijou* rustic villa. Motivated by the glamour of everything that was medieval and baronial, Thomas Davies Lloyd, in the 1850s, employed R. Kyrke Penson to build the mansion of Bronwydd, and purchased for £700 the ruins of the old castle (and surrounding lands) at Newport, part of which was restored as a residence for the Lord Marcher. Expressive of the owner's delusions of grandeur, Bronwydd was an example of full blown romanticism and combined in its bizarre execution of battlements, towers, oriel windows, irregularity of front and roof line 'an air of dignified repose and jovial hospitality, with feasting in the great hall and the yule log crackling in the fireplace'.[18] On a lesser scale Lancych was rebuilt in the late 1850s as a 'cottage ornée', while Rhosygilwen was remodelled in a mixture of the Tudor and Jacobean styles in the 1880s.[19] Many other 'Tivyside' gentry houses were rebuilt or remodelled, as were, for example, Noyadd Trefawr and Clynfyw in a plain but dignified 'domestic' Tudor style, and others like Plas-y-Bridell in what one might describe as 'Victorian institutional' and suitable for a grim school. Cilgwyn is an example of a very large house, built around the former Emlyn Cottage, with a castellated tower, heavy dormers and pyramidal gables—giving an impression of great strength and dominating the countryside.[20]

Not all the 'Tivyside' gentry followed the vogue for the 'Gothick', and Penylan was built in the 1850s with Renaissance features. The wealth of the family is reflected in its grandiose proportions and ornamentation with interior details like painted ceilings, arcaded landings and a cantilevered staircase. Cilbronne, rebuilt in the early 1900s, was a large half-timbered house more in keeping with the style of building in the Welsh marches and border counties.[21]

The grande finale of country-house building in the area was Ffynone which was totally remodelled in 1904 for John Vaughan Colby by the dilettante artist, architect and garden designer F. Inigo Thomas.[22] The house survives to this day with its balustraded front, rusticated quoins and key-stones, together with pedimented elevations. The original Nash interior survives, but the additional rooms with plaster mouldings and carved fireplaces betray the advent into the area of a very 'polite architecture', which by the early 1900s had ousted much native and local taste, as well as craftsmanship, not only in 'Tivyside' but in the country at large.[23]

Ffynone and Cilbronne were the last monuments in the area to a vanishing age. The dénouement of the gentry and their estates was accelerating. Economic and social factors, spurred on by the 1914-18 war, meant a shortage of cheap labour and cheap fuel. Increased taxes on income and transferred property made a large country house no longer a viable asset. Many estates were heavily mortgaged, as has been noticed, and landowners had eventually to abandon the homes their families had lived in for centuries.[24]

The lifestyle of the late nineteenth-century squire in his grand mansion was very different from that of his ancestors two centuries earlier. Increased wealth and prestige, together with sophisticated taste and manners, demanded that a large country house in the nineteenth century was a real mansion and not a glorified farmhouse. Anyone who visited Bronhydden, Ffosesgob, Gilfach, Plas Aberporth or Wstrws would have seen, as in the seventeenth century, 'all the apparatus, the barns and beast houses, the muck and the mire inescapable in a working farm'.[25] The inventories, already examined, suggest a simple and plain lifestyle of farmer-gentry actually exerting themselves in daily farming tasks. The visitor to a nineteenth-century country mansion approached it along a gravel drive through a landscaped park. The 'home farm', where such existed, was discreetly tucked away out of sight. The squire had become removed from soiling his hands, and his house was isolated from the working world. Inside, the setting for gracious living was increasingly separated from the servants who sustained it. A great household was a well oiled machine with a distinct hierarchical division between the family in the main block of the house, and the servants in their own separate quarters or 'offices'.[26] In a gradation of function each room had its own purpose, and the manuals and plans of architects anatomised the country house down to the last square inch—from the ballroom to the soiled linen closet and luggage entrance.[27]

Life in the Victorian country house was extremely formal, with fixed times and routine for meals and strict rules concerning suitable costume for every class within the family and household. Class divisions existed between squire and domestics, and also within the servant class.[28] The principal reception rooms, namely the drawing and dining rooms, library and hall, served the same function as in Georgian houses. The Nash plan for Ffynone provided for the 'eating parlour'; and as houses were rebuilt and enlarged, extra rooms such as breakfast, morning, smoking, music and billiard rooms in houses like

Bronwydd, Pentre, Rhosygilwen and other large 'Tivyside' houses were to provide for the reception and leisure activities of family and guests.[29] In some houses there existed rooms unique to them, such as the 'chapel' at Bronwydd, and the 'prayer room' at Llwyngwair—a survival from the days of the 'Methodistical' Bowens which was used in 1866 for catechising Nevern children.[30] At Highmead a large concert hall, with a splendid pipe organ, was built for Col. Herbert Davies-Evans and his musical friends. Rhosygilwen had a visiting coachman's room, and at Alltyrodyn and Ffynone there was an 'audience' or 'justice' room where (until an act of 1848) poachers and other social miscreants appeared before their betters.[31]

The needs of the squire and his family were provided by a class of domestic servants recruited from the children of farmers, labourers and craftsmen. Inculcated with the virtues of fidelity, honesty, cleanliness and, above all, loyalty, they were not to divulge family confidences and had to avoid prodigality, drunkenness and bad company. They were the essential infrastructure of country-house life. An unlimited pool of cheap labour coped with large house parties, balls and theatricals, and an endless round of cooking, cleaning and carrying fuel. Large houses like Bronwydd and Ffynone each had at one time, about twelve household staff to cater for very small families of two, respectively. But there were often large house parties of relations and friends. On the other hand, the family at Gwernant in 1871 amounted to eleven people served by a staff of seven.[32]

Conditions of work and wages are difficult to assess. While a pool of cheap labour was available, any suggestion of exploitation has to be carefully handled. Inevitably, conditions varied from house to house according to the status and character of the squire. In spite of long hours, arduous tasks and almost 'theoretical' wages, many servants became attached and valued members of the household. The humble *plas* as well as the grand Victorian mansion, provided food, shelter and work for many who would otherwise have to depend on poor relief or the workhouse. In the early eighteenth century, household staff at Cilgwyn carried out a whole variety of tasks in and about the house, farm and garden. Wages varied from half a guinea to about two pounds for a whole year, despicably small, even allowing for the value of money at the time. Additional perquisites would be thrown in, such as a 'pair of close and a lam'; and sums of money were advanced to meet contingencies, for example, 'yards of cloth—10s 7d', 'for a Bible—3s 6d', '2 new shirts—10s 6d'.[33] In 1796 wages at Blaenpant appear to show some increase, with the men receiving something like 3s 6d to 4s 6d per week, while women and boys earned half a crown.[34] A hundred years later a very 'superior nurse' at Tŷ Llwyd earned about £16 a year and lived as one of the household for 30 years. Under-housemaids would earn less than half that sum, but had gifts of clothing and other necessaries as well.[35] Superior servants in the 1880s and '90s at Blaenpant, such as the gardener, earned £60 per annum with allowances for coal, milk, vegetables and a rent-free cottage.[36]

The paternalistic concern of the squire, in some instances, more than compensated for the, seemingly, low wages of the majority of his work force. As hinted, there was the 'security'—an important word in the area—in terms of food, clothes and a roof over one's head. Seasonal diversions such as fairs, markets, chapel activities and considerable freedom for horseplay and spree behind the squire's back, made life infinitely more tolerable for those fortunate enough to 'find a place' in a squire's household. At Bronwydd, for example, old and infirm servants were maintained in demesne cottages with an additional small pension. Surplus food and clothing from the big house supplemented low wages, and a thrifty housewife turned these 'doles' to good advantage in raising large families before the days of the welfare state. Large house parties at Pentre and elsewhere not only provided surplus food but also 'vails' or tips to the staff by departing guests, again according to status—coachman, groom, housekeeper, butler, footman and so on. In the 1920s, the cook at Bronwydd sold surplus dripping to needy cottagers at 6d a basin, and, considering the level of wages and human nature, each servant in the hierarchy used his position to his own advantage.[37]

No doubt dissatisfaction was bound to exist under the surface, especially where the regime was unsympathetic and harsh, as at Highmead in the 1840s, when the 'servants mutinied' because 'all maids ask for £20'. But such examples of open dissent were rare.[38]

When topographical writers in the early 1800s made special mention of the squire's 'neat and elegant villa', 'genteel residence' in a 'romantic valley' with 'thriving plantations' and 'extensive woods', they were directly paying tribute to the aesthetic values applied by the country landowner in laying out his park and pleasure gardens. During the eighteenth century architectural taste and landscape design worked hand in hand. The 'Tivyside' gentry were, on a lesser scale, applying the theories, already adopted by the great English nobles, in order to enhance the approach to and the view from the mansion.[39] Charles

Bridgeman and Lancelot (Capability) Brown were pioneers of the landscaped park (as opposed to the formal garden) surrounding the mansion house. From the 1790s the 'picturesque' movement became fashionable, and its chief apostles were Payne Knight, Uvedale Price and Humphrey Repton, whose theories claimed that every estate had latent natural characteristics to be 'improved' so as to combine the 'sublime and the beautiful'.[40]

Many of the new 'Tivyside' mansions were surrounded by extensive parks where aesthetic norms had influenced their creation. Nash, who worked at Llysnewydd and Ffynone, was closely connected with Payne Knight and Repton,[41] and was prepared to add the 'curious' and 'antique' within the 'thriving plantations'. When Gwernant park was planted, groups of trees were arranged to represent the position of troops in an Indian campaign in which Lloyd Williams had fought.[42] The drive to Bronwydd was recontoured to make it longer and more exciting, and to present the spectacle of the great house with dramatic visual impact on the visitor. As the mansion house had to be furnished with taste and elegance, so the park had to be adorned with grottoes, follies, rustic lodges, dovecotes and icehouses, the latter for a utilitarian as well as an ornamental function.

Cilwendeg and Blaenpant boasted a 'shell house'.[43] Ffynone had a summer house in the form of a Palladian temple, while Llysnewydd amongst others had rustic bowers. Streams were diverted, lakes were created artificially as at Ffynone, and at Llysnewydd a little 'ladies summerhouse' overlooked the Henllan falls. In the grounds of Blaenpant there was a Swiss cottage and an ornamental bridge.

The site of a country house had to take into account other factors, such as a southerly aspect and the social advantages of the area. Thus Aberceri, for example, had the advantage of sporting facilities, fishing, shooting and hunting.[44] A large Victorian family required ample domestic offices along with good stabling, pleasure gardens, a tennis lawn, herbaceous borders and panoramic walks.[45] A lesser house like Dôl near Llechryd was desirable because it was equidistant from two market towns and was advertised as a suitable residence for 'a gentleman of moderate fortune'.[46] The social class of a locality was important; thus, Stradmore Vale was considered to be in an area of 'genteel society' where 'taxes and labour are extremely low and the London post passes daily'.[47] When Emlyn Cottage was let in 1856, in addition to the usual amenities, one advantage was its proximity to a church where 'English services were held'.[48] The crime rate within a locality, the possibility of civil strife and commotion had long been considerations in acquiring a mansion and an estate. Thus, in April 1787, a barrister at the Sessions in Haverfordwest wrote to John George Philipps of Cwmgwili: 'It is reported the judges mean to have two or three for execution, as the observation was made in court, that if he did not, it would lower the price of land for no person would chuse to purchase among us'.[49]

As has been suggested, Welsh gentry houses generally, and those in the Teifi valley especially, were minor derivatives, both aesthetically and architecturally, of the great English palaces of the nobility. The small Tivyside mansion was poor in its possessions by comparison. Even so, it made a distinctive contribution to enrich the taste and culture of an otherwise aesthetically backward area. Although the houses lacked the *objets d'art*, pictures and furniture of famous Welsh houses like Hafod (which was open to the public),[50] a great step forward had been made by the local squires since the early 1700s. In fact, as noticed already, the farm stock at Blaenpant in 1751 was rated at almost four times the value of the contents of the house.[51] But with the building of new houses from the mid-eighteenth century onwards, furnishings in the best contemporary taste were acquired. Thus in the 1790s, John Colby of Ffynone obtained furnishings from such emporia as Gillows of Lancaster.[52] In terms of elegance, Castle Malgwyn in 1812 contained gilt pier and chimney glasses, ormolu French clocks, chandeliers, silver and plate, Brussels carpets, and furniture of every description in rosewood and mahogany.[53] The household effects at Blaenpant in 1832 were worth £978 in comparison with £80 in 1751.[54] The difference in family fortune and wealth is well demonstrated by the relative value of items in other houses too; for example, the contents of the 40-roomed mansion at Ffynone in 1837 amounted to £2,722, its cellars containing 3,500 bottles of choice wines, whereas in 1853 the value of the contents of Noyadd Trefawr amounted to £950.[55] Most country houses contained *objets d'art*, fine furniture and collections of pictures, mainly portraits of ancestors, national heroes like the Duke of Wellington, horrific scenes of battles and of ships in dire distress—to evoke pious and filial memories of long dead heroes.

At Glandovan, a portrait of Admiral Sir Erasmus Gower and a painting of the retreat of Vice Admiral Cornwallis from Yorktown had pride of place.[56] A painting by Rembrandt is supposed to have existed at Llwynbedw in 1850, and a Gainsborough at Blaenpant in 1898.[57] At

Falcondale there were attested items by Sir Thomas Lawrence and George Romney,[58] and paintings of horses by George Stubbs at Llysnewydd. Moreover, the latter could boast of a Ming vase, Waterford glass and rare Chelsea porcelain. At Cilbronne, in the early 1900s, there were splendid treasures from India and the Orient.

As in acreage, rent rolls and county position, the houses of 'Tivyside' deserve the label of lesser Welsh country houses. Perhaps the exception in this area was Ffynone, which continued to sustain its 'gracious living' until the 1920s, and represents, for the area, the acme of display and grandeur. The valuation of the contents of its sixty rooms in 1923 (£24,000+) suggests something of its relative splendour.[59]

It has been said that the 'rich ate and drank freely and accepted gout and apoplexy as things that ran mysteriously in respectable families'.[60] Indeed, Herbert Evans of Highmead suffered badly from the former, and in 1821 sought medical treatment in London.[61] A hundred years earlier Lloyd of Alltyrodyn, by way of contrast, lived simply and thought a great deal of his favourite dish, 'broad beans and bacon'.[62] In the meantime, houses, food and clothing answered more and more to the fashions of English grandees. Country houses possessed cellars which partly ousted butteries and still-rooms for the storage of beer and cider; the latter remained as the beverage of the lower orders of farm servants and labourers. As the wealth of the gentry increased, port, sherry and other continental wines and brandy came to be drunk more and more. These were imported by agents such as Fry of Bristol or the London Commercial Hall Wine Company who had distribution centres in towns such as Carmarthen and Cardigan. The bills paid by Lewes of Gellydywyll are typical of the amount spent on wines and spirits, and during a period of three months in 1770 he paid for eight dozen bottles of port.[63]

From 1800 onwards the Lloyd-Williams family of Gwernant was supplied with tea from Twinings, perfumes, snuff, refined lamp oil and a whole variety of commodities ranging from the ordinary to the very exotic, purchased from London firms who shipped supplies to Cardigan. By the end of the nineteenth century large houses like Bronwydd and Pentre—whose lavish entertainment was unrestrained —obtained supplies of recherché food and liquor from London houses such as Harrods, and Fortnum and Masons. A few of the gentry, on the other hand, had always lived simply, even to the point of parsimony. One of these was Mrs Lloyd of Gilfachwen, who in 1833 retired to a 'neat and quiet cottage where elegance, taste and mental improvement may be attained and cultivated'.[64] This could mean refined manners, intelligent conversation but a frugal lifestyle. E. Crompton Ll. Fitz-Williams of Emlyn Cottage, too, lived almost a spartan existence, avoiding the 'conspicuous display' which was a drain on many an estate.[65] The country squire visiting London imitated metropolitan styles and fashions in varying degree.

Owen Brigstocke of Blaenpant sported fine clothes: a 'claret coloured coat with gold lace', a 'Blew sattan coat with gold lace', 'brocade coats', 'breeches', 'super beaver' hats, and a 'white hat', all very fashionable in the years 1750-72.[66] Lewes of Gellydywyll was supplied with cosmetics such as a 'hair pencil' and vials of 'pomaton of Saturn', 'ruffled shirts and silk hose', which along with horses and saddlers' bills amounted to £1,892 in one year.[67] The Lloyds of Coedmore displayed Regency fashions in the countryside around Cardigan, wearing cord breeches, hunting coats with gilt buttons, greatcoats, capes, shalloon skirts, gaiters and the like.[68] The formal uniform of an officer in the army and navy could prove expensive, especially the 'gold braid' accessories which Webley-Parry of Noyadd Trefawr sported in 1850. A touch of the dandy is suggested, too, in his 'toilet' bills—bottles of lavender, hair oil and a box of 'Odonto'—which was a well known dentifrice.[69]

Whereas the great mansions of the land had, since the end of the seventeenth century, the most advanced sanitary arrangements,[70] the 'Tivyside' squirearchy regarded these as the last in their list of priorities. H. M. Vaughan states that the state of affairs was 'pretty primitive at old Llangoedmore' where baths were not in much demand, and, if required, hip-baths were used. Domestic servants would carry the water up and downstairs in the process of filling and emptying them. At Tŷ Llwyd the drains led to a nearby open field, and a bathroom was not installed until 1930.[71] Lloyd of Coedmore's town house in Cardigan had its 'necessarium' or privy outside in the yard, and at Pentre (before the house was remodelled in the 1820s) a row of 'privies' stood between the house and the farm midden. The idea of a 'water closet' was so novel and unique in the area that Rhosygilwen was singled out as possessing one in 1836 (but even then it had no bathroom).[72]

Ideas concerning personal hygiene and the health of family and servants do not appear to have been of much concern to the country gentry of 'Tivyside'. In spite of public health acts, new medical knowledge, the emphasis on clean water and proper sanitation, it was only towards the last quarter of the nineteenth century that Clemena

Lloyd of Coedmore expressed her worry that 'in spite of the advance of cholera' she could not get the 'seat of the WC finished'.[73] A growing concern with epidemics like cholera and typhoid no doubt spurred the Lloyds to improve matters at Bronwydd and Newport Castle.[74]

In other respects, however, the gentry had wished to move with the times by installing domestic appliances and the manufactured gadgets which the industrial revolution produced. Gone were the dog-driven spits, brass pans and skillets, boilers and cauldrons listed in early eighteenth-century inventories. After 1800, patent stoves, tea and coffee urns, kitchen ranges, neat grates and fireplaces with suitable cleaning tools were installed. A wide variety of tableware, cutlery, napkin rings, asparagus tongs and many more items of stirling silver or heavy plate adorned the squire's dining table. Other amenities, such as central heating installed at Cilgwyn in the 1880s, and from then on electric light and the telephone at Bronwydd,[75] all added to make the life of the squire and his family more comfortable and grand, and in what Queen Victoria would have called—'the high mode'.

An essential appendage of the squire's estate and mansion was his town house in Carmarthen, Cardigan or Haverfordwest. Owing to difficult travelling conditions it was important to have a base near the centre of 'county' affairs, such as Quarter Sessions, meetings of burgesses, visits to houses of correction and the like. In addition, there were the social events like balls, levees, dramatics and horse races, which followed from the presence of the squire and his family in the locality. The Brigstocke's town house in Carmarthen was commodious and well furnished, with contents valued at £120 in 1751.[76] Although much smaller in scale than their country mansions and more modest, a house like the one owned by Lewis of Llwyngrawys in Cardigan had everything in it so as to make life as comfortable as in the squire's country home. Functionally essential items, like the 'two saddle horses, a cow, a horse and cart and a water cart', were complementary and within easy reach in an adjoining yard.[77] Tucked away in genteel and respectable localities, the town houses of the Lloyds of Bronwydd, Coedmore and the Morgan family of Plas Aberporth were situated in St Mary's Street in Cardigan, the Morgan house built in an imposing classical style.[78] Professional exigencies demanded that Dr Davies of Pentre had a town house in Carmarthen and Tenby, as his services were widely needed in the Tywi valley and along the south Pembrokeshire coast as well as nearer home in 'Tivyside'. While many gentry rented temporary accommodation in Bath or London,[79] only the very wealthy like Lady Owen of Orielton, a sister of John Colby of Ffynone, had, in the years about 1800, fashionable London residences, together with Col. Spence-Colby of Ffynone and Col. Davies Evans of Highmead in this century.[80] Improved and quicker modes of travel, as well as the cost of maintaining them, led to the decline of gentry houses in towns like Cardigan and Carmarthen, and the fortunes of many 'Tivyside' gentry were inadequate to support a London home.

NOTES AND SOURCES

[1]P. Jenkins: *op cit.*, p. 250.

[2]R. Warner: *op cit.*, p. 80; Lord Raglan: 'The Origin of Vernacular Architecture' in Sir I. Foster and L. Alcock (eds), *Culture and Environment*, 1963, pp. 373-78.

[3]RCLWM Report 1896, p. 697.

[4]R. Fenton: *op cit.*, pp. 404-06.

[5]S. R. Meyrick: *op cit.*, p. 196; S. Lewis, *op cit. sub.*—Llandysiliogogo and Llandysul.

[6]NLW/Cilgwyn/213.

[7]*Yr Haul*: 1864, t 341.

[8]T. A. Lloyd: 'The Georgian Period in Welsh Building', *Arch Camb*, 1956, pp. 90-93; *DWB*.

[9]*ibid*: p. 91.

[10]P. Smith: *op cit.*, pp. 226, 293.

[11]T. Davis: *The Architecture of John Nash*, 1960, *sub* Ffynone and Llysnewydd; R. Suggett: *John Nash architect*, 1995, pp. 37-58, 72-76, 116-120.

[12]NLW/Highmead/2.

[13]H. M. Colvin: *A Biographical Dictionary of British Architects, 1600-1840*, 1978 and RIBA Archives *sub* Poynter.

[14]P. Smith: *op cit.*, p. 326.

[15]*ibid*: p. 321.

[16]*DWB*; J. J. Thomas: 'The Architectural Development of Hafod', *Ceredigion*, vii, 2, 1973, pp. 153-69.

[17]J. Franklin: *The Gentleman's Country House and its Plan, 1835-1914*, 1981, pp. 1-5.

[18]NLW/Bronwydd/4251-54, 5822-81.

[19]B. Williams (Gwynionydd): *Hanes Castell Newydd Emlyn, Trefhedyn . . .*, 1860, pp. 51-59.

[20]Dates on parts of buildings at Cilgwyn and Rhosygilwen. NLW/Cilgwyn/Ms. LB 40/28/11/1860.

[21]The ceilings at Penylan were painted by an Italian—Ludovici—a Royal Academician [Cd. Ad: 25/8/1905].

[22]T. Davis: *loc cit.*; D. Ottewill: *The Edwardian Garden*, 1989, pp. 13-19.

[23]D. L. Baker-Jones: 'Ffynone, Pembrokeshire—A Country House and its Occupants', *THSC*, i, 1965, pp. 115-36; J. A. Gotch: *The Growth of the English House*, 1909, pp. 246-48.

[24]C. Aslet: *The Last Country Houses*, 1982, pp. 2-7, 50-57.

[25]P. Smith: *op cit.*, p. 323.

[26]J. Franklin: *op cit.*, pp. 39-43.

[27]M. Girouard: *The Victorian Country House*, 1979, pp. 29-45; R. Kerr: *The Gentleman's House or How to Plan English Residences from the Parsonage to the Palace*, 1864.

[28]J. Franklin: *op cit.*, pp. 39-49.

[29]D. L. Baker-Jones: 'Ffynone', *loc cit*; personal knowledge.

[30]*The Welshman*: 12/1/1866.

[31]J. Franklin: *op cit.*, pp. 51-52; personal knowledge; a magistrates court is recorded to have taken place at Alltyrodyn on 1 January 1788 [NLW/Cards/QS/OB/4].

[32]*Gent Mag*, 1768, pp. 470-71; ER/1861, 1871. P. Horn: *The Rise and Fall of the Victorian Servant*, 1995, pp. 1-188, 211-31.

[33]FG/26/138; NLW/Cilgwyn/371.

[34]NLW/Evans George/1587.

[35]NLW Mrs E. B. Wood (Tŷ Llwyd Diary).

[36]CRO/EG/Box/23.

[37]NLW/Howell (Glaspant) Diary/1896; personal knowledge.

[38]NLW/Highmead/2808, 2861.

[39]J. Lees-Milne: *Earls of Creation*, 1962; *The London Magazine* or *The Gentleman's Monthly Intelligence*, May, Sept., 1768; Jan., June, 1769.

[40]P. Willis: *Charles Bridgeman and the English Landscape Garden*, 1977, pp. 1-9; Uvedale Price: *An Essay on the Picturesque . . .*, 1794, i, p. 39; J. Summerson: *John Nash*, 1935, pp. 291-92; *DWB*.

[41]T. Davis: *op cit.*, pp. 11-12.

[42]NLW/Ms/5152 B.

[43]RCAHM Archives *sub*: Cilwendeg, Pembs; Blaenpant, Cards; etc; B. Jones: *Follies and Grottoes*, 1974, p. 412.

[44]*Cd Ad*: 16/5/1873.

[45]*Cm Jnl*: 20/11/1874.

[46]*ibid*: 25/9/1818.

[47]*ibid*: 7/9/1811.

[48]*The Welshman*: 8/2/1856.

[49]CRO/Cwmgwili/231 A.

[50]J. T. Barber: *op cit.*, p. 121.

[51]NLW/Evans George/2426.

[52]NLW/Owen Colby/1856.

[53]*Cm Jnl*: 21/3/1812.

[54]CRO/EG/(Brigstocke)/11/-.

[55]NLW/Owen Colby/1087; NLW/Noyadd Trefawr/1517.

[56]HRO/D/Lew/4/395.

[57]*Cm Jnl*: 15/2/1850; NLW/Evans George/2036.

[58]J. Steegman: *A Survey of Portraits in Welsh Houses*, 1962, ii, South Wales.

[59]CRO/JF (Colby) 22; personal knowledge.

[60]George Eliot: *Silas Marner*, p. 33.

[61]NLW/Lucas/625-30.

[62]NLW/Ms 8742 B (John Davies 32).

[63]NLW/Evans George/3111; *Cm Jnl*: 25/3/1814.

[64]CRO/Talardd/Box/2/31.

[65]NLW/Cilgwyn/LB/56/11 Jan. 1877.

[66]NLW/Evans George/1398-1412, 2421.

[67]*ibid*: 3119, 3319, 3356.

[68]CRO/Coedmore/2/493.

[69]NLW/Noyadd Trefawr/1518-63.

[70]M. Girouard: *Life in the English Country House*, 1978, pp. 252-56.

[71]H. M. Vaughan: *op cit.*, pp. 17-18; E. B. Wood: *op cit.*

[72]*Cm Jnl*: 8/4/1836.

[73]CRO/Coedmore/4/61.

[74]NLW/Bronwydd/3523-27, 7304.

[75]NLW/Cilgwyn/LB/60/29 Apr. 1888; NLW/Bronwydd/5995.

[76]NLW/Evans George/2423.

[77]NLW/Clynfyw/Box/1.

[78]Local recollections.

[79]*Trans Carms Antiq Socy*, 9, pp. 50-2; 29, pp. 96-7.

[80]NLW/Owen Colby/988; Walford: *op cit: sub* Evans.

The Education of the Squire

Family papers, letters, account books, diaries, journals and other personalia, as well as the contents of their libraries, demonstrate that the gentry on the whole possessed a broad educational background. Most of them were, at least, sufficiently literate and numerate to understand the finances of their estates, county business and magisterial matters. In addition to their lands, their farmyards and gardens, horses and hounds, it was part of the ethos of a gentleman's lifestyle to have some basic knowledge of Latin and Greek, an acquaintance with Shakespeare, Milton and other English classics, an appreciation of art and scientific development, along with the manners and social polish which befitted a gentleman.

That the 'Tivyside' gentry were as aware of the need to be educated, as any of their peers elsewhere, becomes clear from wills early in our period. In 1672 Lewis of Pantyrodin provided in his will that his 'friends' and 'cozens' were to be 'tutors' of his children, and responsible for their guardianship, education and general upbringing.[1] Sums of money were left to buy books and Bibles towards 'schooling'. Stephen Parry of Noyadd Trefawr in 1721 made a charge on his estate of £50 a year in order to maintain his nephew at Oxford.[2] Younger sons, without the necessary finance to obtain an army commission and the patronage to acquire government office or university education, were sometimes left money to secure an apprenticeship in a trade. For example, Parry of Troedyraur left his nephew £15 for the purpose.[3] Sons of lesser gentry were (in the early 1700s) expected to have 'schooling' from the age of 8 to about 16 years of age. Lloyd of Coedlannau Fawr considered it unnecessary to educate his eldest son beyond the age of 15; he would inherit the estate and, consequently, additional education for a profession or employment was to no purpose.[4] Nor was the education of girls for a prolonged period regarded as important by the lesser gentry. Thus, in 1784, Evans of Penwenallt left £15 to his daughter for her 'keeping', as well as for all 'necessaries for six months' at a school in Carmarthen[5]—just enough time to learn the rudiments of writing and reading.

The education of the gentry was variously provided for by the employment of a private tutor, 'schooling' at one of the old grammar schools or dissenting academies, or attendance at public schools of national repute (private boarding establishments in the case of girls), often followed by a period of residence at Oxford or Cambridge and the Inns of Court. Many of the grammar schools established after the Reformation were attended, no doubt, by the sons of town burgesses and the sons of yeomen and small landowners.[6] In the county towns of Cardigan, Carmarthen and Haverfordwest the old grammar schools had drawn a fair proportion of gentry boys. Although founded by wealthy gentry for the education of 'poor scholers'—a very ambiguous term—amongst the 'alumni' of these schools were Gen. Sir Thomas Picton at Haverfordwest, and a Bowen of Llwyngwair and Lloyd of Llanwenog, at Carmarthen in the 1780s.[7] The disastrous eviction of dissenting clerics in 1661 had led to the foundation of academies which were a blessing and the backbone of the educational system up to the eighteenth century and later. The Rev. Samuel Jones of Brynllywarch in Glamorgan, attracted to his academy the sons of the Glamorgan gentry.[8]

Likewise, in west Wales, establishments like the Carmarthen Academy attracted young squires like Thomas Lloyd (possibly of Bronwydd, Cilgwyn or Coedmore) in 1746, and John Jenkins (Ifor Ceri) of Cilbronne towards the end of the century.[9] The fear of dissent was no bar to James Brigstocke's entering Thomas Morgan of Laugharne's academy in 1763. Morgan belonged to a circle of prominent dissenters such as David Lloyd of Coedlannau-fawr, Philip Pugh and Christmas Samuel.[10] He was a frequent visitor to west Wales houses, including Gellydywyll in the Teifi valley.[11]

Edward Richard, who kept the well known school at Ystrad Meurig, like Thomas Morgan, was *persona grata* in the mansions of north Cardiganshire like Nanteos, Ffosybleiddiaid, Crosswood and others. The education he imparted, and his literary reputation as one of the Welsh Augustans, added lustre to his name.[12] At least one 'Tivyside' squire received his education at Ystrad Meurig, namely, the Rev. Benjamin Millingchamp of Llangoedmor.[13] The outstanding dissenting academy in 'Tivyside' was that of David Davis at Castell Hywel during the years 1782 to 1827. Davis, a friend of dissenters and anglican clergy, imparted sound scholarship and a broad ecumenism at a time of considerable religious and dogmatic debate.[14] The future squires of Gellydywyll, Waunifor, Maesycrugiau, Highmead, Tŷ Llwyd and others ranked amongst its 'alumni'.[15] Dr Havard of Blaengwthan in 'Tivyside' was educated at the equally famous Ffrwdfâl Academy in the Cothi valley, along with the gentry of that area. Much of the teaching consisted of a thorough grounding in the classics in order to enter English public schools. The ideal dissenting academy emphasised rigour and diligence, while presenting an exacting and broad based curriculum imparted by teachers, who were imbued with the radical and humanistic trends of the time.[16]

In some instances gentry children were educated privately for many reasons, such as lack of local facilities, economy, the hazards of travel, undesirable influences and unsatisfactory regimes. The Brigstocke youngsters in 1761 had a private tutor so as 'not to allow them abroad to be educated in the Roman Catholic way . . . but to [acquire] a virtuous and genteel education in the Protestant way'.[17] The 'Methodistical' leanings of the Bowens of Llwyngwair naturally led to the appointment of the Rev. David Griffiths, the enthusiastic evangelical cleric, as tutor.[18] Not only were the religious and political susceptibilities of tutors under the microscope; they had to be able to fit into the lifestyle of a 'gentleman's family', 'respectable', with 'an unexceptional [sic] character', in addition to their intellectual skills. The regime could often be arduous and even harsh; for example, in the family of Jenkins of Penyrallt, Aberporth, 'the girls were kept at their studies from 5 a.m. until late at night . . . the older girls having undertaken the education of their younger brothers and sisters'[19]—a situation of family tutoring which existed because of the impecunious circumstances of the family. A few years later, in the 1830s, the Colby girls of Rhosygilwen had private tutors at home but 'were bro't up to London occasionally for the better instruction by first masters'.[20] In 'Tivyside' the system of home tutoring under a clergyman survived late into the 1860s (and possibly later), as, for example, at Penylan, Llechryd, to provide for the children of Morgan Jones.[21]

Over the centuries a few gentry families had aspired to widen their cultural and social horizons by sending their sons to be educated at English public schools. As early as 1635 David Lewes of Llysnewydd attended Shrewsbury school. From the 1750s onwards, examples from the families of Brigstocke of Blaenpant, Lewes of Penybenglog, Rice of Penbryn, Jenkins of Cilbronne, amongst others, can be cited from the registers of Christ's Hospital, Harrow and Shrewsbury Schools. From 1800 the major families increasingly sent their sons to Eton, Harrow, Rugby, and Shrewsbury.[22]

Moreover, the older grammar schools had declined, through misuse of endowments and negligence, and could no longer provide for the needs of young gentlemen. The dissenting academies, too, in the early 1800s, were being associated more and more in gentry estimation with expanding nonconformity and radicalism, so that by mid-century the

Tory church periodical, *Yr Haul*, dismissed them as only fit for enlightened labourers and budding pulpit thumpers.[23]

The reforming zeal of Dr Arnold at Rugby, his influence on other public schools and the foundation of new ones like Cheltenham, Marlborough and Wellington, attracted the sons of the squirearchy as suitable places to prepare young gentlemen for a prospective role as rulers in the context of national politics and an ever expanding empire, not to mention the needs of a country estate and local administration. Thus, the small squire from the Teifi valley was able, through attending schools like Eton, Harrow and Rugby, to rub shoulders with the English landed nobility, giving both a sense of common identity and natural superiority within a culturally homogeneous, if hierarchical élite.[24] By helping to consolidate a caste system which was based on birth, wealth, leisure and a special education, the effect upon Welsh Wales, whence the gentry had sprung, was to exacerbate the divisions between social classes in terms of language, culture, politics and religion. Moreover, the final stage in the anglicisation of the gentry must be attributed, in no small measure, to the English public school and what it stood for.

Families, who could afford to send their daughters to private establishments, took advantage of schools in the neighbourhood of London or Bath. Thus, in such schools, from 1784 to 1794 the Colby daughters of Ffynone and Rhosygilwen were taught French, Geography, History, Grammar as the 'core' subjects along with genteel accomplishments like music, dancing, needlework and embroidery.[25] Colby's ward Ann Ferrier had, in addition to her general education, the opportunities and social 'grooming' with a view to finding a suitable match. The regime in some of these schools was, sometimes, unsatisfactory and nothing more than a girls' equivalent to Dotheboys Hall, as the Colby archives demonstrate.[26]

From the 1750s it is possible to trace the growth of private adventure schools in west Wales, less expensive than those of London and Bath, and with a more limited 'clientele' drawn, perhaps, from the less affluent gentry.[27] These were aimed mainly at the daughters of genteel folk, providing what may be summed up as 'useful' and 'ornamental' education. In 1802 the Walters children of Perthgereint attended such schools in Carmarthen and Haverfordwest.[28] From the 1820s to about 1878 the best known and best attended school for gentry daughters in south-west Wales was the Hill Street Boarding School in Haverfordwest, which attracted over the years the daughters of a dozen or more

'Tivyside' gentry.[29] The foundation of girls' public schools, such as the Cheltenham Ladies College in 1854, along with improved travelling facilities, eventually appealed to the squirearchy, as more and more of the well-to-do middle classes 'invaded' the local schools.

From the Tudor period, Welsh gentry looked towards the universities of Oxford and Cambridge in order to complete their education. Possibly on account of the shorter distance to Oxford, as well as its political and religious complexion, it was favoured more than Cambridge by many Welshmen. In this respect the 'Tivyside' gentry, like their counterparts in Glamorgan, favoured Oxford.[30] The steady trickle, from the time of the matriculation of Sir John Lewes of Abernantbychan in 1598, increased to about 40 in the years 1688 to 1714 (interrupted by the troublous times of the Civil War and Interregnum), when most Welshmen were drawn to Jesus College.[31] The early zeal for a university education fell in the years 1715 to 1725 and one can only trace the names of Griffiths of Mountain Hall and Jones of Lletherneuadd from the Teifi valley entering Oxford. The universities had become increasingly unpopular as they could not provide the social polish which the gentry sought. Admissions fluctuated in the middle decades of the eighteenth century, with an increase by about 1800, and a fairly steady intake from the landed classes occurred from then on. During the same period the number of 'Tivyside' gentry who entered Cambridge colleges was, in all, only about one-fifth of those at Oxford. Out of a total of 32 who matriculated from the area in the years 1500 to 1900, only a dozen had done so up to 1800.[32]

There was considerable truth in the claim that the gentry who went to Oxford and Cambridge sought there social rather than intellectual improvement, and were 'scholars only in masquerade', participating in the leisure activities of foxhunting squires or society aristocrats transposed to a university setting.[33] Living in a grand style and indulging in recreations beyond their means could lead to serious financial troubles. In 1683 Sir Erasmus Philipps of Picton Castle (albeit outside our area) had expressed alarm at the wasteful expense of his son at Trinity College, Cambridge, and would tolerate no more 'his foolish frolics', and this behaviour was probably true of many a young squire.[34] About £250 was considered adequate for young Brigstocke of Blaenpant, when he matriculated in the 1750s, to cover '. . . matriculation, fees, gowns and capp, furniture for the chamber, cloaths and apparel, two horses and attendant, tutor, bedmaker, chamber servant, stable rent, common room, library, caution money . . .',[35] all worthy and respectable, but only a fraction of the invisible expenses a young blood might spend on gambling, horse racing, drinking and paramours. Another Sir Erasmus Phillips of Picton Castle is a typical example, spending his time hunting the fox, attending cock fights, horse races, fishing, riding and boating. Nevertheless, there were other interests as well; he tried to learn the violin, attended political gatherings and listened to 'declamations' in hall.[36]

For many undergraduates, being examined in the subject matter of formal lectures was not the purpose of attending a university. But it did not mean that they were all idle or dissolute. Some attended Bradley's lectures on chemistry and Blackstone's on the Common Law; they took part in 'disputations' and 'declamations' in logic and philosophy; they studied the works of Plato, Aristotle and other classical writers, modern authors like Newton and Locke, as well as polite literature. Most students acquired the habits and interests of a liberal education, which was to be reflected more and more in their lifestyle at home and on their estates.

To a lesser extent Cambridge suffered from the same ills as Oxford at the time. Whilst at Oxford by 1770 no serious examination in any modern sense at all was held for a degree, at Cambridge the mathematical Tripos offered a real test for the more ambitious candidates for honours. During the nineteenth century university commissions brought about radical reforms. 'Close' scholarships granted to students from particular areas or families were thrown open, archaic customs were abandoned and a widening academic and scientific interest along with religious and political ferment began to blow away the stupor of centuries.[37]

It is significant that the 'Tivyside' gentry were not reluctant to send their sons to Oxford which, up to about 1760, had been a bastion of Tory politics and strident Stuart loyalism. The Whig image of Oxford as dissolute, as well as its religious and political opposition to the Hanoverians, doubtless alarmed a few anxious parents lest their sons, on account of an Oxford education, might lose some measure of government patronage and preferment. It was only after 1760, with the reconciliation between Crown and university, that the fears of the ruling classes were allayed, although in 1776 Brigstocke of Blaenpant stipulated in his will that his son was not to be educated at either of the English universities but was to be sent abroad for that end.[38] From now on Oxford became more 'respectable' as it progressed steadily to co-operate with the politics of George III. By the end of the eighteenth century the university stood out for church and King, the monarchical

ideal and the Anglican establishment.[39] The landed gentry were bound
to see this very clearly in an age of Jacobin and revolutionary attack on
the established order, and this is reflected perhaps in the number of
gentry who in the nineteenth century received a university education.

With regard to the choice of college, the more fashionable and
wealthiest gentry in Glamorgan in the years 1640 to 1790 dissociated
themselves more and more at the university from their humbler Welsh
compatriots who entered Jesus College. The cult of fashion and urbane
manners, however, did not deter some 'Tivyside' families from sending
their sons to the 'traditional' Welsh college. Thus, David Lloyd of
Alltyrodyn matriculated from Jesus College in 1734, while six members
of the Brigstocke family of Blaenpant were educated there from 1726 to
1849.[40] Other gentry families, such as Lewes of Llysnewydd, showed a
predilection for Brasenose and Trinity—Llysnewydd sending four sons
to those colleges from 1741 to 1814. It would appear that, well into the
nineteenth century, a fair number of 'Tivyside' squires entered at least
half a dozen different Oxford colleges for no obvious reason. It is
noteworthy, however, that one of the 'new' gentry, Evans of
Highmead, in 1791, chose to join Christ Church after a period at
Eton, a college renowned for its wealth and its 'alumni' who were the
rich nobility of the land. This trend was repeated from 1800 onwards
by the wealthiest of the 'Tivyside' squires of Bronwydd, Llwyngwair
and Pentre. Notwithstanding the considerable expense of 'keeping up'
with dukes and earls, the lesser gentry wished to identify themselves
with a superior aristocratic caste and, thereby, they severed themselves
socially from their Welsh cultural origins. Moreover, the sons of
middle-class attorneys, clerics and wealthy merchants were
increasingly entering the universities and acquiring parity with the
gentry in education and manners. Therefore, becoming members of
Christ Church, Magdalen and New Colleges was one way the gentry
could dissociate themselves from lesser folk like the sons of the
Llandysul vicar, who in the 1840s matriculated from Jesus College.[41]

No single Cambridge college seems to have especially attracted the
'Tivyside' squires, except perhaps, St John's, which in the period up to
1800 had provided education for four out of about a dozen from the
area. During the nineteenth century considerably more graduated at
Cambridge, some 20 in all from 'Tivyside' with Trinity College attracting
six of them.[42]

It is claimed that by the nineteenth century the respective colleges at
Oxford and Cambridge had developed characteristics which attracted

particular groups. Thus Christ Church, Oxford, is supposed to have become a school for Tory statesmen, Oriel and Balliol appealed to intellectual men, and, at the latter, Webley Hope of Pigeonsford was an undergraduate during the mastership of the illustrious Jowett. At Cambridge, Trinity College is said to have nurtured Whig statesmen, ousting St John's in that context, while Magdalene and Queens' had the reputation of an evangelical type of churchmanship.[43] It is not possible to see any clear motivation in the choice of college made by the 'Tivyside' gentry (except a predilection during the early period of this study for Jesus College, Oxford, with its strong royalist and Welsh connection). They did not belong to any family of outstanding calibre in terms of politics or connections on a national level, and probably chose their colleges through the influence of the schools they had attended, the level of fees they could afford and the friendships they had made.

Education at what may be termed a 'third university' was provided in the Inns of Court; an ideal sequence of education was provided at the university, one of the Inns and foreign travel.[44] The Inns, according to Maitland, formed associations of lay lawyers which had about them a good deal of the club, something of the College, something of a trade union.[45] From Elizabethan times many entrants had been sent to the Inns of Court to obtain the social cachet so avidly sought by the rising gentry of the period.[46] Moreover, there was a growing demand among the landed classes for a training which both fitted them for local and central office and enabled them to hold their own in the company of virtuosi around a dinner table.[47] The Inns of Court gave a grounding in an important base of English life, namely, an affirmation of the rule of law as something superior to the will of rulers. At the end of the eighteenth and in the early nineteenth centuries, the age of reform and radical challenge demanded a legally informed and educated gentry class, many of whom, as has been seen already, were qualified barristers.

As with the universities, the appeal and popularity of the Inns varied over the centuries. A steady stream of Cardiganshire gentry entered the Inner and Middle Temple from the sixteenth century, representing the old families of Lewes of Abernantbychan, Coedmore and Cwmawen. It is suggested that the popularity of the former was due to the pattern set by the chief families in Cardiganshire, namely, those of Gogerddan and Trawsgoed.[48] In the eighteenth century Lincoln's Inn was regarded as the 'soberest of the Inns',[49] and a tradition arose by the end of the nineteenth century that graduates from the older universities favoured the Inner Temple while would-be practitioners at the Chancery Bar sought their training in Lincoln's Inn.

Almost without exception the 'Tivyside' gentry, throughout the period under study, realised the value of a university and legal education. To quote a cogent phrase, they had the 'wit and acumen' to take advantage of their fortune and the resources which the country could provide, to educate themselves and to acquire all the marks which 'gentility' required from them as a class apart in society.

But the education of the 'compleat man' had to include foreign travel in order to see the antiquities, curiosities, character, manners, language and forms of government of foreign countries.[50] A rage for travel seized Englishmen of all classes, according to their means. The sons of élite families made the Grand Tour of the continent, spending their time in taverns, hostelries or sometimes—according to their degree —in the mansions of foreign nobility. The great English aristocrats returned home with rich spoils and artistic treasures to adorn their homes. They were often accompanied by a well informed 'tutor' and 'guide' who had to be physician, diplomat, literary and artistic adviser, as well as moral preceptor against vice and debauchery.[51] No one could have fulfilled Lord Chesterfield's admonitions concerning behaviour more thoroughly than Thomas Lewes of Gellydywyll who travelled widely from 1760 to 1795. Employed in government missions, and educating himself in the process, he recorded his travels to the major countries and capitals of Europe, as well as Canada and the new United States of America. He collected information on a variety of subjects such as mines, manufactures and taxes; he also made detailed descriptions and notes on the cities of Prague, Vienna and Budapest and the Hapsburg emperors. He communicated with European magnates who, from time to time, received him at their courts.[52]

In Victorian times continental travel and long periods of residence abroad had become part of the lifestyle of the gentry when families took their children to learn foreign languages and to explore the sights. Thus, the Lloyds of Coedmore took the waters at Baden-Baden, traversed cities and byways, writing home to their less fortunate friends of the wonders they had seen. The more ventursome swarmed to the continent for mountaineering and other hazardous pursuits.[53] In the 1850s E. Crompton Ll. Fitzwilliams and his family settled at Poitiers in France for health reasons, and the education of their children: '. . . they learn beside general knowledge, French, German, Music and their drawing mistress is to come next week. Charles has a private tutor grounding him for his college work', he wrote to Beynon his agent.[54] From among many examples, we can also mention that the young Morgan-Richardson of Rhosygilwen was resident in France in 1906; there, to be educated in French, singing, dancing and other social graces by 'polite' masters in those accomplishments.[55]

NOTES AND SOURCES

[1]FG/15/101.

[2]*ibid*: 15/110, 15/335; HRO/D/Pen/9.

[3]FG/18/64.

[4]G. E. Evans: *Lloyd Letters*, 1754-1759, 1908, pp. 59-60.

[5]NLW/St Davids/Wills/1764.

[6]J. Rhys and D. B. Jones: *op cit.*, pp. 479-500.

[7]N. Carlisle: *Endowed Grammar Schools in England and Wales*, 1818, pp. 949-54.

[8]H. P. Roberts: 'Nonconformist Academies in Wales', *THSC*, 1929-29, pp. 8-10; G. D. Owen: *Ysgolion a Chalegau yr Annibynwyr*, 1939, pp. 3-5, 12; *DWB*.

[9]NLW/Ms 5457; *DWB*.

[10]H. Lloyd-Johnes: 'An Account Book of Thomas Morgan', *NLWJ*, ix, 1, 1955, p. 63.

[11]NLW/Ms 5456 A; *DWB*.

[12]M. C Donaldson: 'Edward Richard of Ystrad Meurig', *Ceredigion*, V, 3, 1966, pp. 240-41; S. Lewis: *A School of Welsh Augustans*, 1926; *DWB*.

[13]*DWB*.

[14]NLW/Cwrtmawr/111-113 quoting *The Cambrian Register*, 1796.

[15]NLW/Evans George/3554; D. Davis: *Telyn Dewi 1824* (appendix—list of subscribers and old pupils).

[16]Atgofion am Athrofa Ffrwdfâl. *Y Tyst*, 30/11/1883. (Kindly brought to my attention by Dr Huw Walters of NLW); P. Dodderidge: *Memoirs*, 1766, pp. 87-92; R. T. Jones: 'Agweddau ar Ddiwylliant yr Ymneilltuwyr', *THSC*, 1963, ii. tt 173-74.

[17]NLW/Evans George/2434.

[18]*DWB*.

[19]NLW/Ms 1897E, iv.

[20]NLW/Owen Colby/1103-1115.

[21]*Cd Ad*: 28/12/1888.

[22]NLW/MS 1897 E; J. Foster: *Alumni Oxon*, 1891; J. and J. A. Venn: *Alumni Cantab*, 1922.

[23]*Yr Haul*: 1850, pp. 45-49.

[24]G. K. Clark: *op cit.*, pp. 267-74; Report of the Royal Commission on Public Schools, 1864, xx; J. Foster and J. and J. A. Venn: *op cit.*

[25]NLW/Owen Colby/1061-79.

[26]*ibid*: 1082.

[27]G. E. Evans: 'Carmarthenshire Schools', *Trans Carms Antiq Socy*, XLI, p. 16.

[28]F. Jones: *Walters of Perthgereint*, p. 172.

[29]NLW/Lucas/4293, 4302; *Cm Jnl*: 6/1/1871, 28/1/1878.

[30]P. Jenkins: *op cit.*, pp. 224-26.

[31]*Victoria History of the Counties of England: Oxfordshire*, iii, p. 265; T. Richards: 'The Puritan Visitaton of Jesus College', *THSC*, 1922-23, pp. 1-10.

[32]Venn: *op cit.*

[33]L. S. Sutherland and L. G. M. Mitchell (eds): *The History of the University of Oxford*, V, The Eighteenth Century, 1986, pp. 2-7; *DWB*; G. B. Hill: *Memoirs of the Life of Edward Gibbon*, 1900, p. 58.

[34]NLW/Picton Castle/1450; P. Jenkins: *op cit.*, pp. 224 seq.

[35]NLW/Evans George/2461.

[36]L. S. Sutherland and L. G. Mitchell: *op cit.*, p. 320.

[37]*ibid*: pp. 469-505.

[38]NLW/Evans George/753.

[39]L. S. Sutherland and L. G. Mitchell: *op cit.*, pp. 161-63.

[40]J. Foster: *Alumni Oxon.*

[41]J. Foster: *op cit.*

[42]*loc cit.*

[43]G. K. Clark: *op cit.*, pp. 255-57.

[44]P. Jenkins: *op cit.*, p. 225; for Maitland, see *DWB.*

[45]Maitland: *Collected Papers 11*, p. 482.

[46]W. Prest: 'Legal Education of the Gentry at the Inns of Court, 1560-1640', *Past and Present*, 38, Dec. 1967.

[47]L. Stone: 'The Educational Revolution in England', *ibid*, 28 July 1964.

[48]D. S. Davies: 'Cardiganshire and the Inns of Court to 1850', *CLR*, 1976, pp. 91-99.

[49]NLW/Picton Castle/1473.

[50]Letters of P. D. Stanhope, 4th Earl of Chesterfield, (ed) B. Dobrée, iii, 1932, pp. 773-76, G. Williams: *op cit*; *DWB.*

[51]P. Jenkins: *op cit.*, p. 227.

[52]*Cambrian Register*, 1795, p. 465; NLW/Noyadd Trefawr/1754-57, 1767-68; *DWB.*

[53]CRO/Coedmore/2204, 2637.

[54]NLW/Cilgwyn/LB/38/10 Dec. 1857.

[55]Morgan-Richardson/Diary 1906, in private hands.

Culture

On a visit to the town of Cardigan in 1761, Lewis Morris had expected to meet a 'Mathematician, a Naturalist or an Antiquary', and observed that while in England the Arts were reckoned the necessary qualification of a gentleman, in Cardigan he met nothing but '. . . Bombaglio, Clangor, Stridor, Tarantara . . . not as much as a piece of Welsh poet to be seen or heard of . . . everybody seems to be wetting his bill'. As this visit coincided with the Quarter Sessions then sitting, with half the county gentry present, the inference is that some of them were an uncouth lot and not interested in traditional Welsh or any other culture.[1] Allowing for Morris' bitter experience of some Cardiganshire gentry and bias against them,[2] it is interesting that a century later E. Crompton Ll. Fitzwilliams of Cilgwyn bemoaned the lack of any intellectual stimulus amongst the local gentry compared with the sort of company he had met in 'The Temple' and in foreign capitals. While 'Tivyside folks' were 'a good worthy sort of people', he felt that for years he was isolated and alone amongst them: 'I have found few or none of a congenial intellect or spirit'. In fact, Fitzwilliams went further when he wrote that he had only contempt for the local 'petty princelings and the mole heaps of its [i.e. Tivyside] social strata'.[3]

The question is whether the above indictment is true of many of the gentry in the area, considering their upbringing and education, foreign travel, the impact of metropolitan urbane manners, their libraries and fine houses, antiquarian pursuits and love of the arts—as well as the dilettante's natural curiosity, an important dimension in the squire's claim to gentility. In answer, one must admit that the widening cultural horizons of the gentry resulted in their ambition to build up a collection of books and manuscripts through purchase and inheritance, and the library was an important room in the squire's mansion. One aspect of gentry patronage of culture was their generosity in lending people their books. Well known in this respect was David Price of Llangrannog.[4] The houses of Hengwrt, Wynnstay and Peniarth in north Wales and Hafod in Cardiganshire are famous in Welsh culture for their remarkable collections of books and manuscripts, while in the Teifi valley the library of William Lewes of Llwynderw was described by Theophilus Evans as '. . . y casgliad gwerthfawrocaf o lyfrau a llawysgrifau' (the most valuable collection of books and manuscripts) seen by him.[5] In some cases the manuscripts had remained undisturbed for centuries. A country, house library not only consisted of books and manuscripts but of all sorts of interesting objects like '. . . globes, optic glasses, mathematical instruments as well as a cabinet of fossils',[6] and along with the books they were a good index to the mental calibre and intellectual pursuits of the squire. In Glamorgan, library catalogues are rarely found before the 1740s,[7] and the same can be said of 'Tivyside'. Moreover, in some cases, the books were never listed and were scattered when the houses were sold, abandoned and fell into ruin. The ownership of a book did not necessarily mean that its possessor had himself acquired it, or that the book was ever read. Perhaps, in many instances, the library was only part of the 'display' of the landed classes, and a reflection of the intellectual attainments expected of a gentleman.

Influences other than taste sometimes determined the contents of a library, such as religious fervour, the literary activity of a particular area, and the degree of contact local gentry had with the outside world. In the late seventeenth and early eighteenth centuries, there was great intellectual and literary fervour in the lower Teifi valley which was reflected in the setting up of the first printing press by Isaac Carter in Atpar, Newcastle Emlyn, in 1718.[8] Furthermore, one can visualise the country squire reading reviews of new publications in the *Gentleman's Magazine* and later periodicals, and during periodic sojourning in London or Bath he would have mingled with people who would influence his reading habits and taste.

It has been suggested that two or three thousand volumes was the normal size for the libraries of the greatest Welsh gentry houses such as Chirk, Mostyn and Picton.[9] The small houses of 'Tivyside' could not make such claims with their libraries comprising a hundred books or so, to, at the most, 2,000 books. The Brigstocke library at Blaenpant, amounted to about 700 volumes in 1778 and included publications from as early as 1541. Probably these were added to during the next century and a half, until its dispersal in the 1920s.[10] Other houses possessed roughly the following number of books—Llwyngwair 500 (1820), Ffynone—100 (1820s), Pentre—150 (1829), and Coedmore—535 (1892).[11] Because of the loss of library lists and sale catalogues it is not possible to determine the number of books at Cilgwyn, Bronwydd, Dolhaidd and some other houses. The commodious library and other extensive shelf space at Cilgwyn suggests a large collection of books, but the space allocated to books at Bronwydd was relatively small. The contents of its muniment room—deeds, charters, pedigrees and the like—made it, however, one of the most valuable repositories in the area.[12] In comparison with the library of the scholarly but financially limited Lewis Morris in 1764-65, which contained over 500 volumes covering a wide range of interest, 'Tivyside' gentry house libraries were on the whole modest.[13]

In terms of importance, two or three libraries deserve special mention. The Llwynderw library of William Lewes, probably, housed one of the most important genealogical collections of the day, and it included the famous Golden Grove books.[14] By the early 1800s this collection was housed at Alltyrodyn where, according to Fenton, David Lloyd the '. . . worthy proprietor has with a laudable liberality, thrown them open to the inspection of such persons as wished to peruse them', thereby, displaying a sense of trusteeship of such treasures which were of importance to the public at large.[15] Lloyd's common place book (extending to about 1100 pages of folio) contains detailed analysis of books he had read and are listed under Latin subject headings—Grammatica, Poetica, Phisica, Metallurgica, Architectura and so on—reflecting the intellectual diet of a veritable polymath in every branch of knowledge.[16]

Brigstocke's library at Blaenpant deserves mention on its own, and comprised works under the following broad headings,—

> Ecclesiastical History and Theology
> History, Antiquities and Law
> Dictionaries and Reference Books; especially John Davies of Mallwyd's
> *Dictionarium Duplex* of 1632
> Classics
> Political Philosophy
> Novels, belles lettres
> Drama
> Logic, natural philosophy, architecture.[17]

It cannot be said that any other 'Tivyside' library could compete with the above. On the whole, libraries display perhaps the limited interest of some gentry, namely, guidelines on a variety of subjects like foreign travel, geography, history (such as was the small Ffynone library), along with a few specialist books on estate matters, livestock breeding, agriculture, farriery and home medicine.[18] The average squire needed to reflect a modicum of general education and enough knowledge to indulge in cultural chatter in order to hold his own with his social peers at the dinner table. As a supporter of the established church the squire needed a copy of the Bible and the Book of Common Prayer, and, perhaps, one or two commentaries on the Scriptures.[19]

Law books were much in evidence at Coedmore in 1892; used by the lawyers in the family over many years. In addition, school and college Latin and Greek texts survived, as well as those relating to the claims of the church of Rome, liturgical reform and points of doctrine, which reflect some of the ecclesiastical controversies of the 1850s. Whereas most libraries contained the occasional Welsh Bible or dictionary, the Lloyds of Coedmore had several volumes of *cofiannau* (biographies) of eminent Welshmen, and occasionally books of Welsh poetry such as *Cywydd y Drindod* (Ode to the Trinity) by Dafydd Ionawr.[20]

It is unsafe to assume, however, that Welsh or any other authors were read with any seriousness. Many gentry were satisfied merely to act as subscribers, and bought books because they considered it the right thing to do. Although much maligned for their Anglicised outlook and desertion of the Welsh language, their patronage of printers and authors made it possible for the Welsh vernacular press to survive.

With few exceptions, the reading material of the landed gentry tended to be ephemeral and lightweight. One suspects that in many cases the impressive leatherbound tomes were largely for display and occasional reference. The *Gentleman's Magazine* was regarded as essential reading from the middle of the eighteenth century to the early 1800s. It provided a wide variety of information covering deaths, weddings, dowries, theatrical and book reviews, political comment and foreign 'intelligence', as well as useful hints on farming methods, such as ingenious devices for drilling post holes, catching moles and feeding poultry. From the archives of Clynfyw, Ffynone and Glaspant it is possible to know something of the 'light' reading that appealed to the gentry. The *English Chiswick and Whitehall Evening Post* amongst other London newspapers (although arriving many days late) kept the country squire informed about current affairs as well as items of news concerning those included in the bankruptcy lists, the ups and downs of the stock market, and useful advertisements like Dr Steer's 'Opodeldoc' for sprains and rheumatism.[21] Cardanus Rider's *British Merlin* contained weather forecasts, the dates of fairs, the weight of coins and other essential information for the squire farmer.[22] The squire, not trained in the law, needed a working knowledge of acts relating to stage coaches, buying horses, landlord and tenant rights, wills and revocations.[23] Intelligent discourse at the dinner table required knowledge of voyages and travellers which could be gleaned from books like *Cooke's Universal Geography*; and *The Encyclopeadia of Wit* had a few thousand *bon mots* and humorous anecdotes which the squire could memorise to amuse his guests.[24] Didactic reading was considered essential for the upbringing of the squire's family. The *Critical Review* in October 1812 dealt with topics like juvenile respect towards elders, traits of character in youth, as well as lighter hints on evening recreation, enigmas, posers and charades *pour passer le temps*. Young men were expected to know something of the lives of English monarchs and the Welsh princes, gobbets from Seneca and other classical authors, Chesterfield's advice to his son and other edifying material.[25]

The 'morality' and function of the penal colonies, arguments concerning the 'Civil List', public education and literary matters were gleaned from Tait's *Monthly Magazine*. Victorian ladies had their own journals and periodicals which had information on flower cultivation and other widely separated topics, such as the habits of frogs, the toilet of a Roman lady, and remedies for skin ailments. 'Our Library Table' reviewed new books, and Chambers' *Miscellany*, as the name suggests, comprised notes on handwork, anti-macassars, novelettes, adventures, moral histories and biography, and accounts of foreign countries and people—all aimed at educating as well as providing diversion and entertainment. Social taste and refinement, also, owed much to publications such as *The Ladies Mirror* or *Mental Companion* for guidelines on costume, indoor games like billiards and pyramids (snooker), flimsy tales about daring travellers and ferocious bears, new dances, and a host of fashionable 'nothings', relieved occasionally by intellectual works like James Thompson's *The Seasons* and Goethe's *Sorrows of Werther*.[26]

The common-place books of gentry ladies display the strong religious interest within some families. Thus, Crosby's *Christian Lady's Pocket Book* of 1810 had a wide ecumenical appeal, containing portraits of Anglican parsons and dissenting preachers, notes on civil and religious liberty and headings on private devotion. But any bias towards too much other-wordliness was counterbalanced by a very matter of fact attitude to daily affairs—the buying and selling of stock, British commercial and military successes—were all bundled *sub specie aeternitatis*. It was a benevolent Providence which was behind it all:

> Daughter of Commerce—Empress of the Main!
> Turn to thy God! For he hath girt thy breast
> With iron ramparts and thy loins with strength.[27]

The sacred and the sentimental, the pious and the profane, the banal and the sublime were all the ingredients of an amalgam of patriotism and incipient jingoism, religiosity and often, it has to be admitted, sincere conviction. It was part of the mental diet of the members of a ruling hierarchy, within a ruling nation, which asserted that Providence had ordered their position and status in life as well as the British empire of which they were privileged to be citizens. Even so, Mrs Howell of Glaspant recorded in her scrapbook what was to become the creed of many a Victorian squire, namely, that whereas 'Man proposes, God disposes':

> When our Redeemer on the earth did rest
> Humility he taught those he lov'd best
> So God the victory gave which raised our pride
> To check its force—he spoke,—and Nelson died![28]

The acquisition by the squire of a large library, as the hallmark of what a cultivated gentleman should possess, often meant that his patronage and support was sought by authors. The astonishing increase in the number of books printed from the Restoration to the early decades of the eighteenth century—many of them weighty works of theology and philosophy—brought in gentry patronage because of their strong moral obligation to ameliorate the social and religious woes of the nation.[29]

The considerable output of the printing presses at Trefhedyn and Carmarthen from 1718 onwards brought authorship and publication to the fore in the 'Tivyside' area, where there still remained a gentry circle conscious of their Welsh heritage notwithstanding increasing Anglicisation.

Theophilus Evans made considerable use of Lewes' library at Llwynderw, and the latter commended *Drych y Prif Oesoedd* especially '. . . i ddyrchafu gwybodaeth ac i hyfforddi dynion ynghylch y wir ffydd a'r grefydd Gristionogol'* (. . . to elevate knowledge and to instruct people concerning the true faith and the Christian religion).[30] Like William Lewes of Llwynderw, Captain John Lewis of Gernos gave financial backing to the writers of the area, such as Moses Williams for his *Cydymaith i'r Allor* (Companion to the Altar) in 1715. Alban Thomas was urged by Stephen Parry of Noyadd Trefawr, the county MP, and by Lloyd of Coedmore, the high sheriff, to prepare and publish *Dwys Rym Buchedd Grefyddol* (The Intense Power of a Godly Life) in 1722. Authors realised the important value of influential patrons against possible derogators, of whom there could be plenty. It was the name of a patron of rank which lent authority and respectability to a publication.[31] Some hold the view that the proportion of readers in the Teifi valley was higher

than in any other rural area in Wales.[32] Judging from William Lewes'
muscular idiom and rich vocabulary in his introduction to *Drych y Prif
Oesoedd*, one can fairly conclude that in the early decades of the
eighteenth century his gentry peers had at least a working knowledge
of the Welsh language. It would seem that the early 1700s represents
the high point (in modern times) of the Welsh cultural awareness of the
'Tivyside' gentry. With increasing anglicisation, metropolitan and
continental influences, a cultural gap and final breakdown between the
gentry and traditional Welsh life and letters was to take place from
now on.[33] The degree of patronage of works, published both in Welsh
and English, can be conveniently estimated thus:

Year	Author/Title	Total no. of subscribers	No. of Tivyside gentry
1724	Wm. Gambold— *Welsh Grammar . . . Intoduction to the Welsh Tongue*	130	7
1727	Ed. Lhuyd *Archaeologia Brittanica*	200	6
1730	*Cyfreithiau Hywel Dda . . . seu Leges Wallicae*	400	6
1748	Lewis Morris *Plans of Harbours, Bays and Roads*		5 Those who had estates and manorial rights along the coast.
1784	Ed. Jones—*Musical and Poetical Relicks of the Welsh Bards*	223	2
1790	Thos. Edwards (Twm a'r Nant)— *Gardd o Gerddi neu Gasgliad Caniadau*	650	—
1804	*Celtic Researches on the Origins, Traditions and Language of the Ancient Britons*	1500	3
1808	S. R. Meyrick: *History and Antiquities of County of Cardigan*	188	11
1811	R. Fenton: *A Historical Tour through Pembrokeshire*	301	14

Year	Author/Title	Total no. of subscribers	No. of Tivyside gentry	
1815	J. Walters: An English and Welsh Dictionary	615	16	
1817	R. Williams: *An Analysis of the Medicinal Waters of Llandrindod*	228	3	Two of whom were physicians
1824	D. Davis: *Telyn Dewi.* Castell Hywel	800	40	About half had been pupils under Davis
1824	T. J. Llewelyn Prichard: *Welsh Minstrelsy*	2500	24	
1832	W. Owain Pughe: *A Dictionary of the Welsh Language*	414	3	
1833	S. Lewis: *A Topographical Dictionary of Wales*	2,500	24	
1850/ 1860	*The Cambrian Journal*	135	1	
1986	W. Davies: *Hanes Plwyf Llandysul*	1,100+	10	
1899	D. E. Jones: *Hanes Plwyfi Llangeler a Phenboyr*	800	2	
1906	E. Davies: *Hanes Plwyf Llangunllo*	200	1	

From such evidence it is clear that gentry patronage had almost evaporated by the end of the nineteenth century. The *Cambrian Journal*, with its strong antiquarian flavour in addition to articles on history, geography, natural science, Welsh literature and the like, was subscribed to by distinguished Welshmen including members of parliament, the nobility, bishops and the judiciary, but by only one member of the Tivyside gentry. With the appearance of the parish histories at the end of the nineteenth century D. E. Jones' history of Llangeler and Penboyr was only supported by two landowners who had estates in the parish, namely Col. Lewes of Llysnewydd, to whom the book was dedicated, and Earl Cawdor. Only Mrs Tyler of Gernos subscribed to

Davies' history of Llangunllo. Such limited support at this time reflects, at best, only a patronising attitude to local authors, who were somewhat obsequious to the gentry of their native parishes and always included lavish pedigrees and family information. It betrays only a begrudging interest in a Welsh-language publication, long after the language itself had ceased to be of any use or meaning to the gentry as a class.[34]

The period of the literary activity of the 'Tivyside' gentry (from the late seventeenth to the early nineteenth centuries) falls naturally into two parts. From 1660 to 1730 the south-west counties of Wales had retained, not only their 'Welshness', but a strong literary tradition. Of middling or lesser gentry stock, Theophilus Evans is remembered as the author of the classic *Drych y Prif Oesoedd* (A Mirror of Early Times), a *molawd* (paean) of his people from earliest times. His friend, William Lewes of Llwynderw, was also deeply sensible of the richness of the Welsh literary heritage and translated *Maddeuant i'r Edifeirol* (Forgiveness to the Penitent) and *Dwy Daith i Gaersalem* (Two Journeys to Jerusalem) in collaboration with his father-in-law Evan Pryce of Rhydybenne. Erasmus Saunders and William Gambold, both of them friends of Edward Lhuyd, produced *A View of the State of Religion in the Diocese of St David's* and *A Welsh Dictionary and Grammar* in 1721 and 1727 respectively.[35] Alban Thomas was another prominent figure in the literary ferment of the area, a translator of theological works as well as author of ballads, elegies and diverse poetry in the free and strict meters, especially of *halsingod* (carols in a special metre), a popular medium for didactic and religious purposes. Thus, in one of his *halsingod*, he deplores the rifts and bickerings within the Church:

> *Ni ddylai fod gwân mewn eglwys bur lân*
> *Ond byw yn gytun fel rhannau corff dyn*
> *Aelod trwy glod a ddylem ni fod*
> *I'n gilydd heb falais na llid.*

(There should be no schism in a Church, holy and pure, but harmoniously living together, all should live as parts in one body; we should be praiseworthy members of one another, without malice or indignation).[36]

Following the death of Hector Morgan, the squire of Plas, Aberporth, in *c.*1700, Thomas composed a *cywydd marwnad* (elegy) to his memory and this continued an important function of Welsh poetry since medieval times.[37]

The popular *genre* of the *halsingod* appealed to Siôn Bowen, the squire of Glynllebyng (later Plas Troedyraur), and they were still remembered by country folk up to the 1860s. These simple jingles, drenched with Biblical references, were aimed at teaching a basic morality to an ill-educated and superstitious *gwerin*, and warned them of '*y pechod gwreiddiol*' (original sin): the dire consequences of the temptation and fall of Adam. The Rev. Benjamin Williams (Gwynionydd), recalled some of them:

> *Pam r'yn ni mor ffôl a chanlyn ar ôl,*
> *Lusiffer a'i lu i'r tywyll bwll du . . .*

(Why are we so foolish as to follow Lucifer and his throng to the dark black pit . . .?)

—and such jingles were recited in the home, and more especially at wakes, funerals, festivals, holy days and after Sunday services.

A significant feature of the literary activity of the mid-eighteenth century was the continuing patronage of bards by the lesser gentry of the period (who themselves were not gifted by the muse), as, for example, Dr Philipps, tutor at Blaenpant, Makeig of Llandygwydd, and Beynon of Rhydlogin near Cardigan.[38] In the second half of the eighteenth century, a significant contribution to the literary heritage of the area was made by the gentry family of Lloyd, connected with Llwynrhydowen and neighbouring unitarian 'causes' and descended from the ancient stock of Cadifor ap Dinawal.

David Lloyd of Brynllefrith, and his son Charles, were notable scholars, schoolmasters and preachers. The former's poetic output was considerable. It was varied in content, with the prominent themes of current natural theology, the divine order in creation and the like, coming out very strongly. He also struck a practical note on a very homely level in his admonitions to his children:

> *Fy annwyl blant caredig*
> *Rhowch glust i wrando'n ystig*
> *Ar gynghorion dwysion da*
> *Sydd gennyf yma i'w gynnyg.*

(My dear kind children, give ear to listen carefully to the sound and good counsels I have here to offer you.)

His hymns and poems are equally didactic and reflective, invoking godliness, disdain for worldly vanity and awe of impending doom. A translator of English hymns by Isaac Watts and others, he also wrote in Welsh traditional metres, exchanged verses with poets such as Ioan Siencyn—*y Bardd Bach* (The Little Poet)—and his kinsman Ifan Llwyd of Llanfechan. David Lloyd's son, Charles Lloyd, was a man of great ability—a regular contributor to *The Monthly Repository*—and his auto-biography, *Particulars of the Life of a Dissenting Minister* is a valuable source relating to the history of Arianism and Unitarianism in the Teifi valley, notwithstanding the crankish temperament, biting tongue and vitriolic pen of its author.[39]

The Anglican squire cleric, John Jenkins of Cilbronne (1770-1829), is chiefly remembered as a geneaologist, patron of bards and one of those who revived the Eisteddfod. As vicar of Kerry, Montgomery-shire, he kept open house to anyone who composed poetry, sang or played the harp. The doyen of the '*offeiriaid llengar*' (literary clerics), he made an abiding contribution to the preservation of Welsh culture and the Welsh language.[40]

In spite of the valiant efforts of these squires, their continued devotion to the Welsh language as a desirable medium to express serious history, theology, philosophy, politics, and moral questions as well as literature itself, the growing anglicisation of the gentry as a whole resulted in the increased use of English, rather than Welsh, for their literary compositions. Thomas Lloyd of Cwmgloyn, for example, although himself a strong patron of Welsh bards, chose to use English for his elegy to a young girl killed in a tavern brawl. Although the sentiment is strong and vigorous, his poetic skill is that of an unproved amateur:

> Peace to thy Manes unpolluted maid
> Whose cold remains now in the grave are laid
> In vain alas the pearly tears we shed
> Now that the Fates have cut thy short spun thread
> May wrath Divine its utmost vengeance shower
> On the vile wretch who cropt thy vital hour . . . etc.[41]

A similar 'flirtation with the Muse' is displayed by the Rev. John Lloyd of Alltyrodyn in his pastoral odes, replete with nostalgia for primeval innocence, the idyllic simplicity he derived from Theocritus and Virgil, and a typical Augustan reverence for nature. Amongst his other compos-itions may be mentioned the odes: 'On Cutting Down the Elder Tree in Jesus College Quadrangle', 'To A Spring in Wales', 'The Radnorshire Wells' and 'In Praise of Oxford'. He composed epigrams and satirical poems; one in particular concerned the baronetcy conferred in 1763 upon the notorious Sir Herbert Lloyd of Peterwell:

> Soon tidings came where Tivy flows,
> A tyrants harass'd land,
> That Lloyd to envied honours rose
> And kiss'd the Royal Hand.
> O had our Gracious Sovereign's touch
> But cur'd him of his evil,
> I'd own St. George ne'er boasted such
> A Triumph o'er the Devil.[42]

Some of the 'compositions' of these homely squire bards were only meant as sheer drollery to amuse convivial company at the expense of rival squires in other parts of the county. Evidently, Lloyd thought little of the fuddle-headed Sir Charles Cornwallis of Abermarlais. In another vein, he composed genteel stanzas in praise of Miss Jones of Llanina and Miss Evans of Highmead. Ordinary folk, too, were not beneath the squire's 'literary' attention, such as Sabbath Daniel of Brechfa who brewed very good ale:

> Of genteel Sabbath future times shall tell
> None ever brewed and bottled ale so well,
>
> Rouse each, Sir Toby Brechfa's genius hail
> Whom ale inspires, when all the Muses fail.[43]

On a more serious level, a few of the 'Tivyside' gentry, choosing to write in English, produced works of importance. Thus, Maurice Morgan (c.1725-1802), descended from the Morgans of Blaenbylan and Ffynone, wrote numerous pamphlets on current topics, but is chiefly remembered for his *Essay on the Dramatic Character of Sir John Falstaff*, 1777, a work of literary criticism remarkable for 'style, intellectuality, knowledge of human nature, and consequent profound appreciation of Shakepeare'.[44]

In the late nineteenth and early twentieth centuries, two, at least, of the 'Tivyside' squires could claim a place amongst the Anglo-Welsh school of writers. Charles Evans Davis Morgan-Richardson of Rhosygilwen published a nove,l *Henry Vaughan*, together with tracts on political and agricultural matters. His novel has been variously assessed—'a veracious account of the average life led by a Pembrokeshire squire, containing valuable descriptions of local customs, the fur, fin and feather fraternity; the social structure of mansion, farm and cottage; and the strict social divisions in a caste-ridden rural community'.[45] As a portrait of life in the Welsh countryside, it only narrowly avoids the flagrant errors of the Anglo-Welsh view of Wales—the traditional caricature of Welshmen as strange, superstitious beings with primitive customs, against a backcloth of 'Gothick' ruins haunted by ghosts, phantoms and druids, and speaking a bogus non-language cooked up by the English tourist and satirist.[46]

H. M. Vaughan of Plas Llangoedmore, remembered mainly for his *South Wales Squires*, wrote extensively on historical subjects, including 'The Last of the Royal Stuarts', 'The Last Stuart Queen', 'The Medici Popes', as well as 'The Church in Wales from the Reformation to the Present Day', 1908. His reminiscences of the gentry contribute a little to our knowledge of their social life and pursuits. Vaughan's analysis of the land, church and disestablishment questions, however, is that of a Tory and Anglican. His attitude to the Welsh language shows the condescension and patronising attitude of the ruling classes to their native language which they had long abandoned. It was only natural that his views, as we have seen, were unfavourably and even scathingly received by radical and nationalist alike. Vaughan's excursions into the annals of the debacle of the Stuart Cause are, however, marked by sympathy, skill and an honest investigation of sources.[47] A man of wide and cultivated taste, whose resources had enabled him to travel extensively, he recorded his experiences in *The Naples Riviera, Florence and her Treasures* and *An Australasian Wander Year*, published in 1914. Not so successful, perhaps, as a writer of fiction, his 'novels'—*The Dial of Ahaz* and *Nephelo Coccygia or Letters from Paradise*, were only moderately received as 'fresh and unconventional, and out of the run of the commonplace'.[48]

Vaughan's outlook lacked sympathy with the religious, political and cultural aspirations of Welshmen. The Welsh language, with which he only had a nodding acquaintance, he perceived as a peasant's language only befitting farmyard and byre. Above all, he failed to understand the basic principle that his social inferiors had a moral and indisputable right to present their case, and to endeavour to bring their democratic aspirations to fruition as radical, nonconformist Welshmen.

The onset of radical influences, and the consequent challenge to the *status quo*, prompted some of the gentry to take up writing what may be termed 'apologetic literature'. The useful and informative *Memoir of W. H. Webley Parry Esq., Rear Admiral of the White . . . of Noyadd Trefawr, Cardiganshire*, published in 1847, not only gives a biographical account of his distinguished career, but also makes him out as a model and generous landlord who revitalised an impoverished estate. The memoir is strongly propagandist in praising the squire as generous and liberal, and as one who was regarded with affection by his neighbours, tenantry and 'dependants'. The patrician qualities of the squire have their counterparts in the hard-working, honest, religious and deferential retainer, each representing two social classes co-existing in a state of mutual dependence. Thus in 1849, Miss Webley-Parry of Noyadd Trefawr wrote her pseudo-fictional memoir of David Lloyd of Hafod Fach, which traced the life-story of a man from very humble origins who became a trusted and respected retainer of Noyadd Trefawr. Translated into Welsh for consumption by a deferential *gwerin*, it attempted to extol, a noble work-ethic, based on a Bible-reading morality and enduring submissiveness to the ruling classes.[49]

As the 'Liberationists' and other anti-church groups were advancing like a phalanx against the established church, with cries of disestablishment and disendowment, Miss Webley-Parry also wrote *An Epitome of Anglican Church History*. Although based on not too reliable sources it contained a favourable introductory 'imprimatur' by Bishop Browne of Winchester. It was an attempt to buttress the Anglican position, to demonstrate the unbroken continuity of the church from early times, and to prove the errors of the Papacy—a 'manifesto' against all who dared challenge the church of England.[50]

Very often the curious and the arcane appealed to the gentry. Thus Miss Howell of Glaspant in 1898 published a pamphlet, *Disclosure through Palmistry*, and this is not surprising as fortune-telling was a popular way of idling away the time in country mansions.[51] Family pride and respect for ancestors led Deaconess Hope to compile a short but useful history of *Llangranog and the Pigeonsford Family*.[52] Lady Lloyd of Bronwydd indulged in excessive and sad nostalgia for the Lords Marcher of Kemes, when she wrote a so-called history of the Lloyds of Bronwydd and their 'forebears' Owen and Fitzmartin.[53]

Emily Prichard published in 1904 a book entitled *Cardigan Priory in the Olden Days*, which raised a hornets' nest of unfavourable reviews. Sir John Lynn Thomas (albeit with his distinguished military and medical career behind him) took up archaeology as a hobby and produced a bizarre and eccentric study of the lower Teifi valley entitled 'Key of All Wales'.[54] In the 1880s and '90s a few squires were wiser and indulged their 'literary' craving in harmless ways and about matters which they knew about—like Augustus Brigstocke's stories new and old, or 'Rouge

Noir' who contributed racy accounts of fox hunting and hare coursing. It is said that Fitzwilliams of Cilgwyn, under the *nom-de-plume* of 'TSH' and 'Sixty-Four', was another who wrote for the local press, for the 'benefit of our boys scattered throughout the world, and who duly read with interest all news from the old home of the sport [sc. fox hunting] they love so well'.

The cultural world of Theophilus Evans and William Lewes, Llwynderw, had, by the end of the nineteenth century, disappeared with the mists of antiquity. Not only were their names forgotten by the 'Tivyside' gentry; one questions whether the latter ever knew of the cultural rock whence they were hewn. Antiquarianism, brought together Theophilus Evans and William Lewes of Llwynderw in the early 1700s, and continued to interest David Lloyd of Alltyrodyn at the end of the eighteenth century. These squires had a vision of a remote past, romantic and utopian, which led to the collection of pedigree rolls and the accumulation of manuscripts, books, curios and artefacts as the prized possessions of a squire of ancient lineage. The Brigstocke library at Blaenpant contained editions of Camden, and the Bronwydd library held the works of George Owen of Henllys, such as his *Description of Pembrokeshire, The Taylor's Cussion* and *Baronya de Kemeys.*

The correspondence of some gentry, a vital means of communication in the eighteenth century, was a form of polite literature and an important medium of culture for those intellectually inclined. Through Lewis Morris, whose official duties brought him into contact with the Cardiganshire gentry, some of them were drawn into the peripheral activities of the Welsh Augustans. Dr Philipps of Blaenpant corresponded with the Rev. Evan Evans (Ieuan Fardd), Edward Richard and the Morris brothers, and visited his brother-in-law at Nanteos to discuss ancient manuscripts and kindred matters. Evans stayed at Blaenpant, and was regarded as *'Lingua Cambro Brittanicae facile princeps'* on Welsh etymology. Philipps, for his part, in June 1760 communicated with Edward Richard concerning Saxon grants in Latin Gospel manuscripts presented by Athelstan to Canterbury, and pursued a lengthy correspondence with English antiquaries.[55]

The London cultural and learned societies, founded in the eighteenth century, attracted many gentry because of their social and national appeal, and amongst the early members of the Society of Cymmrodorion, founded in 1751, were very influential Welsh gentry such as Sir Watkin Williams Wynn, Sir John Philipps of Picton Castle and Lewis Pryse of Gogerddan.[56] A few gentry from the Teifi valley were Fellows of the Royal Society and of the Society of Antiquaries, for example, Owen Brigstocke of Blaenpant in 1720, and John Lloyd Williams of Gwernant in the early 1800s. Through these prestige societies, many a backwoods squire came into contact with learned gentry from Wales, such as Banks Hodgkinson of Edwinsford, Sir William Jones, John Campbell of Stackpole Court, Thomas Pennant and Richard Payne Knight. In addition, membership of these societies led to acquaintance with national figures like Horace Walpole and Sir Joshua Reynolds; architects like Salvin, Gwilt the translator of Vitruvius, and topographical writers such as Malkin, Warner and Carlisle.[57]

The cultural repercussions of the London societies and the anti-quarian movement influenced 'Tivyside' squires in other ways too. Walter Lloyd of Coedmore, High Sheriff in 1761, was commended as a '*siryf o ddyn gonest*' (a sheriff and an honest man) for his intervention, when some 'old poetry' was discovered in Cardigan Priory resulting in excited exchanges between Vaughan of Crosswood, the 'doctor of Cryngae' and other gentry. In addition to the preservation of old manuscripts, the conservation of ancient relics was part of the antiquarian 'mystique' of many gentry, and Lewes of Gellydywyll saved the 'Curcagni' stone from the sort of vandalism often perpetrated by boorish rustics when he 'rescued' it to adorn the grounds of Gellydywyll.[58] Fenton, in a letter to Thomas Lloyd of Bronwydd, bemoaned the losses over the centuries of '. . . ancient edifices, church monuments and inscriptions, genealogy . . .' and proposed to survey and record the 'beautiful and interesting country in your vicinity'. Likewise, the Rev. John Jenkins (Ifor Ceri), visited family houses like Llysnewydd to consult and transcribe pedigrees and old manuscripts. Perhaps the greatest contribution of the gentry to Welsh antiquarian studies was their support of the Cambrian Society, founded in 1818, to compile a catalogue of Welsh manuscripts in Britain and on the continent,[59] to transcribe them under the supervision of Edward Williams (Iolo Morganwg), and to print ancient historical documents in the Welsh language.[60] In this project, William Lewes of Llysnewydd, Dr Davies of Pentre and William Philipps of Penralltrheiny were prominent. The revived Eisteddfod in the early 1800s, with its strong antiquarian and druidic dimension, owed much to gentry patronage and participation like that of the Rev. John Jenkins (Ifor Ceri). The Cambrian Archaeological Association was founded through the zeal and impetus of literary clerics and landed gentry, while, on a local level, societies such as the Loyal Lodge of Ancient Druids at Cardigan, were likewise partly aimed at fostering antiquarian interests.[61]

Gentry interest in antiquarian matters was on the wane during the nineteenth century. As a class the gentry were satisfied to pay lip service to Welsh cultural and historical traditions. As part of their 'status' obligation to national and local causes, they lent their patronage and made cash subscriptions where it was deemed proper to do so.[62] Family pride and prestige was, however, to be quantified in a national or British sense. The pursuit of pedigree and genealogy continued, with a view to publication in the volumes of Burke, Walford and Kelly. Here was the hallmark of status and acceptance in an English-speaking world. Pride in native Welshness was shown through gifts by families (such as the Lloyds of Bronwydd) to the Carmarthenshire and other antiquarian societies and by defraying the cost of repairing such things as 'the beautiful wheel window in the banqueting hall of the bishop's palace at St David's'.[63] But, antiquarianism was no longer pursued as the vital key to a rich cultural and national heritage. Like the Welsh language, it only had its quaint and curious, fanciful and esoteric appeal. Moreover, antiquarian interest was limited to mural tablet, stained glass and heraldic achievement, with pious aphorisms in dog Latin or archaic Welsh like '*Asgre lân diogel ei pherchen*' (Safe is the owner of a clean conscience). and '*Da yw ffon amddiffyniad*' (Good is the staff of defence)—the latter being the motto of the Jenkins clan of Cilbronne.[64]

NOTES ANS SOURCES

[1]H. Owen: *Additional Morris Letters*, 1947, ii, p. 531, Letter to Edward Richard 25/4/1761.
[2]*DWB*.
[3]NLW/Cilgwyn/LB/41/14 Aug. 1861.
[4]E. Rees: 'An Introductory Survey of Eighteenth Century Welsh Libraries', *JWBS*, X, 1966-71, pp. 198-221.
[5]G. H. Hughes: *Bywyd a Gwaith Iaco ap Dewi, 1648-1722*, 1953, p. 59; *Myvyrian Archaiology*, 1, 1801, p. ix quoted in F. Jones: 'Genealogy'; *DWB*.
[6]J. H. Davies: *op cit.*, ii, p. 282.
[7]P. Jenkins: *op cit.*, p. 230.
[8]G. H. Jenkins: 'Bywiogrwydd Crefyddol', *Ceredigion*, VIII, 1979, pp. 439-77; *DWB*.
[9]P. Jenkins: *op cit.*, p. 230, note p. 328.
[10]NLW/Morgan Richardson/2364, 2374.
[11]NLW/Llwyngwair/14278; NLW/Owen Colby/623; HRO/D.Pen/1/146.
[12]D. S. Jones: 'Dyffryn Teifi', *Y Geninen*, Ion. 1901, p. 97.
[13]H. Owen: *op cit.*, pp. 794-807; for Lewis Morris, see *DWB*.
[14]F. Jones: *op cit.*
[15]T. Rees: *op cit.*, p. 499; J. Davies: 'The Alltyrodyn Manuscripts', *JWBS*, July 1938.
[16]NLW/Ms/14990 F.
[17]NLW/Morgan Richardson/2364.
[18]*loc cit.*
[19]*loc cit.*
[20]*DWB*; T. Parry: *Hanes Llenyddiaeth Gymraeg hyd 1900*, 1944, pp. 216, 240.
[21]NLW/Owen Colby/229.
[22]*ibid*: 1094.
[23]*The Country Gentleman's Lawyer and Farmers Complete Law Library*, London, 1810.
[24]*Cm Jnl*: 14/3/1812.
[25]NLW/Clynfyw/Box 15.
[26]NLW/Owen Colby/1088.
[27]NLW/Falcondale/Group vii, 162; L. Colley: *op cit.*, pp. 18-25.
[28]NLW/Howell Glaspant/Common Place Book; pious maxims in English, Welsh, French and Latin were carved on the walls inside Bronwydd.
[29]G. H. Jenkins: *Literature, Religion and Society in Wales*, 1978, p. 58.
[30]Theophilus Evans: *Drych y Prif Oesoedd*, 1853 (ed), p. xx; *DWB*.
[31]G. H. Jenkins: *op cit.*, pp. 465-67; *DWB*.
[32]*loc cit.*
[33]G. Bowen: *Traddodiad Llenyddol Deau Ceredigion 1600-1850* (unpublished MA thesis, Wales, 1943), p. 183.
[34]See lists of subscribers to these publications.
[35]G. H. Jenkins: *op cit.*, p. 198.
[36]NLW/Add Ms 6900 A.
[37]G. Bowen: *op cit.*, pp. 85-6.
[38]G. H. Jenkins: *op cit.*, pp. 158-59; *DWB*; NLW/Llanstephan/146, quoted in G. Bowen: *op cit.*, p. 98; *Blodau Dyfed*, 1824, pp. 285-86.
[39]G. E. Evans: *op cit.*, p. 69; *Gwaith Prydyddawl y diweddar Barch. Dafydd Llwyd . . . 1785*; *ibid*: pp. 72-74; *DWB*.
[40]R. T. Jenkins: *op cit.*, pp. 113-116.
[41]NLW/Ms 19B, p. 47.
[42]*loc cit*; for a study of Sir Herbert Lloyd, see B. Phillips: *Peterwell: the History of a Mansion and its Infamous Squire*, 1983.
[43]NLW/Ms 7362B.

[44]F. Jones: *Blaen-bylan* . . . p. 327; *DNB; DWB.*

[45]D. L. Baker-Jones: 'C.E.D. Morgan-Richardson', *Ceredigion*, viii, 2, 1977, pp. 168-71.

[46]For a *critique* of Anglo-Welsh writing see D. Tecwyn Lloyd: 'Cymru yn Saesneg', *THSC*, 1966, ii, pp. 257-80.

[47]*Manchester Guardian*: 18/5/1926; *Church Times*: 6/12/1906; *The Welshman*: 29/11/1906; H. M. Vaughan: *The Church in Wales from the Reformation to the Present Day*, 1908.

[48]CRO/CAS/ix. 1917-18.

[49]*Memoir of David Lloyd of Hafod Fach, Cardiganshire* by EWP, 1849.

[50]E. Webley-Parry: 'An Epitome of Anglican Church History [nd]'; *Yr Haul*, Ionawr 1880, pp. 35-6.

[51]Morgan-Richardson Diary 1906-07, in private hands.

[52]Deaconess Evelyn Hope: *Llangranog and the Pigeonsford Family*, 1931.

[53]Lady K. Lloyd: *The Lords Marcher of Kemes*, 1930.

[54]*Arch Camb.*, 1905, pp. 322-238. *Cd Ad*: 12/3/1897; *The Welshman*: 1/1/1885; NLW/Cilgwyn Ms vol/LB/52/13 Jan 1906.

[55]*DWB*; H. Owen: *op cit.*, i, p. 391 and ii, p. 463; J. H.Davies, *op cit.*, ii, p. 192; *DWB*.

[56]H. Owen: *op cit.*, ii, p. 767; *List of Fellows of the Society of Antiquaries 1717-1796*, London, 1798; NLW/Ms 5152 B.

[57]Society of Antiquaries Library—A. W. Gould: A History of the Society of Antiquaries (unpublished Ms vol 678).

[58]H. Owen: *op cit.*, ii, p. 767; Inventory of Ancient Monuments, Wales and Monmouthshire, V. County of Carmarthen, 1917, p. 13.

[59]NLW/Bronwydd/3937, 7172.

[60]*DWB; Gent Mag*, Jan. 1891, pp. 3-4.

[61]*Cm Jnl*: 4/6/1841; 26/8/1859.

[62]P. Jenkins: *op cit.*, pp. 237-38.

[63]*Trans Carms Antiq Socy*: 1921-23, pp. 23-28; Pembs. Association for the Preservation of Ancient Monuments. *Report*, 1907.

[64]Heraldic window in Cilbronne.

Leisure

Britain's rulers indulged with passionate intensity in field sports. The gentry possessed an amazing versatility in sport, and the hunting field played a big part in their upbringing. The archetypal squire was the 'good natured fox hunter who spends his days on horseback and his evenings eating and drinking'.[1] Macaulay's type-casting of the squires with '. . . a gun on shoulder, a leash of dogs at their heel, and three or four scoundrels for their bosom friends',[2] gave a picturesque gloss to what was a feature of a very cruel age. The most obvious, but least recognised, feature of English life in the eighteenth and early nineteenth centuries was its love of aggression and violent passion. The amusements of all classes were streaked with blood and cruelty— cock fighting, bear baiting, bull baiting, being present to witness executions and the like. The image of the Georgian world with its fine mansions, elegance and taste is far removed from reality.[3] As part of the culture and ethos of the landed society, the 'county' community as well as of 'county' politics, fox hunting encouraged 'vitality, cohesion and stability' between the gentry and the community. It was an expression of an outlook possessed by country landowners which was anti-urban.[4] Fox hunting generated a mythology and mystique which characterised the ruling class.

Keeping hounds and horses was part of the squire's 'display' and added to his social prestige. As a 'central social institution' it helped to keep the 'peace of the country'; it was basic to a vision of a settled society and kept the landed gentry *in situ*.[5] Moreover, it was an unchallengeable English institution at the very time—the late 1870s and '80s—when the old alliances and 'harmony' between the interests of landlord and tenant were strained.[6]

The 'Tivyside' gentry cultivated a strong fox hunting tradition. In the mid-eighteenth century Dr Llwyd of Cryngae kept a famous pack of hounds, and its prowess was extolled in Nathaniel Jenkins' lengthy ballad about the exploits of Dido, Ringwood and Nimrod. Even the dogs had a noble pedigree (like their master) which could be traced back to those of the hounds of princes like Rhys ap Tewdwr. The daring and liberality of Dr Llwyd and his friends of Gernos and Llwyncadfor became part of the folk mythology of the area.[7] The 'Tivyside' hunt (dating from the early 1700s) had amongst its supporters Lewes of Llysnewydd, Lewes-Lloyd of Dolhaidd and Howell of Glaspant. Each new member had to 'quaff the contents of a chased silver cup in the form of a fox head' to toast future success.[8] An aura of chivalry and valour, formerly experienced in battle, was transferred from the battlefield to the hunt meet. When the 'Tivyside' hunt was revived in 1825, Lewes of Llysnewydd was described as a Chevalier Bayard '*sans peure et sans reproché*—in terms of prowess and gallantry, a man of epic reputation.[9] The mastership of the Tivyside hunt was held in turn by squires such as Jones of Penylan, Colonel Howell of Blaendyffryn, George Bowen of Stradmore and Sir Marteine Lloyd. Gallantry and chivalry were attributed to these squires in deferential terms. The *Cardigan and Tivyside Advertiser* described how after a lengthy chase, the escaping fox is pursued no further—'the magnanimous squire's sense of sporting justice decrees that the animal's life shall be spared for that day'!'[10] The sympathetic participation by an impoverished *gwerin* was one means whereby their dull and hard lives were occasionally lightened by the spectacle of the hunt.[11]

Not all gentry regarded fox hunting with enthusiasm. In the 1860s E. Crompton Ll. Fitzwilliams of Cilgwyn was concerned with the wasteful expense of maintaining hunting and hounds, observing that '. . . many men are fond of fox hunting and spare no risk or expense to indulge it. I have no taste that way'.[12] When, years later, his son devoted too much time and money on '. . . this horrid trade of fox hunting', he observed: '. . . curse all fox hunting say I. Foxes should be shot down or poisoned'.[13] What mattered was the expense of maintaining horses and hounds, which could be a very heavy burden on an estate, especially during periods of economic depression.[14]

Fox and otter hunting (the latter taking place in the summer months), and the social round attached to these pursuits, were important events in the calendar of country-house activities, with large house parties and an opportunity to meet squires and squiresses from other areas. Rarely, members of the nobility might be amongst the guests, such as the Duchess of Hamilton, who visited Llwyngwair in 1894.[15] Closely connected with the excitement of fox hunting in the field, were the hunt ball and hunt dinner, attended by the gentry in the assembly rooms of Cardigan, Carmarthen and Haverfordwest. According to a member of the Highmead family in 1843, some west Wales towns were regarded as '. . . the most miserable holes on earth, and the society far worse than none'.[16] Social functions were held not only to provide recreation for the gentry, but also in order to support and sustain the various hunts through subscription, as, very often private means were not available. The amount of monetary support towards these events ranged from a few shillings to about half a guinea, and such events were widely advertised as 'fashionable, gay and numerous'. The presence of distinguished county figures in the early 1800s, such as Colonel Powell of Nanteos and Sir Pryse Pryse of Gogerddan (the respective MPs for the county and boroughs of Cardigan),[17] at these functions had a double purpose of supporting what they regarded as a 'suitable cause' and of fostering their patronage and preserving their political 'interest'. It was indeed important for gentry who wanted to be prominent in public life to subscribe liberally. Significantly, Philipps of Picton's niggardly donation of a very small sum of money in 1880 was received very coldly by his fellow gentry.[18] One important aspect of fox hunting and horse racing was the participation of all sections of the community. Prosperous farmers and middle-class professional people gave financial support. Major events in the sporting calendar depended for their success on the attendance of plebeian spectators drawn from the small close-knit rural community, who, thereby, developed their basic sense of social identity. Moreover, these gatherings provided a safety valve for hostile feelings and tensions within the community, and served to foster group unity and social cohesiveness.[19]

A special gentry pastime was shooting and the pursuit of game. In the eighteenth century, 'driving' the birds had not come in; pheasants and partridges would be flushed out from hedgerows and stubble by faithful spaniels and setters. The reason that hares were coursed or shot along with rabbits was that they were considered as being injurious to crops, not to mention their obvious value as food. By the end of the nineteenth century, society had discovered a new diversion in the 'shooting party'. Railways made it possible to get to country houses more speedily, and what members of the royal family did, provided the social impetus.[20] H. M. Vaughan regarded the practice as unsporting, and thought little of the monied *parvenus* who took over Welsh estates with that end in mind.[21] From the few game books which have survived it appears that such activities in 'Tivyside' were on a very limited scale. While many landowners employed regular game-keepers, those at Bronwydd, Ffynone, Highmead and Llysnewydd, for example were employed mainly to safeguard the squire's sole right to game, a right reinforced by harsh laws which were the cause of grave social unrest. From one or two surviving game books it is clear that pheasants and partridges, hares, wild duck, snipe and woodcock were the usual birds shot. At Highmead in the years 1825-1836, the surplus from a typical 'bag' was sold, and part of the proceeds used to pay for gunpowder, 'shoes', and other incidental expenses, as well as the cost of the necessary task of shooting rooks. The evidence suggests that there was no 'game farming' on a large scale.[22] Likewise, on the small Glaspant estate, later in the century, the picture seems to be the same.[23] However, some squires such as William Lewes of Llysnewydd up to 1952, who employed a gamekeeper, bred pheasants and held the annual *battue,* albeit on a small scale.[24]

Fishing was also a popular pastime for the gentry, privileged as they were with good trout and salmon streams flowing through their estates. They held on tenaciously to their right to fish and woe betide anyone who was caught fishing on their property. The matter of fishing rights was one reason for social conflict, as will be seen later.

The more 'civilised' pursuits of cricket, tennis and croquet caught on in south-west Wales, as in the rest of the country. Cricket had developed gradually from medieval times, and by the mid-eighteenth century noblemen and gentry played with local yeomen and artisans whose womenfolk and children came to see the fun. As in the case of fox hunting, tension and social division were for the time being forgotten. About 1783 the game was taken up in west Carmarthenshire by the Philipps family of Cwmgwili, near Carmarthen.[25] By the early 1800s it was established in 'Tivyside' and, according to Jenkins of Cilbronne, was played on Cardigan Common in 1830.[26] The Cardigan Cricket Club played against the military stationed in the locality in 1846. Amongst the cricket devotees of the area were Thomas Howell of Glaspant, David Arthur Saunders Davies of Pentre and William Price Lewes of Llysnewydd, each of whom played with the Carmarthenshire Club, whose president was Lord Cawdor. Cricket teams were formed at 'Tivyside' houses, such as Pentre and Noyadd Trefawr, and such country-house teams, comprising members of the family and their friends, survived until the end of the century.

Croquet was a polite, and not too strenuous, outdoor activity during the fine summer months. It could be enjoyed by ladies, and there are diary references to the popularity of the game in the 1860s at Gilfachwen and Rhosygilwen, and a Miss Gower of Castle Malgwyn, won an all-England championship in 1899.[27]

After the first lawn tennis championship was played at Wimbledon in 1877, the game seems to have become popular throughout the country. Local clubs, such as the Tivyside Lawn Tennis Club, were formed as one more gentry leisure activity, and in 1883 the winners at a tournament of the Cardigan Club were members of the Llwyngwair and Pentre families.[28] Unlike the rough country pursuits, where the presence of the general populace was essential to stir up the excitement and thrill of the proceedings, the gentry played tennis, croquet and cricket with members of their own social circle. The 'Tivyside' gentry did not wish to welcome into their circle professional and well-to-do middle-class newcomers who had taken up residence in the mansions of the locality. Thus, the Prichards (a medical family from London), who had acquired Cardigan Priory had (according to local gentry standards of good manners) dared to propose themselves as members of the local tennis club and as a result '. . . so many people threatened to black ball them, that they were warned to withdraw their names'.[29]

As an expression of the craze for the 'antique', many gentry held the *fête champetre* as an open air equivalent to the *bal masqué* held within the mansion. The function was an assembly of the 'quality', in fancy dress of a 'pastoral appearance and simplicity', in a setting camouflaged with branches of trees, flowers and greenery. Some aimed at targets with bows and arrows, others kicked and danced around a *tambour de masque*, while others paraded in the guise of 'cupids', 'druids' and 'country swains'. According to tradition, a *fête champetre* was held at Bronwydd in 1780 when Sir William Jones composed complimentary verses to the 'noble houses' and 'fair damsels' of the Teifi valley.[30] Regarded as a 'most splendid entertainment' the *fête champetre* was a spectacle much in vogue in the great houses of the nobility; and through the influence of fashionable stunts, like the ill-fated Eglinton tournament in 1839, became modified as part of the *battue*, and of shooting parties when hot lunches, champagne and choice 'viands' were served by liveried attendants.[31]

While cruel sports like cock fighting, bull and bear baiting had gradually given way to more sophisticated pastimes, rustic and clownish capers continued to be indulged in. The influence of Methodism in the eighteenth century, and a stricter religious attitude later in Victorian times meant that a few squires, like Bowen of Llwyngwair, gave up the coarse sport of cock fighting after their religious conversion. But 'aquatic excursions' and 'rural diversions' provided entertainment for the gentry as well as for ordinary folk; for example, in the summer of 1813 Thomas and James Lloyd of Bronwydd organised a function on Penbryn beach, which was repeated on 'Cwmhyar Downs', Llandysul in 1814. The *pièce de résistance*, amongst other forms of tomfoolery, was catching 'the sticky pig', i.e. a pig whose tail had been 'previously close shaven and soaped'.[32] Some believe that, during the first half of the eighteenth century, many of the gentry were not 'disengaged entirely from the culture of the common people', occupying a half way position between the robust, unpolished lifestyle of the booby-squire in the country and the cosmopolitan, sophisticated culture of London.[33] It appears, however, that old attitudes survived until much later in 'Tivyside'. It was inevitable that a strong element of cruelty attended such practices, and that, in spite of their ostensibly gracious lifestyle, some gentry, no doubt, had only a veneer of culture. In 1842, Collingwood Hall, brother of Edward Crompton Lloyd Hall (later Fitzwilliams), was well aware of this and introduced 'old English sports' of a less coarse nature for his birthday celebrations—donkey races, pushing barrows blindfolded, and the like.[34] While the commonalty were expected to participate in such frivolity, the gentry themselves took part in sophisticated and more skilful pursuits, such as 'archery' in the privacy of their own demesne, as, for example, at Ffynone in 1851 when the 'Tivyside Archery Society' started its season with 'eclat', and 'with all the beauty and fashion' present. Likewise, in the 1880s and '90s hockey and polo were played by Col. Newland of Llanfair, Brigstocke of Blaenpant, and Lewes of Llysnewydd. The 'Tivyside Polo Club' met on Fitzwilliams' land at Newcastle Emlyn.[35]

The benefits of taking the waters and of sea bathing became a salubrious and pleasurable pastime of the gentry. Bath, in the eighteenth century, and Cheltenham in the early nineteenth, drew many of the south-west Wales gentry, where they had permanent residences and where some ended their days. Members of the Llwyngwair family in the early 1800s visited Llandrindod and Llanwrtyd Wells, as well as the spa in Harrogate. The contemplation of the sea and coastal scenery, and the benefits of sea bathing indulged in by royalty such as George III, brought about a new fashion. It was taken up by the gentry, and ladies like the Misses Bowen of Llwyngwair kept a 'machine for bathing' on Newport beach in 1834.[36]

In the 1890s, the bicycle became fashionable, just as soon as the two low wheels superseded the dangerous 'penny farthing'. The new facility added variety to outdoor activities. Women felt emancipated by being allowed to scour the countryside and to see for themselves what life was like outside the high wall of their park. Cycle 'meets' became additional attractions after the hunt week. For example, in the spring of 1896 such a 'meet' was held on Llechryd bridge. The participants then proceeded to Gellydywyll where 'refreshments and social diversion' awaited them. In the following year the cycle club comprised about 50 members made up of gentry, doctors, lawyers and clergy.[37]

With the advent of the motor car a new era was about to begin. Charles Home Lloyd Fitzwilliams of Cilgwyn regarded the motor car as something of purely functional and utilitarian advantage. He only wanted a reliable model, cheap to run and easy to maintain, in order to facilitate estate and official business.[38] Others, like the Morgan-Richardsons of Rhosygilwen, regarded the motor car more as a source of pleasure, to enable them to visit ancient ruins and enjoy seaside picnics, as well as providing a quicker link between widely scattered country houses. Although, in its early days, the motor car was owned only by a few who could afford such a status symbol, it was to bring about the intrusion of urban life into the countryside and to herald a tremendous revolution in days to come. It was to be one of the forces of change which would affect the gentry in no small measure.

Family diaries and papers suggest that time weighed very heavily on the lives of some gentry, especially on the females who had no public and official duties to carry out and did not, but rarely, have to administer an estate. An 'educated' lady would have mastered the 'social refine-ments' of deportment, dancing, singing and playing a musical instrument.[39] Gentlemen also participated in the polite pastimes of the drawing room, mixing with the ladies, and providing diversion and amusement as part of the social etiquette expected of them.

The enjoyment of music, as an important part of polite leisure activity, and the playing of musical instruments were a feature of every genteel drawing room. At Gellydywyll in 1775, for instance, there was a fiddle, guitar, harp and harpsichord. References to the traditional Welsh instrument, the harp, however, are few. Nevertheless, in the years 1827 to 1832, the household at Highmead had their own harper, one Benjamin Jones of the famous family of harpers related to Edward Jones (Wood), harper of Bala.[40] At Tŷ Llwyd, the harp was in use from the early 1800s to the end of the century, and Jenkins of Cilbronne provided a 'harper' for his ship: 'He will be a great acquisition to us, particularly as several young ladies are going out on the ship . . . and it is a National Music that I should be proud to have . . .'[41] That the pianoforte was displacing the harp and harpsichord from the mid-eighteenth century onwards is suggested by the sale of the Trewern harpsichord to St David's Cathedral in the 1790s, and in the 1830s two harpsichords were sold from Bronwydd. Advertisements for the new 'grand forte piano' by makers like Broadwood, Stodhart and others, as well as sheet music—sold by agents such as Richards of Carmarthen—point to more fashionable trends in music.[42]

While it is possible to imagine drollery and salacious behaviour in some gentry circles, one can trace a strong Methodistical and reformist tone in the 'religious' houses of Bronwydd and Llwyngwair. Theological and literary discussions were interspersed with the 'diversion' of listening to edifying music. According to Bishop Burgess, sacred music was the favourite relaxation at many houses like Hafod, Llanayron and Bronwydd; and Mrs Lloyd of Bronwydd '. . . was able, with the assistance of some members of her own family, to gratify the Bishop's taste for it by the united powers of organ and voice'. In many of the grand houses of England and Wales pipe organs had been fashionable for centuries. Later, in the nineteenth century, fine pipe organs were installed at Derry Ormond, Highmead and Gwernant, and at Rhosygilwen the family enjoyed listening to the 'Angelus'—a trade name for a type of harmonium.[43] But the principal music making of the Victorian country house was centred around the grand piano. The repertoire varied from songs apostrophising the Royal Navy and invoking courage and loyalty in defence of our shores, to stock Victorian ballads ranging from the mock heroic—'Rest, Warrior, Rest', 'The Little Hero', 'Staunch and True'—to the pseudo-religious like 'The Lost Chord' or 'The Star of Bethlehem'. Towards the end of the century and the early 1900s devices to provide ready-made music were available; the tinkling bells of the musical box and gramophone records were frequently listened to in houses like Pentre and Rhosygilwen.[44]

The musical interests and talent of the gentry were not confined to leisure activities in their own homes. Deserving public causes drew their patronage and participation as vocalists and instrumentalists. Thus, programmes of 'popular' readings and music for the edification of the lower orders and their instruction in abstinence, sobriety and hard work were held in places like Cenarth in 1866.[45] Distress, caused by the death of workers during the construction of the railways, prompted Mrs Saunders Davies of Pentre to take part as soloist in concerts in aid of widows and orphans. A public-spirited patron of music like C. H. Ll. Fitzwilliams brought in London artistes like the tenor singer Hirwen Jones and the young Henry Wood to give recitals for the benefit of local distress.[46]

Taste for music led the gentry to support causes near their own hearts. Thomas Davies Lloyd of Bronwydd, amongst others, took part in a concert held at Cardigan to raise funds to rebuild Llangunllo church in 1870—when the star attraction was Herr Hauptmann, the distinguished violinist.[47] Because the gentry themselves valued musical and literary culture, there was a conscious attempt on their part to bring these values into the lives of ordinary country folk. Mrs Saunders Davies' household choir, styled 'The Pentre Merry Choir', as well as the Bronwydd and Llysnewydd Brass Bands, were not only attempts at educating the *werin* in a broad sense, but helped too, to extend the cultural influence of the squire families amongst their peers, through their participation in concerts, garden fêtes, tableaux and public spectacles.[48]

The polite pastimes of the gentry sometimes led to specialised professionalism, with members of the Castle Malgwyn, Gellydywyll, Pentre and other families gaining distinctions from national bodies for their skill as performers on musical instruments.[49] Moreover, some gentry eagerly spotted talent and did their best to further the careers of young men from the Teifi valley, such as the singer Hirwen Jones, and the sculptor James Milo Griffith. C. H. Ll. Fitzwilliams of Cilgwyn and Syr Pryse Pryse of Gogerddan mooted the idea of raising an endowment for a Cardiganshire scholarship to enable poor students to study at the Royal Academy of Music.[50]

In addition to hunt balls and race meetings, the gentry found other means of entertainment and amusements in the county towns and watering places of Aberystwyth and Tenby. Urban attractions included the theatre, assembly rooms, coffee houses, clubs and libraries, the latter a means of keeping up acquaintance with the 'polite world' and current events. While cock fighting, bear and bull baiting attracted the grosser types of squire and his lady, there were gatherings where heavy drinkers and boorish squires were excluded and only the polite and well-mannered admitted.[51] South-west Wales towns were visited by strolling players, freak shows of giants and dwarves, mountebanks and men with performing bears and monkeys—all adding to the varied programme of 'entertainment'. The gentry might have had their appetite for the theatre sharpened through visits to London. Plays were frequently read in the household and performed in home theatricals. Strolling players presented entertainment containing much vulgarity, broad jokes and rude wit, as well as sensationalism and violent action.[52] Local magistrates, namely, the gentry took a tolerant view and allowed these dramatic interludes to be held in fairgrounds and near race meetings, and probably enjoyed the ribaldry as much as their social inferiors. But as custodians of the public good, they imposed certain basic conditions. Thus a theatre which opened in Carmarthen in 1815 was to be run with '. . . due regard to decorum of conduct'. Some theatres were circumspect in their productions, such as the Tenby theatre which at the time was presenting mild and innocuous farces such as *The Honeymoon* and *The Spoiled Child*.[53]

In their country houses the tradition of home-produced theatricals survived to the early decades of this century. Actors and audience would gather at houses such as Glandovan, Glanarberth and Pantsaison, where, after a dinner party, light hearted *comediattas* were performed bearing titles such as *Orange Blossoms* and *Oh! For a Thousand a Year*. These performances usually ended with an 'elegant supper' and as many as fifty gentry folk might be present.[54] Visits to other country houses, reciprocating hospitality, a clockwork round of gargantuan meals along with indoor games like backgammon, pyramids (snooker) and bridge, fortune-telling and gossip were the main activities of the Morgan-Richardsons of Rhosygilwen. At Glaspant, one of the lesser houses, leisure activities included perfunctory reading and indulging in a whole range of country gossip concerning the extramarital liaisons and illegitimate offspring of the 'Tivyside' squires, and other scandals concerning local country folk.[55]

In a comparatively poor mansion like Tŷ Llwyd life was almost unbearably dull. The Jones-Parry children regarded with envy the foreign travels of the Lloyds of Coedmore; and the receipt of Christmas cards and the prospect of a ball at Gernos or one of the other mansions enlivened the social scene. 'Papa' Jones-Parry spent the long winter evenings 'knitting nightcaps for his little girls'. A visit to Cardigan fair to buy toffee and India rock was a special treat; a trip to watch croquet or tennis at one of the bigger houses was a change from 'interminable walks around the garden!' Mrs Wood, brought up at Tŷ Llwyd at the end of the last century, summed it up: '. . . it was poor amusement for a child, but in our chill lives all was fish that came to our nets'. In contrast, the Welsh *gwerin* had had their folk dances; had watched the satirical interludes of Twm o'r Nant in tavern-yard or fair, and had later abandoned those aspects of folk culture for the more edifying *eisteddfod, darlith* and *cyfarfod diwylliadol*.[56] It could be argued that it was they (and not the gentry) who were the custodians of an aristocratic, intellectual culture which was admired by eminent persons like Robert Southey, Bishop Thirlwall and Matthew Arnold.[57] Indeed, in contrast to the dialectic of sermon and *darlith* (public lecture), the moral, social and political dimensions of these exercises in improvement and edification, the social gatherings and activities of the gentry were marked by much that was trivial and fatuous.

NOTES AND SOURCES

[1] E. Moir: *op cit.*, p. 82.

[2] Lord Macaulay: *op cit.*, i, pp. 239-41.

[3] J. H. Plumb: *The First Four Georges*, 1956, pp. 13-16.

[4] G. E. Mingay: *English Landed Society*, 1963, pp. 145-54; F. M. L. Thompson: *op cit.*, p. 150; R. B. Munsche: *Gentlemen and Poachers. The English Game Laws 1670-1831*, 1981, p. 18.

[5] R. Carr: *English Fox Hunting*, 1978, pp. 3, 45, 50, 108.

[6] *ibid*: p. 220.

[7] J. Evans: 'The Cryngae Hounds', *Trans Carms Antiq Socy*, 1932-33, pp. 23-24; *DWB*.

[8] *Sporting Magazine*, 1834; *South Wales Daily News*, 7/10/1907.

[9] *Cm. Jnl.* 15/7/1825. [Collier's Encyclopaedia, 1980].

[10] *Cd Ad* 3/3/1871, 10/12/1893; Memorial in Llangunllo church.

[11] *Cd Ad* 18/1/1867; *The Welshman*: 28/1/1870.

[12] NLW/Cilgwyn/LB/38/27 April 1860.

[13] *ibid*: 44/2 Mar. 1876.

[14] *Cd Ad*: 10/2/1893.

[15] *ibid*: 8/5/1894.

[16] NLW/Highmead/2763.

[17] *Cm Jnl*: 26/1/1811, 16/2/1816.

[18] J. Hd. Davies: *op cit.*, p. 78; NLW/Picton Castle/3889.

[19] R. W. Malcolmson: *Popular Recreations in Rural England, 1700-1850*, 1973, pp. 52, 84.

[20] J. G. Ruffer: *The Big Shots—Edwardian Shooting Parties*, 1978, pp. 25-26, 50-52, 133.

[21] H. M. Vaughan: *op cit.*, pp. 188-192, 194.

[22] NLW/Highmead/31.

[23] NLW/Howell, Glaspant/Game Book, 19c.

[24] Pesonal knowledge.

[25] CRO/Cwmgwili/146.

[26] *RSCCI*, 1844, p. 221 [Qu 3161]; *Cm Jnl*: 14/8/1846.

[27] CRO/Talardd/Box 1; Morgan-Richardson Diary 1906-07; *Cd Ad*. 8/9/1899.

[28] *Cm Jnl*: 14/6/1878; *Cd Ad*: 27/6/1883.

[29] Morgan-Richardson Diary; HRO/RW/86.

[30] *Gent Mag*, June 1774, pp. 262-65; Lady K. Lloyd, *op cit.*, p. 93; NLW/Clynfyw/Box 15; C. Cannon: *The Letters of Sir William Jones*, 1969, i, Letter 290, p. 500.

[31] Horace Walpole: *Letters 1857*, ed., vi, p. 88; M. Girouard: *The Return to Camelot*, 1981, pp. 96-110; the Earl of Eglinton organised a great spectacle in the park around Eglinton Castle in Ayrshire in August 1839. Owing to heavy rain the event was a literal 'wash out'.

[32] NLW/Bathafarn/xxiii/p. 19; *The British Press*: 10/8/1813; *Monthly Magazine*, Sept. 1814, p. 201.

[33] R. W. Malcolmson: *op cit.*, p. 68.

[34] *Cm Jnl*: 1/7/1842.

[35] *ibid*: 13/6/1851; Cd Ad. 8/10/1895; *The Welshman*: 12/6/1885; *Cd Ad*: 25/8/1899.

[36] *Trans Carms Antiq Socy*: 9, pp. 50-52, 91; 29, pp. 96-7; Memorials in Bath Abbey and in St Mary's Church, Cheltenham; NLW/Llwyngwair/1696-98; NLW/Highmead/2429.

[37] *Cd Ad*: 24/4/1896; NLW/Llysnewydd/Bundle 37.

[38]NLW/Cilgwyn LB/53/9 May 1909; 31 July 1907.

[39]NLW/Owen Colby/1936, 2002-32.

[40]NLW/Evans George/3130, 3301; NLW/Highmead/2, 6.

[41]NLW/Ms 1896E ii, 1877E iii; E. B. Wood: *op cit.*

[42]*WWHR*, vi, pp. 27-28; *Cm Jnl*: 26/9/1834; 3/3/1815; *DWB*: *sub* Brinley Richards.

[43]J. S. Harford: *Life of Bishop Burgess*, 1841, p. 275; personal knowledge; *DWB*; information from Mrs P. Chalk, Blaenralltddu, Pont-siân, Llandysul.

[44]NLW/Owen Colby/1018; Morgan Richardson Diary 1906-07; *Cd Ad:* 19/12/1902.

[45]*ibid*: 2/11/1866.

[46]*ibid*: 14/12/1883; 3/10/1890; *DWB*.

[47]*ibid*: 7/12/1866; D. L. Baker-Jones: 'The Carmarthen Eisteddfod of 1867', *Carms. Historian*, ix, 1972, p. 46.

[48]*Cd Ad*: 3/8/1866; 28/5/1875; 24/9/1880; *The Welshman*: 1/1/1847.

[49]*Cd Ad*: 5/2/1892.

[50]Local tradition; *DWB*; NLW/Cilgwyn/LB/46/8 May 1882; *DWB*.

[51]C. Price: 'Polite Life in Eighteenth Century Wales', *Welsh Anvil*, V, pp. 89-98.

[52]P. Jenkins: *op cit.*, pp. 248-49, 254; C. Price: 'Portable Theatres in Wales, 1843-1914', *NLWJ*, ix, 1, 1955, pp. 65-92.

[53]*Cm Jnl*: 15/9/1815, 21/5/1815.

[54]*Cd Ad*: 13/8/1899; C.E.D. Morgan Richardson: *Henry Vaughan*, 1902, p. 107.

[55]NLW/Highmead/2828; Morgan-Richardson Diary 1906-07; Howell, Glaspant/Diary 1896.

[56]E. B. Wood: *op cit.*, p. 11; *DWB* (* eisteddfod, public lecture, cultural meeting).

[57]H. Richard: *op cit.*, p. 45.

Status Celebrations

A gentleman's position and status in the community were reflected in the pattern of his social activities. Family events were meant to be celebrated in great style and with lavish display so as to mark the stages in the family's continuity over many generations. Not only were birthdays, anniversaries, marriages and the coming-of-age of the eldest son important in the annals of the family, but also in the life of the estate and its tenants. For such events gave an opportunity to reaffirm old loyalties and to cultivate the good favour of the future squire. The birth of an heir to Col. John Colby of Ffynone was heralded with bells pealed at Tenby and other towns in 1813. Likewise the coming of age of Lloyd Davies of Alltyrodyn and Judith Tyler of Gernos led to general merrymaking— 'potations long and deep', the distribution of wine and *cwrw da*, hunks of roast beef, barley, cheese and gifts of money. On the occasion of Sir Marteine Lloyd's wedding in 1878 one and a half thousand people assembled to welcome him home, to show respect and deference, or, merely, out of curiosity and to partake of the largesse provided by the squire and his lady. Fifty years later Sir Marteine and Lady Lloyd celebrated their Golden Wedding with lavish hospitality to tenants and well-wishers.[1]

One important aspect of gentry status was its relationship to socially superior classes throughout the land, especially to the sovereign as the 'fount of honour'. Thus, fancy-dress balls, masques and other forms of jollification marked the presentation at court of the young ladies of the Saunders Davies family of Pentre.[2] Presentation into high society had its market value. The occasion meant that invitations were sent over a wide area to other gentry and even nobility to share hospitality and entertainment to demonstrate the wealth and position of the hostess, and possibly to lure a well-heeled young man into marrying the debutante. Frequently these gatherings took the form of a *bal masqué* or *bal costumé*, a fashion set by Queen Victoria in 1842.[3] Participants dressed up in rustic and even in the bizarre costumes of legend and fairy tale, folk culture and history, for example, shepherdesses *à la* Wateau, Little Red Riding Hood, Mary Queen of Scots and the like. Of all the 'Tivyside' houses the lifestyle at Pentre and Bronwydd was most lavish, and a typical 'grand supper' might consist of roast turkey, pheasant, chicken, brawn, beef, tongue, ham, crab, lobster, followed by pastries, jellies, creams and dessert, all washed down with champagne and other choice wines.[4] Rooms were lit with wax candles, and were elaborately decorated with floral motifs depicting the valour, chivalry and noble ideals of the family, as occurred at Bronwydd in 1882 when '. . . the lofty open groined roof of the library put one in mind of the olden days, when illustrious barons and their retinue met each other, with a boar's head at the high table'.[5]

In this community of honour, the code of chivalry extended also to servants, who were occasionally privileged to enjoy festivities prepared by their masters, albeit as Dr Girouard reminds us:

> Each knew his place—king, peasant, peer or priest,
> The greatest owed connexion with the least.

Sixty retainers from 'Tivyside' mansions attended a servants' ball at Pentre in 1875. According to Victorian standards of propriety, and mindful that servants had to be kept in their place, the reception rooms in the mansion were not used, but the 'spacious coach house' was arranged as a ballroom and the 'recherché supper' was served in the servants' hall.[6]

As the pillars of the constitution and the custodians of law and order, the gentry had to be seen to fulfil their public duties with commensurate show of loyalty. Thus Abel Gower entertained the 'quality' and official classes to a magnificent ball when he was High Sheriff of Pembrokeshire in 1845. During the 'Rebecca' troubles of the 1840s, regiments of soldiers who had come to put down disorder in the area were lavishly entertained and fêted in the big houses.[7]

Important events in the life of the royal family had to be celebrated locally by the gentry as a sign of their loyalty and devotion. Functions such as tea parties with a 'beautiful repast of choice viands', bell ringing, bonfires and such like were held, as, for example, when the Duke of Edinburgh was married in 1874.[8]

Even during the 1880s and 1890s, a period of intense anti-gentry feeling, there were strong ties within the strata of a class-conscious society. The lower orders took part and rejoiced in public celebrations of family successes, such as C. E. D. Morgan-Richardson's marriage to the daughter of Sir Henry Moore Brownrigg, 3rd, Bart. of Sandhill Park, Somerset. When Lawrence Hugh Jenkins of Cilbronne was appointed a high court judge in India, the event was marked in and around Cardigan with processions, fireworks and abundant food for the community, an example of the gentry reciprocating in a very practical way, and thereby trying to preserve social harmony and the 'status quo'.[9]

These public occurrences were the means whereby the gentry asserted their position vis-à-vis the crown, honoured important national and imperial events, and partly achieved the fulfilment of their moral and social responsibilities towards the lower orders. But the outward façade often concealed the reality. It is significant that the tide of radicalism had for a long time questioned more and more the privileged position of the gentry. Thus, the Alltyrodyn coming-of-age celebrations of 1848 were challenged in the press.[10] There was growing, if smouldering, dissent against a public moral code which accepted as sacred dogma the existence of a privileged idle class of rich folk as against an under-privileged suffering poor. In the aftermath of the 1865 election, when protest was more vocal, the perceptive and challenging press corres-pondence of a 'Llandyssul Preacher' (probably the saintly William Thomas, 'Gwilym Marles') argued that he did not wish to deprive the gentry of their wealth and position. The moral imperative facing them was to use their surplus wealth, not by giving dinners, *cwrw da* and such trifles, like 'sweets to little children' to keep them contented, but rather by supporting agricultural and technical education for their tenants, providing a good water supply to local villages, building libraries and raising the moral tone of the community.[11]

Gentry preoccupation with dignity, status and display extended to the circumstances surrounding the death and burial of the squire and his family. In some instances, the death of the squire could be a local calamity: the loss of the leader of the community and the unifying force in a hierarchical structure which had existed without challenge for centuries. The traditional loyalty of a Welsh community was expressed, in a nutshell, by the rustic parson of Llanymawddwy in Merionethshire during the obsequies for Squire Thomas in 1837: 'Good people of Llanymawddwy we are met here today for a great preachment—a preachment for a dead body—the body of good Squire Thomas, the squire of our parish. We did all love him though he had scolded us shocking'.[12] Doubtless, this was typical of the homespun 'funeral oration' and 'tribute' to the local squire uttered in parish churches throughout Wales; an occasion when everybody turned out to bid a last farewell to someone regarded by the community, as a whole, with a complexity of feeling—reverence, awe, admiration, affection as well as fear and, perhaps, even hatred.

The ceremonies and ritual in connection with the death and funeral of the squire had to be followed scrupulously. These acts of 'pietas' reflected the obligations which affected each social gradation.

Commencing in the mansion a strict procedure was followed: clocks were stopped, door knockers muffled and stair balustrades draped. The aged and infirm in the locality were given clothes and large pieces of black cloth as mourning scarves. The funeral procession was headed by the parish poor followed by the household servants. Kinsmen held aloft the family banner, the helm, crest, coat of arms or hatchment. Then came the preacher or minister and gentry kindred, the eldest son and heir walking alone followed by the immediate family of brothers, sisters and other relations—all wearing black, according to the degree of kinship. Then followed the 'county' gentry in strict order of precedence—baronets, knights, squires and gentlemen, with a sprinkling of professional men such as doctors, lawyers, clergy and even nonconformist ministers. This spectacle of gloom was a pageantry in celebration of death, and examples may be cited from the 'Tivyside' area. When Arthur Henry Saunders Davies, the squire of Pentre, died in 1873, in his forty second year, a local newspaper considered that his funeral 'had eclipsed all predecessors', with five family carriages and ten carriages for pall bearers and gentry from important Pembrokeshire houses. Head servants were conveyed in a pony carriage, with lesser servants, tenants and the general public drawing up the rear. In 1877 there were three family and thirty gentry carriages for the funeral of Mrs Stewart of Rhosygilwen. On these occasions the deference not only of tenants and neighbours of the squire and his estate was in evidence, but also that of other gentry and of the inhabitants of the county towns where the family influence, patronage and acts of charity of the deceased were held in high regard. Thus, when Lady Lloyd of Bronwydd died in 1871 the funeral bell of Cardigan church was tolled all day. The last status funeral in 'Tivyside' was that of Sir Marteine Lloyd in April 1933, with all the traditional pageantry and display.

On the other hand, gentry acceptance of and esteem towards other landowners who possessed lands and mansions (the outward 'indicia' of gentility) could sometimes be muted or even entirely absent. The reporter to the *Cardigan and Tivyside Advertiser* of 10 September 1897, confessed that he had a 'difficult task' in giving an account of the funeral of John Francis Jones-Lloyd of Lancych. According to the *Tivyside* and other county papers not a single member of the local gentry was present; the occasion was exceptional for its lack of ostentation.[13]

Since prehistoric times the commemoration of kings, chiefs and brave leaders in battle has been marked by setting up tumuli, memorial stones, tombs, chantry chapels and the like.[14]

In the eighteenth and nineteenth centuries, the family vault became the burial place of the distinguished and powerful; and this development may be accounted for by the renewed interest in classical antiquities. West Wales gentry took up the fashion, and although their vaults were modest, yet they had a strong sense of purpose. Vaults follow the same general pattern, namely a rectangular subterranean room, vaulted over and firmly built of brick and stone surrounded by iron railings. Some display classical motifs, such as a cubic base, pillars in the Ionic or other order, Venetian arches, entablatures comprising a frieze or cornice, and an arched entrance flanked by niches with devices like medallions, plaques, urns and garlands.[15]

Most 'Tivyside' vaults, as stated, are modest in scale and plain in execution. Perhaps the only vault in 'Tivyside' that can claim to be a 'mausoleum' is the Maesycrugiau vault in Llanllwni churchyard: a solid rectangular building standing above ground, constructed of large blocks of red sandstone, with recesses outside for marble inscribed tablets in memory of the persons buried within. In the churchyard of the old Maenordeifi church, there are vaults belonging to the Clynfyw, Ffynone and Pentre families. Although not elaborate, nor in a grand style, they are exquisite examples of the refined simplicity of spontaneous Georgian craftsmanship in stone, metal and wood.[16]

Within parish churches throughout the land, mural tablets in metal, stone and marble exist to commemorate the landed gentry, often with crests, arms and mottoes. Hatchments of wood are frequently seen. The latter are meant to give a chronicle of family deaths, with technical heraldic variations to distinguish between married persons, widows, bachelors and spinsters. Frequently, heraldic memorials are of a high artistic standard. They reflect the prevailing taste in architecture, and range in style from Palladian, Baroque to Victorian Gothic. Invariably, the lettered panels describe in glowing terms the life and godly works of the deceased. Like vaults, they are often decorated with classical conventions—pilasters, pillars and orders, draped urns, cherubs, and angels as well as pious aphorisms such as *memento mori, beati mortui* and *datur omni mori.*[17] It would be invidious to list the numerous churches with gentry memorials in the 'Tivyside' area. As with stained-glass windows, these memorials commemorate those who held sway in the county and the locality; recording not only past glory but also to secure for the deceased a guaranteed place in history. They emphasise gentry pre-eminence and the 'godly works' of many. On the other hand, they consciously, even blatantly, obliterated the manifold personal weaknesses, private immorality, shortcomings and sometimes public scandals which some gentry were guilty of, but were condemned and despised in the lower orders. One example, may be cited, namely the memorial tablet to the Rev. Thomas Bowen, rector of Troedyraur, landowner, and squire who died in 1842. His grave moral lapses, especially in a priest, were totally ignored by those who erected the memorial.[18] Some gentry had two moral codes—one for themselves and another for the rest of society. In another sense, too, such manifestations of gentry 'values' illustrate their sensitivity concerning status and their eagerness to be well remembered in popular esteem as generous landlords, honest magistrates and humane administrators: the veritable pillars of church and state and of a social order which they thought would never change.

NOTES AND SOURCES

[1]*Cm Jnl*: 23/10/1813, 7/1/1848, 14/1/1848; *The Welshman*: 6/2/1852, 8/11/1878; *Cd. Ad.* 9/11/1928.

[2]*Cd Ad*: 14/10/1878, 18/4/1879.

[3]M. Girouard: *op cit.*, pp. 81-83.

[4]*Cd Ad*: 7/1/1876, 18/4/1879.

[5]*ibid*: 6/1/1882.

[6]M. Girouard: *op cit.*, p. 83; *Cd Ad*: 23/4/1875.

[7]*Cm Jnl*: 14/11/1845, 16/1/1846, 16/7/1847.

[8]*Cd Ad*: 30/1/1874.

[9]*ibid*: 27/2/1885, 20/3/1896.

[10]*loc cit.*

[11]*DWB*; *Cm Jnl*: 3/11/1871, 24/11/1871, 15/12/1871; William Thomas (Gwilym Marles) 1834-79, Unitarian minister, radical and social reformer, writer and schoolmaster; took a prominent part in the 1868 election, and was a strong advocate of the secret ballot.

[12]*Red Dragon*: May 1884, 5, pp. 434-40.

[13]For ceremonial at the obsequies of Sir Hugh Owen, Bt. of Orielton, Pembs—see *Annual Register 1809*, and for the funeral of David Jones, MP of Pantglas, Carms, 7/7/1869 see D. L. Baker-Jones: 'Pantglas and the Jones Families', *Carms Historian*, xii, 1975, pp. 14-15; *Cd Ad*: 20/6/1873, 2/2/1877, 17/11/1871; 14/4/1933; 10/9/1897; an omission also in the Pembrokeshire papers.

[14]J. S. Curl: *A Celebration of Death—an Introduction to some of the buildings monuments and settings of funerary architecture in the Western European tradition*, 1980, pp. 168-79.

[15]D. L Baker-Jones: 'Christian Sepulchral Monuments in and around Carmarthenshire', *Carms Antiq*, iv, 3, 4, 1963, pp. 116-23; *DWB*.

[16]A. D. R. Caröe: *Report on the Old Church of Maenordeifi*, 31/8/1950.

[17]A. Needham: *How to Study an old Church*, 1944.

[18]Memorial tablet in Troedyraur Church; see p. 206.

Gentry Morals

The bucolic squire has been portrayed in lurid and often exaggerated terms in Restoration comedy and in eighteenth-century novels. Squire Western has become the prototype of the 'good-natured fox hunter who spends his day on horseback and his evenings eating and drinking'. One might add that he also indulged in 'wining and wenching' to the full, the 'civilised' and sophisticated 'mores' natural to an affluent and leisured ruling class.[1]

A modern study of eighteenth-century Pembrokeshire squires cites only two instances of scandalous behaviour relating to them: a certain gentleman of large estate entertained his friends in celebration of the birth of his fiftieth 'love child', while another squire, smitten with the charms of a collier's spouse, purchased the lady 'for a crown, a gallon of beer and a calfskin waistcoat'.[2] When H. M. Vaughan in his book *The South Wales Squires* referred to the illegitimate offspring of a Lloyd of Coedmore, it raised a furore in gentry circles.[3] There is, however, a considerable amount of evidence that many of the 'Tivyside' gentry were boors, drunkards, whoremongers, rogues and avaricious knaves, just like the rest of mankind.

That the gentry acquired their great wealth largely through legitimate means has been demonstrated already. But, some of them were not too scrupulous in using every opportunity towards furthering their own ends by fair means or foul. Their close links with the established church easily led to the misappropriation of church revenues. George Bowen of Llwyngwair, in the late 1600s, was 'admonished' for 'substraction of tithes' and had to answer for his conduct on pain of excommunication.[4] On similar charges concerning church rates, prominent gentry like Nathan Griffiths of Mountain Hall, David Lewis of Dolhaidd, Theophilus Jones of Rhosygilwen and Samuel Williams, the renowned man of letters and vicar of Llandyfriog, were summoned in 1701 to the consistory court. It would appear that Lewes of Gernos took £400 of Queen Anne's Bounty fund for his own personal use but, to make amends, added a codicil in his will in 1719 that the money had to be repaid from 'money in house or in bonds' and was to be applied for the maintenance of divine service in 'Cynnon Chappell in Llandysiliogogo parish'.[5] But, such qualms of conscience were not too frequent, and the portrait of an unscrupulous landowner with total disregard for the public good is clear from other examples. Thus, William Warren of Trewern in 1692 had to appear before the Grand

Jury for stopping and diverting the King's highway from St David's to Cardiganshire, 'turning ye said highway through a dangerous bogg from the usual and antient road to the great perill and annoyance of His Majesty's subjects'.[6]

The incidence of excise duties on essential commodities has always been a source of aggravation. In 1754, Thomas Lewis of Llwyngrawys hid many 'salt bags among the corn so as not to pay duty' and bribed the tax collector five guineas when they were discovered. The excise man, on his part, reported the matter to his superiors, which resulted in legal proceedings being taken against Lewis. As the penalty was as high as £100, every attempt was made to quash the matter by asking Sir William Owen of Orielton, MP for Pembrokeshire, and his friend, Mr Webley, to use their influence with the commissioners at the Salt Office. The outcome is not clear, but the incident is probably typical of what always went on. In particular, it illustrated how patronage and the right connections in high places were important, as Mr Webley was 'well acquainted with the Salt Office and with the ways of the Commissioners . . .'![7]

The conduct of John Colby of Ffynone at the end of the eighteenth century is an example of unbridled greed and dishonesty. Taking advantage of his special position as receiver of the Orielton estate during the minority of his nephew Sir Hugh Owen, his personal fortunes were enhanced considerably. Even Colby's own sister Lady Keith, was, at the time, 'divesting herself entirely of his known and universal avaricious character and conduct on all occasions, and which are literally proverbial in his own county'. From 1799 to 1801 his ward Ann Ferrier had great difficulty in obtaining legacies left to her by a will of which Colby was executor.[8] Colby's command of the Pembrokeshire militia around 1800 exploded as a public scandal leading to his court martial and dismissal for '. . . having embezzled and misapplied certain sums of public money . . . at the rate of ten guineas for each man . . . and converted to his private use, coals and candles allowed by the government for the use of the regimental mess . . . and withheld cloathing from the men'.[9]

H. M. Vaughan glossed over the 'one little failing' of the Welsh gentry, namely drunkenness, as something that affected every other class in the community, whether in England or Wales. Nevertheless, it often resulted in the dissipation of family estates and, along with other forms of fast living, brought ruin upon families.[10]

Foreign travel and residence at fashionable centres, such as London and Bath, often exacerbated tendencies which squires had acquired at home. In 1761 Lewis Morris wrote of Pryse of Gogerddan (who, although not a resident 'Tivyside' squire was one who wielded political power in the area): 'Tom Pryse is in the gout. He drinks excessively. *Wfft i'w fath. Fe ddywed rhai na chaiff John Pugh Pryse mo'r mynd i drafaelio Italy eto gan ei fam.* (Shame upon his sort. Some say that his mother will not allow John Pugh Pryse to travel in Italy again.)[11] Gout also affected Major Evans of Highmead in the early 1800s. This was, perhaps, not so much due to over-addiction as to his too generous hospitality. Dr Davies of Pentre wrote thus: 'I do not my dear major mean to censure you of being a sworn votary of Bacchus, but in exercising the common duties of hospitality—you have probably so far exceeded the Bounds of Prudence'. But of Evans's brother-in-law, Vaughan of Tŷ Llwyd, it was said that he was 'an incorrigible drunkard'.

Although there was a growing seriousness of character, a stricter morality, even a fervent righteousness and new enthusiasm in the social conscience of the ruling classes from the early nineteenth century onwards, yet rakes and debauchees remained in plenty.[12] The Thomas family of Dôl-Llan and Llanfair were notorious in this respect. One of them noted in his diary for New Year's Day 1860: 'I find that all my failings and imperfections are entirely attributed to alcoholic drink and that alone'. In terms of quantity, a staggering amount, namely a gallon made up of brandy and gin, was sent up from a Llandysul druggist every day and at his funeral his cleric cousin, Evans of Llaethliw, was hopelessly drunk in Pantydefaid chapel.[13] That drinking led to gambling is not surprising, and was the downfall of many families.[14]

Some of the gentry were quarrelsome and vindictive, even in unimportant matters. Evan Pryce of Rhydybenne, Llangeler, was summoned in 1708 to answer before the consistory court why he had 'usurped' a seat in the parish church which belonged to somebody else. Through some nefarious plot on the part of the infamous Herbert Lloyd of Peterwell, his henchmen managed to start a brawl at Llandysul fair in 1750 against the supporters of Johnes of Llanfair Clydogau which resulted in the latter being taken to Cardigan prison and thence to the court of King's Bench where he was sentenced to languish with Lloyd of Mabws in the Fleet Prison.[15] Brawls and assaults were just as common amongst the gentry as the rest of society; thus, Captain Owen Lloyd of Cardigan in 1784 had to appear at Lincoln Assizes on a charge of assault which cost him and his confederate £70 for their defence. Over-sensitivity to the concept of honour sometimes had serious consequences, as, for example, the duel fought between John James of Pantsaison and Samuel Simmons Fortune in 1799. The latter died of his wounds and James fled to the continent after the coroner had brought in a verdict of wilful murder. Many years later James returned to inherit his estate, and subsequently became a respectable colonel in the Pembrokeshire militia.[16]

A lack of a sense of guilt, seems to have been a mark of some gentry. In addition, there was scorn and disdain towards religious conviction and overt piety. When the 'Methodistical' clerics David Griffiths of Nevern, and David Jones of Llangan, held annual preaching meetings on Goodwick beach to celebrate the French defeat of 1797, large crowds of gentry from south-west Wales attended. Some were so lacking in ordinary decent behaviour that they rode their horses wildly on the beach and tried to shout down the preachers.[17]

Scholars have claimed in recent years that newer attitudes concerning the family, involving the embrace of a more 'middle class' and puritan outlook, can be discerned in the habits of some gentry. But the growing tightening of moral standards and seriousness of character, a revival of piety, strict morality and a new interest in religion, was only limited in its effect in the lower Teifi valley. The constant references to bastardy in the Quarter Sessions Order Books deal with the loose moral fabric of the lower classes, but this in turn was also the normative behaviour of many within the upper strata. As leaders of society, and as magistrates having to deal with problems of illegitimacy, many squires must have found difficulty in setting their faces against vices to which they themselves were all too often susceptible. Johnes of Abermâd and Llanfair Clydogau (albeit in north Cardiganshire) was sent to prison for non-maintenance of his many bastard children, and many Cardiganshire squires were like him.[18] Throughout the eighteenth and nineteenth centuries there is massive evidence of illicit liaisons, which subsequently became public knowledge through court proceedings, and one can imagine many more which were discreetly hushed up.

In 1719 the rector of Llangoedmor was charged with the breach of the ecclesiastical and civil laws of the land, as well as being guilty of 'sundry immoralities'. From 1736 to 1751 Richard Parry and Oliver Howell were accused of 'fornication and incontinency' in the parish of Llangeler, and of 'contempt and contumacy' for not appearing at the consistory court, so that, as a result, they were publicly excommunicated.[19] A squire, who had not yet acquired a suitable bride with an ample dowry, sometimes took a mistress under the genteel guise of housekeeper. When William Brigstocke of Blaenpant in 1739 ultimately found a lady of fortune, namely Mary Lloyd of Glyn, Carmarthenshire, he dismissed his 'housekeeper' who brought a legal action against him which lasted from 1744 to 1747. It was revealed that she had borne him six children; that he had seduced her with 'fair and delusive promises and repeated oaths of constancy'. As an unpaid servant, she had managed his home farm and had carried out duties such as making butter and cheese, tending to poultry and pigs, and taking produce to market. The court found that 'casks of butter, cheeses, flannel and farm animals' were not a sufficient recompense for her 'services' when she was later thrown on the parish. Consequently the court ordered Brigstocke to sign a bond for £500 to support her and her offspring.[20]

Concubinage was common among some gentry. That Lady Griffies Williams of Llwynywermod (daughter of Major Evans of Highmead), for instance, had lived in a 'state of concubinage for many years' was common knowledge in 1836. Such a situation leading to illegitimate offspring could have serious legal consequences, and put the inheritance of an estate in jeopardy. Thus David Edward Lewes of Dolhaidd admitted in his will of 1810 that he was not married to '. . . his beloved Ann Baughan who has borne my name and lived with me for more than thirty years'.[21] Notwithstanding his sincere intention of marrying her, he was deterred from doing so '. . . by the apprehension of a discovery . . . and the disgrace of illegitimacy on my dearly beloved son James Richard Lewes, generally called James Richard Lewes Lloyd . . . [which] thereby prevented him from inheriting the estates entailed on me by my late uncle Richard Lloyd of Wern'.[22]

As has been pointed out, the protection and survival of the good name of the family was an essential constituent of gentility. The Rev. Thomas Bowen, a magistrate and deputy lieutenant, died in 1842 having been rector of Troedyraur for half a century. His good qualities were commemorated in glowing terms, but the other side of his character was carefully concealed: his 'adultery, fornication and incontinency, neglect of his ministerial duties and other enormous Crimes', and, in addition, he 'had absconded and hid himself from the mandatory', i.e. the person carrying out the consistory court order. The summons was issued 'concerning his soul's health and the Lawful Reformation and Correction of his vices and excesses'.[23]

Illicit liaisons were common in every grade of the landed classes. In the mid-eighteenth century, the legitimacy of the heir to Lord Lisburne was in serious doubt on account of the alleged adultery of Lady

Lisburne with the coachman and other servants. The detailed depositions taken at the time reveal in sordid terms what went on in Trawsgoed (Crosswood), one of Cardiganshire's prestige houses. In 'Tivyside' the cause célèbre was the Lloyd of Coedmore divorce case; the vilification of each other by the parties in the proceedings, which lasted from 1775 to 1779, would rank with the worst that the modern media could rake up.[24] Even in the nineteenth century, a more rigorous ethic and respect for fidelity within matrimony as well as the practice of chastity seems to have left some families totally indifferent. Two of the Gernos squires were unmarried, and the estate consequently devolved on illegitimate offspring. It is significant, however, that when Llewellyn Parry of Gernos died in 1836, leaving his estate to an illegitimate daughter by one of his servant maids, a degree of protest and a fervent righteousness characterised the conduct of Thomas Lloyd of Bronwydd in his refusal to act as a trustee and party to the legal arrangements that followed.[25]

Foreign travel and the hazy moral standards of the *demi-monde* of Paris and other European capitals, as well as a posting to distant parts of empire, proved a strain on matrimonial ties. Dorothea Lloyd Williams of Gwernant bemoaned, in her will of 1859, that for upwards of 12 years she was separated from her husband because of his continued absence abroad and desertion.[26] Likewise, the young John Lloyd Davies of Alltyrodyn in the 1870s was another rake 'weak in intellect', who wasted his substance with mistresses and came to an untimely end. Traditions still survive of the smothering of babes (newly born to servant girls) and their burial in the vicinity of the mansion. Towards the end of the century some families still clung to their immoral ways. A private diary mentions several 'Tivyside' gentry, one of them, 'the old man of Llysnewydd', as having numerous illegitimate offspring. The lodge of one country house had 'Rahab's red cord' hanging in the window when the courtesan was at home, a fact that many a squire knew.[27]

The outlook of some of the squirearchy derived, in part at least, from an element deep in their 'psyche' that feudalism still held sway, and that they had unquestionable rights over the mind, will and body of their inferiors: moral imperatives were too often sacrificed for an unabashed lewdness. The growing public criticism of the private lives of the gentry by a more articulate, radical and nonconformist conscience in the latter half of the nineteenth century, which openly assailed the squirearchy for their 'immorality', had little effect.[28]

In the period under study, one discovers a strange ambivalence in the attitude of the gentry. While liaisons with servants and mistresses resulting in illegitimate children was normative behaviour, some squires in such a position followed a strict code of mitigating what they had done by making some sort of financial or alternative provision to set up their offspring in life. Brigstocke of Blaenpant, as cited above, is not typical of the gentry in this respect. In 'Tivyside' only he and Thomas of Llanfair in the 1860s were taken to law and made to pay according to the affiliation order demanded by the courts.[29] Thomas had upon occasion resorted to foul means of shedding his responsibility, such as obtaining potions from the local druggist to procure the miscarriage of pregnant servant maids.

That some gentry practised a certain code of honour is clear from wills, although the term 'natural son . . . or daughter' does not always signify illegitimacy. A few examples must suffice: David Lewes of Llysnewydd in 1706 bequeathed to '. . . my reputed son Sylvanus Lewes on the body of Jane Thomas, twenty yearling sheep, one heifer and five pounds at age fourteen'. Captain Lloyd of Llanfechan, of H. M. Independent Company in Newfoundland, left a fairly large sum of £300 'to my reputed daughter Mary by Rachel Williams of Dolgwm' and 'to my reputed son John by my cozn. Mary Lloyd of [Pantybalden?]'[30]

It is interesting to note that there were no inhibitions about naming the mothers; that the father's family name was given to the child; and that the liaisons were sometimes with other gentry ladies, and not only with rustic lasses or village molls. That mistresses existed in polite circles and were very much part of the social scene is clear. Thus, Thomas James of Trewern in Nevern parish, by his will of 1763, provided £10 to 'my mistress the wife of Phillip Jones of Trewern Esq'—a *ménage à trois*—and the trustees responsible for raising the sum were none other than the two Lewes clerics of Penybenglog, Meline.[31] Another cleric whose condonation was also evident was the Rev. John Williams, rector of Llandyfrïog in 1832, who, in a letter to Major Evans of Highmead, speaks of fostering out a male child with a 'clean tidy woman' and calling him David Lewes after his squire father: 'He is a fine gentlemanly looking child, and looks even now officer like, and who can tell but that he may fight the Battles of his King and Country and indeed become a sort of defender of the Faith, and as a member of the Established Church, bestow some concern for the protection and nourishment of his infantile days'.[32] Whereas the bastard children of the poor and their mothers were regarded as social pariahs and hounded from parish to parish, gentry bastards could redeem their illegitimacy and possibly develop the virtues and characters of their putative gentry sires. In some cases, bastards were often brought up alongside legitimate children and publicly acknowledged by their fathers.[33]

The boarding out of bastard gentry children was common. For example, James Lewes of Gellydywyll in the 1770s paid out several sums of money in respect of such children. Sometimes these payments were part of a bigger transaction, as in the case of Thomas of Gellyorlas who gave Lewes a promissory note in respect of '£30 for value received—security for a bastard child'.[34] Rather than making an outright cash payment, a charge on the estate was sometimes made; for example, Major Evans of Highmead left to '. . . my illegitimate son William Jones Evans now articled, in the firm of William Evans and Powell attorneys Haverfordwest £1,500 and interest @ 4% . . . charged on Llechwedd-y-Cwm, pa. Llanwenog'.[35] Such arrangements could lead to acrimony and litigation on the part of aggrieved relations, whose financial expectations would be greatly diminished by the heavy demands on estate funds. When Bowen Davies of Maesycrugiau left, as we have mentioned earlier, numerous illegitimate offspring (all individually named along with their mothers) and made a charge of £1,000 on the estate for their benefit and a bequest of the residue to 'natural children', a Chancery action in 1848 lasted many years in an attempt to challenge the will.[36] One of the Lloyds of Coedmore made ample provision for his offspring, but without causing any financial shock waves in the direction of his estate and family. In one instance, a son, John Lloyd, was settled as tenant of Pentowin, St Clears, a Coedmore estate farm; and he was also provided with £12 to be charged annually on Forest farm in Cilgerran parish. In 1817 this was surrendered in lieu of a cash sum of £150.[37]

While profligacy and debauchery were rampant in some gentry circles, there were some squires and their ladies who led moral and virtuous lives. Of Thomas Lloyd of Cwmgloyn (1733-1788), a poet was moved to commend his exemplary life—his hospitality, benevolence, patronage of the poor; he was a magistrate who tempered justice with mercy; and, while making allowances for the poetic exuberance of the elegist, Lloyd was singled out as one who did not waste his substance on wild prodigal schemes, nor was he caught on 'horses feet', 'cock fighting' or any 'natural passions'. There was not a gentler or more chaste person.[38] It was with a guilty conscience that David Lloyd of

Alltyrodyn in 1744 confessed to his would-be bride: '. . . I visited neither church nor meeting house [chapel service] this half year'.[39] On the other hand an intense religious commitment involving Bible reading and prayer was the very core of the lifestyle of some gentry. In the late eighteenth century Thomas and Mary Lloyd of Bronwydd followed a 'rule of life', with morning devotions to 'renew the covenant with God, to serve him during the day and at the end of daily toil to . . . cast up the accounts of the day and beg pardon for all done amiss'. Sermons were read, and Christ's divinity had to be upheld in discussions against the heretical doctrines of Dr Priestley and others, especially, the vocal Unitarians up the valley from Llandysul. The resources of the Bronwydd library included a large collection of theological works, and, in search of godliness and 'my blessed master's matchless treasure of love', Mary Lloyd read and summarised sermons, commentaries and Christian authors from the early Christian Fathers to post-Reformation divines of many theological complexions—Fuller, Hooker and Whitfield—as well as Welsh authors like Griffith Jones of Llanddowror, Daniel Rowland and the sermons of a neighbour, the Calvinist, Ebenezer Morris of Rhydlewis.[40]

Eliza Price of Pigeonsford was regular in her devotions and loyalty to the Methodists, frequenting every Sunday the 'meeting house' at Penmorfa. When she died in her eighteenth year, Williams of Pantycelyn, lamented her passing in a somewhat stereotyped ode, wherein he says that all the gold of Peru could not lure back the '*pingcen bur-tan ddeunaw oed*' (the pure rosy-cheeked girl under eighteen) from her heavenly reward.[41]

Family letters, especially those of Bronwydd and Llwyngwair, are full of the burning religious questions of the day and ideas and news were exchanged. Hospitality was given at Llwyngwair to leading Methodists such as John Elias. Indeed, the Bowens 'were present at many of the opportunities'. John Wesley's mission was supported by them and by other families, such as Vaughan of Trecŵn. Financial help was always forthcoming, and Bowen gave a handsome donation towards a nonconformist 'meeting house' at Haverfordwest. Wesley was allowed to use the Llwyngwair sloop to cross to Ireland.[42] Conversion to Christ was a moral imperative, and Easter Bowen of Llwyngwair wrote, in 1781, to her son at the university begging him to pursue 'salvation' and to shun 'entering into scenes of riot and dissipation such as drinking and gambling', to read the Bible and to be 'reconciled by the blood of Jesus'.

A sense of apocalyptic urgency moved the Rev. David Jones of Llangan to warn the Llwyngwair family to be prepared '. . . when the Blessed Lord comes' to be found '. . . *Ymysc y Disglair Lu*' (amongst the Shining Throng).[43]

Unlike most of his gentry peers, E. Crompton Ll. Fitzwilliams of Cilgwyn was one of the few independent-minded intellectuals in the area. With an impressive academic background and a wide range of interests, he corresponded with Jewish rabbis and denominational leaders of all sorts, regarding himself as a Unitarian Christian 'holding the perfect Unity of the Deity' but still accepting the atonement through Christ as Messiah. While resident in France, he had a prolonged theological dialogue with a local curé, using his wide knowledge of church history and patristic texts as his ammunition. When in London, he frequented a 'pure Socinian' conventicle; and in 'Tivyside' was a friend of the Rev. William Thomas (Gwilym Marles), and preached on one occasion at Llwynrhydowen. He was about the only squire of his day who faced up squarely to the church v. chapel controversy, admitting to his agent: 'without prejudice and improper bias it is all over with ye parsons and they know it must be so now'. His critical mind turned to the question of the divine inspiration of the Bible in view of its 'palpable contradictions'. During the years 1860-1862 he crossed swords with Connop Thirlwall, the bishop of St David's, concerning the 'persecution' of 'modernist' theologians like Colenso, and more especially of Rowland Williams of St David's College, Lampeter.[44] He held a view of the Church of England and other dissenters as 'schismatic', having severed itself from 'ye Romish which severed itself from ye Greek Church on ye question of ye third person of the Trinity'.[45]

Many gentry left matters of dogma to clerics and preachers, and were happy to live without any deep commitment to any particular creed. The Thomas brothers of Dôl-Llan and Llanfair (in spite of their excesses) did what was considered proper by regularly attending preaching meetings in their locality. Like other Welshmen of their day, sermon tasting and disputing about what they had heard took up some of their spare time. That it had little effect is seen in his reaction when the worthy divine, the Rev. John Jones of Blaenannerch, preached in December 1861 at the Tabernacle Chapel, Llandysul: '. . . his sermon was descriptive of our state hereafter and our souls when we die. All nonsense', was the comment of Thomas of Dôl-Llan.[46]

The Walters family of Perthgereint and Glanmedeni belonged to a different class of fervent and zealous conviction. Without any profound intellectual base, they were nevertheless avid to save souls; sinners were to be scourged with scorpions, and could only be redeemed by the prayers of the faithful. Frances Walters' life was governed by a fanatical compulsion and—to use the late Major Francis Jones' phrase—'the zeal of a Moslem engaged in a holy war'. In some of the neighbouring country houses and vicarages, prayers and Bible reading were vital to the day's activities. Collections were organised for the local poor and foreign missions, and the unabated enthusiasm of the Walters family led to the building of Watch Tower chapel in the park around Glanmedeni—endowed by Jane Walters and served by a Methodist divine—to perpetuate her apocalyptic zeal and burning faith.[47]

Around the beginning of this century, the Hope family of Pigeonsford were 'touched' in varying degrees by the 'born again' brand of Christianity. Forsaking gambling, horse racing and other vices, they organized open-air missions as—'valiant soldiers in the army of the Lord'—on race courses such as Epsom and Ascot, and in the Midland-town fairs of Peterborough, Nottingham and Leicester. Charles Hope evangelised on the beaches of Llangrannog and other coastal villages of south Cardiganshire, sadly ending his life in an institution as a result of incurable religious mania.[48]

NOTES AND SOURCES

[1]*Gent Mag.* 1788, p. 315; P. Jenkins: *op cit.*, p. 195.

[2]S. and B. Webb: *The Parish and the County*, i, 1906, p. 346, quoted in E. Moir: *op. cit.*, p. 83; J. H. Plumb: 'Nobility and the Gentry in the Early Nineteenth Century', *History Today*, V, 1955, p. 816; D. W. Howell: The Landed Gentry of Pembrokeshire in the Eighteenth Century (unpublished MA thesis, Wales, 1964), p. 178; E. Laws: *A History of Little England beyond Wales*, 1888, p. 406.

[3]H. M. Vaughan: *op cit.*, pp. 100-01.

[4]NLW/SD/CC Cd/(M)G3; for Sir Herbert Lloyd, Bt., the 'Vulture Knight', a classic example, see B. Phillips: *op cit.*, pp. 144, 158-61.

[5]*ibid*: C(G) 78; *DWB*; NLW/Ottley/1347.

[6]FG/14/259.

[7]NLW/Clynfyw/Box 1.

[8]D. L. Baker-Jones: 'Notes on the Orielton Chancery Proceedings', *NLWJ*, 3, 4, 1968, pp. 344-61, 405-22; NLW/Bronwydd/5402; NLW/Owen Colby/693, 1940-45.

[9]*ibid*: 503-79.

[10]H. M. Vaughan: pp. 108-10.

[11]J. H. Davies: *op cit.*, ii, p. 407.

[12]NLW/Highmead/Box P (File 5), 20 Jan. 1827; *ibid*: 3077.

[13]HRO/Wil/226: entries for 1 Jan. 1860, 29 Nov. 1861.

[14]NLW/Bronwydd/3642-52; information from the late Mr John Evans, Felindre (John y Gwas).

[15]NLW/St D/CC Cd/C(G) 86; H. Owen: *op cit.,* ii, pp. 923, 928; NLW/Morgan Richardson/2228-35; The 'gangland' methods of Herbert Lloyd are discussed in B. Phillips: *op cit.*, p. 219 seq.

[16]NLW/Ms 11091 E (margin note by F. Jones).

[17]*DWB*; J. M. Jones a W. Morgan: *Y Tadau Methodistaidd*, i, 1895, p. 331.

[18]P. Jenkins: *op cit.*, pp. 259-60; G. E. Mingay: *English Landed Society*, p. 288; G. H. Jenkins: *op cit.*, pp. 109-10; H. Owen: *op cit.*, ii, p. 928.

[19]NLW/Ottley/24; NLW/St D/CC Cm(G) 343, 343A, 471; 'incontinency'—lack of restraint in sexual matters, O.E.D.

[20]Burke: *op cit. sub* Brigstocke; NLW/Evans George/1322-50.

[21]NLW/Highmead/3075; FG/22/80.

[22]*loc cit.*

[23]Memorial tablet in Troedyraur church; NLW/St D/CC Cm/C(G) 1325.

[24]CRO/Museum/413; NLW/St D/Arches 8 (a-y) 1-50; G. Morgan: *A Welsh House and its Family*, 1997, pp. 77-102.

[25]NLW/Ticehurst Wyatt (Gwernant) Box 7.

[26]*ibid*: Box 7.

[27]RCLWM, iii, p. 487 [Qu 44, 946]; J. Owen: 'The Papers of John Davies Lloyd', Dyfed Archives Annual Report 1983, pp. 13-15. NLW/Howell, Glaspant/Diary 1896; Joshua ii, v. 18.

[28]CRO/Cawdor/2/258; Cd Ad: 7/5/1869, 24/1/1881; see note p. 145.

[29]HRO/D/Wil/226.

[30]G. H. Williams: *op cit.*, p. 10; NLW/St D/Wills; FG/25/70-1.

[31]FG/21/37.

[32]NLW/Highmead/Box P/File 5.

[33]Evidence from various QS/Order Books; based on a conversation with the late Captain Fitzwilliams of Old Cilgwyn; R. Porter: *op cit.*, p. 263.

[34]NLW/Evans George/3203, 3554, 3705; NLW/Noyadd Trefawr/1694.

[35]NLW/Morgan Richardson/1533.

[36]NLW/SD/CC Cm(P).

[37]CRO/Coedmore/1/170.

[38]*Blodau Dyfed*, 1824, Marwnad Thomas Llwyd, Cwmgloyn gan Ioan Siencyn, p. 300; NLW Henry Owen THS 2925 A (Haverfordwest 5).

[39]NLW/Ms 8724 B (John Davies 32).

[40]*DWB*; NLW/Bronwydd/Add mss 1093-1108.

[41]NLW/D. Pryse Williams/15633; G. M. Roberts: *Y Pêr Ganiedydd*, ii, 1958, pp. 204, 212, 258; FG/26/141; *DWB*.

[42]E. Morgan: *John Elias, Life and Letters*, 1973, p. 193; A. H. Williams: *John Wesley in Wales 1739-1790*, 1971, pp. xx, xxxv, 87, 94, 97, 101, 115, 121; L. J. Meyler: 'Wesley in Pembrokeshire', *Proc. West. Hist. Socy*, XXI, 8, 1939, p. 9. *DWB*.

[43]NLW/Llwyngwair/15649; NLW/Ms 894C.

[44]NLW/Cilgwyn/LB/39/18 Mch 1859, 24 Apr. 1859; *ibid*: 40/9 Dec. 1860; 41/15 Feb. 1861; correspondence May to July 1863; *DWB*.

[45]NLW/Cilgwyn/LB/40/15 Dec 1860.

[46]HRO/Wil/226. 12 Dec. 1861; Y Parch. J. Davies: *Cofiant y Parchedig John Jones, Blaenanerch*. N.D.

[47]F. Jones: *Walters of Perthgereint*, pp. 173-76, 183, 190.

[48]*Cd Ad*: 30/2/1900; CRO/Beckingsale/52/2744.

Llanfechan

(Illus. from *History and Antiquities of the County of Cardigan*, S.R. Meyrick, 1808.)

Old Waunifor

Perthyberllan

Perthgereint

Llysnewydd: garden front, 1790s.

(Illus. T. Nicholas.)

Berry Hill

Watch Tower Chapel

Glandovan

Sir Marteine O.M. Lloyd, Bart.,
Bronwydd

John Vaughan Colby, Ffynone
(Illus. from *South Wales Leaders* [ND] c. 1900.)

C.E.D. Morgan-Richardson,
Rhos-y-gilwen
(Illus. from *South Wales Leaders* [ND] c. 1900.)

Col. J.R. Howell, Pant-gwyn
(Illus.: *Wales, Historical, Biographical,
Pictorial, 1908.*)

Arms and Crest of Lloyd, Bronwydd

(Illus.: *Memorials: Llangunllo Church.*)

Arms and Crest of
Brigstocke, Blaenpant

(Illus.: *Landed Gentry*,
Burke, 1906.)

ωS · όφιS · καί · περιστερα

Clynfyw Vault, Maenordeifi

Waunifor Vault, Llanllwni

Section 4

The Squire in Public Life

The Problem of Rural Poverty

According to the norms of gentility, a gentleman's status carried ideals from which duties followed, and his superior wealth was a privilege which entailed responsibilities. As Thomas Smith had laid down in 1582, a gentleman 'must open his purse wider and augment his portion above others or else he doth diminish his portion above others'.[1] The goodwill of the community towards the gentry depended on the latter's patronage and support of the poor and needy; of worthy causes which were focussed around the parish church (and later the dissenting chapel), and of cultural activities like the sponsorship of local talent in poetry, music and craft.

The nagging and ubiquitous problem of poverty constantly faced the gentry. As a class, the poor had to depend on their betters for the right to work and the right to eat.[2]

The poor fell into many categories—cottagers, paupers, vagrants, gypsies, beggars and thieves—the flotsam and jetsam of society. Of these, the local community recognised in its midst the elderly, the orphaned and the sick; the labouring poor subject to the vagaries of the seasons, food prices, sickness and malnutrition; the marginally poor smallholder, craftsman and tradesman; the ex-servicemen, the wounded soldier and his family, and the illegitimate poor through the high incidence of bastardy.[3] The living conditions of the lower classes in terms of their dwellings, food and wages were at worst deplorable, and at best only tolerable.

How far the peasant's dwelling and lifestyle had developed since medieval times is difficult to ascertain.[4] Even in modern times, rural cottages in Wales were, too often, 'mud without and misery within'; they were not the picturesque tidy dwellings of the traditional lady in Welsh costume, but ill-constructed hovels, damp, dark, with mud floors, thatched roofs, wattle and daub chimneys and the *dowlad* or *croglofft* above[5] (i.e. space under the roof ascended to by means of a ladder). Insanitary conditions led to epidemics, such as the outbreak of typhus near Edwinsford in 1808 (although outside our area) and such a situation is typical of what happened generally.[6] While some observers such as *The Quarterly Review*, 1825 (xxxii, p. 194 seq), commented upon the marked improvement in rural dwellings since the 1750s, the same cannot be said of south-west Wales. According to Samuel Lewis, cottages in Cardiganshire in 1833 were 'very wretched'. Leading parishioners in Llangunllo in 1848 voiced grave concern about the dirty and insanitary state of many cottages.[7] In the 1860s, suggestions were mooted to improve the dwellings of working people by building well-lit, properly ventilated houses with decent sanitation, a sufficient number of living and sleeping rooms and even a '. . . sitting room for reading, writing and a little leisure'. Such idealism from radical intellectuals like R. J. Derfel, castigated the gentry for allowing their estate workers, tenants and cottagers to live in unsatisfactory conditions. Many an improving landlord, it must be remembered, had built suitable dwellings for estate workers, and the survival of estate cottages in the vicinity of the mansions of Blaenpant, Ffynone, Cilwendeg, Pentre, amongst others, bears ample testimony to what had been achieved. Nevertheless, in far too many cases, farmhouses and cottages were a 'positive disgrace', according to Dr Enoch Davies' evidence before the Land Commission. Likewise, the parish historians of the area confirm this view of peasant society at the end of the nineteenth century.[8] A recent analysis of the living conditions of the agricultural labourer in nineteenth-century Wales confirms that up to the mid-nineteenth century the agricultural wage earner lived a hard and impoverished existence.[9] Walter Davies had described the peasant's diet in Cardiganshire around 1810 as mainly consisting of pottage made up of bread, salt and water varied with oatmeal mixed with sheep's milk, flavoured with herbs and vegetables. Buttermilk or whey with potatoes, eaten with barley bread, could sometimes be supplemented with salted herrings in coastal districts. W. O. Brigstocke of Blaenpant (in his evidence before the Land Commission) regarded the Welsh tenant farmer as 'most thrifty and frugal, and his diet although somewhat rough is healthy and sufficient . . . fresh meat is rarely seen at table, and the diet of the farmer differs but little from that of the labourer'.[10] The spartan nature of a poor countryman's diet survived in many instances until recent decades—bread soaked in skimmed milk or tea forming a large part of their diet along with salt bacon. Roast meat was a rarity reserved for Sundays.[11]

As has been noticed already, the amount and usefulness of estate information from Tivyside concerning the wages of workmen and commodity prices is, on the whole, very disappointing for arriving at any coherent picture.[12] From a few sporadic references that can be cited, the wages of estate workers on the Gellydywyll estate in the 1770s varied from 6d to 1/6d per day. As the tasks were seasonal, there were long periods of unemployment for the casual labourers. One may suppose that a subsistence livelihood was obtained by cultivating a small area of ground adjoining the 'cotts' scattered over the estate. *The Cambrian Register* for 1796 quotes commodity prices at the main markets of Cardigan, Carmarthen and Haverfordwest: a couple of fat ducks 1s 6d-2s; eggs @ 4d a dozen; bacon @ 5d-8d per lb; beef and mutton @ 6d per lb; coals @ 2½d-3d per bushel, etc. But these reflect the selling price of items in the market towns which by their very nature would, perhaps, be beyond the reach of an ordinary country labourer. Roast meat and poultry would be expensive luxuries, as was wheaten bread; coals would be unnecessary, as gathered firewood and peat turves were the labourer's usual source of fuel. From the 1790s continental wars enriched the large landowner, capitalist and manufacturer, but exacerbated the condition of the impoverished labourer faced with low wages in relation to steeply rising prices.[13] According to Lloyd Hall's evidence before the Poor Law Commission of 1834, labourers' wages in the Newcastle Emlyn area ranged between five to six shillings a week—'generally low', if not worse, in comparison with the seven to eight shillings in other parts of south-west Wales during the period.[14] With farming still in a deep trough of depression in 1852 the casual male and female worker was in dire plight. Thus, a miner's widow in Llandyfrïog parish maintained herself and her six year-old daughter by knitting stockings, which, according to the squire of Cilgwyn, '. . . is too precarious as the farmers now cannot afford to employ her'. The significant increase in agricultural rates, as a whole, came with the construction of the railways from mid-century, which brought easier access to the 'works' and a consequent thinning of the local labour market.[15] A well organised estate, such as Cilgwyn, had to offer in 1862 its skilled key workers, such as the headman, foreman, foreman-mason, carpenter and the like, wages of two to three shillings a day, with women and unskilled labourers receiving something like 11d to 1s 6d,[16] all 'on their own finding'. While wages inevitably varied from estate to estate, employees earning less could be compensated by direct support from the squire in the form of incidental 'vails': clothes from the big house and ample spare food from the kitchens. Thus, the coachman at Dolaucothi, at the end of the last century earned one guinea a month (thirteen guineas paid at the end of the year), while everything necessary to clothe and feed his family during the year came from the mansion. Although this example is outside the 'Tivyside' area, it is typical of what occurred. The head gardener at Blaenpant earned about 24s per week supplemented with coal, milk, vegetables and two loads of potatoes during the year. Likewise, under-gardeners were allowed the 'keep of a cow', while the coachman and bailiff had their food in the big house as well as a rent-free cottage. At Llysnewydd, from 1895 to 1909, workers were paid from 1s to about 3s 6d per day according to their respective skills, which compare with the rates paid on the large Glamorgan estates at that time.[17] Working conditions were arduous and the hours were long. Indoor servants worked indefinite hours from early morning until late at night (and this applied to the squire's mansion as well as to his tenant-farmer's house). There were no fixed holidays, apart from a degree of flexibility in regard to absence from work to attend social gatherings like funerals, weddings, *eisteddfodau*, preaching or singing festivals and fairs. In the squire's mansion and on his home farm, there were various ways whereby employees could 'work the system' during the squire's absence with his family, or when the weather could provide an excuse for general 'hanging about', especially if the squire was not over vigilant.[18]

The general condition of the agricultural worker (apart from employees fortunate to work on a generous and not over regimented estate) was a harsh impoverished existence with strenuously long hours of work, low wages, poor accommodation and a meagre undernourishing diet. The recollections of E. Pan Jones (1834-1922) speak of how his mother earned £3 10s a year as a farm servant, supplemented by one pound of wool, four yards of flannel for clothing, along with wood for clogs as footwear. Low wages could also be supplemented by earnings from seasonal migration to Worcester, Hereford and other parts of England during the hay and corn harvests.[19]

Working conditions gave hardly any leisure time. During long winter evenings up to the early decades of the nineteenth century, the household sat around a peat or log fire, with the women knitting, peeling rushes for lights, and the menfolk carving wooden spoons, ladles or making wicker baskets. Possibly, the Bible was read, and lighter diversions took the form of telling stories or propounding riddles. Folk customs connected with marriages, births or deaths continued to be observed. Religious festivals, the original meaning of which had long been attenuated or forgotten, provided some relief to the hardship of the times. Methodism and dissent were becoming more and more an educative influence on social and moral behaviour, as well as providing a forum for political discussion through sermon, *cyfarfod diwylliadol* (cultural meeting) and general chapel involvement.[20]

NOTES AND SOURCES

[1]T. Smith: *De Republica Anglorum*, 1582, p. 40.

[2]A. Briggs: *op cit.*, pp. 57-8.

[3]J. R. Poynter: *Society and Pauperism, English Ideas and Poor Relief, 1795-1834*, 1969, pp. 21 seq.

[4]C. Wood: *The Age of Chivalry*, 1970, p. 38—for a description of peasant life in the middle ages.

[5]E. Davies: *op cit.*, pp. 31-32; information from B. H. Jones, Penrhiw-llan, Llandysul.

[6]R. J. Colyer: 'The Edwinsford Estate in the Early Nineteenth Century', *BBCS*, xxvi, ii, 1975, pp. 200-17.

[7]S. Lewis: *op cit., sub* Cards; E. Davies: *op cit.*, p. 33.

[8]*Y Beirniad*: 1862-63, 4, pp. 197-204; *Cymru Fydd*, 1888, i, p. 271; *DWB; RCLWM*, iii [Qu. 44, 312]. Robert Jones Derfel (1824-1905) poet and socialist; advocate of reform; one of the promoters of the Manchester and District Fabian Society; *DWB*.

[9]D. W. Howell: 'The Agricultural Labourer in Nineteenth Century Wales', *WHR*, 6, 1973, 3, pp. 262-287.

[10]NLW/Ms 1756. f. 8; W. J. Lewis: 'Labour in Mid Cardiganshire in the Early Nineteenth Century', *Ceredigion*, iv, 4, 1963, pp. 323-24; *RCLWM*, iii [Qu. 43, 281].

[11]Personal knowledge.

[12]cf L. J. Williams and D. Jones: 'The Wages of Agricultural Labourers in the Nineteenth Century—The Evidence from Glamorgan', *BBCS*, 29, 1982, pp. 749-61; NLW/Evans George/3195.

[13]Lloyd and Turnor: *op cit.*, D. W. Howell: *Land and People*, pp. 99-100.

[14]RCAPL 1834 [Qu. 5, 566].

[15]NLW/Cilgwyn/LB/34/12 May 1852; *loc cit.*

[16]NLW/Cilgwyn/LB/44/6 Mar. 1870.

[17]Information from descendants in the 1950s; CRO/EG/Box 23; Llysnewydd Farm Account Book, 1895-1909 in private hands.

[18]Recollections of elderly former employees on local estates.

[19]D. W. Howell: *op cit.*, p. 105; *DWB*; E. Pan Jones: *Oes Gofion* [ND], pp. 5-6; J. Williams-Davies: 'Merched y Gerddi: A Seasonal Migration of Female Labour from Rural Wales', *Folk Life*, 15, 1977, pp. 12-22.

[20]J. Rhys and D. B. Jones: *op cit.*, pp. 598-90; D. E. Jones: *op cit.*, pp. 362-92; H. Evans: *Cwm Eithin*, 1943, pp. 143-79. *RCLWM Report*, 1896, pp. 233-4.

The Gentry, Rural Poverty and the Education of the People

Henry Richard in condemning the Welsh gentry, alleged that '. . . almost everything that has been done in past times for the improvement and elevation of society in Wales, has been done by the people, through their own exertions and from their own resources, with very little help from the upper classes'. Richard was blind to the fact, or as a politician wished to ignore, that it was a moral imperative for the rich to care for the poor within what had been regarded for centuries as a divinely-appointed hierarchical and social stratification of the community.[1] Wealth and poverty existed side by side, and the majority of the squirearchy and the more affluent persons realised their responsibility for the general good of the community which included the concept of 'social harmony'.[2] Despite the widely held view that the church belonged to rich men, many a squire and parson had long been concerned with the administration of poor relief, bequests and charities, in spite of the shortcomings of the system.[3]

In the nineteenth century, increased government legislation could only be put into execution through the gentry acting as the unpaid local officers, who promoted a benevolent paternalism to bring about better working conditions, schools for the labouring classes, friendly and benefit societies, and clothing clubs to foster Victorian virtues of industry, perseverance, tidiness and order. Through the application of the Biblical precepts of piety, gentleness, sobriety, truthfulness, diligence and self denial, a moral and dutiful working class could evolve.[4]

The question to be asked is—how far did the gentry of the lower Teifi valley in the period 1700-1939 create a climate of goodwill and social harmony between themselves and the lower orders? How far did they stretch out their hands in helping those who were struggling for survival and those whose aspirations were often beyond their means? The conclusion reached in a study of the Pembrokeshire gentry of the eighteenth century is that, as landlords, the gentry had a 'sympathetic regard for their tenants and showed consideration for those in distress', and their sympathy was extended towards the labouring poor in the community during hard times, and in Carmarthenshire in the mid-nineteenth century the gentry responded to their Christian duty to defend and befriend the poor. Even if there was a strong element of self interest in what they did, there was a degree of benevolent paternalism on the part of the gentry which it would be churlish not to recognise. On the other hand, with the wide gap between the rich and poor, the gentry could have done much more for the poor given the extent of their incomes spent on entertainment and leisure pursuits.

From an examination of the evidence relating to the gentry of 'Tivyside', one can only come to the conclusion that some of the squires were 'sympathetic patrons in times of distress'.[5] The family estate and its prosperity depended a great deal on the loyalty, long service and devotion of its tenants and workers. The gentry reciprocated by making provision in their wills as a token of their gratitude. To take a few examples: Maurice Morris of Ffynone in 1727 left twenty shillings a year each for life to two loyal retainers; lump sums varied from a few pounds to over £20, as were provided in the wills of Anne Parry of Noyadd Trefawr in 1740 and of Jane Colby in 1787. Occasionally, there were gifts in kind to help a cottager or smallholder, and examples of a sheep and a lamb were by no means uncommon.[6] The well-being in old age of former retainers sometimes prompted concern on the part of the squire, as happened in 1834 when Major Evans of Highmead authorised his agent to spend one guinea to provide 'a Bible and spectacles' for an aged servant on his Dolgadfan estate in Montgomeryshire.[7] In mid-century E. Crompton Ll. Fitzwilliams supported the indigent and aged on his Cilgwyn estate, but stipulated that they had to carry out light tasks in lieu of the cash doles handed out to them. He believed that by receiving money, without giving some equivalent in work, his dependants would lose their self-respect. A similar practice was observed at Bronwydd up to this century.[8]

Seasonal gifts were also a feature of gentry charity, and many examples can be cited of the gift of blankets, clothing, culm, beef, foodstuffs and household necessities from squires such as Thomas Morgan of Cardigan. Foremost in facing up to their social responsibilities towards the lower orders were ladies like Mrs Colby of Ffynone, Mrs Saunders Davies of Pentre and (up to the 1930s) Lady Lloyd of Bronwydd.[9]

The squire's position in society, his affluence and his regard for the public good, meant that his charitable acts were extended to those in the community other than those comprising the dependants on his estate. Gentry wills from the seventeenth century until the last decades of the nineteenth, illustrate the squire's concern for the needs of the local poor, for worthy causes such as almshouses or persons hit by natural calamity or as a result of national events. One cannot resist the conclusion that gentry wills, on the whole, contained some provision for alleviating poverty. To cite a few examples: Lloyd of Pantcilgan, left five shillings to the poor of Llangeler parish in 1684, and the poor of Penrith parish had an almshouse provided for them by Morgan of Blaenbylan, its endowments forming a charge on his estate 'to be payable for ever'.[10] It seems to be the case that sums were bequeathed in proportion to the influence and amount of land owned by the squire in certain parishes. Towards the end of the seventeenth century David Parry of Noyadd Trefawr, for example, bequeathed £5 each to the poor of Llandygwydd and St Dogmael's parishes, but only £1 to Llangrannog. At a time when rights over land were thought to last for ever, many of these bequests were charges upon the estate.[11] Those not beholding to the squire's family as homagers on his common, or those who through some claim could not vote for his clan's interest—such as paupers or 'pensioners' in receipt of parish relief—were sometimes excluded, as in the wills of Thomas of Camnant in 1762, and Price of Pigeonsford in 1786. Although the cash bequests were small in relation to the affluence of some gentry, occasionally fairly substantial sums occur. Thus Hester Bowen's endowment of £300 (the interest from which was to be given in flannel to the deserving poor of Troedyraur parish) in the early 1800s was exceptional.[12] Again, in the 1860s the £2,000 endowment left by Miss Lloyd of Plasybridell for the poor of Cardigan town and its neighbourhood was an act of singular munificence.[13]

The frequent press references in the nineteenth century to gentry liberality, especially at Christmastide, suggest a degree of competition and advertisement of their 'godly works' on the part of the squirearchy. Each vied with his neighbour in attracting the gratitude and goodwill of their inferiors. Doubtless, it cannot be denied that a few like Mrs Lloyd of Bronwydd in 1852, were motivated by pure altruism, and explained that she was only 'carrying out a duty incumbent' on her as 'it was better to give than to receive'.[14]

In addition to gifts of food and clothing, and luxuries like oranges and sweetmeats, gentry charity included the provision of tea parties, games and entertainment, like magic-lantern shows for the children living in the vicinity of the mansion. Even the inmates of local work-houses were sometimes invited to mansions like Rhosygilwen to enjoy special treats.[15] In monetary terms, however, the largesse given could not have been much in relation to the expensive and extravagant display and consumption of the gentry in their lavish parties, hunt suppers, food, wine, horses and equipage. While no gift horse is to be looked in the mouth, Sir Edward Webley-Parry-Pryse's gift, in 1898, of ten rabbits to the Cardigan workhouse could not have stretched his resources unduly![16]

In their strong defence of the established Church of England in Wales and in the face of a mounting tide of nonconformist opposition, it is only fair to state that some, at least, of the gentry tried, through their acts of charity and patronage, to defuse a highly charged political and religious climate in order to retain community deference and loyalty. Thus, it was said of Harford of Falcondale (and this is true of the Lloyds of Bronwydd), that '. . . a fixed principle had been laid down by himself and his wife of absolute religious equality. All sick and needy should be succoured, all farms and cottages let, all children and their elders welcome to entertainments irrespective of creed'. Sums of money were also donated by William Price Lewes of Llysnewydd and William Owen Brigstocke of Blaenpant, amongst others, from the 1850s onward 'irrespective of the creed or denomination' of their recipients.[17]

The degree of community gratitude and response can be partly measured in the columns of the local press, with their lavish praise for gentry 'munificence and liberality'. The 'indulgent landlord' treated his inferiors with 'parent like regard for their welfare'. The liberal charity of John Lloyd Davies of Blaendyffryn during the severe winter of 1859-60 prompted this comment: 'two things are conducive above all others to make society happy and united, namely sympathy and active benevolence on the part of the rich, and a willing honest tribute of respect to their superiors on the part of the poor'.[18] An unhealthy obsequiousness occurs towards Mrs Maria Brigstocke of Blaenpant, admittedly a foremost benefactress in the area, on the occasion of a local school treat: 'it was a pretty sight to see child after child marching up to their kind benefactress, with hand extended and face bright with happy innocence to receive the annual Christmas box'.[19] Nevertheless, the more perceptive, while not begrudging the wealth and 'charitable works' of the gentry, mused philosophically on the passing of many old squires. Death was the great leveller, and in the words of a local rhymester:

> Where Pantgwyn is Squire Griffith?
> Where Penlan is Jones the just?
> So the rich and poor together
> Sweetly slumber in the dust.

A more articulate undercurrent of protest, in response to the frippery and superficial trimmings of seasonal charity, is seen in the comment of a local observer: pretty decorations and baubles were '. . . but very indifferent articles for an empty stomach'.[20]

There was in the outlook of the gentry a concern for public religion, morality, the evils of drunkenness and consequent poverty. The efforts of the Rev. Griffith Jones of Llanddowror (born in Penboyr parish), the SPCK and important south-west Wales gentry like Sir John Philipps of Picton Castle, had had a marked effect on the conscience of 'Tivyside' personalities like Erasmus Saunders, William Brigstocke of Blaenpant, and erudite clerics like Moses Williams.[21] Before the spiritual convulsions of Methodism, squires like Jones of Pantyderi in 1728, bequeathed 20s to endow a Welsh sermon at Llanfair Nantgwyn church 'for the good Edification and Reformation of the Auditories'. Later in the century there was support for and participation in 'Methodist' activities by many families.[22] In the early nineteenth century, societies for encouraging piety, virtue and the prevention of vice drew support from leading dignitaries like Bishop Burgess of St David's and squires like William Lewes of Llysnewydd and James Richard Lewes-Lloyd of Dolhaidd. The distribution of Bibles, Prayer Books and devotional works was paid for through gentry subscription in 1826.[23] Local Bible societies were formed; and, alarmed by the dangers of atheism, republicanism, civil strife, the gentry joined hands in amity with dissenters in their attempts to stem popular movements. Thus, in 1836 and 1857 squires like John Lloyd Williams of Gwernant and Thomas Davies Lloyd of Bronwydd made eloquent speeches in political gatherings, along with nonconformists.[24] A more sectarian aspect of gentry patronage developed in the second half of the century when societies like the Laity Society in Aberbanc, fostered by the Lloyds of Bronwydd, met to study and discuss the Book of Common Prayer, the duties of the Christian layman vis-à-vis the established church, as well as the social and moral questions of the day.[25]

In a classic passage Samuel Smiles wrote: 'No laws however stringent, can make the idle industrious, the thriftless provident or the drunken sober'. Aware of the evils of drunkenness, temperance societies were promoted, especially by the Harfords of Falcondale and other squires, who also made fervent efforts to reduce the number of public houses.[26] In country towns like Cardigan, Newcastle Emlyn and Lampeter, one out of every two houses was a tavern—to the great concern of squires like Archdeacon North. Total abstinence movements followed; rallies were held with prominent gentry taking part, like the one on the Preseli hills in 1875. To combat drunkenness at Llandysul, on fair and market days, the Lloyds of Gilfachwen and Waunifor started a coffee tavern to be financed by the gentry and other well meaning persons.[27] Through provident and friendly societies, the habits of sobriety and thrift were instilled into the labouring classes. These had existed since the end of the eighteenth century, with the government legislating to provide guidelines for their administration. Their aims were well expressed, namely to raise money by subscription and donation for the '. . . Mutual Relief and Maintenance of such members, their Wives and Children, Relations or Nominees in Sickness, Infancy, Advanced Age or Death'. Amongst the many societies, the Oddfellows and Ivorites had gained ground in Wales during the years 1835 to 1880. Although the aims of these societies included support for the Welsh language, Druidism and Antiquarianism, as well as to safeguard against revolutionary influences, the main emphasis was upon the practice of thrift as a basis for future welfare benefits.[28] But earlier in the century, Archdeacon Beynon, who was Lord Cawdor's agent and right-hand man in the area, with Dr Davies of Pentre, had promoted the Edinburgh Savings Bank Plan, which aimed at improving farming and rewarding the long service of agricultural workers. Groups like the True Ivorites and Oddfellows met at inns and chapels and were hospitably received in gentry houses such as Cilwendeg, Ffynone, Pentre, Pantgwyn and Cilgwyn and their processions were led by the Bronwydd band.[29] Gentry support went further than donations and hospitality. Many identified themselves personally with these movements by becoming full members. In the 1860s and '70s gentry, such as Sir Thomas Davies Lloyd, Richard Jenkins of The Priory and Arthur Henry Saunders Davies of Pentre, were 'initiated'. These philanthropic societies, while of immense value in improving the outlook and habits of the lower orders, were also supported by the gentry as they could be used to buttress the *status quo*. Their mottoes were 'patriotism, philanthropy and morality', which were the essential qualities in 'a contented and law abiding community'. The afflicted, such as widows and orphans, were helped in times of distress through these societies, and they also kept thousands from the workhouse and the stigma of pauperism. Moreover, the working classes were educated to be 'good and provident members of society', but the old order of rich man in his castle and pauper at his gate was not to be seriously challenged.[30]

In conjunction with the benefit societies, clothing clubs, with the gentry as prime movers, were aimed at encouraging poor folk to set aside something like a penny every week towards a fund for the purchase of clothes. Their organisation and financial support depended on ladies like Mrs Lloyd of Bronwydd.[31] These clothing clubs were only partially successful because some took unfair advantage of the scheme. In 1861 Fitzwilliams sought to resolve the problem by setting up a Charitable Loan Society, to lend blankets and provide household needs at cost price to the poor only.[32]

While many charitable acts of the gentry to dependants on the estate or in the local community were done, they were also sensitive of the needs of those far outside their own areas. Events of national or international importance resulting in suffering or hardship invariably touched their heartstrings. The relief of necessitous clergy, their widows and orphans prompted a very sympathetic response. Gentry support can be traced from 1785 until the end of the nineteenth century.[33] Families whose menfolk were mainly engaged in sailing and fishing along the Cardiganshire and north Pembrokeshire coast suffered frequently from shipwreck and drowning. Similarly, the construction of the railway to places like Llandysul, Newcastle Emlyn and Cardigan resulted in serious and often fatal accidents. Consequently, the squire felt it his duty to respond by helping deprived and bereaved families.[34]

The loyal support of the gentry to the government's conduct of affairs, at both a national and international level, claimed from them a public assertion of their position and authority. Times of social crisis and suffering elicited a response from the gentry towards relieving hardship, which was seen to be a veritable duty on their part as a natural concomitant of their status. During food riots in Haverfordwest in 1800, John Colby of Ffynone had to take prompt measures to minimise the effect of civil commotion by ordering the sale of corn at reduced prices, because '. . . unless some immediate means were adopted for the relief of the poor they were determined to [acquire] relief themselves'.[35] The quality of corn sold and its weight were strictly enforced by Cardigan gentry from the 1790s.[36] During the 1840s Lewis of Clynfyw sold all his barley to his workmen and local poor for 4/2d a bushel, while other gentry and farmers sold theirs to merchants at twice the price. The ravages of the Napoleonic Wars in Germany prompted Thomas Lloyd of Bronwydd and other gentry to organise a relief fund. Likewise, famine in Ireland from 1822 onwards, and the distress of the Lancashire cotton workers in 1863, met with a generous response from the 'Tivyside' gentry.[37]

As an important part of their functions as magistrates, the gentry visited prisons from time to time to examine the state of the buildings and the welfare of prisoners. Frequently, there are references of gifts of money from the pockets of the gentry to provide a few comforts for indigent prisoners in Cardigan and Carmarthen prisons.[38]

When medical services were crude and primitive, the gentry were foremost in promoting welfare schemes. Thus, in 1821 Mrs Brigstocke made a donation to a 'lying in charity', and William Lewes of Llysnewydd supported a new 'dispensary' in Aberystwyth. Later, the establishment of the infirmary in Carmarthen in 1847 was largely brought about through the generosity and patronage of west Wales gentry families, such as Saunders Davies of Pentre, Colby of Ffynone and Lewes of Llysnewydd. Likewise, through gentry support towards the end of the century, the Joint Counties' Asylum at Carmarthen came into being.[39]

Public hygiene, like applying limewash to cottages in Felindre in 1862 to prevent cholera, the acquisition of copious quantities of disinfectant for Cilgerran, and the supply of pure drinking water for the townsfolk of Lampeter, all provided for by the gentry, illustrate their concern for the health and welfare of the community.[40] All this amounted to a practical gesture against poverty, ill-health and disease, it is readily conceded; and one which also enhanced their position and prestige as custodians of public welfare.

The view that the gentry as a class were not committed to the support of popular education, but were concerned rather with keeping the poor 'in their due place in society', does less than justice to those who supported schools in south-west Wales in the eighteenth and nine-teenth centuries. From the sixteenth century, grammar schools in Cardigan, Carmarthen and Haverfordwest had been founded through the aristocratic patronage of persons like Thomas Lloyd, precentor of St David's, Lady Cornwallis and Thomas Lloyd of Cilciffeth.[41] In 'Tivyside', in particular, there is some evidence for gentry encouragement of schools, dating back at least to the mid-eighteenth century. The Rev. Dr Philipps, chaplain at Blaenpant, supported centres for instruction in reading and writing, and especially the school at Ystrad Meurig. Early in the 1800s, the Rev. Daniel Bowen of Waunifor and his son provided over £2,000 to endow schools in west Wales and a scholarship at St David's College, Lampeter. Archdeacon Beynon, in providing a school in Penboyr parish, aimed at the 'gratuitous' instruction of 'poor children'.[42] Contributions towards maintaining schools in London and the provinces, were freely given by wealthy squiresses such as Dame Anna Owen.[43]

As the clamour for universal education gained momentum in the nineteenth century, certain values had to be shed. Education, merely as a means to instil sound principles and good moral behaviour, was deemed insufficient. The 'utilitarian' view spoke of the 'greatest good for the greatest number' and of 'the universal diffusion of general knowledge'. Some wished to hasten slowly lest the education of those doomed to toil and drudgery might lead to discontent and revolt.[44] The British and National School Societies (founded in 1808 and 1811) were born when revolutionary theories re-echoed, especially in Wales, in the propaganda of Jac Glan y Gors and Tomos Glyn Cothi. The 'Tivyside' gentry responded by donating land and money to build new schools in Cardigan, Cenarth and Newcastle Emlyn, to cite a few examples.[45] While the 'Blue Books' *Report* on education in 1847 commented unfavourably on so many schools in Wales, an exception to be singled out was the one at Llandygwydd in our area, '. . . housed in excellent classrooms . . . chiefly due to Mrs Brigstocke of Blaenpant'. There is, nevertheless, considerable truth in the charge made by William Williams (MP for Coventry) concerning the neglect by Welsh landlords of their duty in giving aid to educate the people. If they had done so, they would have been repaid tenfold by the improved condition of their estates and by having an intelligent 'superior' tenantry.[46] With increasing awareness of political, religious and sectarian issues on the part of Tory churchmen and radical dissenters, bias and prejudice crept into the organisation of new schools. At the new school in Newcastle Emlyn 'for the labouring classes', religious knowledge was taught by the incumbent of the parish. 'Other knowledge' had to be approved by the 'Committee', namely the local gentry. Education in the 'doctrine of the church of England' was a proviso demanded by Lord Cawdor, and Lewes of Llysnewydd, if they were to support the new schools at Cenarth and Llanfihangel-ar-Arth.[47] Although cautious of their vested interests, a minority of gentry like Jenkins of The Priory, Lloyd Hall and Brigstocke, in giving evidence before the commissioners of 1847 deplored the lack of good schools and the deficient knowlege of the majority in secular subjects as opposed to Sunday school instruction.[48]

The principle of state aid for education was not officially accepted in England and Wales until about 1853, and while some gentry blamed the lack of government support, Thomas Lloyd of Coedmore admitted his dread of state interference in education, promulgating, instead, voluntaryist methods to secure adequate facilities. He was more in tune with a vocal dissenting lobby who maintained that it was the duty of the religious denominations to provide education for their children.[49]

Denominational and anti-church bias prompted a liberal reaction from the Rev. Lewis Davies of Cenarth and Thomas Davies Lloyd of Bronwydd, who sought a *modus vivendi* between church and chapel. Bible teaching, they maintained, should be without sectarian bias in church schools, and pupils should be allowed to attend their own places of worship.[50] In 1853 Thomas Davies Lloyd, no doubt aware of the adverse reaction to the 'Blue Books' and of suggestions by Sir Thomas Phillips for a comprehensive Welsh educational system, urged the 'application of industrial principles to the schools, to further commercial and mechanical interests', especially, with the expansion of industry and the railways which was taking place. In addition, Davies Lloyd, at the time of the Reform Bill of 1867, argued for an educated working class, because the extension of the franchise, giving more political power to them, would be an unmitigated evil unless there was a corresponding provision of education.

Other motives stimulated gentry patronage of schools. A small landowner, like Griffiths of Pantgwyn, in view of heavy rates on the community, hoped for understanding and co-operation between churchmen and dissenters to lessen the burden.[51] The spread of Church (National) Schools aroused bitterness within nonconformist ranks, to be exacerbated after the Education Bill of 1870 on account of the provision of religious teaching with an Anglican bias to nonconformist pupils. In hundreds of rural parishes, the Church retained its monopoly of primary education. Lloyd George and O. M. Edwards were themselves rebellious products of these schools. The gentry rejected the argument of dissenters that the people of Wales would, on account of church schools, suffer under a 'clerical' yoke.[52]

Teifi valley gentry, living amongst their tenants who were often nonconformist, possibly responded with greater sensitivity to local needs than what the vociferous propagandists on national platforms alleged. Griffiths of Pantgwyn, as we have seen, had in 1854 sought co-operation and understanding, between churchmen and dissenters to lessen the heavy burden of rates on the community.[53] And, in the acrimonious climate of political and religious controversy after 1870, wealthy gentry families like Colby, Brigstocke and Gower were determined to shoulder the cost themselves. Thus, John Colby of Ffynone built the Maenordeifi schoolroom and master's house in 1872 for £700, and the family continued to support the school until 1927.[54] In fairness, the motives of some gentry, at least, were not only to avoid a school board and heavy rates, but also to provide a religious education to ensure that their dependants in the community were free from 'godless and secular influences'. Moreover, in so doing, these gentry succeeded in retaining the good will of the community, who on account of the bonds between them were '. . . undisturbed by the agitation which has taken place in other parishes'.[55]

Genuine attempts were made to respond in a conciliatory manner to the attacks from dissenting and radical quarters. In reply to the criticism of church schools by politicians like Henry Richard, who regarded the teaching of the catechism and the creeds to nonconformist children as an influence to 'pervert' them from 'the faith of their fathers', a few gentry like W. O. Brigstocke and George Bowen displayed a radically ecumenical approach. While questioning whether any Biblical teaching could profitably be given without doctrinal or exegetical comment, they proposed that local nonconformist ministers could, with 'increased vigilance', visit church schools to hear for themselves what religious teaching was being given.[56]

The foundation of the Anglican St David's College at Lampeter in 1827 had met with a generous response from the local gentry. Money poured in to support the building fund and to establish bursaries. Harford, owner of the Peterwell estate, gave the land for the college, and, as the primary purpose of St David's College was to educate clergymen, the gentry as pillars of the established church did not fail in their patronage.[57]

By way of contrast, half a century later the landlord class in Tivyside did not show any marked enthusiasm towards the founding of the first university college of Wales at Aberystwyth. In the flux of conflicting religious dogma, acrimonious political and educational debate, only a few 'Tivyside' gentry gave it unqualified support. The 'Liberal' Sir Thomas Davies Lloyd of Bronwydd, MP for Cardiganshire, used the college opening celebrations to share the limelight with other politicians like Henry Richard, E. M. Richards and Osborne Morgan.[58] Commenting on the work of the Aberdare Committee of 1881, W. O Brigstocke took a line totally alien to his fellow gentry: 'Wales has a distinct nationality of its own', and there was no greater mistake than to look at Welsh affairs through English spectacles. St David's College,

Lampeter, he argued, was on a par with Oxford and Cambridge, but 'because of its theological teaching in accordance with the view of a minority of Welsh people, it was practically a Church of England establishment and never can become a great national institution'.[59]

The movement to provide secondary education, culminating in the Welsh Intermediate Education Act of 1889, only found a limited response from the Teifi valley gentry.[60] But Morgan Richardson, Miles of The Priory and W. O. Brigstocke, supported the Cardigan Intermediate School with donations and a gift of land. The Lloyds of Waunifor gave their blessing to the new county school at Llandysul, allowing their family arms and motto to be adapted as the badge of the new school.[61]

The need for 'profitable means of recreation' and 'popular education to put the people in the way of amusing and refreshing themselves in a rational manner' was legitimately advocated by public figures within the Liberal ranks of Welsh society, such as D. Lleufer Thomas and T. E. Ellis.[62] But in fairness, from the 1860s, the 'Tivyside' gentry had gone some way in promoting activities where workers would learn new interests and improve themselves. The 'penny readings' at Newcastle Emlyn were aimed at giving the lower classes some insight into popular English literature of quality, and had the backing of squires like Fitzwilliams. Village reading rooms and institutes were fashionable, with gentry like Webley-Parry of Noyadd Trefawr, Colby of Ffynone and Gower of Castle Malgwyn, amongst others, providing books and wholesome reading matter.[63] The Maesllyn Club and Reading Room was built by the Tylers of Mount Gernos 'for the convenience of the employees of the Maesllyn Mill and the working men and youths of the locality'. Doubtless, books, newspapers and games like chess and draughts were harmless pastimes, which the squire's generosity provided for the genuine improvement of his dependants. The labouring community could hear lectures on sensitive topics like the new local government acts of the 1880s by broad-minded gentry like Jones-Parry of Tŷ Llwyd.[64] While there was, on the whole, no obvious attempt by the gentry who founded reading rooms and institutes to suppress religious and political debate, Col. William Price Lewes of Llysnewydd, however, laid down that 'no politics be allowed' in the Velindre Reading Room, as a condition of granting a lease. Likewise, David Davies of Cardigan Castle, protested at the management of the Mechanics' Institute in the town as being 'too sectarian and political'.[65] Provided that the reading room, club or institute sustained a placid deference to the gentry in political and social attitudes, they were to be promoted and nurtured. Once they became a forum for the debate of burning topical matters they were to be tamed and restrained like dangerous animals. All in all, the efforts of the gentry to educate the people were limited in outlook, inadequate and aimed in the main towards Church of England families, estate tenants and such sections of the community who remained submissive to the existing order. The charges levelled by William Williams MP against the gentry in the decades up to 1850, as already mentioned, were still largely true at the end of the nineteenth century.

NOTES AND SOURCES

[1] H. Richard: *op cit.*, pp. 115-16; A. Briggs: 'Middle Class Consciousness in English Politics 1780-1846', *P and P*, 1946, ix, p. 65.

[2] H. Perkin: *op cit.*, p. 28; A. Smith: *Wealth of Nations*, i, 1776, p. 263; E. Moir: *op cit.*, p. 104.

[3] J. P. D. Dunbabin: *Rural Discontent in Nineteenth Century Britain*, 1974, p. 14; O. Chadwick: *op cit.*, ii, 1971, p. 158.

[4] D. Roberts: *Victorian Origins of the British Welfare State*, 1960, pp. 177-79, 193.

[5] D. W. Howell: 'The Pembrokeshire Gentry in the Eighteenth Century', *Carms Studies*, pp. 183-84; R. J. Colyer: 'The Gentry and County in Nineteenth Century Cardiganshire', *WHR*, 10 Dec. 1981, 4, pp. 497-535. M. Cragoe, i. *op cit.*, p. 94.

[6] NLW/OwenColby/362; FG/19/241-42; 239; NLW/Ms 8716B.

[7] NLW/D. Pryse Williams/15623E.

[8] *Cd Ad*: 27/12/1872; recollections of the late Mrs R. Davies, Glen View, Llangunllo.

[9] *ibid*: 23/4/1875, 10/1/1896.

[10] NLW/Wills/St D/1684; FG/16/238-39.

[11] NLW/Noyadd Trefawr/465, 484.

[12] NLW/D. Pryse Williams/15658A; NLW/Morgan-Richardson (Pigeonsford) 1870; NLW/Ms/5152B.

[13] CRO/Coedmore/4/435-46; HRO/D/WIL/-.

[14] *Cm Jnl*: 16/1/1852.

[15] *The Welshman*: 21/1/1870; 28/12/1877; 4/1/1884; 2/1/1891; 3/9/1897.

[16] *ibid*: 3/2/1898.

[17] A. M. Harford: *op cit.*, pp. 147-48; *Cm Jnl*: 31/3/1854; *Cd Ad*: 1/1/1875.

[18] *Cm Jnl*: 11/1/1856, 6/1/1860.

[19] *Cd Ad*: 12/1/1872.

[20] *ibid*: 15/2/1867, 4/1/1867.

[21] M. Clement: *Correspondence and Minutes of the SPCK relating to Wales, 1699-1740*, 1952, pp. 28, 45, 70, 78-9, 82, 194; *DWB*.

[22] HRO/D/Pen/27/28.

[23] *Cm Jnl*: 26/11/1813, 11/8/1826.

[24] *ibid*: 4/3/1836; 23/11/1857.

[25] *Yr Haul*: 1865, p. 197.

[26] *Self Help*, 1859, ch 1; A. M. Harford: *op cit.*, p. 136.

[27] *Yr Haul*: 1859; pp. 59-60; *ibid*: 1860, p. 58; *Cd Ad*: 25/6/1875; *The Welshman*: 2/3/1879.

[28]*Instructions for the Establishment of Friendly Societies with a Form of Rules and Tables* . . . 1835; E. Scourfield: 'Rhai Cyfrinfeydd Iforaidd ac Odyddol Sir Gaerfyrddin yn y Bedwaredd Ganrif ar Bymtheg', *Carms Antiq*, vii, 1971, p. 103; D. L. Baker-Jones: 'The Carmarthen Eisteddfod, 1867', *loc cit*, pp. 44-70.

[29]*Cm Jnl*: 10/11/1815; 24/5/1844; *Yr Haul*: 1841, p. 154.

[30]*Cd Ad*: 8/3/1872, 1/9/1876; *The Welshman*: 26/12/1873.

[31]*Cm Jnl*: 2/2/1855, 18/1/1864.

[32]NLW/Cilgwyn/LB/23/23 June 1861; *RCALW*, 1893-94, p. 26, para vi.

[33]NLW/D. Pryse Williams/15623E; *Cm Jnl*: 4/8/1820; NLW/Cilgwyn/LB/34/30, June 1854.

[34]*Cm Jnl*: 1/12/1815, 9/4/1869; *Cd Ad*: 14/12/1853, 12/3/1885.

[35]NLW/Owen Colby/2150.

[36]NLW/Cards/QS/OB/4; *Yr Haul* 1847, pp. 185-86.

[37]*Cm Jnl*: 15/5/1814, 21/6/1822; *Yr Haul*: 1863, p. 28. During the American Civil War the North imposed a blockade on the Southern Ports and exports of raw cotton ceased for four years. Lancashire endured a cotton famine and unemployment, with some 350,000 persons in receipt of poor relief.

[38]*ibid*: 27/12/1822, 18/3/1842; CRO/Ms 4916.

[39]NLW/Evans George/1435; CRO/T/Hos/1; D. L. Baker-Jones: 'To Supply the Sick Poor', *Carms Historian*, XV, 1978, pp. 3-28; CRO/Joint Counties Asylum Report, 1886; *Cm Jnl*: 17/11/1854; *Cd Ad*: 28/9/1866.

[40]*The Welshman*: 31/10/1862, 14/11/1862.

[41]A. Briggs: *op cit.*, p. 216; S. Lewis, *op cit.* sub Cardigan, Carmarthen and Haverfordwest; F. Jones: 'Lloyd of Cilciffeth', *Pembs Hist*, 4, 1972, p. 37; J. E. Lloyd: *op cit.*, ii, p. 126; M. Cragoe: *op cit.*, p. 72.

[42]W. Howells: 'The Library of Edward Richard, Ystrad Meurig', *Ceredigion*, IX, 3, pp. 233-34; W. J. Davies: *op cit.*, pp. 97-8; *Cm Jnl*: 12/11/1847; S. Lewis: *op cit.* sub Penboyr.

[43]NLW/Owen Colby/1086.

[44]S. C. Carpenter: *Church and People, 1789-1889*, 1933, pp. 70-2.

[45]*Cm Jnl*: 3/3/1815, 9/2/1844; NLW/D. Pryse Williams/156359A.

[46]RCISEdW, 1847, 1848, 2, p. 162; D. Evans: *The Life and Work of Wm Williams, MP for Coventry*, 1939, p. 85; *DWB*.

[47]NLW/D. Pryse Williams/15622E; NLW/Amphlett Lewis and Evans/-.

[48]*loc cit.*

[49]G. G. Davies: 'Addysg Elfennol yn Sir Aberteifi, 1870-1902', *Ceredigion*, IV, 1963, p. 354.

[50]RCISEdW, 1847, pp. 31, 76, 81-4; *Cm Jnl*: 25/6/1847; 13/3/1848.

[51]Sir T. Phillips: *Wales, the Language, Social Condition . . . Education*, 1849, pp. 478-83; *Cm Jnl*: 2/9/1853; *Cd Ad*: 14/8/1868; *The Welshman*: 14/2/1874; *DWB*.

[52]K. O. Morgan: *op cit.*, pp. 43-46, 183-86; *DWB*.

[53]*The Welshman*: 14/7/1854.

[54]CRO/JF (Colby)/595.

[55]*Cd Ad*: 16/1/1885, 25/10/1885, 3/5/1892; *Cm Jnl*: 4/5/1888; *The Welshman*: 16/3/1888.

[56]H. Richard: *op cit.*, p. 75; NLW/Evans George/1837-38, 1983.

[57]*Cm Jnl*: 23/3/1827, 20/6/1834.

[58]E. L. Ellis: 'Some Aspects of the Early History of the University of Wales', *THSC*, 1967, ii, p. 211; *Cd Ad*: 18/10/1872; K. O. Morgan: *op cit.*, p. 59n; V. H. H. Green: *The Universities*, 1969, pp. 107, 113.

[59]NLW/Evans George/1941.

[60]W. G. Evans: 'The Aberdare Report and Cardiganshire', *Ceredigion*, IX, 1982, 3, pp. 125, 209.

[61]RCHEW, 1881, p. 436; *Cd Ad*: 6/6/1890.

[62]RCLWM, ii, 1893-94, pp. 31-34, para ix; A. J. Ellis: *op cit.*, p. 137; *DWB*.

[63]*Cm Jnl*: 19/2/1864; *Cd Ad*: 5/2/1869, 3/3/1882.

[64]*ibid*: 11/1/1889, 28/2/1902.

[65]*ibid*: 26/5/1876, 11/2/1887; NLW/Llysnewydd/Bundle 37.

The Gentry and Religion

After the Revolution of 1688, the position of the Anglican church was consolidated, in spite of the Toleration Act of 1689, and was buttressed by the law of the land as well as by the alliance between clergy and gentry. The threat of Jacobitism and of the revival of Popery had secured the position and supremacy of the established church through political force. The gentry held a key position in maintaining law and order, and in upholding a protestant religious settlement which united the English, Scots and Welsh notwithstanding the tensions and rivalries between Anglicans and Dissenters. Churchmanship and good citizenship were synonymous, and a clergyman's task was to get his flock to regard the church as '. . . a monolithic institution to which they owed affection as well as obedience'.[1] As pillars of the church and constitution, the gentry were put in an invidious position when penal laws against dissenters were relaxed from 1689 to 1719, and, likewise later on, when the authority of the established church was being challenged by the increase of nonconformity and dissent, by the impact of 'Methodism' in the mid-century, and by the tide of deistic Unitarian and atheistic Jacobin forces by 1800. The gentry had to accommodate their social and official rôles in the face of latitudinarian and disruptive elements within their own community of kinsmen, tenants, labourers and domestic servants. Their Laodicean and lax temperament with regard to dogma and religious observance no doubt helped. A few gentry were 'touched', as we have examined already, with 'Methodistical' charisma and conviction; others veered towards unitarianism or a 'rational' ethic. Such an outlook, in part at least, defused tension between their expected loyalty to the established church and the forces of dissent.

The gentry of 'Tivyside' in the eighteenth century were, perhaps, typical of their class in their response to the flexible dogma and practice of the Georgian church. The niceties of liturgical practice, pastoral ministration and the upkeep of the church fabric were not paramount in their limited vision of their Christian duty. Doctrine, as such, only reared its head when it related to the political situation.[2] David Lloyd of Alltyrodyn admitted that he had not attended a place of worship for six months. A survey of the content of gentry libraries (with the exception of Bronwydd and Blaenpant) has shown that theology and philosophy were not high on their list. One suspects that the 'bibliophile' Lloyd of Alltyrodyn, at the end of the eighteenth century, regarded such subjects only as suitable intellectual exercises along with the many other interests which occupied his time. Nevertheless, the average squire in the area was not insensitive to the claims of the established church. A frequent bequest in gentry wills is of small sums of money, often only a few shillings, towards St David's Cathedral. Thus Lewis of Gernos in 1719 left 5s for that purpose, and a similar custom prevailed in other Welsh dioceses, such as Bangor.[3] The funeral sermon, invariably an eulogium of the deceased, was one way of asserting his future beatitude and to instruct the local community. In 1731 the squire of Ffosesgob in Llandysul parish left his vicar 10s to that end.[4]

The maintenance of the church fabric was, from time to time, an opportunity for the gentry to show their religious allegiance as protectors of the Anglican establishment. In 1702 and 1748 over sixty of them contributed to the repair of Cardigan church, amongst whom were most of the squires of the locality. Another reason for such patronage was that it could be an attempt to cultivate the squire's interest for the sake of political and social advancement, as in the case of the infamous Herbert Lloyd of Peterwell, who in 1762 presented a clock for the tower of Cardigan church.[5] The danger of the spread of 'anabaptist and methodist meeting houses', in the neighbourhood of Newcastle Emlyn, led to a petition by the church folk of the town to prominent gentry for money to build a chapel to counteract the increasing influence of their 'mistaken and deluded neighbours'. Vaughan of Golden Grove (owner of considerable land in the area) responded with a donation of £100, and drew the support of about fifty gentry.[6] A similar sum was left in his will by Thomas Howell of Penbeili in 1799 to lessen the burden on the parish of Llangunllo by paying 'for all dilapidations'. Personal religious commitment, perhaps, more than sectarian fear or political opportunism, led to the restoration of about half a dozen churches by the squires of Troedyraur and Bronwydd in the early 1800s.[7] Growing dissent and attacks on the church, supposed to be in decline, led to the building of Capel Dewi church in Llandysul parish in 1835 through the efforts of the Rev. Daniel Bowen of Waunifor. The provision of work for some two hundred labourers— 'thus dispensing his wealth profusely'—as well as providing a decent place of worship led Morgan Jones of Cilwendeg to rebuild Capel Colman church.[8]

While the temper of the eighteenth-century church had inclined to trust in the enlightenment of its own age and in cool rationalism rather than in ecstatic revelation, the nineteenth century brought forth a reaction to atheism, anticlericalism and republicanism. The French Revolution had stirred the British aristocracy to reassess their position *vis-à-vis* the church and they now emerged as buttresses of the established church against an active and radical nonconformity.[9]

An ever widening chasm separated the English-speaking gentry of Wales, who were churchmen and Tories, from the Welsh-speaking farming and labouring classes who were dissenters. Radical nonconformity more and more challenged the privileged position of the church; fought for the removal of disabilities and burdens on non-church people; and as a final goal looked to the disestablishment of the Anglican Church in Wales.[10] An articulate press produced a well informed public, and newspapers and journals, such as *Seren Gomer, Yr Amserau, Y Dysgedydd* and *Baner ac Amserau Cymru*, were to mould opinion. With Liberal members of parliament of the calibre of Henry Richard, Lloyd George and T. E. Ellis, the nonconformist conscience had its vociferous champions in the second half of the nineteenth century. Welsh 'nonconformity' from the 1850s took the first steps towards becoming a movement of pronounced political significance.[11]

The Religious Census of 1851 showed that the Welsh church provided the largest number of places of worship, but in terms of members it was weak. Its bishops, men like Burgess and Thirlwall of St David's, were English and of aristocratic background. Bishop Basil Jones was one of the landed gentry and was totally English in culture and outlook.[12] Within the church itself, there was criticism of the neglect of parishes, the trading in advowsons, anglicisation, ruined churches and the misappropriation of tithes and revenues—voiced over the years by clergy like David James (Dewi o Ddyfed) and his association of Welsh clergy in the West Riding of Yorkshire, along with Dean Edwards of Bangor and obscure but valiant clerics, like the Rev. David Jones of Llanfair in Anglesey.[13]

While the 'Tivyside' gentry had for generations been tolerant of dissenting groups, and were prepared to help in establishing chapels, as long as their orthodoxy was not in question, and their political loyalty safe, any move towards Catholic Emancipation was strenuously opposed. From the early 1800s Bishop Burgess and prominent gentry in their own localities, like Lewes-Lloyd of Dolhaidd, the Bowens of Llwyngwair, Howell of Glaspant and Archdeacon Millingchamp, had stirred up opposition, arguing that Catholic Emancipation was not consistent with the principles of the protestant constitution in church and state.[14] A meeting at Cardigan in 1825 had overwhelmingly voted against the measure, except for the single voice of the curate of Llangoedmor who, as a result, was removed from his parish by Bishop Burgess. Such intolerance was doubtless fanned by the thought of 'Anti Christ', 'Romish troubles in Ireland', the 'machinations' of Roman Catholics and the fear of people with fresh memories of the French landing of 1797 and of Irish support. Squires like Dr Davies of Pentre and the Rev. Daniel Bowen of Waunifor led a campaign by gentry and clergy, in the 1820s, to petition the King and parliament.[15] But it has to be remembered that anti-Catholic and anti-Irish sentiment was current amongst other sections of the community. During the 'No Popery' campaign after 1829, the 'Tivyside' gentry were only concerned with the possible dangers to the constitution and the political and religious settlement as it was. Thus, in 1850-51 the 'aggression' of Pope Pius IX in dividing Britain into dioceses, and the appointment of Catholic bishops, were to the likes of Saunders Davies and Thomas Davies Lloyd an 'interference in the prerogative of the Crown'.[16] Grievances felt by dissenters led to a resolution of the Church Rate Abolition Society in 1836 that the church rate was an inequitable burden on those whose conscience had led them to worship elsewhere.[17] As these issues were linked with tithes, disestablishment and contentious feelings from other directions against the church as a privileged body, John Lloyd Davies of Blaendyffryn in 1834 petitioned the King on the need for national loyalty to the crown and the established church. The Lloyds of Coedmore, by way of contrast, were conciliatory in respect of tithes and were prepared to meet the bishops' representatives to find an amicable solution.[18]

Opponents of the church were able to voice their opinion and channel their energies through the Liberation Society from 1844 onwards, which had amongst its followers in the locality ardent dissenting radicals like Thomas Harries of Llechryd.[19] Legitimate protest against harsh burdens was interpreted by church people as nonconformist malice. Periodically, from 1854 to 1868, public agitation occurred in Llandysul and elsewhere concerning church rates demanded from a predominantly nonconformist public.[20] On the other hand, when Sir Thomas Davies Lloyd of Bronwydd in the 1870s recommended, in a Llangunllo parish vestry meeting, abandoning the church rate, dissenters, who were in a majority, disagreed because it was *hen gwstwm* (ancient custom)—so strong were the traditional ties towards the squire's church in that parish. It is suggested that in some areas, in the early nineteenth century, there was little objection to church rate as such. Even in those parishes where nonconformity was strong, men felt a great respect for the parish church where they had been married and for the churchyard where their loved ones lay buried. As the pressure for disestablishment intensified from the 1870s, and the forces of liberalism could not be restrained after 1868, gentry reaction was to form the Church Defence Alliance, comprising leading gentry like Bowen of Llwyngwair, Colby of Ffynone, Archdeacon North and others. Their aim was to defend church revenues and endowment in reply to anti-church agitation.[21] As will be seen later, Thomas Davies Lloyd of Bronwydd had reason for defending the gentry as a class who had the best feeling towards their nonconformist tenants. He claimed that he never knew of a landlord to refuse land for chapel purposes. Even nonconformist congregations were not always united in demanding the disestablishment of the church.[22] When overwhelmingly dissenting pressure seemed to overstate the case against the church, Sir Marteine Lloyd and Gwinnett Tyler of Mount Gernos organised campaigns to enlighten farmers concerning church endowments, and to answer the Liberationist charge that the Anglican church had failed in her mission and was not an '. . . essential part of the history of England'.[23]

A few squires, like the colourful General Jenkins of Penrallt, Aberporth, entered the fray with passionate and colourful speeches, but with little grasp of the principles involved.[24]

Gentry with literary inclinations responded with alacrity to the charges levelled against the church. Miss Webley-Parry produced in 1854 *A Sketch of the British Church from the Earliest Ages to the Present Time*, and in 1879 *An Epitome of Anglican Church History*. Both were didactic and polemical, aimed at informing those in Welsh National Schools and their families of the catholicity of the established church from the earliest times before Augustine of Canterbury introduced 'superstitious customs and useless ceremonies' into Britain. Facile arguments are used to justify tithes, and 'Romish practices' are scourged mercilessly. The author had scant respect for Independents, regarding them as the spiritual descendants of the evicted clergy of 1662, '. . . many of whom had been deeply concerned in the guilt of the rebellion'. Unwittingly, perhaps, Miss Webley-Parry promulgated a view of the catholicity of the church held by Welsh writers since the days of Salesbury and Bishop Richard Davies.[25] It was a view that the true church in Wales had existed long before the Church of Rome.[26] Re-examined in recent years, it imagined a mythical and glorified antiquity alleged by church champions wherein '. . . the Reformation [was] a return to the pristine purity of the church of the Ancient British . . . the fulfilment at its most sublimated level of the prophecy of the restoration of the ancient glories of Wales'.[27] This was a dangerous argument for apologists of the church to use, as nonconformist leaders could equally claim it to justify their own position. They argued that the 'spirit' of the Celtic or pre-Roman Catholic church lived on in Welsh nonconformity. The Anglican church in Wales was in no respect the ancient Welsh church or its legitimate successor.[28] H. M. Vaughan continued the church v. chapel argument in his book *The Church in Wales from the Reformation to the Present Day*, 1908, reminding nonconformists of their indebtedness to the translators of the Bible. But as an anglicised squire he questioned whether the salvation of the ancient Cambro-British tongue, i.e. Welsh, had proved to be a 'benefit or hindrance in the development of the Cymric race'. Dissenters like Vavasor Powell he castigated as 'ignorant fanatics' and 'violent oppressors' of the church during the Commonwealth. Grudgingly, he admitted the loss to the church when clerics like Stephen Hughes were evicted in 1662. Vaughan's 'apologia' provided valuable ammunition to the opponents of the church. Nonconformist attitudes he dismissed as 'sectarian jealousy', and the arguments of the 'notorious Baner' as a threat to 'law and order'.[29] Such attempts to defend the church only added to the bitterness, and created an almost unbridgeable gulf between squires of his persuasion and the rest of the community.

It may be claimed that a second reformation took place in the annals of the established church during the last century. The Ecclesiastical Commission of 1836 started a movement to redistribute revenues, stamp out nepotism and provide a resident clergy in commodious, well-built parsonages. In addition, public opinion and the inspiration of an evangelical conviction or Puseyite sacramentalism, as well as the ideals of a Christian socialism, were all ingredients in a great wave of reform throughout the land.[30] In Wales, the movements militating against the church brought about a reaction which was not confined to defence and excuse, as has been noticed already, but a concerted effort by leading churchmen and landowners to put their house in order. In the diocese of St David's, the pioneering work of the bishops Connop Thirlwall and Basil Jones brought about a significant change, as in the rest of the country.[31] The ruinous state of churches had been noticed early in the eighteenth century by Archdeacon

Tenison, and the picture in some cases was equally dismal up to the 1850s.[32] A number of 'Tivyside' churches like Capel Mair in Clydai parish, Cilfowyr in Maenordeifi, Llanannerch near Aberporth, Llanfair Trefhelygen, and many others had virtually disappeared.[33] On the other hand, an effort was made to restore churches, and by 1854 about ten had already been rebuilt.[34] The stimulus from the Incorporated Church Building Society, together with the zeal of church dignitaries and the landed gentry, resulted in the restoration of churches and the building of new ones in every parish by the early 1900s. The threat from radical dissent was not the only motive. Wealthy gentry were able to display their wealth and generosity for the public good. Thus, John Lloyd Davies of Blaendyffryn and Alltyrodyn rebuilt St John's Church, Pont-siân, and Bangor Teifi church in 1854 and 1857 respectively. The former was in the strong Unitarian 'Black Spot' of Cardiganshire, and so warm was the response to this 'magnanimous gesture' whereby the inhabitants of the parish were relieved from the burden of church rates, that the congregation at the consecration included Unitarian laymen and ministers. Lord Cawdor in 1862 had built, at his own expense, St Barnabas Church in the village of Felindre in Penboyr parish as well as Penboyr school to meet the requirements of an expanding population in the centre of a growing woollen industry.[35] At the opening of Cenarth church in 1868, built through the generosity of Lord Cawdor and local gentry, one basic motive for such benevolence was neatly summed up: 'Every lord and landed proprietor deemed it his duty to build a church for his retainers and tenants, and not only so, but to devote a tenth of his revenues to maintain it'—a timely, but subtle, reminder to the parish at large to pay tithe.[36] The needs of Welsh-speaking church folk in Llandygwydd parish were provided for by Mrs Brigstocke of Blaenpant, when, in 1882, she built the mission church of Capel Tygwydd and paid the curate's stipend. A deep sense of *pietas* led Battersby Harford of Falcondale to build Maestir church in Lampeter parish, with its adjoining burial ground as the family *machpelah*. The needs of her family, retainers and servants, as well as a commemoration for her deceased husband, resulted in the building of Holy Trinity Chapel in the grounds of Pentre mansion by Mrs Saunders Davies.[37]

A survey of churches like Llandygwydd, Llangunllo and Llanwenog, replete with rich stained glass and ornate memorials to local gentry, has in some ways given birth to folk belief that these and other churches were gifts to the parish from a wealthy, generous and devout aristocracy. While this is partly true, there is one aspect of church patronage which needs scrutiny. A strong element of 'voluntaryism' and community effort can be traced as far back as the late eighteenth century, and the local gentry have been given credit for much church repair and rebuilding. In fact, they were, sometimes, only the instigators of what was done by the parish as a whole. In the case of a popular and benevolent landowner, farmers and labourers would, doubtless, rally to his call as the wise and prudent response of a deferential community. Although most of the credit went to local squires, it must not be forgotten that Troedyraur, Llangunllo and Llangeler, amongst many others, were restored through public subscription, the parish rate and outside grant, in addition to gentry support.[38] How far gentry pressure and duress (as the witnesses before the Land Commission of the 1890s alleged) were factors in the support which the public (especially the chapel-going nonconformists) gave towards church building, is difficult to judge. A press report of 1857 tells how the farmers of Bangor Teifi parish 'undertook the haulage without any dissentient in lieu of the 1/- in the £ rate' towards the church.[39] At Bethesda Independent chapel in Llandygwydd parish, a public collection (at the instigation of the squire Webley-Parry and the chapel minister) was made for the benefit of the parish church, so that as a result '. . . people contributed liberally and cheerfully, and were glad to have the opportunity to show their good feeling towards the Church of England'. Similar sentiments moved the inhabitants of Eglwyswrw (a parish in north Pembrokeshire *with* Bronwydd influence *very* strong) where 'different denominations' in 1883 contributed towards the rebuilding of the church.[40] No doubt the squire continued to hold sway in his locality; in part, the subtle influence of custom, deference, and the fear of unpopularity or of vindictiveness by a ruling caste, were factors which caused many to display outward show, at least, of loyalty to the church because it was, after all, the squire's church. In their enthusiasm for church building the gentry were sensitive to the charge that their cause was in decline. On the contrary, they argued, old ruined churches 'were giving way for larger and handsomer edifices worthy of the divine truths taught there, and as monuments that church lethargy has passed away, and her most bitter enemies have been forced to acknowledge her influence'.[41] Such was the press comment on the restoration of Bridell church in 1866; a few years later the new Llangrannog church was regarded as tangible proof of 'the great advance which church principles are making in south Wales'. Consequently, gentry families over a wide area joined in fund-raising activities for church restoration. They took part as vocalists, instrumentalists and impresarios, rallying around the squire of the parish where church restoration was taking place. Concerts, bazaars, garden fêtes, soirées and other social gatherings brought the gentry together.[42]

During the process of providing places of worship, the gentry were inspired by current aesthetic and cultural values. New churches were commodious, attractive and a reflection of contemporary architectural style befitting the status and outlook of their patrons. No longer could the country squire, living in a stylish mansion, continue to worship in a building that was damp, mouldy, the floor ill-paved and subsiding to reveal the bones of past generations. As Gothic had become a polite style for the squire's home, so the ideas of Pugin and the Cambridge Camden Society spread to west Wales. Gothic was regarded as the only Christian style of architecture, and, unlike other parts of the country, there was no Evangelical reaction to it in the area as a sign of resurgent Popery. Heavy carving, encaustic tiles, stained glass and altar (as at Llangunllo especially) were not dismissed as foolish vanities.[43] A campaign of church building over many decades led to gentry patronage of many talented architects who prospered through the squire's favour in designing mansion and church. To take a few examples: John Jones (Talhaiarn), worked at Tremain church in 1848, and later distinguished himself under Sir Joseph Paxton in building the Crystal Palace and at the Rothschilds' chateau in France; J. Middleton of Cheltenham had several 'restorations' to his credit, for example Llangunllo (1865-70), Llandysul (1870-74) and Newport (1878).[44] Some 'restorations' were so drastic, however, that much of what was traditional and native was removed to accord with the fancy of the squire patron rather than the strict rules of the ecclesiologist. Although alien to the *genius loci*, Llangunllo church stands out as an ambitious exercise in high Victorian Gothic, with its interior of brick polychromy, elaborate freestone and alabaster embellishments.[45] In response to liturgical innovation and more dignified worship, the gentry sponsored surpliced choirs and pipe organs to lead the singing, as for instance at Llandygwydd, Cardigan and Llandysul. Ritualistic objects such as patens, chalices, fonts, ewers and many other things besides, were given to commemorate the squire's family. Churches were heated and lit by gas and electricity, so that elegance and comfort should prevail in the squire's church as much as in his mansion.[46]

The militancy of the gentry on behalf of the established church in the nineteenth and early twentieth centuries raises the crucial question as to the extent of their opposition to dissent and radical noncon-formity. Detractors of the squirearchy, like Henry Richard, T. E. Ellis and Lloyd George, were merciless in their condemnation of the church as a religious arm of a secular tyranny. These 'parliamentary pests' (as they were labelled) hated the Church as a church, and not simply as an establishment.[47] Was this bitterness reciprocated by the gentry?

Although the gentry had a unique relationship with the established church over the centuries, the evidence suggests a broad tolerance towards dissent and nonconformity. As JPs in Quarter Sessions they carried out fairly the duty of licensing 'meeting houses'. Examples, however, do exist of the refusal to grant this concession because, it was argued, there was already a sufficient number of preachers and 'meeting houses', as at Holyhead in Anglesey in 1763. But none seems to have been refused in the 'Tivyside' area where, up to 1851, over a hundred had been registered.[48]

In granting leases of land for chapel building, conditions were usually generous. For example, in 1763, Stephen Colby of Ffynone granted a piece of land on Cilgwyn (one of his farms near Boncath) to erect a chapel for a term of 99 years at 1s per annum. Again John Lloyd of Alltyrodyn in 1779 granted a 99-year lease for Llwynrhyd-owen 'meeting house' (this had disastrous consequences after 1868 owing to causes not entirely related to the conditions of the lease).[49] Far from persecuting nonconformists, leases on generous terms were granted up to the end of the nineteenth century. Thus, Sir Thomas Davies Lloyd of Bronwydd granted a lease to 'his friends who worshipped at Bryngwenith chapel', and Mrs Lloyd of Cilrhiwe allowed the full occupation of a house by a nonconformist minister in order that '. . . he had a dwelling house without paying rent'.[50] When leases had subsisted for many years, and estates had to be sold piecemeal, the chapel and adjoining land were invariably conveyed by the squire to the minister and congregation. In 1892 Bowen of Llwyngwair gave Elim chapel and burial ground to the chapel folk on the sale of the Pantyrhead estate near Eglwys Gymyn, Carmarthen-shire.[51] Likewise, Mrs Davies Evans of Highmead, gave to the Methodists their chapel at Llanbryn-mair, Montgomeryshire, on the sale of her Dolgadfan estate in 1894.[52] It is significant that these gifts were in no wise aimed at cultivating the squire's influence to secure the good will of the community in those localities—as the sale of these

distant estates meant a complete break with the landowner's connection with the area.

In spite of their broad tolerance of dissent, there were occasions
when doctrinal considerations were much in the mind of the gentry.
When Unitarianism was spreading in the Teifi valley, and was feared
as one symptom of the political and religious turbulence at the end of
the eighteenth century, Thomas Lloyd of Bronwydd, in 1795, founded
and endowed Capel y Drindod (Holy Trinity Chapel) at Aberbanc,
Henllan, and within sight of his mansion. The Gospel preached there
had to be in the Calvinistic line and according to the Thirty Nine
Articles of the established church. Similar orthodoxy was demanded
by Llewellyn Parry of Gernos, who leased land for Twrgwyn chapel '. . .
for preaching and hearing divine worship according to the doctrinal
articles of the Church of England'.[53]

In some quarters, Methodism and 'enthusiastic' manifestations of
faith were disliked. The puritan 'ethic' of the reformers ran against the
natural instincts of the gentry who saw nothing wrong with wild
behaviour at races and cock fights, and in drinking and carousing.[54]
Amongst early converts to Methodism was Evans of Penwenallt in
1742, who organised meetings for Hywel Harris near Newcastle
Emlyn. In 1764 Ensign Bowen of Pengelly was in raptures because
Harris was to pay a visit which would be 'to the glory of God, and
Edification of the People'.[55] Such attitudes could alienate some gentry
from their more worldy minded peer group. Examples have been cited
of devout gentry—the paragons of virtue—who espoused Methodism
and other brands of religious conviction. Along with the families of
Vaughan of Trecŵn, Fenton of Glyn-y-Mêl and Higgon of Pontfaen
(albeit a short distance outside our area), they were typical of many
Welsh gentry, whose strong faith in personal salvation was, perhaps, a
rejection of the metropolitan standards of the important English
centres and of the outer world. So suspect were these squires of
political as well as religious deviation that Thomas Charles had to rally
to their defence. It was argued that their loyalty to church and state
was unimpeachable: they stood for 'regular' government, had rejoiced
at the French defeat of 1797 and accepted wholeheartedly the divine
revelation in Holy Writ.[56] When overactive displays of 'enthusiasm'
occurred, as, for example, in Llandysul church, the 'aggravation' was
reported to the bishop, and Thomas Bowen of Waunifor was blamed
for supporting Methodists. He had built Waunifor or Blaenborthin
chapel in 1760 and left it to them in his will in 1805; his strong sense of

ecumenical tolerance was aimed to protect the basic freedom of people: '. . . the liberty to preach . . . and of worshipping God without molestation or interruption'.[57] As has been noticed, few of the 'Tivyside' gentry could claim any depth of intellectual curiosity concerning theology, politics or moral philosophy. Amongst the exceptions, the 'Unitarian' Lloyds were stimulated by rationalism and theories of enlightenment. Immune from the morbid self-analysis and ecstatic extravagance of 'ranters' and 'Methodists', they put theological, political and social fundamentals under their microscope, such as the equality of the citizen before the law, the emancipation of Catholics and universal franchise. The ideas of Priestley and other national intellectuals were current coin, and the Unitarians were to the fore as political radicals. David Lloyd and Charles Lloyd were the apostles of this deistic freedom, but, as their disputations were from the pulpit and the lecture room, and their social pedigree was beyond question, they were free from the harassment that daring and volatile propagandists like Tomos Glyn Cothi suffered.[58] In the nineteenth century Edward Crompton Lloyd Hall (who as we have seen changed his surname to Fitzwilliams in 1849) had scant respect for the other Tivyside gentry. He displayed a broad liberalism in matters of religious dogma. In 1846 a request to him from the Baptist Quarterly Meeting to refuse a lease of land to a schismatic group from the Newcastle Emlyn Baptists, met with a sharp reply which deserves to be quoted *in extenso*:

> Everyman's religious tenets are between himself and our Maker, and I believe that every man, who to the best of his ability, without prejudice of any sort searches the Scripture, and holds the tenets which he individually believes to be the most pleasing to the Great Spirit is right, however much he may differ in his view from his equally right neighbour. Where two or three are gathered together, in a building or in a field, yr [sc. your] dwelling house or mine—yr chapel or the parish church—I therefore hold it sinful to throw the slight impediment in the way of any two or three worshipping our Master in the mode they fancy best and most agreeable to him—and I consider it a portion of any duty I owe Him to aid them in every way in my power, however much they may differ from me in the construction they put on the Holy writings and this whether Jews or Gentiles. None of us mortals can 'fulfil the Law'.[59]

His broad ecumenism led him to admire that *bête noir* of the landlord class, Rev. William Thomas (Gwilym Marles). He was no blind follower of tradition and, while being prepared to support church building, made a point of calling himself an '. . . Arian Landowner of Llandyssil'. In December 1860 Fitzwilliams preached at Llwynrhydowen chapel—the Mecca of Unitarianism.[60] To him the established church was in schism as much as other dissenters: 'your Church is ye daughter of ye Romish, which severed itself from ye Greek church on ye question of ye Third person of the Trinity'. No respecter of persons, he wrote to the vicar of Llandysul: '. . . I can therefore no more canvass for you than I could for a Jumper Ranter or Mormon, all of whom I consider with ye orthodox to have more or less fallen away from ye truth which is in Christ'. Church schools he would not support, unless they were conducted on unsectarian principles. Had he the chance he would have opposed their foundation— 'to counter the mischief they were doing'.[61] He was convinced that Trinitarians would eventually become Unitarians through study of the Bible and independent thinking, and (as noted above) he reflected that '. . . without prejudice and improper bias it is all over with ye parsons and they know it must be so now'. Armed with his remarkable knowledge of Biblical exegesis, patristics and church history, he carried on a lengthy correspondence with the 'liberal' Anglican Bishop Thirlwall. Uppermost in E. Crompton Ll. Fitzwilliams' quest for moral and religious truth was impartial investigation, and the sad affair of Rowland Williams he regarded as 'persecution'.[62] But, as with the rest of the 'Tivyside' gentry, Catholics were to him still beyond the pale. Writing to Ford Hughes of Aberceri, he enquired: 'Is it true that your sister has joined the Roman Catholic Church? More's ye pity if she has been so deluded'.[63]

In the second half of the nineteenth century, when the church and the squire had to fight off more intense attacks from radical and dissenter, the spirit of magnanimous toleration which had largely been the case during the previous one hundred and fifty years largely continued in some families. Sir Thomas Davies Lloyd expressed concern whether prisoners in Cardigan gaol had access to ministers of their own creed. James Bevan Bowen of Llwyngwair supported the Association for the Freedom of Worship, one of its aims being to secure free places in parish churches without social or doctrinal limitations.[64] Some of the gentry attended from time to time nonconformist places of worship along with their dissenting tenants and neighbours. Generous gestures created harmony between the gentry and the rest of the community, and donations were made to chapel building funds, for example Fitzwilliams gave £50 towards Llwynrhydowen chapel. Gifts of musical instruments, Bibles and articles of furniture, and hospitality at country mansions to visiting preachers during *cyrddau mawr* (big preaching meetings), can be cited as further evidence of the tolerant spirit and patronage of the more enlightened gentry towards dissenters.[65] Reflecting the outlook of his fellow radicals in politics, and Independents in religion, Dr Lloyd of Newcastle Emlyn praised '. . . the generous, tolerant and kind feelings towards nonconformists, which have ever characterised the family of Bronwydd'.[66] Such a claim could be made on behalf of other gentry, too, but not of all.

NOTES AND SOURCES

[1]G. H. Jenkins: *op cit.*, pp. 19-20; L. Colley: *Britons Forging the Nation 1707-1837*, 1992, p. 18.
[2]N. Sykes: *Church and State in England in the Eighteenth Century*, 1934, pp. 23, 231, 250, 257.
[3]NLW/St D/Wills, G. H. Jenkins: *The Foundations of Modern Wales*, 1993, pp. 172 seq.
[4]NLW/Ms 8167 D.
[5]S. R. Meyrick: *op cit.*, pp. 173-74; NLW/Ms 19 B (Sir John Williams 223).
[6]CRO/Cawdor (Vaughan) 41/5771, 103/8044.
[7]HRO/Wi./83; NLW/St D/Archdeacons Visitations/Box 1; S. Lewis: *op cit.*, *sub* Llangunllo.
[8]*Cm Jnl*: 28/8/1836, 19/9/1837.
[9]S. C. Carpenter: *op cit.*, p. 25.
[10]E. T. Davies: *Religion and Society in Wales in the Nineteenth Century*, 1981, pp. 17, 21.
[11]I. G. Jones: 'The Elections of 1865 and 1868 in Wales . . . to Cardiganshire', *THSC*, 1964, i, p. 45.
[12]C. Thirlwall: *Letters to a Friend*, Dean Stanley (ed), 1881; *DWB*, I. G. Jones and D. Williams (eds): *The Religious Census of 1851, a calendar of the Returns Relating to Wales*, vol. i, South Wales, 1976.
[13]*DWB*; D. Jones: *The Welsh Church and Nationality* [ND]; 'advowson'—right of presentation to a living.
[14]*Cm Jn*: 2/1/1813; J. S. Harford: *op cit.*, p. 238.
[15]NLW/Add Ms/1896 E iv: *Cm Jnl*: 22/4/1825; 24/4/1829; L. Colley: *op cit.*, pp. 35, 329.
[16]G. F. A. Best: 'Popular Protestantism in Victorian Britain' in R. Robson (ed): *Ideas and Institutions of Victorian Britain. Essays in Honour of G. Kitson Clark*, 1967, pp. 115-142; *Cm Jnl*: 29/11/1850; 10/1/1851.
[17]NLW/Ms 7993 C; L. Colley: *op cit.*, pp. 322-34.
[18]*Cm Jnl*: 13/6/1834; 2/12/1836.
[19]I. G. Jones: 'The Liberation Society and Welsh Politics, 1844 to 1868', *WHR*, 1/2/1961, pp. 193-94; *The Llanelly Telegraph*: 5/11/1863; R. T. Jones: 'The Origins of the Disestablishment Campaign', *JHSCW*, 25, 1970, pp. 39-56.
[20]R. T. Jenkins: *op cit.*, pp. 104-06; W. J. Davies: *op cit.*, pp. 345-46.
[21]*Cm Jnl*: 6/10/1865; W. T. Morgan: 'The Diocese of St Davids in the Nineteenth Century—B. The Unreformed Church ii', *JHSCW* 26, 1972, p. 23; *Cd Ad*: 16/2/1872; *The Welshman*: 18/2/1876.
[22]*ibid*: 10/3/1875; *Cd Ad*: 12/5/1876.
[23]*ibid*: 19/1/1884; 1/2/1884; *The Welshman*: 15/2/1884.
[24]*Cd Ad*: 17/3/1893; 15/5/1893.
[25]*loc cit*: pp. iii-iv, 26-7, 61, 76-7, 82, 187-88; G. H. Jenkins: *op cit.*, p. 193; *DWB*.
[26]E. J. Newell: *A Popular History of the Ancient British Church* . . ., 1887, p. 31; *Yr Haul*: 1884, pp. 370-73.

[27]Saunders Lewis: *Meistri'r Canrifoedd*, G. Gruffydd (gol), 1972, pp. 116-39; Glanmor Williams: *op cit.*, p. 134.

[28]Rev. D. Davies: *The Ancient Celtic Church of Wales*, [N.D.], p. 34.

[29]*loc cit*, pp. 3, 15, 59, 103, 115; *Baner ac Amserau Cymru*, a Welsh radical newspaper edited by Thomas Gee (1815-98)—Methodist preacher and liberal propagandist.

[30]S. C. Carpenter: *op cit.*, pp. 100-02; O. Chadwick: *op cit.*, i, pp. 126-27.

[31]RCWC (St Davids), 1907; *DNB*, *DWB*.

[32]G.M. Griffiths: 'A Visitation of the Archdeaconry of Carmarthen, 1710', *NLWJ*, xviii, 1974, pp. 287-311, xix, 1976, pp. 311-26; Sir S. Glynne: *The Older Churches*, 1824-74, 1903.

[33]*Arch Camb*: 1864, pp. 178-79; S. Lewis: *op cit.*, *sub* Llanfair Trevlygen.

[34]*Cm Jnl*: 10/3/1854.

[35]*Cm Jnl*: 13/10/1854; *The Welshman*: 26/2/1857; NLW/SD/C/222.

[36]NLW/D. Pryse Williams/156 23 E.

[37]*Cd Ad*: 7/4/1882; 3/11/1882; 19/2/1884; A. M. Harford: *op cit.*, p. 148; *The Welshman*: 7/1/1869; D. L. Baker-Jones: 'The Pentre Memorial Chapel', *Pembs Historian*, No. 7, 1981, pp. 24-28; the cave of Machpelah in Hebron, Palestine, was regarded as the traditional burial-place of Abraham.

[38]S. Lewis: *op cit.*, *sub* Troedyraur, Capel Colman, Llangeler, etc.

[39]*The Welshman*: 26/2/1857.

[40]*Cm Jnl*: 5/8/1864; *Cd Ad*: 19/1/1883.

[41]*ibid*: 12/2/1866.

[42]*ibid*: 10/6/1870, 12/6/1874, 29/8/1882, 6/9/1895.

[43]C. L. Eastlake: *op cit.*, pp. 190-91, 199.

[44]*Yr Haul*: 1848, p. 330; *Cm Jnl*: 16/6/1848, 8/9/1848; *DWB*.

[45]For a detailed description of Llangunllo church, *see* E. Davies: *op cit.*, pp. 72-77.

[46]*Cd Ad*: 4/4/1871; 20/5/1887; 7/7/1893.

[47]K. O. Morgan: *op cit.*, p. 117.

[48]J. H. Davies: *op cit.*, ii, p. 588; NLW/SD/Diss/1-209.

[49]CRO/JF (Colby) 199; NLW/Morgan Richardson/1084-85.

[50]NLW/D. Pryse Williams/15664 A; NLW/Bronwydd/6054.

[51]*Cd Ad*: 16/12/1892.

[52]*Cm Jnl*: 21/7/1892.

[53]NLW/Bronwydd/1779; NLW/Morgan Richardson/824.

[54]P. Morgan: *op cit.*, pp. 49-50; M. H. Jones: *Trevecka Letters* . . . , pp. 78-9.

[55]NLW/Trevecka Letters/1/559, 2591.

[56]G. M. Roberts: 'Y Morafiaid yn Neheudir Cymru', *NLWJ*, xx, 3, 1978, pp. 61-3; *DWB*; *Gent. Mag*, Jan. 1800, pp. 46-7; E. H. Stuart Jones: *The Last Invasion of Britain*, 1950.

[57]NLW/SD/Misc/1200; CRO/Museum/224; *Cm Jnl*: 6/10/1857: Y Parch W. J. Davies: *Hanes Plwyf Llandysul*, 1896, pp. 67-8.

[58]Dd Williams: *op cit*; *DWB*, *sub* Thomas Evans.

[59]NLW/D. Pryse Williams/15633 A; NLW/Cilgwyn/LB/15 Nov. 1846.

[60]*ibid*: 9 Dec. 1860, 14 Dec. 1860.

[61]*ibid*: 15 Dec. 1860.

[62]*ibid*: 15 Feb. 1861; O. G. Rees: 'Connop Thirlwall, Liberal Anglican', *JHSCW*, 19, 1964, pp. 66-76; *DWB*.

[63]*DNB*; *DWB*; NLW/Cilgwyn/LB/41/14 July 1863; *ibid*: 44/16 Nov. 1876.

[64]*Cm Jnl*: 3/7/1863; *Cd Ad*: 8/11/1867.

[65]NLW/Cilgwyn/LB/40/17 May 1861; *Cd Ad*: 8/8/1890, 29/7/1890, 11/2/1898.

[66]*The Welshman*, 6/4/1883.

Patronage and Community Response

The radical Liberal W. Llewelyn Williams, in a significant observation before the Land Commission of the 1890s, said: '. . . Nothing is more remarkable than the loyalty which is expressed to the old Welsh families [i.e. the gentry] . . . often this attachment to the descendants of the old national leaders is carried to such an extreme that it has come to be a mere fawning servility'. Deference from the lower orders was the consequence of prolonged and sustained conditioning of their inferiors by the ruling classes, and their continued expectation of a 'perpetual tribute of respect and complaisance'.[1] In Wales, unrestrained praise of the *uchelwyr* (high men, sc. aristocracy) had, since medieval times, been a special feature of the bardic tradition. Loyalty to a chief was the governing idea of tribal society and, perhaps, the Welsh erred too much in their praise of the princeling's moral and martial virtue, aristocratic lineage, hospitality, culture and bearing. A strong literary tradition survived in 'Tivyside' in post-Tudor times, with the squires of Llwyngwair, Henllys, Parcyprat, Tywyn, Gwernant and Cryngae, amongst others, receiving their due meed of praise.[2] Although the golden age of poetry in the strict metres had by the end of the sixteenth century almost disappeared, much of what was traditional was handed down over the centuries, albeit in a weakened form. Bardic lore was preserved by circles of enthusiasts—lesser squires and parsons; but as the squirearchy became more anglicised they were no longer interested (and perhaps did not have the means) in sustaining the favoured and privileged life of the bards, a phenomenon which applied to Gaelic Scotland and Ireland in the same period. Moreover, a puritanical Methodism and the adoption by the gentry of western European etiquette and manners, militated against a native Welsh culture, which was to be associated more and more with the lower orders.[3] The basic latent urge of Welshmen to praise their 'natural leaders', however, remained strong—often expressed in the homely and unrefined rhymes of rural bards. Nurtured by literary personages, too, the aim of the eighteenth-century Welsh Augustans was to keep aflame the concept of praise. Thus, Lewis Morris in 1746 wrote to Evan Evans (Ieuan Fardd) that one poetic essential was '. . . ye praise of some of ye family, the Hospitality of the House, the agreeable situation'.[4] In 1876 the same sentiment prompted Thomas James (Llallawg) to write to the Rev. Benjamin Williams (Gwynionydd) a *Galareb Goffadwriaethol* (Elegy) after the death of Morgan Jones of

Cilwendeg—a 'Tivyside' squire described as '*Hen Gymro trwyadl oedd efe*' (He was a thorough Welshman) 'of ancient lineage and charitable works'.[5]

Perhaps, the model which the poets in the lower Teifi valley could follow was the famous elegy of the classical poet Lewis Glyn Cothi (fl. 1447-1486) to Hywel ap Dafydd ap Thomas o Wernan (i.e. Gwernant). In his elegy for William Warren of Trewern in 1606 Dafydd Llwyd Mathew extolled the squire's virtues; sadness spread throughout Cemaes; there was a universal lament as for a hero slain in battle:

> Marw gŵr dryd mae oergri'r drin
> Mawrwaed Mastr William Warin,
> Mae oer lef holl Gymru las
> Maith wayw aml mab Mathias?[6]

(The death of a precious hero William Warren, of noble lineage, rings out like the chill cry of those slain in battle; prolonged pain and a sad wail is heard throughout Wales after the death of Mathias' son?)

Generosity and Christian charity were essential to the ethos of gentility. Thus, centuries later, according to the poet Dafydd Llwyd of Gwernlogws, Thomas Lloyd (1704-76), incumbent of Troedyraur, never let a suppliant beggar leave his door empty handed:

> Hael yn y drws a'r aelwyd
> Ydyw llaw y ffeirad Llwyd,
> Nid â o'i ddôr heb nod o'i dda
> Undyn o Gapel Gwnda.[7]

(Generous on the doorstep and on his hearth is the hand of cleric Lloyd. No one leaves his door without some token of his bounty—no one from Capel Gwnda.)[7]

While many of the laments to departed squires are in traditional stereotype moulds, occasionally the poet singles out special and unusual qualities, and often meditates on the fate of rich and poor alike. On the death of Thomas Lloyd of Cwmgloyn (1733-88), lineage, generosity, kindliness and other virtues are listed, but with special mention of the deceased's patronage of schools, gifts of books, and avoidance of prodigal pursuits and intemperate passions. Moreover, equity and justice he meted out impartially:

Er maint eu gallu a'u dichellion,
Ni châi'r na'r traws anwir—dreisio'r union.[8]

(In spite of their power and intrigue—the wicked and evil he never allowed to do iniquity to the just.)

Amongst many elegies of the end of the eighteenth century, 'Methodistical' piety, justice for high and low, and the rights of men are singled out as of particular concern to the deceased squire. In the obsequies of John Lewis of Dinas Cerdin, in 1788 the poet strikes a particularly felicitous note in Welsh, reminiscent of the medieval masters:

Rhoddwyd y gŵr wiwgorff gwâr
Dan glo dyrus glawr daear.[9]

(The body of our handsome noble hero was placed beneath the steel lock of the earth's cover.)

From the pen of the Rev. Benjamin Evans, a dissenting minister of Trewen, his *cywydd marwnad* (memorial ode) to Thomas Lloyd of Bronwydd in 1807 expresses in classical form, not the chivalrous knight of medieval chronicle, but the 'Methodistical' piety, open handedness and concern for lesser mortals, on the part of a good squire who was sure of his 'beatitude':

Ei enaid aeth yn union
Gyda llu angylaidd llon,
Byr hediad i Baradwys
Gwiwle Duw mewn golau dwys.[10]

(His soul went without delay, along with a throng of happy angels—a short flight to Paradise, God's blessed realm and light perpetual.)

Generosity to paupers and to those who had fallen on bad times, teaching the poor to read, to write and to sew, qualified his widow Mary Lloyd as a true Dorcas in the community.[11]

In 1844 Evan Thomas, a bard from Llandysul parish, composed a series of *englynion* of considerable merit on the death of James Lewes, the squire of Cwmhyar in 1844. The keynote, as always, is praise of the squire in traditional terms, and in a verse form which still retained the skill, freshness and vivacity of its medieval counterparts.[12] While there is often unquestionable sincerity in these verse tributes to departed squires, and which reflect gentry response to poverty, hardship, injustice and the like, occasionally another facet of patronage is seen. In 1862 the lament for Morgan, the squire doctor of Llwyncadfor, singled out other qualities, namely his curative skills and knowledge of plants and medicinal herbs, which he generously shared with everyone in the community.[13]

Printed elegies, to be circulated in the countryside, became fashionable. In indifferent poetry, some of these elegies often reek of maudlin sentimentality and a servile outlook based on a simple theology. The Divine Order has created gradations in society with the lower orders thankful and obedient to their God-chosen betters. Thus, a local muse lamented the godly works of Mrs Brigstocke in 1833: the benefactress of '. . . *y bobl fach dylodion*' (the little poor people). Clergy dependent on gentry favour, like the Rev. John Jones (Tegid) and the Rev. Benjamin Williams (Gwynionydd), were always ready with pen and paper to glorify gentry ladies and robust fox-hunting squires, and to present the respectable face of the upper classes against the attacks of radical and dissenter.[14] As opposition increased, so did the volume of deferential elegies—indirectly reflecting the current controversies. The squires Lloyd of Waunifor and Gilfachwen were praised not only for the old-fashioned virtues of largesse, bravery and prowess in the martial arts, but also for new values in the community—their tolerant views towards nonconformists and temperate attitudes on the magisterial bench and in public life.[15] The Whiggism of Sir Thomas Davies Lloyd, and the Toryism of Lloyd of Coedmore had become saintly virtues. In *Y Genhinen Eisteddfodol* of 1902 the recently deceased William Owen Brigstocke of Blaenpant is praised as one who had been a radical-liberal, had campaigned for the disestablishment of the Anglican church in Wales, and as one endowed with a sense of equity and fair play:

> Trist fu daearu ein Brigstocke dirion
> Llyw Byrddau ein gwlad, doeth Ynad union,
> Hardd frodor hyawdl, Rhyddfrydwr ëon,
> A grëai degwch drwy Geredigion
> Da, oludog, i dlodion—bu'n dad
> A'i dyner gariad o dan aur goron.[16]

(It was sad to lay to rest our gentle Brigstocke, the Rudder and Guide of public bodies, a wise and just magistrate, a bold liberal, an eloquent and an estimable native—who created justice and fair play in Cardiganshire. He was good and generous to poor people—as a father in his gentle affection, now he wears his golden crown.)

Community deference also identified itself with the prosperity and misfortune of the ruling classes. The jubilation and sorrow of the mansion were felt in many a humble cottage, even after political loyalty in the polling booth had been withdrawn. The squire's welfare was essential to the welfare of those dependent on him. Tied down to a routine of poverty, humdrum lives and often unrelieved misery, the lower orders could depend on largess of food and clothing from some of the mansions during times of joy and sadness. Rejoicing and jubilation concerning royal events had its localised counterpart in the response of a static community whose cultural and emotional horizons saw no further than the squire's mansion (and on whose land many country folk lived). The application for a coat of arms by the squire, his wooing of an heiress or a death in the mansion led to verse-making, complimentary odes or the ringing of church bells. Thus, on the death of young Colby of Ffynone the bells of Cardigan church were tolled for a whole day, and the ringers were quick to tell the family that '. . . whatever you will be pleased to bestow upon us shall be thankfully received'.[17] In addition to verse and prose eulogies (and of the latter there are endless examples), community goodwill was manifested in dramatic gestures like firing a cannon, drawing of the squire's carriages (as when E. Crompton Ll. Fitzwilliams returned from France in 1857), bonfires and the like, all aimed at asserting the 'kindly and honourable feeling' between squire and tenant.[18]

Thereby tensions were defused, an explosive situation rendered harmless and old loyalties reaffirmed. Nevertheless, the old order was changing and new attitudes were in the air. A significant example of this is the occasion of John Vaughan Colby's return home in the early 1900s, after a long sojourn abroad. A reception party met him on Cilgerran station to present an illuminated address, with all the pomp and ceremony of such occasions—but everything had been discreetly and carefully organised by the agent John Francis, who had also chosen the participants and was prepared to allow speeches and poems 'so long as there was no reference to politics'.[19] Although the real power of the gentry had evaporated, and political forces were by the early 1900s turning on the side of the *werin*, servility and deference still survived. A nonconformist minister greeted Lieutenant Robert Lawrence Colby's return from the South African War in a lengthy poem in English which praised his bravery, his wealth and broad acres. Colby stood for all that was 'great and good' with 'ancient blood and virtues coursing in thy veins':

I see an angel hand entwine
A garland fair to deck thy brow,
And to the Colby's honoured line
In reverence and submission bow.

When war demanded Britain's might
Afar on Afric's rolling veldt,
Stout beat thy heart, and in the fight
No coward fear by thee was felt.[20]

The community (so the poem continues) was happy to share with Colby his pride in 'ancestral halls of nobler rank and Norman blood'! Such identification with the cultural, political and jingoistic outlook of the squirearchy by a *gwerin* far removed in language, religion and economic level is difficult to explain in a social structure which was dissolving, but without sudden crisis, revolution or naked expropriation.[21]

NOTES AND SOURCES

[1]RCLWM Report, 1896, p. 296, para. 239 [Qu. 37, 826]; G. E. Mingay: *op cit.*, pp. 287-88; *DWB.*

[2]E. J. Evans: 'Noddwyr y Beirdd yn Sir Benfro', *THSC*, 1972-73, pp. 123-69; D. H. E. Roberts: 'Noddi Beirdd yng Ngheredigion', *Ceredigion*, vii, 1972, pp. 14-39; G. Bowen: *op cit.*, covers bardic patronage from 1600-1850.

[3]P. Morgan: *op cit.*, pp. 223-29.

[4]*DWB*; J. H. Owen: *op cit.*, i, pp. 159-60.

[5]*DWB*; NLW/D. Pryse Williams/15774 B, 15648 B.

[6]E. D. Jones: *Gwaith Lewis Glyn Cothi*, 1953, pp. 54-6; *DWB*; FG/11/147-51, *WWHR*, ii, 1913, p. 78, note 4.

[7]NLW/D. Pryse Williams/15658 A.

[8]Ioan Siencyn: *Marwnad Thomas Lloyd, Cwmgloyn. 'Blodau Dyfed'*, 1824, pp. 300 seq.

[9]NLW/D. Pryse Williams/15758.

[10]NLW/Ms 2102 D.

[11]NLW/D. Pryse Williams/15660 B; Dorcas—the charitable woman at Joppa, who made garments for the poor. Acts ix 36-42.

[12]*Cm Jnl*: 24/5/1844.

[13]*Yr Haul*: 1862, p. 68.

[14]NLW/D. Pryse Williams/15638 A, 15653 C; *DWB*.

[15]W. E. Evans: *Dwy Farwnad Arobryn yn Eisteddfod Llandysil 1877*, 1879.

[16]NLW/D. Pryse Williams/15653 C; *Yr Haul*: Mai 1882, pp. 226-27; *Y Genhinen Eisteddfodol*, Awst 1902, p. 61.

[17]NLW/D. Pryse Williams/15625 B; NLW/Owen Colby/2010.

[18]*Cambrian Register*, iii, pp. 177-81; *Cm Jnl*: 16/8/1816; HRO/D/Pen/26/1; *The Welshman*: 11/2/1870; NLW/Cilgwyn/LB/37/19 Mch 1857; *Cd Ad*: 28/2/1868, 9/2/1872.

[19]CRO/JF (Colby) 61.

[20]*loc cit*; Capt. Robert Lawrence Colby (1880-1914); Grenadier Guards; killed at Ypres, Nov. 1914.

[21]D. Cannadine: *op cit.*, pp. 697-709.

The 'Governance' of the County

An important public function of the squire was to act as a magistrate, with powers so varied as to make justices of the peace the most influential class of men in Britain, as the unchallenged rulers of their counties.[1] As the system was extended all over Britain (in Wales after the Acts of Union of 1536-41) the reality of government lay with the local justice of the peace—in his own front parlour, local inn or with the whole county gathered in Quarter Sessions. As central government was remote in London, its irrelevance to the lives of the community added to the strength of the local JP, who knew his locality and understood its people and their needs.

The possession of property had been the fundamental qualification for appointment to the magistracy, and it was laid down in 1731, and 1744, that every justice for a county had to have an estate worth £100 a year or a reversion or remainder with rents of £300 a year. Not until 1875 was the occupation of a dwelling house of the annual value of £100 a condition of eligibility for the magistracy. In 1906 the property and residential qualification was abolished.[2] The eagerness of the west Wales gentry to become the ruling hierarchy is reflected in the attitude of David Lloyd of Alltyrodyn upon expressing anxiety to John Jones of Pantglas, Llanfynydd, Carmarthenshire in 1745 whether a judgment bond of £300 prevented his qualifying as a JP. He argued that this would be a 'hard case', when he already had £200 a year in possession. As has happened in other periods of patronage through social and political connections, Philipps of Cwmgwili, for example, in 1749 was asked to use his influence to 'get Mr Hector Jones (of Coedstre-isaf, in Llangeler parish) put into ye new commission'.[3] Over a hundred years later, William Owen Brigstocke of Gellydywyll solicited the support of James Bowen Summers of Milton, Pembrokeshire '. . . [in order] to qualify as a magistrate for co. Pemb. Please see that I am on the Commission'. As a landowner already in Carmarthenshire and Cardiganshire, his influence would be further extended in Pembrokeshire.[4]

Before the days of clear-cut party politics in the nineteenth century, political affiliation and activity were not criteria for appointment. While political allegiance cannot be discounted, opposition to the central power was not a serious bar to holding office. Appointed theoretically by the Crown through the Lord Chancellor, the lords-lieutenant as *custodes rotulorum* had a decisive voice, and while the county justices were a symbol of political interest and family loyalties, greater prominence was given to their administrative and judicial functions in the county.

Provided a JP followed the formal procedures of taking out his *dedimus potestatem*, took oaths of supremacy and allegiance, the oath of office after 1744, and received the sacrament in the established church, Welsh JPs held a position of autonomy in relation to the central government on an equal footing with their English counterparts. Legal training was not a prerequisite for appointment to the bench. While the absence of professional lawyers sometimes led to confusion concerning the exact nature and limits of their authority, on the credit side many of the squire-justices possessed a legal education. Their libraries contained works by Coke, Fitzherbert and Blackstone and useful justices' guides like those of Dalton and Burns. They also occasionally kept handy copy books of procedures and precedents, as at Llysnewydd.[5] At Quarter Sessions, county administration was left to a handful of conscientious squires, who transacted an amazing amount of business in the time available. For the 'Tivyside' area, the earliest recorded appointment of a JP is that of Thomas Bryne of Pantdafydd in 1542, and for the next century and a half members of the following prominent families were placed on the commission:

Phillips (The Priory, Cardigan)	
Lloyd (Bronwydd)	Phillips (Dolhaidd)
Lewis (Cwmawen)	Williams (Dolgwm)
Bowen (Llwyngwair)	Lewis (Coedmore)
Lloyd (Cilgwyn)	Parry (Noyadd Trefawr)
Lewis (Gernos)	Lloyd (Castell Hywel)
Williams (Abernantbychan)	Lewis (Pantyrodyn)
Warren (Trewern)	Lloyd (Morvil)

At the apex of power in the years around 1700 were the 'Tivyside' families of Lewis (Lewes) of Coedmore and Gernos, Williams of Abernantbychan, and Brigstocke of Llechdwnny and Blaenpant, whose heads were deputy lieutenants of the county as well as magistrates.[6] Rarely were names removed from the commission, as happened, however, in 1729, when Lewis of Dolhaidd-uchaf and James Lewis of Gellydywyll (from 'Tivyside') were removed, possibly because they were Sea Serjeants and Jacobite in sympathy. Because there were comparatively few active local JPs this was partly remedied from the mid-eighteenth century by the appointment of clerical justices, such as Erasmus Lewis, *clericus*, and the Rev. James Philipps, DD. The appointment of the Rev. William Williams, a nonconformist minister and landowner, as JP and deputy lieutenant reflects an interesting development towards the end of the century. The changing complexion of landownership, and the rise of new families to the upper ranks of landownership and industrial wealth—like the Colby family of Ffynone and Sir Benjamin Hammett of Castle Malgwyn—meant that they, amongst others, found a place on the commission of the peace.[7]

A more sensitive political consciousness in the appointment of JPs is discernible as the nineteenth century wore on. In the Teifi valley, political pressure was gradually making itself felt, and in the political ferment after 1868 Thomas Harries of Llechryd, a vocal nonconformist radical, and a shopkeeper by calling, was placed on the commission through the influence of E. M. Richards, the Liberal politician. Professional status and middle-class affluence in support of radical nonconformists resulted in the appointment of Dr Lloyd of Newcastle Emlyn as justice of the peace. A further erosion of gentry power and status values occurred when the Local Government Act of 1894 allowed persons active as council chairmen, such as Dr Enoch Davies of Bryn Teifi, to sit on the local bench alongside those gentry who had always considered it their special preserve.[8]

Attendance at the Court of Great Sessions and Quarter Sessions often depended on their venue. In general, squire JPs attended these courts more regularly when they were held in towns within easy distance of their homes, and when pressing local matters were being dealt with. At the October 1767 Quarter Sessions, held at Cardigan, the bench was made up of local gentry like Lloyd of Coedmore, Lloyd of Cryngae, and Lewis of Llwyngrawys amongst others. And a similar pattern can be traced in gentry attendances at courts held in the counties of Carmarthen and Pembroke during the eighteenth and nineteenth centuries.[9]

Non-attendance, especially on the part of persons holding a particular office, was frowned upon and led to monetary penalties, for example, James Lewis (of Gellydywyll?), the deputy under sheriff for Cardiganshire, was fined '£10 for contempt of this court' in 1752. His fellow justices were not prepared to condone open dereliction of duty. That the administration of these courts was rickety is gleaned from a remark of Daniel Bowen of Waunifor, high sheriff of Cardiganshire in 1741, that '. . . he did not know when the Quarter Sessions was' when fined £50 for non-attendance. Occasionally, objections were raised that certain sessions were not valid as 'legal sessions', as in the case of one held at Tregaron in 1741 when the proceedings were revoked 'as they had never been'. Some historians contend that only about a quarter of the personnel of the whole bench carried out their functions conscientiously. The conclusion one reaches of the Teifi valley gentry is that, as elsewhere in England and Wales, many justices neglected to do so—save for a nucleus of dedicated squires.[10]

As the nineteenth century wore on, gentry attendance improved to a certain extent, due to factors like improved roads and the railway, and a greater sense of public duty, partly stimulated by radical and democratic challenge to gentry power. As has been suggested, the attendance of squire JPs at Quarter Sessions was more regular when the court was held in their own locality. Thus, to cite a few examples only: in May 1741 five out of ten justices sitting at Cardigan comprised the local gentry of Coedmore, Bronwydd, Cilgwyn and Gellydywyll, when one problem was the purchase of '6 sets of manacles' for Cardigan gaol; in April 1752 John Morgan of Cardigan, Lewis of Llwyngrawys, Lloyd of Cilgwyn, Erasmus Saunders and Lloyd of Coedmore sitting at Cardigan considered the building of a new house of correction in the town; likewise in April 1766 the state of Cardigan bridge and gaol, amongst other matters, was deliberated and the local gentry present were delegated with the task of making a proper survey.

But there are instances of squires attending the court of Quarter Sessions when held at distant venues, because matters affecting their own locality were to be considered. Thus, in January 1741 James Lewes of Gellydywyll sat with five north Cardiganshire JPs at Aberystwyth, when a dispute was heard between the neighbouring parishes of Troedyraur and Betws Evan in the lower Teifi valley, as well as less serious matters like the preservation of 'carpets and cushions' at the Cardigan Town Hall. The 'decay' of the Cardigan Town Hall again figured in proceedings over the years, and in January 1777 Thomas Lloyd of Bronwydd, Walter Lloyd of Cardigan and two other local JPs present were instructed to look into the matter. It would appear that it was the sensible policy to place the responsibility for major plans in a particular area on the shoulders of local justices with local knowledge and where their vigilant supervision was required. In May 1791, for example, the squires of Blaenpant, Llwyngrawys, Bronwydd, Coedmore, Trefach and Pigeonsford, or 'any three of them', were delegated to examine the specifications and estimates which John Nash was preparing for the new gaol at Cardigan. In this way it is plausible to argue that absenteeism from the Quarter Sessions may not have been a serious deterrent to efficient county administration, as at first might be thought.[11]

A wide variety of public duties were performed by the squire JPs as, for example, the supervision of poor relief, bastardy matters and the oversight of conditions in houses of correction. Fines were imposed on those neglecting their jury service or upon constables of hundreds for not carrying out public works. Drovers were licensed, orders were made concerning 'contagious distemper on horned cattle', depositions were heard after shipping losses, and 'meeting houses' were licensed without disfavour, such as Tŷ Gwyn, Llangoedmor 1770, Horeb Llandysul 1785, Esgergraig, Troedyraur 1793 and Capel y Wig, Llangrannog 1813 and many others.

A not uncommon vice amongst south-west Wales farmers generally was selling butter with short measure, and in January 1774 the Cardigan Quarter Sessions warned farmers of this offence. During times of trouble and unrest, special measures were taken to erect gallows, provide for the militia and the housing of undesirable vagrants, 'strolling players and jugglers', and fringe groups living on their wits. In the 1790s and the years 1800-09 the gentry were, perhaps, too ready to call in the military during the corn disturbances. In the 1840s the Rebecca Riots demanded the swearing in of special constables and calling in the military. Any increase in robberies and burglaries meant warning innkeepers to give information to the justices. Although Friendly Societies were sometimes, as in the 1790s, suspected of harbouring Jacobins and other enemies of the state, the 'Tivyside' gentry, as we have already shown, looked tolerantly at these groups. Thus, at Cardigan in April 1796 the articles of 'The Tradesmen and Inhabitants Club at Cardigan' were registered.

The interest and patronage displayed by the gentry towards local projects, beneficial to both themselves and the locality, does suggest that it was not always personal gain that motivated their action. The effort of John Lloyd Davies of Blaendyffryn and Alltyrodyn in building Alltcafan bridge over the Teifi at Pentrecwrt was a boon to farmers and travellers, as well as to his own estate. Lewes-Lloyd of Dolhaidd, Fitzwilliams, Lewes of Llysnewydd and Webley-Parry of Noyadd Trefawr were active members of the roads board operating under the aegis of the Quarter Sessions. As the Cardigan bridge was a vital link in the economic and social life of the area, Bowen of Llwyngwair, secured in 1878 at the Pembrokeshire Quarter Sessions £250 for its repair.

Other matters, too, took up their time. For instance, John Griffiths of Treforgan was assiduous in prison visiting and concerned with conditions in Cardigan gaol. Likewise, Sir Thomas Davies Lloyd and others formed local committees of landowners and farmers to raise funds to counter the cattle plague in 1866. While tolerant of nonconformist sects, Roman Catholicism, as we have seen, brought about a neurotic reaction in defence of conformity to the established church. Thus, a 'vagrant Roman Catholic' was committed to the 'house of correction' at Cardigan in 1749. The personal vendettas of some gentry led to court proceedings, as in 1749 when one Richard Jones, gent., was committed for daring to call Herbert Lloyd of Peterwell 'a scoundrelly dog'.[12]

The criminal jurisdiction of the justices of Quarter Sessions comprised all manner of cases, including homicide, assault, theft, burglary, rioting, thefts from wrecks and 'wrecking'—every offence against persons and property and against the peace of the realm. Very grave offences were committed for trial at the Court of Great Sessions, but within their own jurisdiction JPs could impose the severe penalties of hard labour, transportation, whipping and committal to the 'hulks', as well as fines and the 'stocks' for lesser crimes. It is difficult to assess whether they tempered justice with mercy. In 1755 a Cardigan woman was sentenced to be 'strippt from the waist upwards and whipped in the porch of the common gaol till her body be bloody', and in 1782 one David Evan Daniel was sent to the 'hulks'. The question is whether in the former it was a form of public ridicule and mob derision, or the imposition of actual physical pain. It must be remembered that the eighteenth century was not only the age of reason, elegance and of an aristocracy living in Palladian mansions, but also of appalling cruelty—bear baiting, cock fighting, man traps, the mass hysteria attending public executions and other spectacles enjoyed by rich and poor alike.

Petty Sessions records (which unfortunately only survive from the nineteenth century) and reports in the local papers may be more revealing of gentry attitudes in dispensing local justice. Most offences at Petty Sessions were less important than those tried at the higher courts. The phrase 'to appear before one's betters' spoke of the social stigma affecting the under-privileged, deprived and poor having to answer before socially and supposedly morally superior beings. The administration of poor relief and highway rates, the examination of unmarried mothers, the consideration of alleged breaches of contract between employer and employee, and making lists of idiots and lunatics were only some of the many duties of the Petty Sessions. Criminal matters included destroying fences, cutting birch twigs, assaults, thefts, cruelty to animals and operating carts and waggons with insecure loads. But the perennial game and poaching laws were constantly invoked with vigour, suggesting that these were in the squire's eyes the most important element in their case load. Some idea of the penalties invoked may be gleaned from the following instances: William Lewes of Llysnewydd, sitting as a JP in Aberaeron (in virtue of his Llanayron estate), in the 1820s, imposed a 3s fine or public whipping on an offender for destroying fences around Gwynne of Mynachdy's nurseries while cutting birch twigs to make brooms, met with a 2s fine; aggravated assaults in 1861 before William Lewes of Llysnewydd and Thomas Elliott of Dolhaidd resulted in a two months' prison sentence, while non payment of a 6d road toll meant a fine of 13s 6d.[13]

A degree of capriciousness is observed in sentencing policy (which, it has to be remembered, is a criticism of the lay magistracy today). Fines for the movement of cattle during the cattle plague of 1866 illustrate this tendency: a farmer moving nine calves on the highway was fined 4s 6d, whereas another with only one cow suffered a penalty of one penny but costs of 8s. Fitzwilliams was particularly sensitive to certain offences like drunkenness in public and the ill-treatment of animals. Thus, in 1877 a Llandysul innkeeper was given hard labour for fourteen days for working an unfit mare.[14]

In assessing the rule of the squirearchy of the Teifi valley in the community, one must ask the question—did they use their powers wisely, 'without fear or favour, affection or ill will'? The Hammonds took the view that '. . . through the system of magistracy the English constitution rid itself of feudalism . . . and ultimately gave back to the landlords in another form the power they had lost when feudalism disappeared'. An unfavourable view is that, by the nineteenth century, the continued sway of the gentry through the courts, their unchanged and largely unchallenged administration of justice and local government were the main causes '. . . of the unhealthy social life which prevailed in West Wales'. They had become alienated from the community over which they ruled.[15] As has been seen, a few conscientious gentry took their magisterial duties seriously, especially when the higher courts were held within reasonable distance of their homes. But for all their regularity in attendance and attention to duty, social factors, such as pressing rural poverty, the lack of a Welsh educated middle class and the language barrier, inevitably served to widen the gulf between the ruler and those ruled. The legal system was weighted in favour of the landlord class, and self interest, power and status were paramount values.

The average attendance of about three JPs on local benches out of a complement of seven was usual. It was here in the Petty Sessional Division that the impact of gentry influence over the local community was most intense in terms of psychological and moral pressure. Even in cases where the harsh penal system was not invoked, domestic and human problems resulted in humiliating remedies. Thus, the unmarried mother and 'bastard' child, to save a charge on the parish, were hounded from parish to parish by censorious squire JPs whose own private lives were often scandalous. The petty larceny of turnips, bread and items of food during periods of extreme scarcity, which resulted in a public whipping or imprisonment for the guilty, inevitably rankled with an impoverished peasantry who knew of the feasting and roistering in the squire's mansion. The harshness of three or four powerful squires can be demonstrated by a few examples. Following a court action in 1817 Lewes of Llysnewydd refused to relet a holding to a bereaved widow, who offered £12 per annum (the agreement with her late husband being for £6 10s), but accepted a higher rent from a third person. A labourer cutting twigs for baskets was fined a total of 7s 6d (compensation 3s; constable 1s 6d, witness 1s; summons 2s). This case, amongst others, illustrates the iniquity of nineteenth-century means of acquiring evidence, which often rested on spying and hole-and-corner methods of neighbour informing against neighbour in the hope of some small reward. Failure to maintain a family was frowned upon (perhaps not because of the husband's breach of duty, but rather in order to save parish funds) and could lead to a period of imprisonment—a totally negative sentence unlikely to help the offender or his family. Glaring variations in fines highlighted class values, as, for instance, when a local constable was assaulted the culprit was fined 1s 2d, while a similar assault on a squire resulted in a fine of 20s.[16] Theft of different kinds was harshly dealt with; for example in 1857 a vagrant was imprisoned for two months with hard labour for stealing a counterpane from Newcastle Emlyn workhouse, and another offender went to prison for six months for stealing bacon worth 6d. Even allowing for the unreformed state of the penal code and methods of sentencing, the severity of some penalties bore no relation to the offence. Thus, in 1860, village urchins from Llandysul, who had stolen apples from the orchard of squire Thomas of Dôl-Llan, were fined 20s each by the local bench of magistrates, namely Lloyd of Gilfachwen, Lewes of Llysnewydd, Elliot of Dolhaidd and Pryse of Bwlchbychan.[17] The inequity of magisterial decisions led to adverse press comment, which was symptomatic of a seething discontent concerning the treatment of offenders. Typically, in 1893 a farm labourer was fined 5s for keeping a dog without a licence whereas the local squire was only fined 2s 6d for the same offence. Over the years E. Crompton Ll. Fitzwilliams (who died in 1880) had been a solitary voice amongst the gentry in trying to mollify the process of the law. Contending with overweening local gentry, he admitted '. . . all of them [are] extremely jealous of poor me, and annoyed that ye common people do not hesitate to say that without my presence on ye bench they cannot get justice and even then I was very frequently outvoted'. The partiality of squire justices became another weapon in the armoury of radical politicians, and E. M. Richards, MP for Cardiganshire, 1868-71, openly challenged the Cardigan bench, citing in particular Richard David Jenkins of The Priory as the worst culprit.[18]

In addition to dissatisfaction with the treatment of offenders, there were also serious faults endemic to the magisterial system. Courts were held in tippling houses, as, for example, at the Penrhiwpâl Inn, in taverns in Newcastle Emlyn and the Serjeants Inn at Eglwyswrw. These venues were hardly conducive to dignity and decorum; and liquour was supplied during sittings when bench and public indulged too well during court proceedings.[19] The burden of the County Stock and the capriciousness of JPs in Quarter Sessions in allocating county funds was a grievance in the years before the Rebecca Riots. The auditors of public funds were county gentry with vested interests and with strong ties of loyalty to other gentry, the very persons whose activities were being investigated. In 1824, for example, Lloyd Williams of Gwernant, James Bowen of Cardigan and William Owen Brigstocke of Blaenpant were some of the people appointed as auditors. As late as 1863 it was argued that ratepayers' money was squandered through the ineptitude of magistrates. The salaries of magistrates' clerks were paid through fines and costs, a practice which according to the evidence of gentry like Goring Thomas, Saunders Davies and John Beynon led to prolonged litigation and verdicts weighted against defendants.[20] The implementation on the part of all powerful JPs of statutes relating to poor relief following Gilbert's Act of 1782 led to anomalies and variation in allowances through the 'sovereign will' of JPs in their local petty kingdom. The threat of the 'poor house' over paupers, and a fine or custody in a 'house of correction' for such offences as non-payment of the poor rate, loomed over the heads of rich and poor alike. Gentry like John Lloyd Davies of Blaendyffryn, Lewes Lloyd of Dolhaidd, Jordan of Pigeonsford and Howell of Glaspant were criticised in connection with the Newcastle Emlyn workhouse in 1838. Saunders Davies of Pentre and Evans of Highmead were chairmen of the Cardigan and Lampeter Unions, but, although the squire JPs could direct policies, any benefits from the Poor Law Amendment Act of 1834 were not implemented in 'Tivyside' because it was alleged, the better informed persons of property had exercised little influence over parish matters.[21]

In fairness, it can be argued that the poor law, its bureaucracy and means of raising poor relief were all disliked and that the burden fell entirely on owners of property. Jenkins of The Priory, Cardigan, argued that '. . . the poor of this county ought to be supported by the nation at large', a valid point when fortunes were by then being made in industry. In 1871 Sir Thomas Davies Lloyd, on behalf of Cardiganshire land-owners, petitioned parliament for a more equitable local tax controlled by all ratepayers and based on personalty as well as other forms of wealth. Moreover, the private philanthropy of some enlightened gentry and their patronage of worthy causes was their response to the failure of the state system to help the indigent and infirm.

Lastly, the squirearchy held tenaciously to their power, they were free agents not answerable to anybody and ruled their communities as by divine right. Allowing for the vagaries and frailty of human nature, perceptive and reforming thinkers regarded the magisterial bench (as constituted up to the end of the nineteenth century) as the last bastion of the hoary-headed Tory relics of ancient times, irrelevant in a more progressive and democratic age.[22]

The traditional and coveted county office of High Sheriff, as the 'chief officer of trust and credit in the shire', became the prerogative of leading families and was a criterion of royal favour, loyalty to the crown, and county prestige. With the appointment of lords lieutenant in Elizabeth I's reign, the judicial and executive functions of govern-ment and command of county military forces passed from the sheriff.[23] During his year of office the sheriff's functions were honorary and expensive, and for that reason gentry had tried to avoid being chosen by the sovereign. To take examples outside the Teifi valley, Lort of

Stackpole and Sir Erasmus Philipps of Picton Castle, at the end of the seventeenth century, had tried to avoid the office which they regarded as 'trouble and expense'. In the eighteenth century the office had become more honourable and expensive but, many leading families, nevertheless, undertook the burden as it gave status and prestige to a country squire.[24] Of the 'Tivyside' gentry between 1700 and 1871, sixty-seven were high sheriffs of Cardiganshire, twelve for Carmarthenshire and twenty-two for Pembrokeshire.[25] During his year of office a sheriff had to entertain the judges on circuit, and attend at Assizes, but many duties were carried out by the under sheriff. In terms of their contribution to the office of sheriff, the following Teifi valley gentry families made a major and significant contribution: Lewes (Dolhaidd, Gernos, Llysnewydd), 11; Lloyd (Bronwydd, Cilrhiwe), 6; Bowen (Llwyngwair, Troedyraur), 5; Lloyd (Alltyrodyn, Llanfechan), 4; Lloyd (Coedmore), 4; and Colby (Ffynone, Rhosygilwen), 4. These figures suggest families which could best bear the financial strain of the office and were prepared to do so to acquire honour and prestige. Expenses could be considerable and a heavy drain on impecunious estates. Whilst the paucity of evidence makes comparisons difficult, the following sums are indicative of what an incumbrance upon estate finances the office could be. Henry Jones of Tyglyn in north Cardiganshire paid over £200 during his one-year term of office in 1780. In 1828 John Griffiths of Llwynduris ran up expenses of £405, a large sum compared to that paid by John Vaughan Colby of Ffynone in 1891, namely, £163 for filing oaths, judges' lodgings, trumpeters, ringers, carriages, and other expenses. Colby was regarded in 'Tivyside' as a miser, yet could not well avoid accepting the office. Some gentry were no longer interested in the gloss and glamour of the shrievalty, and regarded it as the 'sheriff calamity' and an 'expensive chore'. In the early 1900s, William Lewes of Llysnewydd wrote to his solicitor: '. . . is there no law regarding this that will protect me? It seems very hard that any one should have to waste a heap of money in this way'.[26]

From 1557, the Lord Lieutenant took the place of the sheriff as commander and organiser of the militia in each shire, with himself and his subordinates making frequent reviews of men, armour and munitions. Each locality and every man of property had to find men, through compulsion or voluntarily, to fulfil their national duty. In spite of a national dislike of a standing army, various Militia Bills from the 1750s onwards, enabled men to be trained in the face of any possible threat from the continent. The militia, serving at home, could be recruited locally through the influence and authority of the squire. An Act of 1757 allowed Parliament to fix the number of recruits and bear the burden of provision and pay. Recruitment fell on parishes, and while subsequent legislation tended towards the gradual absorption of the militia into the regular forces, its organisation and performance were largely in the hands of the landed gentry. The Lord Lieutenant appointed the various officers whose ranks were graded according to income from land. Consequently, the militia reflected exactly the social hierarchy of the county landowners, and the social cachet of rank in the militia was aspired to, like other official county positions. Thus, in the 1790s, John Colby of Ffynone claimed the rank of lieutenant-colonel in respect of landownership in eleven Pembrokeshire parishes, while John Tucker of Sealyham and John Meares of Eastington could only qualify for the rank of major and captain respectively. Apart from the prestige of rank, there were incidental perquisites for officers, such as tax exemption on items like 'hair powder', 'horse taxes' and 'road tolls' when on duty. Moreover, under Lord Cawdor's command of the Carmarthenshire militia from 1798 to 1829, large sums of money were offered to induce 'fine men to enlist . . . and leading families in the county were the serving officers'.[27]

Surviving records from 1781 to about 1900, show that every land-owning family of consequence in 'Tivyside' contributed to the commissioned personnel of the militia, not only of the three counties of Cardigan, Carmarthen and Pembroke, but also of militia troops from other counties passing through south-west Wales. Thus, from 1811 to 1813, W. O. Brigstocke of Blaenpant was Captain of the North Gloucester Militia, and Owen Lloyd of Bronwydd and George Price of Pigeonsford were lieutenant colonels of the Royal Clarence Militia. At the end of the century the number of 'Tivyside' gentry serving as officers in the militia were approximately as follows: Cardiganshire (11), Carmarthenshire (14), Pembrokeshire (14), with from 350 to 450 men in each county regiment.[28] In terms of actual military engagement the activity of the militia was limited. The 'zeal, alacrity and spirited exertion', together with the 'loyalty, spirit and unanimity', of the 'militia and populace', reached epic proportions in the folklore of Pembrokeshire following the French landing in 1797. Major Bowen of Llwyngwair and Lieutenant Colonel Colby of Ffynone were singled out for their participation in the face of what was regarded as a serious crisis. Otherwise, the campaign record of the militia was undistinguished because no serious challenge ever arose. The general attitude to the militia was probably unfavourable, as it was considered to be the gloved fist of the squirearchy trying to impose a military hold on the community. Additional rates for housing, feeding and maintaining the militia were authorised in parish vestry and Quarter Sessions. Legal sanctions could be invoked for non-payment. In addition to the defence of the realm, any symptom of civil strife, protest or disaffection could be put down by the militia. It could be used against mobs pillaging wrecks, which was a valuable if sordid means of subsistence to poverty-stricken peasants. Welsh folk bitterly objected to the compulsion to join the militia, and dissenting ministers preached against voluntary enlistment so that officers were sometimes unable to fulfil their quotas. For many reasons the 'militia' had a bad name. The brutal methods of discipline, like flogging, imposed by officers such as Colonel Howell were deeply resented. On the other hand, isolated incidents in the militia's history were regarded as 'providential' justification for its existence, and local poets like Dafydd Morgan of Trelech indulged in euphoric praise of the 'Tivyside' gentry for their valour in repulsing the French invasion in 1797.[29]

While it has to be conceded that the militia often performed a valuable service as a peace-keeping force, its short period of training, service and lack of co-ordination rather as a motley rabble of 'raw recruits' made it less effective as a law enforcement agency. A more serious criticism is that, in the face of social unrest, it might cause dissension within local communities when neighbour and kinsman were ordered to take action against each other. It constituted another official weapon in the armoury of the gentry over the community, satisfying an instinct for aggressiveness without facing the real dangers of war, imperial conquest or the hazards of foreign exploration. Many members of leading families acquired only limited distinction in the military field, and remained the 'Blimps' of the local militia. It must not be forgotten, however, that members of some gentry families distinguished themselves in extending and defending the frontiers of Empire (a 'role' which was expected of persons of their class, culture and education), and one recalls the distinguished service of Sir Erasmus Gower (1742-1814), the Webley and Hope families and the record of Lieut. Col. Edward Crawford Lloyd Fitzwilliams in the South African War and during the European War of 1914-18.[30]

In the days of patronage and family influence, offices other than that of JP and High Sheriff, but forming an integral part of local government, were held by the county gentry. The Clerk of the Peace, appointed by the *Custos Rotulorum*, carried out the routine work of administering the Quarter Sessions—drawing up indictments, arraigning prisoners, recording judgements and such matters. Gentry with 'Tivyside' connections, like Thomas Lloyd and James Lloyd of Ffosybleiddiaid held the office in 1734 and 1746 for Cardiganshire. John Beynon, the Newcastle Emlyn attorney, held the office from 1814 to 1844. The official salary was not always the main inducement, but the office carried fees and emoluments—a hundred and one pretexts for further charges—and clerks like John Beynon and Herbert Lloyd of Carmarthen were notorious for their unscrupulous methods.[31]

The Treasurer of the County Stock had the task of raising money from recalcitrant hundreds and parishes, and again there was the temptation for officials to feather their own nests. In 1766 Gwynne of Mynachdy was paid £4 for the 'carriage of arms and ammunition . . .' belonging to the militia, from Cardigan to Aberystwyth. In 1795 three guineas were paid to messengers operating throughout the county on 'navy business', thus reflecting perhaps the danger of French invasion. An instance of family influence becomes clear when, on the death of William Lewes of Llysnewydd in 1794, his kinsman James Bowen, gent., of Cardigan, was appointed to succeed him.

For Cardiganshire, two coroners held office, one for the north and one for the south of the county. In 1754 John Phillips of Dolhaidd-isaf acted as a coroner and in 1757 Jeremiah Lloyd. The coroner's tasks comprised making an 'inquisition' on dead bodies, shipwrecks and death due to violence, plague or other causes. They were paid a fee of £1 for every corpse examined, and a travelling allowance of 9d per mile. In 1794 John Ferrier was appointed coroner of Cardigan town, a person who (it is not without significance) had family connections with Colby of Ffynone.

Lesser offices proved useful as a further source of income to younger sons. The post of 'harbour keeper' at Cardigan could provide a living and extras from tolls, contraband or anything else that fell into their hands. A clerkship to the local justices brought in fees and fines, and a member of the Bowen family of Llwyngwair and Troedyraur was appointed in 1796. 'Scavengers' were the overseers of the general health and hygiene of towns, and four prominent local gentry were appointed in 1800 for the town of Cardigan. The post of surveyor of roads and bridges had long been held by amateurs, usually gentry magistrates living in the locality of the public works being carried out.[32]

The 'Tivyside' gentry wormed their way into the 'governance' of the market towns of Cardigan, Atpar and Lampeter which, with Aberystwyth, returned a member of parliament. As burgesses they had the power to elect a ruling élite who could vote in parliamentary elections. Thus, in 1767, Herbert Lloyd of Peterwell decided to create a thousand burgesses to defend his interest at Lampeter against the opposition of Pryse of Gogerddan, Lloyd of Bronwydd and Brigstocke of Blaenpant.[33] As mayors of towns, the gentry acted as returning officers, and thereby had control over those who could vote. The keys of power were in the hands of the gentry, who held in addition the lesser offices of common councilmen, bailiffs, sword bearers and serjeants at mace, as well as the control of fairs, markets and traditional courts.[34]

From early Stuart times, the office of Portreeve of Atpar had been held mainly by the families of Gernos, Noyadd Trefawr and Penybeili, but the actual control of the borough was largely in the hands of the Lloyds of Cilgwyn from 1659 to 1684 and from 1696 to 1730. These petty boroughs were a nettlebed of intrigue, rivalry and ineptitude which could lead to serious litigation. From 1736 to 1741, for example, it was alleged in a King's Bench action that Matthew Griffiths, of Pantybetws, through the connivance of Hector Jones of Coedstre, indulged in corrupt practices by consorting 'with disorderly persons without pretence or right [who] were for half a crown apiece admitted burgesses thereof'.[35] After the 1740s the jurisdiction of the borough of Atpar lapsed, so that by the year 1831 Lloyd Hall opposed any attempt to revive it in view of the expansion of Newcastle Emlyn as a thriving market town and the possibility of joint parliamentary representation.[36] After the Reform Act of 1832 it still remained one of the Cardigan Boroughs returning an MP until 1884, but its significance, and gentry participation in its affairs, had declined.

Cardigan also provided privileges and local power to its burgesses, amongst whom the lower Teifi valley gentry were prominent in the eighteenth and nineteenth centuries. When Owen Brigstocke of Blaenpant in the 1750s was sworn in as burgess, his privileges included the right to vote, to pasture cattle on the commons, to be free from tolls and dues within the borough, and those throughout Wales and Ireland payable by drovers and masters of vessels. One suspects a degree of manipulation of the town's affairs by certain gentry, like R. D. Jenkins who managed to become mayor on several occasions though not a member of its council.[37] In the affairs of the town of

Lampeter, the Jenkins clan of Cilbronne held a key position in the disputed Cardigan Boroughs election of 1812 and in the contest between the Hon. John Vaughan of Crosswood and Herbert Evans of Highmead. As in other towns, burgesses were free from tolls, and in the 1760s local squires were eager to establish their claims, which could be of benefit to them when selling produce from their home farms. More importantly, the manipulation of burgess lists had a political significance, in that the 'interest' of parliamentary candidates could be preserved over a wide area far away from the small towns. In 1774, for example, the 400+ Lampeter burgesses were drawn from 40 Cardiganshire, 30 Carmarthenshire, 2 Pembrokeshire, 2 Glamorgan and 1 Breconshire parish. From the late seventeenth century, every 'Tivyside' family provided burgesses for Carmarthen; many held the office of mayor and thereby qualified for several freehold estates within the borough. In 1763, for example, Owen Brigstocke, Dr Phillips and David Jordan were a few of those holding freehold property; and up to the Municipal Corporations' Act of 1835 the affairs of the town were largely a matter of family privilege with scant regard for the rights of the inhabitants.[38] The corruption of the ruling oligarchy led to protest and dissent: '. . . God damn the corporation and all those that wish it well; they call us Levellers. We will Levell them and their troop of Horse'. Amongst these ruling 'Just Asses' were some of the 'Tivyside' gentry, singled out as 'senile nincompoops' in *An Essay on the Character . . . of the Governors of the Boro of Carmarthen c. 1789*. John Lloyd of Alltyrodyn and Arthur Jones of Carmarthen and Aberdwylan, near Cenarth, were satirised thus:

> Dull Alltyrodyn in love with Power's shade
> To please his whim is now a Justice made,
> Sits in the Hall, with cover'd head, his joy
> Pleased with a Bauble as a Child with Toy.
>
> Old Arthur dull whom every Person knows
> Sans eyes, sans teeth, he hobbles as he goes.[39]

While self interest seems to have been the main motivation in gentry participation in the affairs of the towns, occasionally attempts were made to benefit the public at large. Thus, towards the end of the eighteenth century, Howells of Penralltcuch, Lewes of Gellydywyll, Saunders of Clunfelin, amongst others, petitioned the Post Master General for a 'new bye-post office' for Newcastle Emlyn, a 'flourishing market town' on the road of the 'stage [coach] to Cardigan'.[40] But, in the main, gentry activities were aimed at promoting their own well being. They were not subject to any review or criticism, except by those of the same social circle who shared the same standards of loyalty to family, status and whatever enhanced their power.

NOTES AND SOURCES

[1]J. H. Gleason: *The Justice of the Peace in England 1558-1640*, 1969, p. 7; for a study of the functions of justices of the peace and other 'county offices' see A. L. Rowse: *The England of Elizabeth, London 1950*, 'Administration: Central and Local Government', pp. 339-55.

[2]Earl Jowitt: *The Dictionary of English Law*, 1959.

[3]NLW/Highmead/Box P/File 1; CRO/Cwmgwili/36.

[4]FG/22/pp. 407-09.

[5]K. Williams-Jones: *A Calendar of the Merionethshire Quarter Sessions Rolls 1733-65 with a critical and historical introduction*, 1967 (NLW/124 Q), p. xxiv; The Lord Lieutenant of the county is the official who represents the Sovereign; is the 'custos rotulorum' or Keeper of the records for the county and recommends the names of persons for appointment as magistrates, 'nomina ministrorum'— the names of those persons on the Commission of the Peace, i.e. magistrates. L. J. K. Glassey and N. Landau: *op cit.*, pp. 255, 259-60; K. Williams-Jones: *op cit.*, pp. lii-lvii; B. Phillips: *op cit.*, p. 69. Copy in private hands: 'dedimus'—writ giving authority to act as a magistrate; PRO/C 193/44, 45; C 420/9/8/9; Crown Office Dedimus Books, 1738-63; 1763-1835; C 234/80 (Cds), 81 (Cms), 90 (Pembs), NLW Ms 17071 E.

[6]*Patriarchs and Parasites . . .*, 169; F. Jones: 'Ave atque Vale', *Carms. Historian*, ix, 1972, pp. 5-30. J. R. S. Phillips: *op cit.*, pp. ix, 185-228. T. H. Lewis: 'The Justices of the Peace in Wales', *THSC*, 1943-44, pp. 125-26. NLW/17071 E.

[7]Sea Serjeants—Tory gentry sympathetic to the Stuarts, but whose activities were largely social.

[8]NLW/Gt Sessions/Wales 4/889/1-9, Geo II, 1/5; *ibid*: 897/2, Geo III. *Cd Ad*: 3/2/1872. *ibid*: 16/12/1887, 18/1/1895; in Cardiganshire, in 1893, 105 JPs were Tory in politics and 17 were Liberals. D. Cannadine: *op cit.*, p. 154.

[9]*loc cit.* NLW/Cards/QS/OB; CRO/Carms/QS/OB; HRO/Pembs/QS/OB.

[10]NLW/Cards/QS/OB/1; G. E. Mingay: *op cit.*, p. 128. D. W. Howell: *op cit.*, pp. 143-44.

[11]Cards, Carms, Pembs/QS/OB. *loc cit. DNB.*

[12]NLW/Cards/QS/OB. *ibid*: 1841; *Cd Ad*: 10/8/1866; 7/1/1878. *ibid*: 29/6/1866; NLW/ D. Pryse Williams/15664 A. NLW/Cards/QS/OB. *loc cit.*

[13]NLW/Ms 11488 E; CRO/QS/Files/1861.

[14]CRO/QS/Files/1866, 1877.

[15]J. L. and B. Hammond: *op cit.*, p. 16; Dd Williams: *op cit.*, pp. 4, 34.

[16]NLW/Ms 11488 E. CRO/QS/Files/1859.

[17]*ibid.*, 1859; HRO/Wil/226.

[18]*Cd Ad*: 28/7/1893. NLW/Cilgwyn/LB/4/3 May 1871; *Cd Ad*: 12/1/1872; 16/2/1872.

[19]'Recollections of T. Lewis, Penrhiwpâl', *Yr Efangylydd*, Chwef. 1833, pp. 63-4; *Cm Jnl*: 5/11/ 1824; 8/5/1863.

[20]*RCISW*, 1844, pp. 220 [Qus 5070-78], 221 [Qus 5079-5102], 222 [Qus 5113-14], 238 [Qus 5544].

[21]D. Fraser: *The Evolution of the British Welfare State*, 1973, pp. 31 seq; J. D. Marshall: *The Old Poor Law 1795-1834*, 1968, pp. 13, 48 seq; A. E. Davies: 'Some Aspects of the Old Poor Law in Cardiganshire, 1750-1834', *Ceredigion*, vi, 2, 1968, pp. 12-13; NLW/D. Pryse Williams/15623 E; A. E. Davies: 'The New Poor Law in a Rural Area, 1834-1850', *Ceredigion*, viii, 3, 1978, pp. 248-51, 258; *The Welshman*: 26/1/1844.

[22]*The Welshman*: 5/2/1847; *Cm Jnl*: 31/3/1871; *Cymru Fydd*, ii, 12, Rhagfyr 1890, p. 709.

[23]H. Owen (ed): *The Description of Pembrokeshire by George Owen of Henllys*, 1906 (ed), iii, pp. 64-8; H. Potter: *Historical Introduction to English Law*, 1942, pp. 83-6.

[24]D. W. Howell: *op cit.*, p. 140; M. Cragoe: *op cit.*, p. 75.

[25]T. Nicholas: *op cit.*, i, pp. 82-4, ii, pp. 884-86; F. Jones in D. Miles (ed): *The Sheriffs of the County of Pembroke 1541-1972*, [nd], pp. 8-14.

[26]NLW/Ms/4706 D; NLW/Owen Colby/740. Information from the late Miss D. Lewis-Bowen, 1987.

[27]NLW/Llwynduris/45; NLW/Owen Colby/433-35; NLW/Ms/11558 C.

[28]NLW/Evans George/1491, 1590; NLW/Ms/11105 D; *Cm Jnl*: 23/2/1811, 12/6/1812. 11/6/1813. E. H. Stuart Jones: *The Last Invasion of Britain*, 1950, pp. 77, 85-88, 91-99.

[29]NLW/Owen Colby/2181; Dd Williams: *op cit.*, p. 52; NLW/Cilgwyn/LB/36/28 Nov. 1854. CRO/Derwydd/CA 44.

[30]*Who's Who in Wales*, 1920; information from the late Major Francis Jones.

[31]NLW/Cards/QS/OB/1; R. G. Thorne: 'Herbert Lloyd of Carmarthen', *THSC*, 1977, pp. 108-09; Sir Edgar Stephens: *Clerks to the Counties, 1360-1960*, 1961, pp. 65-66, 148.

[32]NLW/Cards/QS/OB/2, 4.

[33]CRO/Cwmgwili/109.

[34]S. Lewis: *op cit.*, *sub* Atpar, Cardigan.

[35]NLW/D. Pryse Williams/15622 E, 15623 E; NLW/Cilgwyn/342.

[36]*ibid*: LB/32/21 Mch 1831; T. F. Ellis: *Report upon the Borough of Atpar*, 1832 (NLW/Cilgwyn 352); for the ante-diluvian attitude and ineptitude in the governance of county towns, f. also D. L. Baker-Jones: 'Local Government 1815-1974' in *Pembrokeshire County History*, vol iv, *Modern Pembrokeshire 1815-1974*, ed. by David W. Howell 1993, pp. 272-304.

[37]NLW/F. C. Winchester, Hove/7, 10-12, 20-21, 38; NLW/Evans George/1413; FG/19/295-97; H. M. Vaughan; *op cit.*, pp. 125-27 (for the fact but a different explanation).

[38]NLW/Falcondale/GP, iv, 65, vi, 54; NLW/Ms 12366 D; CRO/Plas Llanstephan/325.

[39]G. Roberts: 'Political Affairs from 1536 to 1900', in J. E. Lloyd (ed): *op cit.*, pp. 18-21, 54-63; D. J. V. Jones: *op cit.*, pp. 40-41, 120-132; CRO/Plas Llanstephan/336; NLW/Ms 12169 E.

[40]NLW/Noyadd Trefawr/1680-82.

The Gentry and National Politics

Parliament in the eighteenth century represented only a fraction of the nation, namely, the great landowners and country gentlemen. The candidates themselves were generally chosen by small cliques of local magnates;[1] MPs represented their localities and estates; they were returned by the general feeling of their neighbours, as spokesmen for independent, self-governing communities. In their eyes central government contributed little to the business of life. As rural squires, they were more interested in the pursuits of the countryside than in parliamentary duty, the niceties of constitutional theory or foreign affairs. Important matters were dealt with locally by the squirearchy. To them local affairs were real, and Westminster rather a distant irrelevance.[2]

The Welsh member of parliament had to be influential in terms of lineage, possessed of sufficient income and estate—as MPs received no salary—and equipped with the virtues of independence, constitutional loyalty and concern for the common good. To be the community's representative in parliament was a mark of esteem granted to families of note who had been established for centuries in the Principality, while the outsider stood little chance of support. 'Independence' was a term of approbation, and signified freedom from the pressure of an aristocratic patron or dominant family junta.[3]

The qualifications for Welsh parliamentary representation had been laid down by acts from 1536 to 1543. Candidates for 'county' seats had to have an annual income of at least £600 from land, while 'borough' candidates needed only half that sum. The three south-west Wales shires of Cardigan, Carmarthen and Pembroke each returned a 'knight', and, in addition, the following each returned a member of parliament: the Cardigan Boroughs, Carmarthen Borough, Pembroke Boroughs and the 'town and county' of Haverfordwest.[4]

The political struggle in these areas was virtually a dynastic one between the major ruling families of Crosswood, Gogerddan and Nanteos in Cardiganshire, Orielton and Picton Castle in Pembrokeshire, and Dynevor, Edwinsford and Golden Grove in Carmarthenshire. From 1700 to about 1850 Cardiganshire had (with hardly an exception) been ruled by the great houses of Gogerddan, Crosswood and Nanteos. Any attempt by the Tivyside gentry to represent the 'county' had been stifled after 1698 when John Lewis of Coedmore surrendered the seat. The Cardigan Boroughs were held by Owen

Brigstocke of Blaenpant and Stephen Parry of Noyadd Trefawr for most of the period 1700 to 1724. But, afterwards, 'Tivyside' gentry influence was directed in favour of various powerful contestants, especially Herbert Lloyd of Peterwell, who had strong support around Lampeter and mid-Cardiganshire in the 1760s. As with the 'county' seat, the 'boroughs' became, more or less, the preserve of the greater magnates of north Cardiganshire, allied with newcomers connected to them by marriage, like the Campbells of Stackpole Court, Pembrokeshire, and Glanfread, Cardiganshire.[5]

The active role of the lesser 'Tivyside' gentry was confined to jockeying and canvassing in the interests of the influential candidate, the creation of burgesses and involvement in manipulation and intrigue in towns like Cardigan and Carmarthen. The significance of their participation cannot, however, be ignored, because in their own localities they could muster support and 'preserve the interest'. Thus, in 1761, Walter Lloyd of Coedmore actively campaigned for Pryse of Gogerddan in the contest for the 'county' seat; and in 1796 Pryse Loveden (from 1798 Pryse Pryse) of Gogerddan solicited the aid of William Owen Brigstocke of Blaenpant against the Crosswood and Hafod coalition.[6] As in Cardiganshire, 'Tivyside' gentry who were burgesses of the Carmarthen Borough threw in their lot on behalf of the major contestants. In Pembrokeshire, their participation was virtually limited, and their influence operated only slightly on the periphery.

It is difficult to discern any commited political affiliation on the part of the gentry within the 'Tivyside' area during the eighteenth century. The firm Jacobitism of Gogerddan, Nanteos and Slebech cannot be traced, with the exception of George Bowen of Llwyngwair and a few others who had refused to swear oaths of supremacy and allegiance after 1688. While a body of opinion existed which was hostile to the Glorious Revolution, it is significant that not a single south-west Wales squire joined the risings of 1715 and 1745. Some ten or more 'Tivyside' squires were active Sea Serjeants, whose Jacobitism, one surmises, was skin deep and limited to the polite fictions of drinking the health of the king 'over the water'. Nineteenth-century traditions of cloak and dagger activities by Parry of Noyadd Trefawr, to bring back the Young Pretender from overseas cannot be substantiated and belong to the realms of country-house mythology. As staunch Tories, the Sea Serjeants supported their own party in elections, but not all 'Tivyside' squires were Sea Serjeants and Tories. The rare evidence of surviving poll books shows how many behaved as definable groups in support of candidates from the great county power houses, but with a strong element of changing loyalties from time to time. In the Pembrokeshire election of 1714 there was fairly even support for the Whig—Owen of Orielton—and for the Tory—Barlow of Slebech.[7] During the contests of 1722, 1727 and 1754 for the Carmarthen 'county' seat, about half of the identifiable 'Tivyside' gentry voted for the Tory candidates, and were prominent Sea Serjeants, as against the rest who supported the Whigs. In the strife-torn borough of Carmarthen, the Sea Serjeants were active as the hard core of Tory interest, and allegedly encouraged the mob in the violence which took place during elections.[8]

No doubt the survival of the Sea Serjeants up to mid-century coincided with that of the old type of Toryism, but from the 1760s Whig and Tory differences played a less significant part. By this time, divisions of loyalty were very much a case of family tradition without a real political element. The geographical spread of lands, the influence of a major house on lesser neighbouring gentry, the congruency of estates as well as interest, patronage and personal relationships must also be considered as significant factors in voting patterns. Thus, in 1802, the agent of the Golden Grove estate in the Newcastle Emlyn area was paid £10 for assembling freeholders and '. . . conducting them to the Election at Llandeilo and attending them there several days, till they were polled in Mr Vaughan's interest'.[9]

A feature of late eighteenth and early nineteenth-century politics was the emergence of the 'independent' candidate, as in the contest between Lord Milford and Owen of Orielton in 1760 for the Pembrokeshire county seat. How far 'independence' developed and was influenced by the Association Movement of 1779-82 is not clear. Oldfield, writing in the 1790s, observed that the Pembrokeshire freeholders had 'upon many occasions' revealed a spirit of independence and supported the Owen family of Orielton because of their 'invariable attachment to the cause of liberty'.[10] The contest of 1812 is more revealing. The freehold supporters of Sir John Owen of Orielton, against Campbell of Stackpole, resolved to oppose the combinations of powerful individuals in support of Campbell, and to assert the right of the independent freeholder to exercise his vote. Owen had a 'stake in the county' and (as against the son of a nobleman from outside) was more suited. Amongst Owen's supporters in 'Tivyside' were James Bowen of Llwyngwair and Morris Williams of Cwmgloyn, who asserted that they were not 'destitute of character or property', and that 'wishing to mark that character with independence we are willing to contribute our property to that end'.[11] A few other gentry, however, led by Thomas Lloyd of Bronwydd, supported Campbell, making a point of denying that he was 'trying to deprive the county of an independent free choice'. The ideology of 'independence' could be used to buttress the power of the great magnates and to preserve the *status quo*; for example, Vaughan of Crosswood held the Cardigan Boroughs seat from 1796 to 1818, sustaining support by slogans of concern for the 'Interest and Prosperity of the Boroughs'.[12] The bitter contest between him and Major Evans of Highmead in 1812 was marked by all the abuses of electioneering—bribery, personation of voters, the 'mysterious' loss of poll books and scurrilous attacks on Vaughan's poor attendance at Westminster, his dubious military rank and service record. Evans (a brother-in-law of Sir Watkin Lewes) was, possibly, in the Wilkes tradition representing a new radicalism, fostered, too, by the Arminian and Unitarian Lloyds of the Llandysul-Lampeter area, where a 'new' family was to challenge traditional county politics based on clan loyalties. Vaughan's victory led to a parliamentary petition by Evans' supporters, who included Richard Hart Davis, the Bristol banker and owner of the Peterwell estate and who was regarded by native gentry as an 'outsider and foreigner'. The old families of Bronwydd, Coedmore, Llwyngwair and others ('the Tivyside confederates of Crosswood') rallied solidly behind Vaughan, who held the seat for a further six years. Old-fashioned values of 'fidelity and integrity' were invoked, the 'independence' of the united boroughs was defended, displaying agile pragmatism to support the old regime.[13]

In subsequent elections up to the 1850s and later, the 'Tivyside' gentry continued very much in the same mould. Few issues of principle or daring policies were raised. Traditional sentiments, like 'attachment to the excellent constitution', 'the strictest economy' and support of 'every measure for the good of the country', were the innocuous slogans poured out from the houses of Gogerddan and Nanteos. William Edward Powell of Nanteos held the county seat through seven elections from 1818 to 1854, while Pryse Pryse of Gogerddan held the Boroughs until his death in 1849. In these contests the gentry of 'Tivyside' were content to support the great ruling houses as they had always done.[14]

For over fifty years after 1815 government and parliamentary power still remained in the hands of the aristocracy and gentry. But the nature of politics had changed remarkably since the previous century; the vague slogans of Whig and Tory gave way to party politics. Politicians were faced with the task of presenting in intelligible form the conflicts of thought and interest that divided the country. The power of the ruling party, and the strength of opposition to it, was drawn from organised public opinion.[15] But even with the emergence of new wealth from industry and commerce, the landed caste system seemed impregnable. Any attempts to reform parliament and the franchise had been thwarted by fear of the excesses of the French Revolution and deep-rooted traditionalism. But after 1832, while the landed interest still remained powerful, an era of reforms which commenced in the late 1830s and '40s deeply affected life in town and country. Consequently, Westminster legislation was no longer remote from the lives of ordinary people, and MPs now faced the challenge of 'community well-being' rather than 'preserving the interest' of class and privilege.[16] Further reform of parliament in 1867 and the Ballot Act of 1872 increased the pace of change. In Wales, the year 1868 (especially with the election of Henry Richard as Liberal MP for Merthyr Tydfil) was the *annus mirabilis* in politics which meant the beginning of the end of gentry power.

In the ferment of reform and radical progress the 'Tivyside' gentry still clung to the concepts of patronage and deference. Thus, in the Cardigan Boroughs' election after the Reform Act of 1832, Pryse of Gogerddan, won gentry support for charitable gifts to the town; for example, buoys at the Cardigan Bar to help 'shipowners and mariners', a gallery and clock to the church, and gifts to the poor.[17] His response to public issues of the day was couched in vague generalities, like the support of religious liberty, but without committing himself to asserting the rights of nonconformists and Catholic Emancipation. On less contentious issues, Pryse was more forthcoming and had everything to gain from the mass of voters by resisting tithes on two commodities, namely, milk and wood, and by voting for a penny rather than a shilling postage on London letters. As in a previous election, personal denigration of opponents was a useful weapon. Pryse's *coup de grace* against his opponent, John Scandrett Harford, was his claim that his ancestors had lived for five-hundred years in Cardiganshire, while Harford was only a recent arrival.[18]

A constantly recurring theme in the political thinking of the 'Tivyside' gentry was loyalty to the constitution and the ultimate sovereignty of parliament as the final umpire in a dispute between established groups, but not as an active force in matters faced by people from day to day. Profuse manifestations of loyalty to the sovereign, as head of the constitution, emanated from churchman and dissenter alike. Thus, Williams of Trefach, a dissenting squire JP, pledged loyalty to the King and government in a three-counties' religious assembly held in Cardigan in 1793. In 1810 a *fête champetre* was held at Bronwydd to celebrate the King's birthday. Attacks on the person of the Prince Regent led to messages of 'sympathy and outrage'. Even liberal-minded and self-confessed 'republican' dissenters, like the Rev. Timothy Davis (son of David Davis, of Castle Hywel), condemned demagogues lusting for power, maintaining that 'Civil communities must acquire probity and honesty of character' and that the loud cries of—'*la liberté, egalité and fraternité*—had been mere Fudge!' No wonder that Whigs and Tories found the idea of democracy an unpalatable and dangerous form of government. 'A stake in the country' was still regarded by the landowning classes as an essential title to political power, and they thought that the possession of landed property was a factor in guaranteeing the stability of the social order and the authority of the constitution.[19]

The slowness of the 'Tivyside' gentry to abandon tradition and the support of 'safe' candidates, and to embrace deliberate national political stances is significant. Thus, in 1847, they still supported candidates from the major south-west Wales houses like Dynevor, Golden Grove and Nanteos, whose policies were only a lame re-statement of well-worn platitudes. The ineptitude of the Welsh MPs led to criticism from E. Crompton Ll. Fitzwilliams, who wrote in 1853: 'It is a pity that we cannot get someone to represent us who has both the strength and nerve, as well as the capacity to fight the battle of Cambria in Parliament'. Moral and political conviction, and the intellectual stamina to bring about reform and redress of grievances, were sadly lacking in the south-west Wales members of parliament.[20]

Catholic Emancipation was a persistent British domestic problem of the early nineteenth century. The 'Tivyside' gentry, following blind prejudice rather than enlightened conviction, were generally against any move to ameliorate the fortunes of Catholics. As has been seen, they practised a broad ecumenism in their patronage of orthodox nonconformity, but Roman Catholicism was regarded as a samsonite attempt to pull down the pillars which held the state and constitution intact. On the other hand, by 1829, a few landowners like Lord Cawdor, realising government fears of an Irish rebellion, supported moves towards Irish liberty and the removal of laws against Roman Catholics. He argued that in 1715 and 1745 the Irish had not supported the Stuarts, and the 'United Irishmen' of 1794 had no Catholic support.[21] His moderate Toryism was more akin to the radical liberalism of dissenters like Timothy Davis who welcomed Catholic Emancipation. In spite of the persecution of Protestants by Catholics in the past, he conceded that 'without freedom, man is in worse plight than the captive beast'. David Arthur Saunders Davies of Pentre, a member of parliament for Carmarthenshire, gave support to the Irish Colleges Bill and 'Maynooth' grant in 1845, against Welsh-Irish landowners like Windham-Quin.[22] But the Newport Court Leet (mainly Lloyd of Bronwydd homagers) campaigned against these '. . . malignant schemes [i.e. concessions] . . . detrimental to the common weal, subversive of our constitution, derogatory to the prerogatives of the Crown and hostile to the protestant faith'.[23] Jane Walters of Glanmedeni, and John Vaughan of Brynog, in the Aeron valley, and with family connections in Tivyside were more virulent in damning Roman Catholics as idol worshippers in the train of 'Baal and the whore of Babylon'.[24]

The attitude of the 'Tivyside' gentry towards the reform of parliament could be described as only fairly progressive, albeit perhaps for the wrong reasons. It is questionable whether they wished to extend the franchise to the lower orders, but factors such as agrarian discontent and the continental revolutions—'the portentous change which is now insinuating itself into the stratum of European society'—were dire warnings to those who did not 'bend to the spirit of the age'.[25] Fair representation of the great manufacturing towns was not an argument to stir the political conscience of country gentry.

Not since the early eighteenth century had a 'Tivyside' squire sat in parliament. John Lewis of Coedmore, Owen Brigstocke of Blaenpant and Stephen Parry of Noyadd Trefawr had been examples of the relatively small squire in Cardiganshire who were later overpowered for a century and a half by the great houses. From 1842 to 1880 the following gentry represent a newer type of MP:

D. A. Saunders Davies of Pentre (Carmarthen County), 1842-57;
J. Scandrett Harford of Falcondale (Cardigan Boroughs), 1845-47;
John Lloyd Davies of Blaendyffryn and Alltyrodyn (Cardigan Boroughs), 1855-57;
J. Bevan Bowen of Llwyngwair (Pembroke County), 1866-68; 1876-80;
Sir T. Davies Lloyd of Bronwydd (Cardigan County), 1865-68;
Sir T. Davies Lloyd of Bronwydd (Cardigan Boroughs), 1868-71;
T. Edward Lloyd of Coedmore (Cardigan County), 1874-80.[26]

They were not only squires and landowners, but, in addition, Saunders Davies, Bowen, Lloyd Davies and Lloyd of Coedmore were practising lawyers, who added a 'professional' dimension to their background. Harford represented the new, ambitious, commercial and banking classes, having acquired a landed estate as an important symbol of traditional power. Lloyd Davies, as has been pointed out already, rose to wealth, influence and a seat in parliament from very humble origins. Sir Thomas Davies Lloyd, unlike the others who accepted Peel's label of 'Conservative', regarded himself as an old-fashioned Whig. His new-found 'Liberalism' was not, however, entirely convincing, according to some observers, on account of his antecedents —ancient lineage, family prestige and landed wealth.[27] The ineptitude of Welsh MPs alleged by E. Crompton Ll. Fitzwilliams, was part of wider criticism, namely their poor attendance in the House, aloofness from constituents and over-indulgence in country pursuits like fox hunting—charges levelled against Loveden Pryse of Gogerddan and applicable to many others. The overall performance in parliament of the above-mentioned 'Tivyside' squires was poor and ineffectual.

Before examining their record in detail, their lack of political acumen and backward-looking traditionalism have to be judged against the challenge of new political awareness in Wales. The incipient republicanism since the War of American Independence (1775-83), the French Revolution, the theological ferment surrounding Unitarianism, the gospel of civil liberty, all gave birth to local dissatisfaction against gentry privilege as embodied in tithes, game laws and feudal dues. The Jacobin experience gave men a new vision, and the old order was no longer sacrosanct.

In view of these factors, it was not surprising that gentry politicians were very circumscribed in their outlook by a dogma that the govern-ance of the state and its well-being depended on traditional sources of power. Moreover, ordinary folk had not yet cultivated a truly political consciousness, especially in south-west Wales, and even in the circumstances that led to Rebeccaism. It was only in the 1860s that there were articulate and clamant forces to wrest power from inept squire MPs. The advent of the purposeful businessman standing for parliament had a deeper revolutionary effect than mob violence in challenging aristocratic monopoly.[28] These new men, with their new wealth, were soon to make their impact. The Reform Act of 1867 finally accepted the principle of democracy just as the Reform Act of 1832 had meant the acceptance of progressive reform. In modern

Welsh history the 1860s constitute a watershed, with (as has been noticed) the return of Henry Richard as Liberal MP for Merthyr Tydfil and E. M. Richards for Cardiganshire. It was an era of new politics, which broke up the age-old idea that communities on estates voted as communities with their lords.[29] The political events of the 1860s in Cardiganshire were to bring about a 'national' view of Welsh politics, with the breakdown of traditional values and loyalties.

Of the 'Tivyside' squirearchy who sat as MPs in the two decades leading up to the 1860s, it cannot be said that they were able to read the signs of the times. Harford made one short speech on the need to review and improve prisons with more accommodation and better drainage. Saunders Davies never made a major speech. During various debates he welcomed the Poor Law Amendment Act, as the previous legislation had been the cause of the '. . . disturbances in south Wales'.[30] He argued for greater powers for JPs in the administration of asylums, defended the record of landowners in providing schools and complimented the success of St David's College at Lampeter.[31] Bowen of Llwyngwair raised two questions concerning the authenticity of signatures from rural areas in support of liquor sales on Sunday, and whether a royal residence in Ireland would be a means to pacify the Irish.[32]

John Lloyd Davies, the member for the Cardigan Boroughs from 1855 to 1857, was of entirely superior calibre. Taking part in some twenty debates, he combined political acumen, cogent reasoning and a diversity of interest with a degree of dedication unmatched by any of his circle. He reflected a puritan streak in opposing the opening of museums on Sundays, and using theological argument he foresaw divine vengeance for Sabbath desecration.[33] On a more mundane and practical level, he foresaw a rising tide of dissent and radicalism, and tried to mollify anti-church bitterness on account of church rates. His remedy was to exempt nonconformists from payment, if they could prove that they had already contributed to the maintenance of their own meeting houses and ministry. The imposition of a charge on land values towards church rates, he argued, would only help the landowner who would in turn raise rents. Unlike many of his contemporaries, he foresaw the dire consequence to the established church if the question of church rates was not settled.[34] But other matters drew his attention as well, as for example, the amount of Sir Charles Barry's remuneration for designing the new Palace of Westminster, and the Metropolis Local Management Bill, the Militia

(Scotland Bill), and the Civil Service Estimates.[35] In addition, his regular attendance marks him out as a new breed of MP. Concerned for local welfare, he advocated a harbour of refuge in Cardigan Bay and gave detailed statistics of shipwrecks, loss of crew and cargo, and the increased trade. He argued that, strategically, the lessons of the French landing of 1797 had not been learnt, and with the increasing size of the French navy and the repercussions of the Crimean War it was common prudence to increase maritime defences. The construction of a harbour would absorb much of the convict population, and his theories of penology were akin to modern thinking concerning the ill effects of overcrowded prisons, the corruption of young offenders, and the rehabilitation of convicted persons in some honest calling, with any remuneration during custody invested to accumulate by the time of their release.[36]

In sharp contrast, Sir Thomas Davies Lloyd of Bronwydd attempted during his career as MP to reassert paternalistic values against nonconformist radical opposition, and to allay the fears generated amongst landowners by the Reform Act of 1867. He conceded that church rates were a grievance among the majority of people in Cardiganshire, and that 'Parliament must redress any well-grounded grievance'. A romantic and a sentimentalist at heart, he argued that the established church still held the affections of the people, not '. . . because of external ornament but its intrinsic worth, the beauty of its liturgy, the comprehensiveness of her articles, the piety and activity of its clergy'.[37] In favour of disestablishing the Irish church, Lloyd argued that there was no analogy between the Irish and Welsh ecclesiastical position. The nonconformist majority amongst Welsh worshippers looked to the church with respect—united by a bond of 'a common reformed faith'. As a Welshman, he owed a debt to the Irish. The badge of conquest would be effaced: 'Let there be no strife between you and us, for we are brethren'—a pan-Celtic embrace indeed![38] Trusting in time-honoured ideology, he personally had no fear of the Reform Bill of 1867, emphasising that 'the influence of the county gentlemen of England rested on a more solid basis that electoral franchises . . . namely on the tradition of centuries, on identity of interests and friendly intercourse. A country gentleman, one of the large territorial possessions, living with his people, and for his people, wielded an influence superior to any other class in this or in any other nation in the world'. Against Henry Richard's catalogue of evictions after 1868, his (Lloyd's) tenants, he claimed, had been allowed to vote for whomsoever they wished. As a Whig landlord, he condemned his friends who still maintained that 'the vote belonged to the landlord and the tenant was only an incident in the matter'.[39] Asserting that the vote should be used without condition, he advocated, too, 'mutual forbearance and kindness' in the face of the rising tide of Liberalism. The extension of the franchise would in time, he hoped, work for the common good, 'landlord uniting with tenant and manufacturer with artisan'.[40] In fact, he was only reaffirming a stale doctrine of a benevolent paternalism, a rosy-hued view of wealth, authority, class and their social imperatives. He failed to foresee the gathering momentum of change, which in less than twenty years would uproot finally, by the Reform Act of 1884, the power of the gentry and the social structure and values which they represented.

In fighting a rearguard action, the 'Tivyside' gentry could no longer command community support to acquire a seat in Parliament. They were compelled to confine their activities to local patronage of worthy causes and 'godly works', their political efforts centering around election meetings and local branches of the Primrose League. The 'success' of Sir Thomas Davies Lloyd was due to his accommodation with Liberals and radicals on the questions of the day; for example, in 1865 he argued against church rates, for equal opportunities, for a moderate extension of the suffrage to the working classes and for the perennial 'bread and butter' issues like reducing taxes.[41] In Cardiganshire, an innate conservatism and deference to the landed interest still survived. Country folk, it might be argued, preferred the *status quo*, taking a long view of things and were conditioned by a traditional outlook and lifestyle. Lloyd's rival, the entrepreneur David Davies of Llandinam was a newly rich, self-made man and had not the 'intellectual' qualities to decide upon important issues, whereas Lloyd was a 'gentleman and scholar'—according to the conservative orientated *Carmarthen Journal*. Lloyd was considered to possess the ability to act on 'perfect independent principles, judging matters on their merits'. Nevertheless, his 'equivocation' and so-called 'sincerity' were doubted by some critics, who failed to see how a member of a centuries-old landed establishment could embrace the Liberal creed. To them there was no longer a place for romantic sentiments about the past. In the House of Commons he should speak on 'matters which are really relevant to the welfare of constituents', or otherwise apply for the Chiltern Hundreds to live the life of a good natured country gentleman. In other respects, too, Lloyd's politics were suspect and motivated by ambition in soliciting privately for a peerage through family connections with Sir Cornewall Lewis, one-time Home Secretary, and Lord Cawdor, by promising his political support and voting influence for the 'house of Campbell' in Carmarthenshire. It is to be surmised that his 'Whiggism' was a strategy to this end. Writing to Gladstone in April 1872 he reaffirmed his loyalty to the Liberal cause, and with a higher ambition in mind argued that '. . . in the counties of Cardigan [i.e. the county of Cardigan and the Cardigan Boroughs] there is not a single resident Peer of the Realm. In the whole of Wales there are only five resident peers of the United Kingdom and these are I think without exception Conservatives, so that Wales which is decidedly a Liberal country is unrepresented in the House of Lords . . . my elevation to the Peerage through the influence of a Liberal Ministry would be considered by the great majority of the inhabitants of the Principality as a grateful compliment . . . hailed with almost universal approbation'.[42]

Although it appears that his secret intrigue was not common knowledge, many Cardiganshire nonconformists continued to support him because of his stand on sabbatarianism, the liquor trade, the Ballot and the religious clauses of the Education Bill. But thorough-going Liberals were no longer satisfied with 'Bronwydd Liberalism', even allowing for Lloyd's own personal qualities. The sedate assumptions of a happy dialogue between church and chapel, landlord and tenant were devoured in the clamour for an MP identifiable with the people in background and religion. Whatever Lloyd's true motives were, in his short political career, he made a gracious exit, still loyal to the Constitution, the union between church and state, the rights and liberties of the people, and Bible-based education. Of David Davies of Llandinam, Lloyd admitted that 'as a nonconformist [he] must necessarily enlist the sympathies of his co-religionists and as a successful man of business [he] has it in his power to develop the commercial resources of the United Boroughs [sc. Cardigan]'. Such capitulation to the forces of trade, commerce and enterprise, to the personal ambition and utilitarian values of new men, was as epoch making as any reform bill or constitutional innovation.

James Bevan Bowen of Llwyngwair, successfully contested the Pembrokeshire seat of 1866, appealing to the 'independent' electors to support his stand concerning the country's welfare, defence, and a settlement of the church question 'by mutual forbearance and concession on the part of the agricultural interest'. These pious sentiments were merely a restatement of the politics of deference of earlier times. Likewise, Thomas Edward Lloyd of Coedmore, winning the Cardigan county seat in 1874, stood very much as a traditionalist, although he called himself a Liberal Conservative. Old attitudes die hard, and the lingering loyalty of many towards the squirearchy was expressed *vis-à-vis* the emergence of the new men of industry. It was argued that: 'Mr Richards [sc. E. M. Richards, the Swansea industrialist] being engaged in a large manufacturing business and also being a stranger to the county . . . cannot feel the sympathy in the welfare of the farmers that a resident landowner naturally does'. Moreover, Richards had shown the 'cloven hoof' by requesting that the county pay his 1868 election expenses! Lloyd was no advanced political thinker: thus, he was opposed to the Ballot as '. . . an un-English way of voting, and one which has the tendency to destroy the keeness of a man's character'. He assumed, too, that as an MP he could (like his eighteenth-century counterparts) influence ecclesiastical patronage, only to be sharply reminded by Bishop Basil Jones that as an MP his opinion was '. . . merely that of a gentleman in whose judgment he [sc. the Bishop] had some confidence'. J. B. Bowen of Llwyngwair held the seat for Pembrokeshire from 1866 to 1868 and from 1876 to 1880.[43] He was a politician in the traditional mould appealing to traditional values and loyalties, namely his position in society as a popular landlord, enterprising farmer-squire and patron of good causes. His patriotism bordered on jingoism, as a staunch supporter of Disraeli, and, although sympathetic to social and humane questions, dismissed the challenge of Liberal and Liberationist issues. Grievances emanating from church and landlord power he dismissed as 'revolutionary agitation' and the effects of the 'chapel screw' operating upon discontented country folk. His election successes can only be explained by the abiding loyalty to the ruling classes which was entrenched in the countryside. In Wales, there was a lack of political awareness and activity in rural constituencies. A hierarchical, stratified society persisted where people knew their place, recognising obligations and rights—attitudes that they were born into. It was well nigh impossible for conflict to disrupt such harmony where deference operated reciprocally, and where class conflict was not of the essence of the situation—although the elements of proletariat uprising were grimly present.[44] This is true of the *gwerin* in the 'Tivyside' area towards the end of the century.

By the early 1880s the political structure of Britain was being totally transformed. Up to this period the House of Commons was a landowners' club, an élite of wealth, status and power. The Reform Act of 1884 added new voters, and the Redistribution of Seats Act of 1885 abolished the Cardigan Boroughs. A larger injection of urban voters meant that in Cardiganshire, as elsewhere, the politics of deference gave way to the politics of democracy; the balance of the Constitution was shifted from notables to members. Addressing 'Tivyside' Conservatives, Lord Emlyn referred to the reforms as bringing about '. . . as wide a representation of opinion as possible'—a reluctant admission of Gladstone's great aim to give to '. . . capable citizens . . . the minor tradesmen and the skilled labourers and artizans . . . the peasants . . . this last and highest privilege of the constitution'.[45]

Gentry response, in some quarters, was to campaign for the preservation of '. . . religion and monarchical government' against the attacks of 'atheism and republicanism'. Their hegemony was further damaged by the intervention of prominent squires like Walter Rice Howell Powell of Maesgwynne, Carmarthenshire (later to be elected MP for west Carmarthen in 1880), campaigning on behalf of Liberals like Davies of Llandinam. W. O. Brigstocke's 'defection' from gentry orthodoxy went further than the call for the disestablishment of the church. He advocated control of the police by democratically elected representatives, stipendiary magistrates to replace lay justices, free unsectarian education and the appropriation of tithes as national property. Although a landowner, magistrate and tithe improprietor, he openly condemned the main grievances borne by the Welsh community for which his own class had been largely responsible. Alone in his social class, he thought that 'Conservatism would not raise its hand again in Wales'.[46]

But even in the 1890s, time honoured assumptions were still invoked; for example, Bonsall the squire of Cwm in north Cardiganshire urged 'Tivyside' gentry to continue to fight elections: '. . . the people, the rank and file look first to the old families . . . their natural leaders, and when they fail the preachers step in. The trimmer, the apostate, the self seeker could not win the hearts of a people that have experience of moneyed Iscariots'. There was a considerable measure of truth in this, as local rhymesters still representing a deferential *gwerin* found it difficult to accept the 'newly rich' like Davies, Llandinam, who boasted of his lands, mines, money and houses, and that he was a 'chum of Gladstone'! A fair-minded dissenter like the Rev. David Adams of Rhydlewis, while dissociating himself from Sir Marteine Lloyd's Tory politics, reminded the public of Bronwydd generosity in providing endowments and land for nonconformist chapels. Even radical nonconformists were totally in alliance with Tory squires on matters like Irish Home Rule, fearing Roman Catholic intrigue, the loss of civil rights, disorder and bloodshed.[47]

Rarely did squire politicians come to grips with new political remedies for the basic problems of their communities. Perhaps A. P. Saunders Davies of Pentre in his election campaign of 1895 came nearest to understanding the tenant farmers' problems in advocating compensation for improvements, reduced rates on agricultural properties, and restrictions on foreign imports of meat and foodstuffs. Too many of the gentry were content to shout slogans of honour about the Empire, and loyalty to the British flag—matters which had little relevance to their tenants and dependants. Even so, the spirit of deference had not died completely: Saunders Davies, an opponent of disestablishment, Irish Home Rule, and other sectarian issues arising out of the nonconformist and nationalist conscience, lost to his Liberal opponent in Pembrokeshire, by only 560 votes in a poll of 8,500.[48]

With the reform of local government in the 1880s gentry influence declined still further, so that whereas they had once ruled counties, their power had virtually disappeared in their own parishes. The signs of the times had been apparent earlier when Sir Thomas Davies Lloyd of Bronwydd, and his brother, the Rev. Rhys Jones Lloyd, were placed seventh and twelfth respectively in the School Board Elections. Even those squires who stood as 'independents' in local elections were defeated by farmers, professional men and woollen manufacturers. It is significant that, in 1891, only three out of forty-four members of the Cardiganshire County Council were landed gentry. The defeat of the gentry was attributed by the pro-Tory press as due to 'preachers and agitators'[49] together with the radical issues already mentioned, concerning which the gentry were dismissive. John Vaughan Colby of Ffynone was sixth out of ten candidates in a district council election of 1894, and was little comforted when he was returned for the parish council, as was S. L. Jones-Parry of Tŷ Llwyd. When John Vaughan Colby made a last bid for the county council in 1904, C. E. D. Morgan-Richardson spoke of his '. . . right qualifications . . . as a landed gentleman with ample leisure time and one who would protect local interests'. But paternalism was to give way to the democratic choice of a nonconformist farmer for the seat. It was not the prerogative of class, as such, that deprived the gentry of continuing to hold the reins of power. It was their deep rooted, entrenched attitudes, and their lack of understanding and sympathy as Tory churchmen versus Liberal nonconformists, which lost them power. A Liberal radical like W. O. Brigstocke had all the insignia of the squire—land, wealth, education and leisure—but became the first chairman of the Carmarthenshire County Council from 1889 to 1892 because he advocated new policies to suit the needs of the day, and which the majority of the electorate espoused. The politics of deference to an oligarchy had given way to the politics of democracy; in time, the politics of democracy would give way to bureaucracy.[50]

NOTES AND SOURCES

[1]B. Williams: *The Whig Supremacy, 1714-1760*, (re ed) C. H. Stuart, 1965, pp. 21-3.

[2]J. S. Watson: *The Reign of George III*, 1960, pp. 51-2.

[3]R. D. Rees: 'Electioneering Ideals Current in South Wales, 1790-1832', *WHR*, 2, 1965, 3, pp. 233-36, 249-50; F. O'Gorman: *op cit.*, pp. 392-93.

[4]A. J. James and J. E. Thomas: *A History of the Parliamentary Representation of Wales, 1800-1979*, 1981, pp. 19-22.

[5]D. W. Howell: *op cit.*, pp. 114-19; T. Nicholas: *op cit.*, i, pp. 185-89, ii, 887-90; W. R. Williams: *op cit.*, pp. 32-36, 38-42.

[6]J. H. Davies: *op cit.*, ii, p. 293; NLW/Evans George/1575.

[7]F. Jones: 'The Society of Sea Serjeants', *THSC*, 1967, i, pp. 57-60, 78-91; NLW/Ms/4706 D; J. B. Burke: *Visitations of the Seats of Arms of the Noblemen, Gentlemen . . .*, 1853, i, p. 32.

[8]FG/27/1-3; NLW/Mss 6108 E, 6099 E; CRO/Dynevor/160/1-3; D. W. Howell: *op cit.*, p. 119; CRO/Cawdor (Vaughan) 1/42/ (5817).

[9]N. Gash: *Politics in the Age of Peel*, 1953, p. 47; CRO/Cawdor (Vaughan) 38/5289.

[10]E. D. Evans: *op cit.*, pp. 214-15; T. H. B. Oldfield: *An Entire and Complete History of the Boroughs of Great Britain* (2 vv, 2nd ed, 1794), ii, p. 413.

[11]D. W. Howell: *op cit.*, pp. 120-21; *Cm Jnl*: 4/1/1812.

[12]*loc cit*; NLW/MS 12169 E.

[13]NLW/Highmead/Box P/File 17; NLW/Falcondale/Gp iv/62, 69, 158; *ibid*: 48-9, 62, 158, 183; NLW/Highmead/Box P/File 18; *DNB*.

[14]*Cm Jnl*: 17/5/1816, 19/6/1818, 17/3/1820; T. Nicholas: *loc cit.*

[15]G. K. Clark: *op cit.*, pp. 208-10.

[16]*ibid*: p. 211.

[17]NLW/Highmead/Box P/File 17.

[18]NLW/Falcondale/Gp iv/62, 69, 158; NLW/Highmead/Box P/File 17.

[19]J. S. Watson: *op cit.*, p. 55; *Cm Jnl*: 19/6/1810, 10/7/1840; George IV (1762-1830) regent during the periods of insanity of his father George III: *DNB*; G. H. Jenkins: *op. cit.* p. 315.

[20]NLW/Ms 4367 E (Rees Jenkin Jones/8); A. Briggs: *op cit.*, p. 239; *Cm Jnl*: 20/8/1847; NLW/Cilgwyn/LB/35/30 Dec 1853.

[21]Lord Cawdor: *Address to the Freeholders of the County of Pembroke*, Milford, 1829.

[22]NLW/Mss 43623 B-4363 B; *The Welshman*: 23/5/1845; *DWB*; Burke: *Peerage, Baronetage and Knightage*, 1893 for Cawdor (Campell) and Dunraven (Windham-Quin).

[23]NLW/Bronwydd/7038-40; L. Colley: *loc. cit.*

[24]F. Jones: *Walters of Perthgereint . . .*, p. 180.

[25]*Cm Jnl*: 24/10/1830.

[26]T. Nicholas, W. R. Williams: *loc cit.*

[27]*Cd Ad*: 27/12/1867.

[28]P. M. L. Thompson: *op cit.*, pp. 184-211.

[29]I. G. Jones: *The Dynamics of Politics in Nineteenth Century Wales*, 1971, pp. 21-24; K. O. Morgan: *Rebirth of a Nation 1880-1980*, 1982, pp. 11-12.

[30]*Hansard*/Parl. Debates/3 ser., 60, 1/3/1842; 72, 10/2/1844.

[31]*ibid*: 26/3/1844; 76, 23/7/1844; 84, 10/3/1846; 122, 7/6/1852.

[32]*ibid*: 190, 18/3/1868; 192, 15/5/1868.

[33]*ibid*: 137, 20/3/1855.

[34]*ibid*: 137, 29/3/1855; 138, 16/5/1855; 140, 13/7/1855.

[35]*ibid*: 137, 16/4/1855; 27/4/1855; 12/6/1855; 13/6/1855; 139, 13/7/1855; 141, 31/3/1856.

[36]*ibid*: 140, 12/2/1856; 141, 3/4/1856.

[37]*ibid*: 181, 7/3/1866.

[38]*ibid*: 191, 3/4/1868.

[39]*ibid*: 188, 27/5/1867; 197, 6/7/1869.

[40]*loc cit.*

[41]*Cm Jnl*: 14/7/1865.

[42]Election Address, 5/7/1865; *Y Traethodydd*: xx, 1865, pp. 488 seq; *The Welshman*: 7/11/1865; *Cd Ad*: 27/2/1867. *DWB*; Letters dated 9/12/1859 to 17/1/1865 from Davies Lloyd of Bronwydd to Lloyd of Nantgwillt, Rads (kindly lent to me by the late Lt Col. R. Stedman Lewis); M. Cragoe: *op cit.*, pp. 132-33; NLW/Bronwydd/6520-29.

[43]*Cd Ad*: 23/6/1871, 15/12/1871; *Cm Jnl*: 3/2/1871; *The Welshman*: 30/1/1874; 6/2/1874; *Cd Ad*: 6/2/1874; *ibid*: 16/11/1866; *ibid*: 26/1/1877; CRO/Coedmore/4/244; J. Llewelyn (Borth): *Cofiant y Parch. Thos. Jones, Cilcennin*, 1899, pp. 80-1; W. R. Williams: *op cit.*, *sub* Pembroke County.

[44]*Cd Ad*: 10/7/1868, 26/5/1876, 23/6/1876. I. G. Jones: *op cit.*, pp. 21-4.

[45]K. O. Morgan: 'Cardiganshire Politics, the Liberal Ascendancy, 1885-1923', *Ceredigion*, v, 1967, 4, pp. 313-17; *Cm Jnl*: 1/2/1884; D. Cannadine: *op cit.*, pp. 14, 17, 24; C. S. Emden: *Selected Speeches on the Constitution*, 1939, ii, pp. 193-94.

[46]*The Welshman*: 12/2/1885; *Cd Ad*: 24/10/1890; *ibid*: 30/10/1885; *ibid*: 7/10/1887, 3/4/1891, 15/1/1892, 26/2/1892.

[47]*Cm Jnl*: 2/2/1894; NLW/Ms 8716 D; *Cd Ad*: 28/11/1885, 20/5/1892.

[48]*ibid*: 12/7/1895.

[49]CRO/EG/Box 7/-; *Cd Ad*: 28/10/1889; *The Welshman*: 30/1/1891; *Cm Jnl*: 18/1/1889.

[50]*Cd Ad*: 4/3/1904; Information from Dyfed Archives Service; D. Cannadine: *op cit.*, pp. 141, 147, 153.

Dissaffection and Protest

Until the middle decades of the nineteenth century, a politically unenlightened Welsh rural community had for a long time slumbered under the protection of a dominant family or had been bribed and befuddled into a state of acquiescence and apathy.[1] Gentry patronage and deference on the part of the lower orders had always been accepted, and was assumed to be part of the fabric of social harmony. Even at the end of the nineteenth century, it has been argued, the squire, in some instances at least, was *personally* liked by the rest of the community in spite of the bitter political and religious tension of the time which rendered his class unpopular.[2]

But before the traditional ties between gentry and community were loosened from the 1860s onwards, there were rumblings of protest in Wales as in the rest of the country. 'The covetous mighty gentry', 'oppressors of the land' and 'rack renting profiteers' were some of the labels attached to rapacious landowners and avaricious lawyers.[3] Satirists throughout the whole spectrum of religious and political persuasion, like Ellis Wynne in the early 1700s to Thomas Roberts, Llwynrhudol, and Thomas Edwards (Twm o'r Nant) at the end of the eighteenth century, had attacked social injustice.[4] As has been seen, a new political awakening emerged by the late 1700s, stimulated by international movements. According to one historian, the period was the 'hinge of fate' for Welsh people, 'beginning their long march out of Establishment into the spiritual world of Dissent'. An 'alternative society' would challenge the church and king ideology and give Welshmen a new vision of society.[5] The new radicalism rejected passive obedience to landowners, church and constitution—which continued with increasing momentum through propagandists in press and pulpit. Joseph Harris (Gomer), David Rees of Llanelli and S.R. of Llanbryn-mair, were some of the torch bearers in the nineteenth century, culminating in the parliamentary careers of Henry Richard, T. E. Ellis and Lloyd George, who brought the grievances of Welsh rural communities into the arena of British national politics.[6]

The countryside was always charged with combustible material for disaffection and protest—poverty, the vagaries of weather, disease and plague—which could only be alleviated through gentry charity and an unsatisfactory system of poor relief. In addition, religious and political issues, landlord and tenant relationships (as noticed already), along with Game Laws and Tithes caused constant friction. Game Laws had, since the end of the seventeenth century, given the aristocracy and gentry the exclusive right to hunt game. Administered by squire JPs, these laws were bitterly resented by the lower orders. The field sports of hunting, fishing and shooting were a symbol of a privileged landed class, reinforced by a series of stringent acts, whereby fines and imprisonment were imposed on offenders. In 1816 a further punishment of transportation to penal settlements like Australia could be meted out to poachers. Persons other than gentry could not keep dogs, nets or guns which could be used for poaching. The majority of country folk were not allowed to shoot even on their own land. Legally, only the gentry or nobility could include game as part of their diet.[7]

It is difficult to assess the degree of poaching in the 'Tivyside' area during the eighteenth century. One of the problems is that game cases were heard in Petty Sessions for which records have not survived. It is likely, too, that many a poacher was dealt with summarily in the squire's 'justice room', without any permanent record of the proceedings being kept.

When a new breed of landowner indulged in 'genteel entertainment' such as the 'battue', i.e. game preservation on a big scale for mass slaughter, more punitive measures were introduced to guard gentry privileges. With the Game Reform Acts of 1818 and 1831 poaching increased, giving rise in turn to increased prison sentences, the murder of gamekeepers, and incensed feelings on the part of ordinary folk that the game laws were immoral.[8] Farmers were not compensated for damage done by pheasants; the labouring classes were denied the occasional rabbit to relieve their 'dire poverty'. By the mid-nineteenth century poaching and defiance of the Game Laws, such as the vigorous Night Poaching Act of 1844 and the Poaching Prevention Act of 1862, extended the definition of 'game' and increased police powers of search and confiscation, thereby exacerbating an already bitter situation.[9] The Ground Game Act of 1880, limited the landowner's monopoly by granting tenants the right to destroy rabbits and hares on their holdings, notwithstanding any provision to the contrary in their agreements. But subtle social pressures were still operative as tenants were understandably afraid to exercise their rights if their landlord was openly hostile to the legislation.[10]

The gentry of the Teifi valley were not slow to acquire the privilege of employing gamekeepers on their estates. The Act of 1784 required every person of property qualified to kill game to register his name and abode and the appointment of a gamekeeper with the Clerk of the

Peace. These registrations were announced in the press, so that the gentry thereby publicly established their rights. Thus, from 1784 onwards, the squires of Blaenpant, Bronwydd and Coedmore, amongst others, recorded their Game Licences. Lesser gentry and freeholders like George Saunders of Perthyberllan followed suit, a practice which continued up to mid-century.[11]

In asserting their privileges in this way, many of the traditional rights or customs of localities were ignored; for example, Thomas Lloyd of Bronwydd prohibited all persons from 'sporting' within the barony of 'Kemes' on pain of a £5 fine. A very severe fine of £20 was imposed for encroaching on fishing rights in the river Nevern in 1818.[12] Lord Cawdor openly solicited the help of informers with the promise of reward for information concerning poachers on his 'Emlyn Uwch Cuch' estate in north-west Carmarthenshire, and squires like Webley-Parry of Noyadd Trefawr and Jenkins of The Priory were equally adamant in asserting their rights.[13] The effect of the Game Act of 1831 partly increased the value of estates economically '. . . as affording hereafter not only pleasure but profit'. The attitude of some squires was extremely reactionary towards poachers, whether they were 'professional' or merely humble rustics driven by hunger and poverty to break the law. Thus, in 1862, John Boultbee of Gwernant, chairman of Cardiganshire Quarter Sessions, supported a parliamentary petition to make stiffer laws against persons '. . . spending their time in idleness and dissipation illegally trespassing in pursuit of game and rabbits . . . as present laws are insufficient to put an end to so great an evil'. Far too often, the view prevailed that only harsh laws and severely hard work would prevent the poor from crime and immorality and socially unacceptable 'sins' like poaching. A squire determined to assert his rights, like John Scandrett Harford, owner of the Peterwell estate, ordered a tenant in 1828 to have his dog destroyed.[14] He represented those who believed that privileges like shooting, owning dogs and the like were the sole right of the landed classes. Thus, the obsequious parson of Llandyfríog in 1832, on receiving the gift of a hare from Major Evans of Highmead, acknowledged that only '. . . Gentle Folks are better entitled to the Sports of the Field than persons in my station and profession in life'.[15]

As the gentry dominated the legal system, and as the enforcement of the Game Laws was their prerogative, the question to be asked is whether natural justice suffered or not on a general scale. As has been observed, considerable variation existed between various fines and penalties imposed by different magistrates, possibly because of the personal attitudes of gentry towards offenders such as the latter's past record, or because of 'community' connexions as tenants, estate workers, members of the same church and the like. Indeed, as with other offences, a noticeable degree of capriciousness is evident in the sentencing policy of different benches of magistrates. To take a few examples: in 1839 a fine of £2 with 9s costs was imposed by the Rev. Benjamin Lewis of Cilrhedyn, while in 1847 Lloyd of Coedmore and Griffiths of Llwynduris gave a sentence of 'bail for two years not to commit a similar offence'.[16] Sometimes the sentence could be very harsh, as in the case of a Llangeler cottager fined £5 and costs, with the alternative of three months' imprisonment with hard labour. How far the ability of the offender to pay the fine was taken into account is difficult to ascertain. The Cilgerran magistrates in 1863 fined a person £5 for illegal fishing '. . . because the defendant was in good circumstances'.[17] Sometimes a degree of leniency is clear; for example, a poacher was fined a mere 1s 2d by the Newcastle Emlyn bench in 1868, the landlord concerned, Howell Jones of Penrallt (Llangeler), not 'pressing the charge, but wished the defendant to know he was breaking the law'.[18] On the other hand, gentry magistrates like Vaughan of Plas Llangoedmore and Davies of Castle Green, Cardigan, sentenced a poacher to a long term of imprisonment for being in possession of a rabbit, with the result that the inhabitants of Cardigan petitioned the Home Secretary for mitigation of sentence. Perhaps, the ire of the squirearchy was unleashed against those who openly defied their authority and status, as happened when the Llandysul justices fined a poacher £5 and costs (with the alternative of hard labour) for openly 'carrying game and gun on the road'.[19] As has been suggested, the perverse and cruel arrogance of some magisterial benches was not usually practised by the 'Tivyside' justices. The excessive prison sentence on the Llangoedmore poacher was rare. Tyrannical outbursts by overweening magistrates are hard to trace, such as in a notorious case before the Llandovery magistrates when a boy was fined £3 and costs for snaring pheasants. Campbell Davys of Neuadd Fawr, Cilycwm in announcing the verdict, said: '. . . if a lad of mine were to do such a thing I would take him by the heels and knock his head against the wall'—to the approving 'Hear, hear' of his colleague justices![20]

Some 'Tivyside' justices, it must be conceded, were prepared to dismiss, as too trivial, charges such as the one brought against workhouse boys for poaching hares and rabbits, or another against a farmer killing rabbits because of damage to his crops. When the defence to a charge rested on a point of law, and the ruling of a High Court case, the Newcastle Emlyn bench upheld this in favour of the defendant, as '. . . it would be a lesser hardship for the Board of Conservators [of Fisheries] to seek the decision of the superior courts than the defendant who was a poor man'.[21]

The inhabitants of the banks of the Teifi had over the centuries supported themselves, in part, by fishing. This was particularly true of villages such as Llechryd and St Dogmael's. The right to fish, notwithstanding landlord and manorial rights, was part of the customary practice of 'Tivyside'. In 1877 an old inhabitant of Newcastle Emlyn recalled how— 'humble though his position [was] . . . [through] the geniality of some fine old local gentleman—one of the olden time'—he was allowed to fish without hindrance.[22] But nineteenth-century legislation concerning fisheries' conservation largely destroyed that convention, resulting in distress and ill-feeling between the squire and the community. Rural peasantry, living on a hand to mouth basis, could not appreciate the long-term advantages of fish conservation following the 1818 act to introduce a 'close season'—a measure which had to be enforced by local gentry.[23] The private monopoly of the Lloyds of Coedmore of catching salmon at the Cilgerran weir was a source of contention, leading to its destruction during the Rebecca riots.[24] Even certain gentry like Lloyd Williams of Gwernant and John Lloyd Davies of Blaendyffryn regarded the Coedmore monopoly as inimical to good relations, and a provocation to lawlessness. The use of the police to act against poachers, and the appointment of salaried 'water guards', rewarded with bonuses for successful convictions, further incensed the populace.[25]

Thomas Davies Lloyd of Bronwydd in 1860 rejected any legislative threat to his fishing rights within the Barony of Kemes, relying on his position as Lord Marcher.[26] The arguments for fish conservation (supported by squires like Bowen of Llwyngwair and Brigstocke of Blaenpant), namely the improved quality of fishing, general advantages to hoteliers and fishermen, the clearance of quarry rubbish in the river bed at Cilgerran and the like, were strongly opposed as an attack on the working class. Proposed taxes on rods, nets and tackle, as well as fishing licences, were regarded as an attempt by the gentry to grind the last penny from the pockets of the poor.[27] Legislation in the 1860s led to protest meetings, and fishermen resorted to self help by fishing without permits. Moreover, when workmen were blasting rocks at Cenarth as part of 'river works' carried out by the Fishery Commissioners, local people pelted the workmen with stones from nearby woods. Tools and equipment were broken up, and the lives of workmen threatened. E. C. Ll. Fitzwilliams wrote to the Home Secretary requesting troops to be sent to Cenarth and Cardigan to guard the workmen, adding that 'thereby ye matter would probably be nipped in ye bud'. Landlords like Thomas Davies Lloyd and Fitzwilliams, while accepting the 'conservation' argument, were also concerned with mitigating the effects on the poorer sections of the community. The impasse was temporarily solved by the setting up of 'The Teivy Fishermen's Club and Voluntary Association', wherein the interests of all sections of the community were to be taken into account.[28] In spite of gentry arguments in favour of conservation, and denials that fisheries' costs were a measure 'for landowners to take the river into their own hands', the hardship to many could not be ignored. Some two-hundred fishermen in the St Dogmael's area, 'with a thousand souls to provide for', were singled out as suffering particular hardship, especially as their wages from other occupations were so low. Gentry attitudes and objective arguments for fish conservation were also regarded as *Gormes y Sais* (The Englishman's oppression), and became a political issue against Thomas Davies Lloyd of Bronwydd during his 1868 election campaign.[29] The privileged position of the gentry remained a stumbling block, in spite of the appointment of a radical like Thomas Harries of Llechryd as chairman of local fisheries' groups.[30] As part of a wider pattern of disaffection, the appointment of officials such as water bailiffs with police powers, the payment of subscriptions which could only be afforded by the affluent section of society, and the overall administration of river boards mainly by gentry, could only lead to a sense of deprivation and the extension of class privilege. It was only with the setting up of a Board of Conservators comprising a much wider cross-section of the community, with a Welsh-speaking chairman able to understand the grievances of farmers and labourers, that river conservation became reasonable and fair to the public at large, and no longer a sectional issue.[31] Even so, the right to grant or withhold permission to fish still remained with the riparian owners— mainly the squires. The imperatives of deference and underprivilege had not been removed.

The open and public nature of the opposition, however, did not reach the level of an organised 'Rebeccaite' body, behaving with ritual, disguise and intimidation, as occurred on the river Wye. But even so it was part of social reaction, where crime and protest were clearly allied.[32]

Large-scale reaction to the privilege and power of the gentry country-wide seems to have been absent or at least very muted in the eighteenth century. While poverty and deprivation existed all the time, dissatisfaction never got out of hand, possibly, because the squire's protection and patronage ameliorated the lot of the lower orders. If there were no major rebellions, there was undoubtedly a high incidence of small-scale disturbances at various periods, such as the 1740s, 1760s and 1790s, on account of harvest failure, depression following continental wars, unemployment and rising prices.[33] It was only natural for ordinary people to demand fair prices and customary rights, and one must concede that many of the gentry were not unsympathetic to their claims. Certainly, the gentry of 'Tivyside' sitting in Quarter Sessions were quick to deal with profiteers and dishonest vendors of corn and foodstuffs.[34]

From Great Sessions and Quarter Sessions records, it can be gleaned that a degree of civil turmoil, fomented by a disaffected populace, took place in 1744. During the 1760s, '70s and '90s assaults, burglaries and thefts are recorded for the 'Tivyside' area, and in 1783 Cardigan justices were concerned with increasing crime attributed to 'vagrants and strollers'. Some historians hold the view that outsiders were often blamed for crimes committed by local people. Incidents of throwing down the 'battlements of bridges', 'defacing milestones' and anything purporting to have a link with the official classes, namely the gentry, suggest an orchestrated protest by the lower orders against their betters, and a form of legitimised crime. The nature of the criminal offences (carried out in counties like Pembrokeshire in the early 1800s) reflects the desperation of the poor, such as the theft of oatmeal, barley, cheese and butter from farmsteads, as well as livestock and comestibles, potatoes and turnips from the fields.[35] The malicious destruction of property in the countryside was a persistent and important element in the story of rural crime. Attacks on houses, buildings, machines, enclosures, weirs, trees and plantations, and the killing and maiming of animals and birds, were acts of personal and social revenge. Together with arson, all these were means of attacking the 'upper class', comprising the landowner, magistrate, farmer, clergyman and poor-law guardian.[36]

In spite of centuries of bardic deference to the gentry, many country poets were sensitive to oppression and were not afraid to be the voice of disaffection. Nurtured in the radical and Unitarian traditions of the vale of Cletwr were poet-critics like John Thomas of Pont-siân (1775-1836), known as Jaci'r Gweydd (Jaci the Weaver). In *Cwyn y Cristion* (The Christian's Complaint) he meditates on the divine order. Oppression can only be brought to an end in the next world:

> Dwg bawb i ddidranc wynfyd, nid aiff
> un dyn ar goll

(God will lead all [sc. of those who have suffered] to an endless beatitude—not a single soul will be lost.)

Rees Jones, Pwllffein (1797-1844), was a vitriolic critic of the gentry. He likened the workhouse to the Bastille, where the indigent poor were 'bent under the oppressive lineage yoke of the gentry'—(*yn plygu wrth ach ormesawl y mawrion*). Calling the poor to rise against their masters —the 'devouring wolves'—he inveighs against the workhouse system and the gentry who did nothing to alleviate the suffering of the poor. The old protest theme:

> When Adam delved and Eve span
> Who was then the gentleman?

recurred in the writings of Thomas Jones, Rhiwsiôn, Cwmcou (1782-1869), and was aimed against Lewes of Llysnewydd, Lewes Lloyd of Dolhaidd and others, who would one day be reduced to penury. A man of considerable moral courage to attack the gentry by name, he sees the time coming when inept squire-justices will be replaced by the people's leaders.[37] Those sentiments were no mere propaganda outbursts. Acts of arson, theft and malicious damage were perpetrated against some gentry in the Teifi valley. In the years 1819-20 such acts were committed against Lloyd Williams of Gwernant, and a pattern of criminality throughout the century suggests deep-rooted grievances against the gentry by an embittered and deprived proletariat.[38]

At various times civil disturbance and illegal acts reached a high point: in particular, during the Rebecca troubles the gentry were a prime target because they failed to come to their tenants' rescue by shouldering part of what were unbearable financial burdens. To quote a few examples from Tobit Evans' long catalogue of dissaffection at the time, threats were made against the persons of the vicar of Penbryn and John Lloyd Davies of Blaendyffryn; and other landlords and their agents were threatened and their property damaged.[39] Walter David Jones of Lancych was a particularly unpopular squire, harsh and merciless towards law breakers, especially poachers. As indicated, the Poor Law generated great bitterness, and the building of the workhouse at Newcastle Emlyn caused ill-feeling for which Lewes-Lloyd of Dolhaidd, Howell of Glaspant, Jordan of Pigeonsford and the Rev. Benjamin Lewis of Cilrhedyn were held to be responsible.[40] The project was castigated by a local bard, Gwallter y Gelltydd (Walter of the Woodlands), as an 'improvident folly', 'unspeakable craziness' and an additional burden on the rates.[41] There can be no denying that particular grievance was caused by the levying of tolls by the Turnpike Trusts owned largely by the gentry. The new poor law of 1834 added to the rates. Again tithes, following the Commutation Act 1836, had to be paid in money and not in kind. Instances of violent attacks on persons were frequently the result of rural unrest and protest, as when Lord Cawdor's agent was attacked and robbed after rent collecting in Newcastle Emlyn in 1838. Shadrach Lewis, woodward and gamekeeper, was murdered near Ffynone, the home of squire Colby, in 1840. Such brutal attacks took place elsewhere in south-west Wales later in the century against the gamekeepers of Crosswood, Cresselly and Slebech.[42]

The introduction of new farm machinery seems to have been the cause of protest by labourers, who saw such innovations as a threat to their livelihood, as, for example, when damage was caused at Blaenpant in 1867. During the charged atmosphere following the 1868 election, gentry like Vaughan of Plas Llangoedmore, Thomas of Llanfair and Jordan of Pigeonsford were singled out as targets for revenge.[43]

The 'contentious tithe' had been a source of disaffection as an irksome and unpopular tax, subject to violent fluctuations, and hated by nonconformists as an immoral imposition. Farmers, too, opposed it as a disincentive to better husbandry. Tithe owners, on the other hand, went to great lengths to safeguard their rights to tithe as the key link in the vital association between church and state, mutually dependent as bulwarks of the constitution. In Wales, this tradition had been forcibly held by Walter Davies, who claimed that lay impropriators had the 'permanency of title to tithes' which rested on the law to protect property and every 'individual's private rights'.[44] An undercurrent of disaffection with the legal title, misappropriation and unfair administration of tithes had rumbled since the early decades of the eighteenth century. In the 1730s Cenarth tithes had been appropriated *trwy drais* (through oppression). It was felt that squires like Powell of Nanteos in the north of the county were becoming too powerful as lay improprietors of tithes in areas unconnected with their estates. Poor farmers were dragged before ecclesiastical courts. By the end of the eighteenth century tithe commutation was mooted as a favourable solution to many tithe owners, clergy and farmers.[45] Even after the passing of the Tithe Commutation Act in 1836, however, bitter arguments followed concerning the amounts payable, the greediness of absentee improprietors, and tithe maps were not always accurate in respect of acreages, land use, rough grazing, glebe and such matters. The tithes of Penbryn parish, for example, were worth about £525 in the years 1825 to 1829 but were commuted to £700 after 1836 (two thirds of which went to Major Walter Rice of Llwynybrain, in north Carmarthenshire), causing a furore amongst the Dissenters who predominated in the parish.[46]

From the 1850s a mounting radical campaign was led by Asa Evans, a Cardigan attorney, against tithes, church and squire domination. County bards fanned the flames of condemnation against squires like Parry of Gernos, Saunders Davies of Pentre and Jordan of Pigeonsford. A satirical *Carol Nadolig i'r Eglwyswyr* (A Christmas Carol for Churchmen) called them oppressors and the dregs of society:

> *Ysgubion, carthion bro a bryn*
> *Er dyddiau'r cynddilywiaid*

(The filthy sweepings of hill and dale since ante-diluvian times.)

The overwhelming case against tithes, voiced by radicals like the Rev. William Thomas of Whitland, was regarded by churchmen like David Owen (Brutus) as unashamed heresy.[47] In addition to the denominational grievance, the resolutions of local assessment committees, largely made up of Tory gentry, weighed heavily against the farmers. In some fifty 'Tivyside' parishes twenty lay improprietors were landlords, of whom about a third were absentee or total outsiders. To take a few examples: Miles the owner of The Priory estate in Cardigan lived in England and claimed the tithes of three parishes; Llangeler tithes were partly claimed by Lewes of Llysnewydd and the Principal of St David's College, Lampeter; and Jesus College, Oxford, received the tithes from Llandysul.[48]

The economic depression which increasingly hit the agricultural community from 1879 to the late '90s resulted in direct action protest on the part of the farmers, with local nonconformist preachers, along with politicians, fanning genuine grievances but sometimes for sectarian and political goals. Economic difficulties alone cannot explain the 'Tithe War', as they were soon merged in political and religious issues.[49] These appear strongly in *Cymru Fydd*, the Welsh nationalist organ edited by T. J. Hughes (Adfyfyr), and in the political speeches of T. E. Ellis and pulpit demagogues lilke E. Pan Jones. Although landlords, for their part, were prepared to make some rent reductions for their farms, insufficient measures were taken to settle unrest with regard to tithe. In September 1886, 'The Farmers' Tithe Defence League' was formed to compel tithe owners to make reductions in rent, and it called upon farmers not to pay tithes even if distraint of goods followed.[50] The recalcitrant attitude of tithe owners towards making reductions led to a concerted effort to rouse popular opposition by nonconformist preachers in the 'Tivyside' area like the Rev. Edward Jeffreys of Saron, and the Rev. T. Thomas of Llandysul, predictably described by their enemies as 'disturbers of society'. In Llangeler parish, Jeffreys refused on principle to pay a paltry sum of 1s 3d whereupon his goods were distrained, while most of the other dissenting parishioners surrendered to Lewes, Llysnewydd pressure. Even some of Jeffreys' own flock formed a schism church in protest against the fusion of religious and political issues.[51]

In many parishes like Penbryn, Moylegrove, Bangor Teifi, Whitechurch (Eglwys Newydd) and Llanfair Nantgwyn, tithe sales were accompanied by mob violence. Nonconformist ministers in Cardigan formed the Rhos Hill Anti-Tithe Society, organised marches and harangued the crowd.[52] The persistent refusal to pay tithes resulted in west Wales parishes being dubbed the 'Wild West'. Board schools were closed for pupils to take part; crowd violence, verbal abuse, damage to property and general mayhem followed. Sober observers came to the conclusion that the Queen's Writ had ceased in Cardiganshire, giving way to the rule of King Mob. Attempts to restrain violence by Quaker radicals, like Tobit Evans, failed. Even prominent nonconformists were forced to condemn the agitation as a disgrace to Welsh nonconformity.[53]

Very few gentry emerged from the strife with an enhanced reputation. Refusal to lower tithes, the increased cost to public funds of a bigger police force to ensure law and order, their position as magistrates adjudicating on matters in which they had a vested interest —all contributed to an unfavourable portrait of the squire. To take a typical example: when Tithe cases were heard before the Llandysul bench in July 1892 all the magistrates were Tory squires.[54] Non-payment of tithes became part of a larger protest against the existing order. A *Twm-Shôn-Catti* (A Welsh Robin Hood-like folk hero) ethic of robbing the robber and cheating the cheat became common:

> *Nid twyll yw twyllo twyllwr*
> *Nid brad bradychu bradwr,*
> *Nid lladrad lladrata ar latratawr.*

[It is not cheating to cheat the cheat; nor treachery to betray the traitor nor theft to steal from a thief.][55]

General reaction to the deprivation suffered by ordinary people and the economic difficulties of the farming community, soon embraced wider problems. The economic and religious grievances of the farmers became intermingled, and the land question and the disestablishment of the church were brought to the notice of the country at the highest level. Most of the unrest ceased after the passing of the Tithe Rent Charge Act of 1891 (with the exception of trouble in Penbryn parish until 1895). Tithes were now recognised as the responsibility of the landlord. However, the situation remained virtually unchanged, for from now on the tithe charge was included in the rent. While the criticisms and grievances voiced against landlords and social injustice were often trenchant, what is remarkable is that, as on many occasions during previous generations when disaffection and dissent had reared up their heads against the landlord class, no mass movement sprang up to destroy the gentry. At least some landlords were personally liked and respected even after they had been rejected as political leaders and replaced by prominent Nonconformists.[56]

NOTES AND SOURCES

[1] I. G. Jones: *op cit.*, p. 23.

[2] K. O. Morgan: *Wales in British Politics* . . . , p. 67.

[3] G. H. Jenkins: *op cit.*, pp. 166-70.

[4] *DWB.*

[5] G. A. Williams: *The Search for Beulah Land*, 1980, pp. 1, 7-8, 11.

[6] *DWB.*

[7] P. B. Munsche: *Gentlemen and Poachers*, 1981, pp. 1-7; P. Jenkins: *op cit.*, p. 265.

[8] *id: op cit.*, pp. 132-58.

[9] D. J. V. Jones: 'The Poacher, A Study in Victorian Crime and Protest', *Hist Jnl*, 22 (4), 1979, pp. 827-29.

[10] D. W. Howell: *Land and People* . . ., pp. 77-9.

[11] 24 Geo III C43. HRO/PQ/1784-1801; *Cm Jnl*: 4/10/1816, 5/9/1817, 7/12/1821; *ibid*: 19/11/1841, 29/6/1845.

[12] *ibid*: 5/8/1814, 24/2/1815; NLW/ Bronwydd/601.

[13] *Cm Jnl*: 7/8/1818, 9/8/1822; NLW/Falcondale/191, 192, 208.

[14] *Cm Jnl*: 11/11/1831; *ibid*: 3/1/1862; NLW/Falcondale/Gp. vi/171.

[15] NLW/Highmead/Box P/File 5.

[16] *Cm Jnl*: 11/1/1839, 15/2/1839; *The Welshman*: 17/12/1847.

[17] *ibid*: 13/10/1856; *Cm Jnl*: 8/5/1863.

[18] *Cd Ad*: 21/12/1868.

[19] CRO/QS/Files/1860; *Cm Jnl*: 22/12/1865; *The Welshman*: 30/12/1881.

[20] *Cm Jnl*: 17/11/1882.

[21] *Cd Ad*: 22/11/1867, 13/3/1891; *The Welshman*: 27/12/1889.

[22] S. Lewis: *op cit.*, *sub* Llechryd, St. Dogmaels; *Cd Ad*: 20/4/1877.

[23] CRO/Coedmore/2490.

[24] J. R. Phillips: *op cit.*, pp. 178-81.

[25] *The Welshman*: 10/1/1845, 24/12/1852; NLW/Cilgwyn Mss/LB/44/22/8/1868.

[26] NLW/Bronwydd/6851.

[27] *Cm Jnl*: 24/1/1862; *The Welshman*: 1/1/1864; *Cd Ad*: 8/3/1867.

[28] *The Welshman*: 12/4/1867, 19/4/1867, 17/5/1867; 7/1/1870.

[29] *Cm Jnl*: 24/4/1867; *Cd Ad*: 1/11/1867, 14/8/1868.

[30] *ibid*: 1/7/1881.

[31] *ibid*: 4/4/1890.

[32] D. J. V. Jones: 'The Second Rebecca Riots, A Study of Poaching on the River Wye', *Llafur*, 2, 1, 1976, pp. 32-6; NLW/Cilgwyn/Ms LB/22/2/1868.

[33] G. Rudé: *The Crowd in History*, 1964, pp. 36-8.

[34] J. G. Parry: 'Terfysgoedd Yd yng Ngogledd Cymru, 1740-50', *Tr Caerns Hist Soc.*, 1978, 39, pp. 74-98.

[35] NLW/Gt Sessions/Wales/4/897/1 Geo iii; 3/893/2 Geo iii; 4/757/2-5; 4/1893/21 Geo iii; NLW/Cards/QS/OB/3; *ibid:*/QS/OB/4; NLW/Gt Sessions/Wales/4/828/41-43.

[36] D. J. V. Jones: *Crime, Protest, Community and Police in Nineteenth Century Britain*, 1982, pp. 33, 47.

[37] R. J. Jones (Aberdâr): 'John Thomas o Pontsiân, 1775-1836', *Cymru*, vi, 1893, p. 43; J. Griffiths: 'Rees Jones, 1797-1844', *Cymru*, vii, 1894; J. Jones: *Crwth Dyffryn Cletwr*, 1848; J. Jones (Machynlleth): 'Hen Emynwr, Mr Thomas Jones, Rhiw Siôn, ger Emlyn', *Cenad Hedd*, 1888, viii, p. 50.

[38] *Cm Jnl*: 30/4/1819, 26/2/1847; *Carms Antiq*, 11-12, 1916-18, p. 58; *The Welshman*: 13/4/1865, 5/4/1867; *Tarian y Gweithiwr*: 7/10/1886.

[39] H. T. Evans: *Rebecca and her Daughters*, 1910, pp. 21, 52, 57, 67-8, 70-77, 81-91, 126-27; Dd Williams: *op cit.*, pp. 211-25.

[40] RCEdSW, 1844, p. 224; *Tarian y Gweithiwr*: 7/10/1866; NLW/D. Pryse Williams/15625 B.

[41]*ibid*: 15655 C.

[42]*Cm Jnl*: 22/3/1839, 5/4/1839; G. Phillips: *Llofruddiaeth Shadrach Lewis*, 1986, pp. 1-30; *The Welshman*: 16/6/1871, 22/12/1871, 9/2/1875; *Pembs Herald*: 2/2/1877.

[43]*ibid*: 5/4/1867; *Cm Jnl*: 8/1/1869; NLW/Ms 8167 D; NLW/Amphlett Lewis and Evans, Box I (Penrhiwpâl P.S.D. minute book 1872-78).

[44]E. J. Evans: *The Contentious Tithe, 1750-1850*, 1976, pp. 9, 16, 25-7, 35, 76-8, 86-8. W. Davies: *op cit.*, i, p. 184.

[45]NLW/D. Pryse Williams/15622 E; H. Owen: *op cit.*, i, p. 204; NLW/Lucas/2864-65; *Gent. Mag*: 1790, pp. 101-02.

[46]J. M. Powell: 'Tithe Surveys and Schedules', *NLWJ*, xvi, 1, 1969, p. 86; Dd Williams: *op cit.*, p. 134.

[47]*Yr Haul*: 1888, tt, 88-90, 119-20; *The Welshman*: 30/5/1852. E. J. Evans: *op cit.*, p. 84; *DWB*; W. Thomas: *The Anti Tithe Movement in Wales, 1891*; *DWB*.

[48]*Cd Ad*: 17/8/1866. R.C.Ecc.R.E.W., 1835, Table E iv, pp. 288-327.

[49]D. W. Howell: *op cit.*, pp. 84-5, 155; J. D. D. Dunbabin: *op cit.*, pp. 286-87; *DWB*.

[50]*RSCT*, 1881, pp. 3-5; *DWB*.

[51]*Cd Ad*: 12/11/1886, 26/11/1886, 28/1/1887; D. E. Jones: *op cit.*, p. 339; J. James: *Hanes Eglwysi Annibynnol, Saron, Llangeler*, 1937, p. 21.

[52]*Cm Jnl*: 15/10/1886, 26/11/1886, 21/9/1888; *Cd Ad*: 15/8/1887, 15/2/1889, 22/3/1889, 29/3/1889, 5/4/1889, 14/2/1888, 31/8/1888; P. Horn: *The Tithe War in Pembrokeshire*, 1982, pp. 3, 7, 10, 15, 18-19; *Pembs. Herald*: 5/8/1885.

[53]NLW/Ms 15321 D; *The Welshman*: 11/6/1892; *Y Celt*: 17/7/1891; *DWB*.

[54]*Cm Jnl*: 1/7/1892.

[55]*The Welshman*: 27/11/1896; *DWB*.

[56]K. O. Morgan: *op cit.*, p. 87; D. W. Howell: *op cit.*, p. 85; *id: op cit.*, p. 152.

The Gentry and the Welsh Language

Bitter censure of the anglicised gentry and clergy has for generations been the war cry of populist and nonconformist radicalism. The language clause of the Act of Union, and jibes concerning the 'sinister usages and customes' of Welshmen, the 'native gibberish . . . prattled throughout the whole of Taphydom', cut deeply into the Welsh psyche. The appointment of monoglot English clerics to Welsh parishes was a policy buttressed by English official opinion that as '. . . Wales is a conquered country, it is proper to introduce the English language'. This attitude, together with the vituperative remarks of the Commissioners of Inquiry for South Wales 1844, have been regarded as acts of treachery against Welsh people, their language and customs. The religious and political radicals of the late nineteenth century, and the modern nationalist movement in Wales, have argued that the Welsh gentry were not only defectors from Welsh cultural orthodoxy, but also traitors to their own heritage.[1]

In addition to the decree of the Act of Union that English was to be the language of government, law and administration in Wales, there were other more subtle influences at work. Economically, Wales drew closer to England from the sixteenth century onwards. Socially, the 'cult of gentryhood', the acquisition of English manners along with the values of 'curtisie, humanite and civillite', the lure of Renaissance culture and the printing and circulation of English books, led inevitably to conflict between the 'new learning', with its new fashions, and traditional Welsh bardic, aristocratic culture. Although the official classes supported the translation and publication of the Scriptures, by the mid-seventeenth century the Welsh language was in decline in gentry circles. By the nineteenth century it was only a crude medium of communication between the squire and his social inferiors.[2] While the above statement is generally true of the Welsh gentry as a whole, any analysis of the 'Tivyside' gentry's sympathy towards, knowledge of and use of the Welsh language reflects a variety of attitudes. It is possible to trace a utilitarian and empirical approach, condescending patronage through affection for historical tradition and institutions, to outright opposition.

It can be argued that upper-class desertion of 'popular culture' characterised much of Europe in the late seventeenth and eighteenth centuries; examples such as Scotland, Norway, Bohemia, Ireland and other countries spring to mind.[3] For Glamorgan, social factors and the profound change in the composition of the gentry community, with older families dying out to be replaced by new lines, often English, who had no sympathy with native culture, account for the non-use of the Welsh language. Whereas the Teifi valley comprised families of unquestionable ancient Welsh stock, such as Lloyd of Bronwydd, Bowen of Llwyngwair, and Lewes of Gernos, to cite only a few, nevertheless Englsh *advenae* families had over many centuries settled in the area. Thus, Birt of Llwynduris, Brigstocke of Blaenpant and Colby of Ffynone, to be followed by Gower of Castle Malgwyn, and Lloyd Hall of Cilgwyn, were some of the outsiders. Intermarriage and the fusion of cultural attitudes, and the legal and official status of the English language in government and administration, inevitably led to a linguistic polarisation between landowner and the common people. The gentry cannot be blamed entirely, as educated Welsh people too, bards and literati, became anglicised to the extent of using the English language as the medium of communication, and often of intellectual discourse. To quote a few examples: the Morris brothers and their 'Augustan' circle, the Unitarian Lloyds and schoolmasters like Davis of Castell Hywel, all used English widely, especially, in their correspondence.[4]

Whilst the majority of Welshmen in the early eighteenth century were monoglot Welsh speakers, and as long as Wales remained a country of localised agrarian communities, the language could survive. Welsh was little used as a written language, save in the field of religion and literature, and had failed to make the leap from traditional medieval culture to what was modern, urbanised and secular. The gentry were gradually moving away from their former role to a more limited concept of their 'Welshness'. The descendants of medieval *uchelwyr* had been influenced by English education, the glitter of London fashion, foreign travel and all the ingredients of the social and intellectual standards of their counterparts in other countries—factors which created a division between the gentry and the lower classes of their own country. That they did abandon their traditional culture is clear, but in terms of betrayal or defection 'they were the scapegoat for some deeper malaise'.[5] By the mid-nineteenth century, the strong forces of religious dissent and political radicalism were pushing the Welsh language and its culture more and more into the lap of a peasant, nonconformist and protesting 'Mother Wales'. The national culture of Wales was also becoming a weapon against the ruling classes; the 'true' Wales became peasant, Welsh-speaking and nonconformist.[6]

Not even *y werin* remained true to the language, in spite of patriotic rhetoric about Wales as the land of poetry and song. Having realised on which side their bread was buttered, the ordinary Welshman faced a far more pernicious threat to his language from the cultural and economic forces within the British and European world than from the local gentry. The retention of a language as the vehicle of poetic musings, homiletic fervour and apocalyptic doom, it could be argued, could only hinder the advance of Welshmen. A Welsh élite, sprung from *y werin* and making a career in commerce, industry, politics and the professions, were not going to be hampered by a sentimental adherence to an ancient tongue. That this Welsh élite regarded the disappearance of the Welsh language as inevitable and a good thing, might at first sight seem questionable.[7] The bread and butter argument was, however, too strong. In spite of cultural ties and innate patriotism, and forces like the emergence of a periodical literature in Wales through the work of pioneers like Joseph Harris (Gomer), the utilitarian argument was clear. 'This is not the age of poesy only, still less of chivalry merely but of Railways and Steam Appliances of all kinds, Science is putting on her full strength'—so wrote a London correspondent of *The Welshman*.[8] He was only expressing the reluctance of the Welsh farmer and labourer to send his children to school, unless they were to learn English to get on in the world, and in the world of science and technology.[9] It was advantageous, too, for the Welsh *gwerinwr* to learn English, because it was the language of the gentry of the land, so enabling him to hold his own against squire and agent and to secure the best paid posts. The argument for 'Welshness' received its *coup de grace* in 1883 in *Y Geninen*: '*Os ydych i barhau i fwyta bara tywyll a gorwedd ar wely gwellt, gwaeddwch chwi eich gorau*—'*Oes y Byd i'r iaith Gymraeg*'—*ond os ydych chwi yn chwenychu bwyta bara gwyn a chig eidion rhost mae yn rhaid i chwi ddysgu Saesneg . . . nis gwyddom ni gymaint ag un Cymro uniaith a gasglodd gyfoeth heb wybod Saesneg*'.[10] (If you wish to continue eating dark bread and to lie on a bed of straw, shout loudly 'May the Welsh language live for ever', but if you wish to eat white bread and roast beef you will have to learn English . . . we do not know of a single monoglot Welshman who has acquired wealth without a knowledge of English.) It is against a very mixed background of traditional loyalties, the challenge of widening horizons, and the lure of social and economic advantage—which affected people throughout the whole spectrum of Welsh society—that the 'Welshness' of the gentry, and of those of 'Tivyside' in particular, has to be measured.

That the Welsh language was not abandoned by the gentry immed-iately following the Union of Wales with England, becomes clear from scattered evidence over two or three centuries. The rigorous literary activity of cultured gentry in the lower Teifi valley (as has been noticed) centred around such figures as Siôn Bowen of Glynllebyng, William Lewes of Llwynderw, Theophilus Evans, William Gambold and others. Welsh speaking and fervent in their patriotism, they were consciously the custodians of a precious heritage in the early years of the eighteenth century.[11]

But lesser known squires also clung to their Welsh endowment, continuing to use the language in their daily lives. In 1727 Morice Morris of 'Finnoney Bychan' bequeathed to his godson, Thomas Colby, 'my new large Welsh Bible with the Apocrypha in it, which I use for my own reading'. A minor squire like David Havard of Goitre-uchaf in Penboyr parish dabbled in Welsh verse, although his skill was limited.[12] That there was no prejudice against the Welsh language in cultured gentry circles in the 1750s is demonstrated by the publication of Welsh poetry in *The Gentleman's Magazine*.[13] An eclectic, enquiring and essentially cultured gentry throughout England and Wales, imbued with the cult of the new Romanticism, did not regard the Welsh language as *tabu*—archaic, antique and curious, perhaps. Depositions, in a Chancery action in 1778, relating to the disputed will of Mary Lloyd of Cryngae reflect the use of Welsh as the language of the household of a lesser gentry family.[14] In the crisis of 1797, John Colby of Ffynone knew sufficient Welsh to 'harangue' the men of the Pembroke Fencibles in connection with some matter of discipline.[15] H. M. Vaughan considered that the transition between 'the bilingual status of the landed gentry from its later monoglot attitude' took place in the earlier half of the nineteenth century.[16] Albeit, ties of affection made some gentry cling to the Welsh language throughout the nineteenth century. Thus, for example, the Rev. Samuel Fenton in the 1820s complained of Oxford University's philistine attitude towards the Welsh language, and yearned to return to Wales where he could hear the language daily.[17] The Lloyd family of Gilfachwen attended the Calan Hen festival in Llandysul church in 1860 to hear 'the schools answering', i.e. the local church Sunday schools being catechised in Welsh.[18] In the second half of the nineteenth century, lesser squires like the Thomas family of Dôl-Llan and Llanfair worshipped in the local Welsh Unitarian chapel. Howell of Glaspant, too, was Welsh speaking and read Welsh periodicals such as *Y Geninen*.[19] Perhaps these backwoods gentry represent a traditional and inward-looking section of the squirearchy, who were without social and political aspirations, contented in their own small communities, and unaffected by, if not oblivious to, the outside world.

Broadly speaking, one can agree with H. M. Vaughan that the landed gentry became anglicised in varying degrees during the early years of the nineteenth century, when their more pragmatic and utilitarian outlook was to prevail over cultural values. Probably, the chief importance of the Welsh language in the daily lives of the gentry from now on, was its usefulness in dealing with estate matters, and so it became merely a means of communication with a Welsh-speaking and socially inferior local community. Thus to cite a few examples: it was deemed that his knowledge of Welsh was of 'considerable value' during Colby of Ffynone's period as receiver of the Orielton estate about the year 1800;[20] again when the young Sir Hugh Owen of Orielton (whose estate was mainly in south Pembrokeshire and in the Welsh-speaking counties of Carmarthenshire and Anglesey) was a pupil at Eton, the sum of £100 was set aside '. . . To a Welch Clergyman's Board and Instruction of Sr. Hugh in ye Welsh language, during ye Vacations'.[21] It is difficult to ascertain the degree of competence in Welsh acquired by the gentry. Judging from rare correspondence in Welsh, like that between Major Evans of Highmead and his nephew the Rev. Thackeray Griffies Williams in the 1830s, one notices in the letters a fairly idiomatic grasp of the language, colloquialisms and Biblical phrases, but considerable orthographic inaccuracy and ignorance of mutations, which suggest that the writer was more conversant with English. Although educated with other local squires and country lads at the Castell Hywel academy, Evans had to admit: '. . . *Nid yw y llithir hwn yn cael ei escrivemni uel copy neu pathrwm y ty— Yr wyf yn gnabod y bod lawer gair a lawer llithiren maes oi lle.*' (This letter is not written to you as a copy or pattern . . . I acknowledge that many a word and many a letter (sc. of the alphabet) are out of place . . .)[22]

In the 1840s the degree of competence and commitment to the Welsh language varied. The squires on the poor law board, advertising for a master and matron of the new workhouse at Newcastle Emlyn, specified categorically that '. . . both must understand the Welsh language'.[23] Goring Thomas told the Poor Law Commissioners: 'I know so little of Welsh that I am not as *useful* as I would wish'. Capt. Prichard of Tŷ Llwyd had a more limited concept of 'usefulness' and, in answer to the question, 'Do you speak Welsh?', replied: 'Only a little to find my way about the country'.[24] On the other hand, John Lloyd Williams of Gwernant was in a happier position: 'I employ many men and women who do not understand a word of English and I can converse with them'.[25]

Some gentry turned the utilitarian argument on its head in order to oppose the Welsh language. In the 1840s E. Crompton Lloyd Hall attributed the maladministration of justice, perjury and corruption in the courts of law within the Principality to the survival of the Welsh language. In his view, '. . . the Welsh language is peculiarly evasive, which originates from its having been the language of slavery'. Likewise William Owen Brigstocke of Blaenpant regarded the language as a '. . . vast drawback to Wales, and a manifold barrier to the oral progress and commercial prosperity of the people'. This opinion was not confined to the gentry. The basic formula was to learn English, for without it no advancement in life could be made. The general public attitude was summed up by the Rev. H. L. Davies, curate of Cenarth, *à propos* the school at Llandyfrïog: '. . . [it] is the only exclusively Welsh school that I know of in South Wales. Had the master been able to teach English, I believe he would have had three times the number of children in his school'.[26]

The anti-Welsh argument was used to repeat a centuries-old canard against the Welsh character. As has been pointed out for Glamorgan in an earlier period, 'Welsh' was synonymous with drunken, ignorant and superstitious ragamuffins. To 'Welsh' on a business transaction implied dishonesty, while 'Welshy' in modern times has denoted the mark of the illiterate and uncouth. Likewise, in 1863 E. Crompton Ll. Fitzwilliams (i.e. Lloyd Hall supra) persisted to attack the Welsh language as a 'great curse' upon Wales '. . . as it is abroad when there is a double language'. Moreover, the Welsh people were 'treacherous', 'deceitful', and every Welshman '. . . a mighty big liar and thief'.[27]

The native-born gentry were more sober in their comments and, aware that their roots went back deep into Welsh history, they often displayed a sentimental 'pietas' towards the language of their ancestors. But this attitude was also coloured by their eagerness to cultivate the goodwill of the community in the context of nineteenth-century British imperialism. Thus, Thomas Edward Lloyd of Coedmore (MP for the county of Cardigan, 1874-80), speaking in English at a Tregaron eisteddfod in 1876, reaffirmed the usual platitudes concerning Welsh culture, and viewed with dismay any danger which threatened it. Its usefulness was measured: 'if it has been the medium of forming, as peaceable, as loyal a people as any in the British dominions, it deserved to be encouraged'.[28] In reality, the utilitarian argument was thus changing over the generations. No longer was the language useful to transact 'the ordinary duties of life', as Sir Thomas Davies Lloyd had admitted,[29] but a weapon towards forging social harmony in a community of *gwerin* in danger of contamination by Welsh radicalism and dissent. In terms of the British Empire, a minority language, localised and limited in its use, could only be justified if it was compliant to the concept of '*Prydeindod*' (Britishness), and subservient to its political, cultural and territorial claims. An example of the tension between British imperialist ideology embraced by the privileged landed classes, and what they regarded as 'inferior' Welshmen on account of birth, language and 'non-culture', occurs in a letter written by Major Lawrence Colby of Ffynone from the front shortly before his death at Ypres in 1914: '. . . Tell Bellamy, that in spite of the War and its distractions he must look after the pheasants . . . and the trout . . . and that, because there is a war in Europe, that is no reason for every Welsh good-for-nothing, who is too careful for his own skin to take up arms, to think that he has now an excuse for stealing *from his betters* . . . *Our Welsh are hopeless, they are a craven people*'.[30]

In fairness to the majority of the 'Tivyside' gentry, and taking into account their 'limited concept of Welshness', they were consistent in their patronage of Welsh cultural activities. Notwithstanding Rhys and Jones' criticism of lack of gentry support for eisteddfod and literary meeting, and their failure to participate in activities which would have encouraged the people in the development of their own ideas of culture, as a means to defuse the explosive situation of the day,[31] there is some evidence to the contrary. Their patronage of Welsh can be traced during the period covered in this study: Brigstocke of Blaenpant donated one guinea annually for a Welsh sermon to be preached each Sunday in St Peter's Church, Carmarthen;[32] the Society of Ancient Britons held meetings in St James' Church, Piccadilly, in 1811 to support the Welsh school in Grays Inn Road and to pray for 'the Ancient British Language', even when squires of English origin like Hart Davis were present, and the eisteddfodic successes of the Rev. Daniel Evans (Daniel Ddu o Geredigion) were celebrated in 1823 by some thirty 'Tivyside' gentry with a presentation of a piece of silver plate for the bard.[33]

During national eisteddfodau in the nineteenth century, held at places like Carmarthen and Cardigan, the gentry were generous donors of prizes and loud in their praise of 'nationality'.[34] Sir Thomas Davies Lloyd combined praise for the cultural and intellectual wealth of Wales with the names of Kossuth and Cavour, and proposed a national memorial to Llywelyn the Last. Local chapel literary meetings were graced by the presence of squires like Colby of Pantyderi and Lewis of Clynfyw.[35]

But rarely was the language considered to be suitable for anything other than for literary meeting, eisteddfod and pulpit. A young squire would learn Welsh, 'if practicable', according to Lewis Bowen of Clynfyw in 1902.[36] But practicability was of little meaning when the lifestyle of the gentry was orientated to values of English public schools and universities, a career in the services or in the colonies, where British imperialist values prevailed. In spite of the pious and patriotic sentiments the gentry might have held towards the language, they never attempted a full command of the language so as to be able to appreciate the poetry of Dafydd ap Gwilym, the prose epics and romances of the Mabinogi and '*chwedlau*', and other classics down the ages. Thomas Edward Lloyd of Coedmore, for example, in response to a diatribe in *The Times* concerning Wales, held up a list of illustrious Welsh names to refute the charges—General Sir Thomas Picton, Sir Cornewall Lewis, Lord Chief Justice Kenyon and the like. They were distinguished people born in Wales or of Welsh blood, but their importance lay in the part they played upon the stage of English history.[37]

It is true that a few gentry like Sir Marteine Lloyd learnt a form of Welsh which was more akin to the patois of servant boys from English 'ragged' schools. Public occasions like St David's Day were celebrated with dinners, stereotyped patriotic speeches, and loyal toasts in a syncretism of conservative politics and Welsh national culture—oratorical dope to gull churchman and dissenter, tenant and labourer.[38]

The appointment of non-Welsh-speaking clerics as parish priests and church dignitaries in Wales had long been a source of sorrow and aggravation. Stephen Hughes and Erasmus Saunders had foreseen the decline of the Welsh language and the estrangement of a monoglot majority from the ministrations of the church.[39] The Right Rev. the Hon. Robert H. Drummond, D.D., bishop of St Asaph (1748-61), '*yr ysgotyn gwenwynllyd hwnnw*' (that poisonous Scot), had urged the Welsh '. . . to enlarge their views . . . and to unite with the rest of their fellow subjects in language as well as government'.[40] But more farseeing Englishmen, like Bishop Zachary Pearce, a former dean of Windsor, on his nomination to the see of Bangor in 1747, '. . . established in himself a resolution conferring Welsh preferments or benefices only on Welshmen'. In 1723, too, White Kennet, bishop of Peterborough (1715-29), had observed to Archbishop Wake, in connection with the appointment of bishops in Wales, that it would have been 'very just and generous to the good estate of that country [sc. Wales] to have given them a man of their own mother tongue'.[41]

Wise counsels within and outside Wales were not heeded until 1870, when a Welsh-speaking Welshman, Joshua Hughes, was appointed by Gladstone to the see of St Asaph.[42] Meanwhile, a chorus of protest had been orchestrated from the beginning of the century against the anglicisation of the Church of England in Wales. The Venerable John Williams, the archdeacon of Cardigan, had attacked a 'Barbarian Episcopate'. Sir Thomas Phillips, in reply to the 'Blue Books', had argued that the ills of Wales were partly due to the dichotomy of a Welsh-speaking clergy denied recognition and forced to serve in parishes outside Wales, like the 'Association of Welsh Clergy in the West Riding of the County of York', who were fervent in their attack on the grave linguistic shortcomings of the church.[43] It was argued that the uncouth attempts of an English-speaking clergy officiating in a tongue unintelligible to themselves and their congregation was a profanation of the worship of God. The press took up the campaign against non-Welsh clergy, who were often identified with the gentry class, and this became a burning issue in the weaponry of radical politicians like Henry Richard.[44] The 'pidgin' Welsh of some clergy, and their absurd mangling of the liturgy, were serious impediments in the way of Salvation. Allowing for apocryphal embellishments to the utterances of 'English' clergy, there was, no doubt, firm ground for the allegations.

In some respects, however, the case against them has been overstated. Ordination lists for the diocese of St David's from 1700 onwards, show that a considerable number of clergy were drawn from the gentry class, with familiar names from the Teifi valley such as Brigstocke, Lloyd, Havard, Bowen and Lewes.[45] In spite of increasing anglicisation there are grounds for presuming that these gentry clerics grew up with a knowledge of Welsh derived from contact with farmers, tenants, maids and grooms, as well as from their own kinsfolk—even allowing that English was becoming more and more the language of the mansion. Clerics like Theophilus Evans and John Jenkins (Ifor Ceri) were illustrious literary men and, perhaps, exceptional, but there were undoubtedly many educated clergymen scattered over the diocese who could minister to their flock in the 'vulgar tongue', i. e. 'the language of the people', according to the Book of Common Prayer. The image of the absentee English-speaking cleric cannot be the whole truth, as has been demonstrated.[46] Examples spring to mind of clerics born and bred in the localities wherein they ministered later on in life, like the Rev. Sutton Morgan, MA, of the old family of Pengwern and Llwynbedw, who was vicar of Nevern for ten years up to 1720. His successor was none other than the Rev. Dr Philipps, late rector of Llangoedmore, a keen antiquary who corresponded with the Morysiaid and their circle.[47]

In the second half of the eighteenth century the clerical family of Lewes in Meline parish continued to hold the living, and to reside in the parish as they had done for generations. The Rev. Watkin Lewes sent his son to Shrewsbury school and to Cambridge. Sir Watkin's colourful career, in fashionable London circles, did not deprive him of his interest in Welsh literature and music, nor prevent him from being a prime mover of the Societies of Ancient Britons and the Cymmrodorion.[48] Such a cultural outlook could only have been nurtured in a clerical house where sympathy to, and knowledge of Welsh were significant.

By the end of the century, Llwyngwair, Bronwydd and other houses had welcomed 'Methodistical' preachers and had supported their mission in open-air meetings, where the exhortation and the 'opportunities' were in the Welsh language. The intellectual and religious climate of the period and the atmosphere in which the 'squarsons' grew up, cannot but support the view that they knew Welsh and used it. The primary function of a language is as a means of communication —in the highways and byways, in field, farmhouse, cow byre, public house and pulpit. Any 'squarson' of common sense was not deterred, by the genteel sophistication of drawing room or salon, from making himself understood to his parishioners.

Faced with the zeal of Methodism, and the rising tide of dissent, a bilingual clergyman was vital to the spiritual needs of a parish. Jenkins of Pantirion in 1826 commented on the clergyman named as the new incumbent of the parish of St Dogmael's, thus: '. . . a young man of good character and classed among the first rate of the extemporary, [i.e. preaching without strictly following written notes] clergy both in English and Welsh'.[49] The well known Rev. David Jones, Llangan, Glamorgan, born in the parish of Llanllwni (1736-1810), preached to west-Wales gentry congregations in English and in impeccable Welsh as his sermon notes over forty years show.[50] The high standard of pulpit Welsh becomes clear likewise in the sermons of the Rev. Thomas Davies of Cilrhedyn in the 1790s, whose 'auditors' included Howell of Glaspant and Saunders of Clunfelin. To oblige members of the congregation not over-familiar with Welsh, the Rev. John Jones (Tegid), (vicar of Nevern 1842-1852), who, like Jones of Llangan, may be considered among the upper ranks of the clergy of the day, used a singular device of preaching his complete sermon in Welsh followed by a short summary in English, in the ratio of about twenty pages of notes in Welsh to four in English.[51]

The Welsh 'squarson' has been caricatured and his Welsh speech dismissed as *llediaith* (affectation). The 'Welshness' of many a 'squarson' deserves a more generous view than that given by politicians like Henry Richard. During a ministry extending for almost half a century, the Rev. Augustus Brigstocke preached Welsh sermons to his congre-gations in the Teifi valley which were well expressed, and, judging from the 'flow' of the language, delivered with the full fervour of the Welsh *hwyl*. Possibly, in the somewhat stilted and prolix style of the Welsh prose of the period, they nevertheless display sound Biblical scholarship and the evangelical doctrinal imperatives of repentance, forgiveness and ultimate salvation.[52]

One of the best known 'squarsons' of the area, the Rev. Rhys Jones Lloyd, had a thorough command of the Welsh language. He, along with Augustus Brigstocke, Thomas Lloyd of Gilfachwen and John Jenkins of Cilbronne, amongst others, had had a classical education.[53] Their mastery of Latin and Greek syntax and accidence, and hard practice in translation and composition, were vital in their mastery of the Welsh language. Jones Lloyd used two methods: firstly, the sermon composed in impeccable Welsh, rhetorical and emotional, geared to the 'Hallelujah' and 'Amen' exhortations of Welsh congregations; the other type of sermon was equally well composed, yet was constantly garnished with English words at key points in its delivery, presumably to provide verbal guidelines to aid any English-speaking person present. On the Bench and in public committees, too, Lloyd was known for his rare skill in coining new Welsh terms of a technical nature.[54]

In conclusion, one can agree with H. M. Vaughan that the Welsh gentry (on the whole) were not unpatriotic. There was no overt gentry plot to jettison the language. Even taking into account the ill-effects of the Act of Union, in ceasing to speak their native language the Welsh gentry were merely following in the wake of a larger unifying process that was at work throughout the whole kingdom. It affected all classes of Welshmen, and it was inevitable that the upper classes, with their superior advantages of education and travel, should feel it first and succumb to it.[55] But such a plea in mitigation cannot, wholly, exonerate the gentry for deserting their heritage through default, carelessness and disregard for their roots. In short, the lure of advancement and the acquisition of the Anglo-Saxon polish through public school, university, and contact with the high society of the metropolis, was the lucre they were eager to acquire in lieu of the ancient language of the Welsh *uchelwyr*, from whom many of them claimed to be descended. They deliberately allowed themselves to be alienated from the Welsh language, which they came to regard as the expression of a culture belonging to inferiors, who over many generations had become nonconformist in religion and radical in politics. It has been strongly held that the Welsh gentry often pretended not to understand Welsh and used the language as a social weapon in order to put ordinary folk at a disadvantage, and deliberately to distance themselves from their tenants and the Welsh-speaking community.[56] By the nineteenth century the gentry and squirearchy were no longer an organic part of Welsh rural society. Although resident for most of the time on their estates, their lifestyle, outlook, reading habits and language were totally different from those of the local community. In spite of bardic patronage, cultural support and the homilies of 'squarsons', one can only conclude that the gentry of the Teifi valley, as in the rest of Wales, spoke English and had come to despise the Welsh language, and what they considered to be Welsh peasant culture as inferior.[57]

NOTES AND SOURCES

[1] W. Rees: *The Union of England and Wales*, 1937, pp. 81-100; J. Rhys and D. B. Jones: *op cit.*, p. 515; A. O. H. Jarman: 'Cymru'n Rhan o Loegr, 1485-1900' in *Seiliau Hanesyddol Plaid Cymru*, 1950, pp. 79-97.

[2] W. O. Williams: 'The Survival of the Welsh Language after the Union of England and Wales, 1536-1642', *WHR*, 2, 1964, i, pp. 67-93; H. M. Vaughan: *op cit.*, p. 200.

[3] P. Jenkins: *op cit.*, p 214.

[4] J. H. Davies: *op cit.*, i, ii; H. Owen: *op cit.*, i, ii; G. E. Evans, *op cit.*

[5] P. Morgan: *The Eighteenth Century Renaissance*, 1981, p. 21-5.

[6] D. J. V. Jones: *Before Rebecca . . .*, 1973, p. 63.

[7] I. G. Jones: 'Language and Community in Nineteenth Century Wales', in D. Smith (ed.): *A People and Proletariat*, 1980, pp. 47-51.

[8] G. Williams: *Gomer . . . Llenyddiaeth Gyfnodol*, *THSC*, 1982, pp. 111-18; *The Welshman*: 12/6/1846.

[9] *RCIEdSW*, 1847, pp. 330-33; G. W. Roderick and M. D. Stevens: 'The Influence of Welsh Culture on Scientific and Technical Education in Wales in the Nineteenth Century', *THSC*, 1981, p. 104.

[10] *Y Traethodydd*: xiv, 1858, pp. 384-97; *Y Geninen*: i, 1883, pp. 19-20.

[11] *Yr Haul*: 1864, p. 347; G. H. Jenkins: 'Bywiogrwydd Crefyddol a Llenyddol Dyffryn Teifi 1689-1740', *Ceredigion*, viii, 4, 1979, pp. 439-77.

[12] NLW/Owen Colby/362; NLW/Penboyr Vestry Book, 1748-80.

[13] *Gent. Mag*, Feb. 1752, p. 87.

[14] HRO/D/Pen/11/37.

[15] E. H. Stuart Jones: *op cit.*, p. 202.

[16] H. M. Vaughan: *op cit.*, pp. 201-04.

[17] NLW/Ticehurst Wyatt (Gwernant) Box 1, 11.

[18] CRO/Talardd/Box 1.

[19] HRO/D/Wil/p. 15; NLW/Howell, Glaspant/Diary 1896.

[20] NLE/Owen Colby/2128.

[21] NLW/Bronwydd/5836.

[22] NLW/Highmead/Box P/File 10.

[23] NLWE/D. Pryse Williams/15625 B.

[24] *RCISW*, 1844: p. 219 [Qu. 5059], p. 224 [Qu. 5207].

[25] *ibid*, p. 234 [Qu 5492].

[26] *ibid*, p. 61-7, 303-33.

[27] P. Jenkins: *op cit.*, p. 213; NLW/Cilgwyn/LB/42/28 July 1863; 44/4/Jan. 1875, 25 Oct. 1875; G. H. Jenkins: *op. cit.*, pp. 218-22.

[28] *Cd. Ad*: 30/6/1876.

[29] *ibid*: 28/7/1876.

[30] NLW/Owen Colby/2410-69.

[31] J. Rhys and D. B. Jones: *op cit.*, pp. 524-5.

[32] NLW/Evans George/1296.

[33] NLW/*Cm Jnl*: 16/2/1811; *DWB*; NLW/Ms/1896 E iv.

[34] *Cm Jnl*: 30/4/1840; *The Welshman*: 3/8/1866; D. L. Baker-Jones: 'The Carmarthen Eisteddfod of 1867', *Carms Hist.*, ix, 1972, pp. 44-70; Lajos Kossuth (1802-94): Hungarian patriot and soldier; Count C. Cavour (1810-61): Italian staresman.

[35] *Cm Jnl*: 18/10/1872; *The Welshman* 17/1/1873; *Cd Ad*: 21/5/1873, 31/8/1878.

[36] *ibid*: 12/12/1902.

[37] *ibid*: 14/6/1878.

[38] *ibid*: 10/10/1890, 3/3/1893.

[39] G. H. Jenkins: *op cit.*, pp. 7-9; *DWB*.

[40]J. H. Davies: *op cit.*, i, p. 288.

[41]N. Sykes: *op cit.*, pp. 182, 363; see W. Hughes, Diocesan Histories: Bangor, 1911, p. 171.

[42]K. O. Morgan: *op cit.*, pp. 30-3; *DWB*.

[43]*DWB*; The Independence, Folly and Sin of a Barbarian Episcopate in a Christian Principality, 1858; Sir T. Phillips: *op cit.*, pp. ii-vi, 15; O. Ll. Owain: 'Cymdeithas Swydd Efrog Ganrif yn ôl', *Y Traethodydd*, iii (xviii), 1950, pp. 67-74.

[44]A. J. Johnes: *An Essay on the Causes of Dissent in the Principality of Wales*, 1832, p. 63; M. H. Jones: 'The Additional Letters of Arthur James Johnes', *NLWJ*, xiv, 2, 1965, pp. 129-82; *The Welshman*: 2/6/1868; H. Richard, *op cit.*, pp. 153-55.

[45]NLW/StD/O/144 seq.

[46]S. R. Thomas: The Diocese of St Davids 1703-1803 . . ., esp. pp. 1-32; (unpublished M.A., dissertation, University of Wales, 1983).

[47]*WWHR*, iii, p. 219; *DWB*.

[48]*ibid.*

[49]NLW/Ms/1896E iv.

[50]*DWB*; NLW/Mss 6869-6870 A.

[51]NLW/Ms 6955 B (Sir Lewis Morris 55); *DWB*; NLW/Mss 11342-52; 11542-45 C.

[52]NLW/Pryse Williams/15925 B.

[53]CRO/Talardd/Box 2/31.

[54]NLW/D. Pryse Williams/15872 B, 15925 B; *Yr Haul*: 15 Awst 1904, vi, p. 370.

[55]H. M. Vaughan: *op cit.*, pp. 199-205.

[56]An opinion strongly held by the late W. Beynon Davies, M.A., Aberystwyth, concerning the gentry in the vale of Aeron, Cardiganshire.

[57]D. W. Howell: *Land and People* . . ., p. 151; personal knowledge.

Conclusion

To conclude this study of the 'Tivyside' gentry, a ruling élite in a remote corner of Wales for some hundreds of years, a verdict has to be reached concerning the nature, quality and above all the 'character' of their rule as a privileged social class. In considering the notion of 'character' it is necessary to evaluate the evidence which has been presented concerning the various aspects of gentry activity in their 'rôle' as landowners and rentiers of land. The degree of their commitment and responsibility to their estates and their tenants who toiled on these estates has to be assessed. It is legitimate to ask how far were the gentry the protectors of those over whom they ruled and to what extent did they show concern for the rest of the community? Living a superior and often lavishly ostentatious lifestyle in commodious mansions, did they add to the sum total of the native culture of their localities, and of Wales as a whole, or did they intentionally alienate themselves from 'the rock whence they were hewn'? As holders of important public office, as members of parliament and magistrates, were they motivated by high ideals of public service or rather, by narrow sectional interests, closing their eyes to the imperatives of probity and integrity, the welfare of their fellow citizens and the common weal? In their response to the perennial problem of poverty, did they go deep into their pockets as became their class as gentlefolk? In exercising support and patronage to churches, chapels, schools, reading rooms and educational institutes, did the gentry act from pure altruism and godly conviction or were they primarily concerned with the preservation of their own privileges as a caste and 'estate of the realm'? Lastly, a particularly sensitive issue in Wales with regard to gentry domination, is whether they intentionally betrayed their own language so as to distance themselves further from the rest of the community which they had come to regard as inferior.

The gentry through their 'wit and acumen' and often through patient work over many generations had consolidated large areas of land in the possession of a few families. As has become clear, their estates were run as units of consumption rather than of production. Notwithstanding any setback to the profitability of their land, due to the vagaries of weather and economic forces, any surplus that the squire's rental produced was not, in any significant degree, ploughed back to support the viability and success of an improved agriculture. There was insufficient outlay in developing the income-producing capacity of their estates. On the whole, the estate's rental had to bolster up the increasingly ostentatious and conspicuous 'display' of the squire and his family in more elegant mansions, with numerous servants and workmen, horses and hounds, carriages and equipage, and in some cases, a too well-stocked cellar.

The country squire, farming his own land in the late seventeenth and early eighteenth centuries, had almost totally disappeared over the next two hundred years. A simple and even rustic lifestyle had given way to cosmopolitan sophistication acquired from London, Bath and foreign capital cities. In a few cases, it can be argued, the home farm and support of the local agricultural society fostered new techniques, an improved livestock and more advanced cultivation, Thomas Lloyd of Bronwydd in the 1780s and '90s, Lloyd Williams of Gwernant in the 1840s and Mark Anthony Saurin of Cilwendeg in the late decades of the last century can be singled out amongst the 'improving' landlords. On the other hand, inept, rakish and feckless squires like Ford Hughes and Capt. Thomas of Llanfair were far too prevalent. Since the late eighteenth century the reports of Lloyd and Turnor, Hassall, Walter Davies and others up to the Land Commission in the 1890s, had observed the generally backward-looking attitude of ill-educated tenants, living in insanitary and primitive dwellings. A conscious effort had been made, however, by a few enlightened squires to improve and ameliorate matters. Amongst these may be mentioned Vaughan of Golden Grove towards the end of the eighteenth century, Fitzwilliams of Cilgwyn in the 1850s and '60s and Lewis of Clynfyw in the 1880s. The condition of many of the latter's properties were regarded as far above the average for the area. In contrast, and far more typically, Sir Thomas Davies Lloyd of Bronwydd only spent a mere fraction of his resources on improved drainage, houses and farm buildings. He spent a fortune on his new baronial mansion, in pursuit of a bogus peerage and in electioneering for a seat in parliament. Generally, rent increases during times of prosperity were not matched by an appreciable lowering of rent during periods of adversity. Rents were increased irrespective of the ability of the tenant to pay, and while there were numerous instances of rent abatement in varying degrees, estate rentals all too often show large arrears. While it is understandable that no prudent landlord could tolerate indolent and feckless tenants, the economic viability of the estate which a landlord, like Fitzwilliams of Cilgwyn, regarded as paramount, meant that human values were secondary. It meant too, that the rent 'screw', to keep tenants 'up to ye mark' (as the Cilgwyn letter books show), could only result in hardship even to the hard working and thrifty. It is true that, during the depression after 1815, Colby of Ffynone amongst others took a sympathethic view and allowed rent abatements, and that later in the century, other gentry adopted a similar attitude from time to time. The unique example of Lady Lloyd, in the 1920s, who argued with the Bronwydd agent that she and the tenants had to 'help one another to survive' by lowering rents, is illustrative of paternalism at its best. But taking everything into account it can fairly be concluded that, on the whole, the 'Tivyside' gentry as a class did not provide sufficient financial backing to their tenants. They had other priorities, an extravagant lifestyle, over-indulgence and a selfish, hedonistic outlook. E. Pan Jones and Dr Rhys Jones may have exaggerated the 'Epicureanism' and licentiousness of the gentry, but in many cases it was palpably true. Added to the economic hardships of tenants were the burdens of dues and services, a symbol of the squire's feudal sway and a real imposition in practice. The payment of tithes and church rate were resented because the squire and the Anglican episcopal church were identified as forces inimical to radicalism and dissent. The gentry and the church had become English in language, sentiment and sympathy, an aristocratic force dominating the majority of the common people, who were Welsh speaking, radical and nonconformist. Harsh conditions in leases, especially with regard to the pursuit of game, the 'keep' of dogs for the squire's pleasure, and (towards the end of the nineteenth century) exceptive clauses in leases nullifying any parliamentary legislation in favour of the tenant, added to a deep distrust and even hatred towards many of the gentry. Often the employment of English-speaking, anti-Welsh agents like the nefarious Allen, who acted for the squire of Alltyrodyn in the 1870s, added to long held grievances. New fishery laws were interpreted as depriving ordinary folk of their time-honoured means of survival, and river conservation (whatever the merits of the argument) was seen by many as the enhancement of the squire's privilege, especially as he had a monopoly over riparian rights, and alone, with others of his class, could afford to pay for the fishing licences demanded. Indeed, W. O. Brigstocke, although a deviationist from the 'values' of his class, and a Liberal, and who was in sympathy with Welsh radical aspirations concerning the church, the challenge to landowners' rights and their power in local government, became the target for attack because of his support for river conservation.

The squire at home, at the beginning of our period, lived a simple and unsophisticated lifestyle, judging from the inventories of household goods and possessions examined. Certainly, from the mid-eighteenth century onwards cosmopolitan ideas displaced an almost rustic lifestyle. The simply furnished *plas* gradually gave way to larger mansions. As has been seen, the lives of many gentry were conspicuous for their debauchery, vices which were condemned in the lower orders such as tramps, gipsies, labourers and village 'molls'—the latter very often the prey of the squire's unbridled passion. Sexual immorality was frowned upon in the lower classes, and the order books of Quarter Sessions illustrate how bastardy was regarded as a plague on the parish. In polite circles, however, another standard prevailed where illicit liaisons were condoned, and debauchery and drunkenness regarded as 'manly vices'. A glaring pattern of immoral behaviour can be traced in gentry circles throughout our period. Many an uncouth 'Squire Western' lived in 'Tivyside' in the eighteenth century, and, despite the challenge of Methodism and a more sober and pious Victorian respectability, there were many examples of seducers and roués late into the nineteenth century. Names like Brigstocke of Blaenpant in the 1750s followed by Lloyd of Coedmore, 'the old man' of Llysnewydd, Davies of Maesycrugiau, Parry of Gernos and Bowen, the rector of Troedyraur, readily come to mind. It must not be forgotten, however, that there were paragons of virtue in some of the 'Tivyside' mansions, devout persons smitten by the evangelical zeal of Wesley and of Welsh Methodist leaders like Hywel Harris, William Williams of Pantycelyn and Daniel Rowland. Among such gentry were the Llwyngwair Bowens and Thomas and Mary Lloyd of Bronwydd, in the 1790s and early 1800s, while nineteenth-century Evangelicism spurred the Walters sisters of Glanmedeni to wage a holy war against vice of every kind.

A few squires could claim a fair degree of intellectualism, as can be demonstrated in the case of Brigstocke of Blaenpant and Lloyd of Alltyrodyn in the second half of the eighteenth century, while the Unitarian Lloyds of the Cletwr valley reached a pinnacle of academic fame. In the nineteenth century, Edward Crompton Lloyd Hall (later to style himself Fitzwilliams) was a highly qualified lawyer with a far ranging interest in almost every branch of human knowledge, as the voluminous Cilgwyn letter books illustrate. The reasonably well-stocked libraries in most 'Tivyside' houses, however, do not prove that their owners had any deep attachment to reading, and one suspects that, for the most part, they were merely ornamental and decorative appendages to a gentleman's house. A few country squires and their ladies pursued literary activities, like Miss Webley-Parry who wrote didactically to encourage a religious work-ethic, as exemplified in the sober and industrious life of the old retainer of Hafod Fach. Her history of the ancient British church was a sincere but inadequate answer to radical nonconformist polemics. H. M. Vaughan of Plas Llangoedmore, with a superior educational background, described the amusing 'oddities and quiddities' of the South Wales squires and sought to defend their anglicisation, their demeanour, treatment of tenants and attitudes to controversial issues like the game laws, the Land Question and disestablishment of the Welsh church, albeit, with the prejudices of his class. His other literary efforts initially received reasonable acclaim but cannot be regarded as of permanent significance. One can ask, what was the contribution of the country house to the broad culture of the locality? The 'mores' of the mansion and its occupants had become increasingly divorced from the traditional and native culture of Welsh country folk of the eighteenth century. The old Welsh aristocratic culture had long disappeared since Tudor times. For various reasons the patronage of *uchelwyr* was no longer practised. Although a Welsh harper was employed at Highmead during the early decades of the last century, life in most gentry houses reflected more and more an indulgence in food and drink, facile and fatuous pursuits like fortune telling, gossip and flirtatious intrigue, and the presentation of trite dramatic episodes, as the pages of local newspapers, diaries and Morgan Richardson's novel *Henry Vaughan* amply show. The true custodians of an intellectual culture thriving in literary, theological, philosophical and political discourse were the common people who thronged to the *cyrddau mawr* (big preaching meetings), the cultural and self-educating societies of Welsh noncon-formity. Here, too, the Welsh language, abandoned by the gentry, was to survive amongst *y werin* inspired by a 'Puritan' ethic, a zeal for religion and eagerness for educational enlightenment.

It is true that ordinary folk gladly enjoyed the plentiful largesse of food and drink at the big house during times of rejoicing in the squire's family. Celebrations like weddings or the heir's coming of age enlivened the dull monotony of their lives and relieved, to a slight degree, the deprivation of many. The Rev. William Thomas (Gwilym Marles)—and one must agree with his sentiment—would have preferred the gentry to provide a water supply, sanitary improvements and hygienic living conditions within the community rather than occasional gifts of roast beef and beer—mere flimsy tokens of generosity. Such a perceptive outlook was also shared by a few homely rhymesters who dared to express the latent tensions of a disaffected class. As the mansion was the most important component of parish life and a force in bringing society together, one can properly ponder how far it influenced in any degree the sum total of the culture of the locality. Its lifestyle, as has been noticed, was far removed from that of the neighbourhood, and disparity of wealth created a wide chasm between the squire and the other inhabitants of the parish. Only in a very small way did the knowledge, skills and accomplishments of domestic and estate workers like kitchen and dairy maids, cooks, housekeepers, estate gardeners, carpenters, masons, farriers and wood-wards to mention only a few, in the complex hierarchy of the country house, percolate into the way of life of the locality. While many 'Tivyside' mansions have disappeared or are in ruins, in surviving estate cottages and in villages along the Teifi valley there are traces of architectural taste which are definite, if distant, derivatives from the former local mansions and which add to the unique personality of the area.

It has been demonstrated that only a dedicated few of the county gentry took their duties as JPs seriously. The nucleus of conscientious gentry who attended Quarter and Petty Sessions regularly, to discharge county business and to administer the criminal law, probably made the biggest impact on the community. Added to their power and authority as landowners was the opportunity as JPs to regulate the daily lives of everyone. With regard to matters of local government, the evidence points strongly to gentry concern for bridge building and repair, the maintenance of gaols and houses of correction and the harrying of loafers, miscreants and bastards in administering the Poor Laws, especially within their own locality, and paid for out of the public purse.

Considering their cool response and minimal financial investment towards developing the new turnpike roads and later the railways, one suspects that their support for road and bridge improvement in the vicinity of their estates was sometimes exercised for personal and selfish ends. Lloyd Davies of Blaendyffryn and Alltyrodyn was highly praised for his efforts in causing a massive stone bridge to be built over the Teifi at Pentrecwrt. What must not be forgotten is the fact that it added greatly to the value of his two estates, in facilitating travel and his own personal convenience. The gentry as a class were not always motivated by pure altruism, in spite of their talk of the public good. The character of the gentry JPs as the personnel of local government does not always add to their credit. As the appointment of county officials was entirely in their hands, one traces more than a degree of nepotism and patronage in the appointment of persons from their own ranks to public posts such as the clerk of the county, treasurer, coroners and the like, right down to minor parish officials. Blatant corruption and graft, and the misuse of public funds could always flourish where there was no democratic *vox populi* to challenge gentry authority.

Amongst other grievances which led to distrust and even hatred of some gentry, was the harshness of some squires on the magisterial bench. In the case of gentry JPs like Walter D. Jones of Lancych, one can agree with the Hammonds that the jurisdiction of the gentry, as magistrates, was in reality feudalism in a new guise. Vaughan of Plas Llangoedmore was openly castigated for the inordinately severe sentences he imposed on those convicted for minor offences like shooting rabbits. Not only were Game Laws sacrosanct in the eyes of the gentry, and harsh penalties meted out for snaring a pheasant or like offences, but trivial pranks could also bring upon the offender a viciously punitive fine, as in the case of Llandysul urchins who were caught stealing apples from a squire's orchard. E. Crompton Ll. Fitzwilliams, who had little regard for the 'Tivyside' squirearchy and who dubbed them 'petty princelings', complained that when he was absent from court common people had no hope of a fair trial. But the 'Tivyside' gentry, as a whole, were not as consistently severe as some magisterial benches in other parts of south-west Wales. As inhabitants, dwelling in their areas of jurisdiction, it appears that some of them at least knew who was who and tempered justice with mercy, knowing that factors like family circumstances, poverty and fecklessness of temperament had often to be taken into account. Moreover, local harmony and the respect of the governed towards those who governed had to be won in a closely knit community where there was a strong element of mutual dependence. One way to secure this was in the sympathetic attitude of a few gentry towards the wrongdoer.

With regard to political issues, the 'Tivyside' gentry were inward looking and, above all, concerned with maintaining the 'constitution' and the existing order in church and state. Fearful of internecine strife and the revival of Popery, they regarded proposals for removing disabilities affecting Roman Catholics as political and religious heresy.

Initially, the 'Tivyside' squires were opposed to the reform of parliament, and only because of the swell of middle-class opinion in towns like Carmarthen and Cardigan in favour of reform, and fearful of revolution spreading from the continent, did they ultimately yield and reluctantly accept the Reform Act of 1832. But there was no warm welcome to the extension of the franchise for its own sake. For the rest of the century, the gentry clung to the politics of deference long after such an outlook had had to give way to the politics of democracy. They opposed the introduction of the ballot as an intrusion into the traditional relationship between the squire and the community. The freedom of tenants to vote according to their conscience was anathema to some half dozen landowners who evicted those tenants who had voted Liberal, and further harsh pressures were brought by many landlords against 'defectors' in the years following 1868.

The parliamentary performance of the 'Tivyside' gentry was largely undistinguished; few of them even participated in parliamentary debate, far less made a valuable contribution. Lloyd Davies of Blaendyffryn and Alltyrodyn was the exception. Regular in his attendance and taking part in debate and during question time, he displayed a remarkable versatility of interest and concern about national and local issues. Although a Tory, and clinging to much of the old ideology, his contribution as a parliamentarian was nevertheless in many ways admirable. Sir Thomas Davies Lloyd was an enigmatic character who espoused an old-fashioned Whiggism with radical Liberalism. In the debates on the second Reform Bill of 1867 and later on the Ballot, he challenged the sacrosanct theory of some of the local landowning classes that the tenant's vote belonged to the lord just as much as the land held by the tenant. But his ambivalence on issues like disestablishment, and flirtation with radicalism, makes one suspect that he was an opportunist whose real aim was to obtain a peerage with the social cachet that went with it.

Although only involved in local government, W. O. Brigstocke was the only true Liberal amongst the 'Tivyside' gentry. He espoused the cause nearest to the hearts of the nonconformist *gwerin*, namely, the disestablishment of the church and removal of disabilities like tithes and the teaching of church doctrine in schools, much to the chagrin and disgust of his fellow gentry. He sympathised with Welsh national aspirations, and was one of the few gentry not to be rejected as a political leader by the community, becoming the first chairman of Carmarthenshire County Council.

What is difficult to explain is that a number of people remained
sentimentally attached to the squire. Many of them were personally
liked, although in national and local elections the common people
chose, instead, farmers and chapel deacons to be their leaders.
Perhaps, Sir Marteine Lloyd of Bronwydd deserves to be remembered
as the best example of the old-fashioned country squire, the ideal of
the Victorian *pater familias* at its best, and one can admire his simple
tastes, frank manners and generous friendship.' As has been demonstrated, the Lloyd family of Bronwydd, towards the end of our period,
were still regarded as real *gwŷr mawr* (big people), continuing a long
family tradition of benevolent paternalism. The Rev. Rhys Jones
Lloyd was a generous parish priest who helped ailing and
impoverished nonconformists during the tithe agitation. It has been
claimed that country folk expected the squire of an old family to adopt
a certain *hauteur*, and that they reacted with servility believing that the
squire could not consort with ordinary folk.[2] The Lloyds of Bronwydd
were, by contrast, not regarded as 'snobs' but regularly attended local
events such as preaching meetings in nonconformist chapels, concerts
and *eisteddfodau*, funerals of local inhabitants and the *cymanfa bwnc*
(catechism festival).[3] By way of contrast, C. Home Ll. Fitzwilliams, the
Thomas family of Dôl-llan and Llanfair, and the Lewes clan of
Llysnewydd were remembered as aloof and authoritarian, like certain
others of the 'Tivyside' gentry.[4] But in spite of occasional personal
dislike, and the religious and political conflict which erupted in the
'Land Question', there was no complete breakdown in relations
between the squire and the community.

At the beginning of this study the sentimental nostalgia expressed
by many at the passing of the old country squire was mentioned.
Indeed, the countryside has lost the spectacle of the colourful and
often eccentric squire riding with his hounds, addressing public
meetings in 'pidgin' Welsh or snoring in his pew during morning
prayer. It is sad to see ruined mansions and overgrown gardens, the
work of skilled craftsmen destroyed, the imagination of architects like
Nash desecrated, the aesthetic appeal of a landscaped park defiled to
give place to modern and often ugly development, all in the name of
progress. On the other hand, one cannot but agree with a comment of
the Land Commission Report that the gentry ruled the countryside as
if by divine right. One might add that they confidently regarded
themselves as 'a superior people' on account of pedigree and lineage.
In spite of the many noble ideals in the concept of gentility which they

boasted, they fell short of those ideals. On the whole, but not in every case, it must be emphasised, they were niggardly in the concern for those less fortunate than themselves.

While it has to be conceded in mitigation that the gentry displayed a readiness to provide leadership in public affairs (especially in the absence of any challenge from a middle class which was non-existent), it must be said that they manipulated the opportunities of public office to serve their own ends. Their patronage of church, chapel and school was often a means to 'educate' their dependants to be content with their station. They failed to recognise the rightful ambitions of the lower classes, and, at heart, were opposed to educational and labour movements which were aimed at affording the *gwerin* greater chances of rising in the world. They wielded power on the bench too often as petty despots. When challenged by the radical awakening and noncon-formist protest many retaliated with spite and vindictiveness.

Where the regime was sympathetic and benevolent, an unquest-ioning deference, often to the extent of obsequiousness and servility, was the price demanded by those who ruled over whom they ruled.

How and why the Welsh folk of the Teifi valley, as in other parts of Wales, continued to be long-suffering is hard to explain. The maudlin sentiment and bardic hyperbole of radical preachers and dissenting deacons addressed to the squire and his family whose political creed and religious dogma were totally opposed, is incomprehensible. Had the native Welshman been conditioned and indoctrinated by centuries of Anglo-Saxon domination? Was the Welshman servile and hypocritical by nature, or merely, docile and kind-hearted? These are questions which have to remain unanswered, and are beyond the scope of this study.

NOTES AND SOURCES

[1] Recollections of local inhabitants.
[2] G. E. Mingay: *Rural Life in Victorian England*, 1977, p. 185.
[3] D. Jenkins: *The Agricultural Community in South West Wales at the Turn of the Twentieth Century*, 1971, p. 29.
[4] The late Mr S. Jones, Beulah, Newcastle Emlyn.

APPENDIX 1 Outline Pedigrees

Bowen of Llwyngwair

Descended from Gwrwared of Cemaes, Gwilym ap Gwrwared ap Gwilym constable of Cardigan Castle in 1260, Sir James Bowen (ap Owen) of Pentre Ifan living during the reign of Henry VII (1485-1509) and through marriage related to the Wogan of Wiston, Warren of Trewern and Philipps family of Picton.

George Bowen of Llwyngwair, H.S. co. Pemb, 1632; will dated 4 July 1659 and proved 16 July 1660
= Dorothy, dau. of John Scourfield of Moat.

James Bowen, born before 1591; will dated 24 January 1677-78 and proved the following April. Mayor of Newport 1660-61; H.S. co. Pemb, 1671.
= Elizabeth, dau. of John Owen of Orielton.

George Bowen (1651-1708) H. S. co. Pemb, 1682.
= i Mary, dau. of Lewis Barlow of Cresswell.
  ii Dorothy, dau. of Essex Meyrick of Bush.

James Bowen (1696-1752)
= Alice, dau. of Richard Rowe of Linney, Castlemartin.

George Bowen (1722-1810) Mayor of Cardigan 1754, 1759, 1761; J.P., co Pemb in 1761 and H.S. in 1803.
= Easter (Hesther) dau. and co-heir of William Thomas of Pentowin, Mydrim and of her uncle Rice Thomas of Castell Gorfod.

James Bowen (1758-1816) Mayor of Cardigan five times from 1780 to 1805; Newport 1787-88; J.P., co Pemb; D.L. for co Pemb 1797.
= Martha, dau. of Evan Jenkins of Glog, Llanfyrnach.

George Bowen (1800-1856) D.L. co Pemb in 1824; H.S. 1825; burgess of Cardigan.
= Sarah, dau. of John Thomas of Longhouse, Mathry.

James Bevan Bowen (1828-1905), educated at King's College, London and Worcester College, Oxford; Barrister of the Inner Temple; J.P., D.L. for co Pemb, Chairman Pembs Quarter Sessions; Alderman Pembs C.C. 1889-1894; H.S. 1862; M.P. for Pembrokeshire 1866-68, 1876-80.
= Harriette, dau. of the Rev. John Standley of Southoe, Hants.

Sir George Bevan Bowen (1858-1940) educated at Cheltenham and Magdalen College, Oxford; J.P., D.L., co Pemb; H.S. Pemb 1914; Lieut. Pembs, Yeomanry; Mayor of Newport 1913; in 1928 he was knighted K.B.E. for public services.
= Florence Emma, only surviving dau. of Deputy-Surgeon-General Federick Corbyn, H.M.I.S.

Brigstocke of Llechdwnny and Gellydywyll, co Carmarthen and Blaenpant, co. Cardigan

Richard Brigstocke of Croydon, d. 1604; a tenant of the Manor of Waldon, 24 June 1583 = Mary ?

Robert Brigstocke, 3rd son of Richard Brigstocke (1578-1619) = Elizabeth, dau. of Edward Heighton of Croydon.

John Brigstocke of Llechdwnny, co Carm. (1604-1640) = Mary, youngest dau. and co-heir of Morris Bowen of Llechdwnny.

Owen Brigstocke of Llechdwnny and Llandybïe, co Carm; H.S.co Carm, 1657, 1669; Mayor of Carmarthen 1682. His will of 1 Oct. 1689 was proved 14 March 1690. = i. Jane, dau. of Sir William Vaugan, D.C.L. of Torycoed, co Carm, and brother of the Earl of Carbery.
ii. Elizabeth, dau. of David Lloyd of Porthwred and Castell Hywel.
iii. Elizbaeth, widow of John Gwyn of Piode and dau. of Arthur Wogan, 5th son of Sir William Wogan of Wiston.

William Brigstocke of Llechdwnny and Capel Evan, co Carm. (? - 1713). = Winifred, dau. and co-heir of Robert Byrtte of Llwynduris, co. Card.

William Brigstocke (1686-1721 or 1726?) 3rd and youngest son. = Elizabeth, dau. and sole heir of William Jenkins of Blaenpant and Carrog, co. Card by Bridget his wife sole heir of James Lewes of Gellydywyll; g. dau. of Reginald Jenkins and his wife Eleanor, only child of David Parry of Blaenpant.

William Brigstocke (1708-1751). H. S. co Card., 1735. = Mary, only child and heir of Francis Lloyd of Glyn, co Carm.

Owen Brigstocke of Llechdwnny, Capel Evan and Blaenpant (1740-78). Mayor of Cardigan 1765, 1772. = Anne, elder dau. and co-heir of John Williams of Corngafr and Bwlch-gwynt, co Carm.

William Owen Brigstocke (1761-1831) H.S. co Card., 1794; Col. Carms. Militia. = Anne, eldest dau. of Edmund Probyn of Newland and Huntley, co. Gloucester.

William Owen Brigstocke of Blaenpant, Gellydywyll and Llechdwnny (1784-1861) J.P., D.L. co Card., H.S. 1833. He died without issue and was succeeded by his nephew. = i. Harriet, 3 dau. of Sir William Mansel, 7th Bart.
ii. Maria, 2 dau. of Adml. Webley-Parry of Noyadd Trefawr.

Willian Owen Brigstocke (1831-1900) J.P., cos Card., Carm., and Pemb.; D.L. co Card. Chairman Carm. C.C., 1888-92; B.A. Jesus Coll. Oxford; Barrister of the Inner Temple. = i. Emmeline, dau. and co-heir of Oliver Lloyd of Coedmore and Dolhaidd.
ii. Anne Gregory, dau. of William Forsyth-Grant of Ecclesgreig, Kincardine.

Augustus (1854-)

Fitzwilliams of Cilgwyn

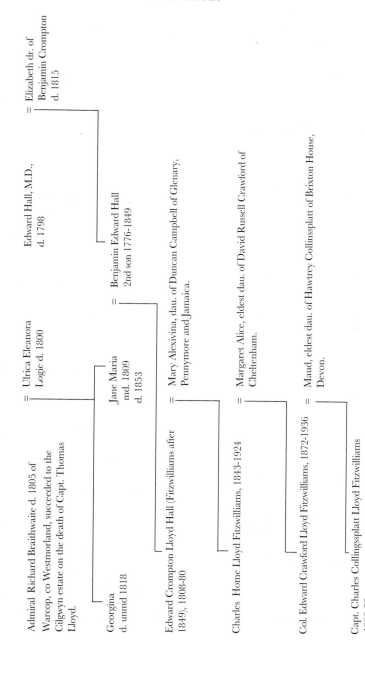

Admiral Richard Braithwaite d. 1805 of Warcop, co Westmorland, succeeded to the Cilgwyn estate on the death of Capt. Thomas Lloyd.

= Ulrica Eleanora Logie d. 1800

Edward Hall, M.D., d. 1798

= Elizabeth dr. of Benjamin Crompton d. 1815

Georgina d. ummd 1818

Jane Maria md. 1809 d. 1853

= Benjamin Edward Hall 2nd son 1776-1849 .

Edward Crompton Lloyd Hall (Fitzwilliams after 1849), 1808-80

= Mary Alexivina, dau. of Duncan Campbell of Glenary, Pennymore and Jamaica.

Charles Home Lloyd Fitzwilliams, 1843-1924

= Margaret Alice, eldest dau. of David Russell Crawford of Cheltenham.

Col. Edward Crawford Lloyd Fitzwilliams, 1872-1936

= Maud, eldest dau. of Hawtrey Collinssplatt of Brixton House, Devon.

Capt. Charles Collingssplatt Lloyd Fitzwilliams ,1900-83

Lewes of Llysnewydd

Ednywain ap Bradwen, head of the 15th noble tribe of North Wales; among his descendants were Rhys Nanmor (fl. 1480-1513), Judge Lewis Owen (y Barwn Owen) who died in 1555 at the hand of Gwylliaid Cochion Mawddwy—'the Red Bandits of Mawddwy'; John Owen the Puritan divine (d. 1683); the genealogist William Lewes, Llwynderw (1652-1722) and Sir Watkin Lewes (1740-1821) Lord Mayor of London in 1780 and one of the four M.P.s for the City of London from 1780-96.

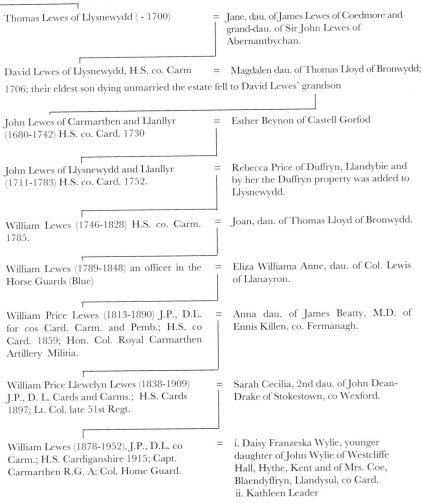

Thomas Lewes of Llysnewydd (- 1700) = Jane, dau. of James Lewes of Coedmore and grand-dau. of Sir John Lewes of Abernantbychan.

David Lewes of Llysnewydd, H.S. co. Carm = Magdalen dau. of Thomas Lloyd of Bronwydd; 1706; their eldest son dying unmarried the estate fell to David Lewes' grandson

John Lewes of Carmarthen and Llanllyr = Esther Beynon of Castell Gorfod (1680-1742) H.S. co. Card. 1730

John Lewes of Llysnewydd and Llanllyr = Rebecca Price of Duffryn, Llandybie and (1711-1783) H.S. co. Card. 1752. by her the Duffryn property was added to Llysnewydd.

William Lewes (1746-1828) H.S. co. Carm. = Joan, dau. of Thomas Lloyd of Bronwydd. 1785.

William Lewes (1789-1848) an officer in the = Eliza Williama Anne, dau. of Col. Lewis Horse Guards (Blue) of Llanayron.

William Price Lewes (1813-1890) J.P., D.L. = Anna dau. of James Beatty, M.D. of for cos Card. Carm. and Pemb.; H.S. co Ennis Killen, co. Fermanagh. Card. 1859; Hon. Col. Royal Carmarthen Artillery Militia.

William Price Llewelyn Lewes (1838-1909) = Sarah Cecilia, 2nd dau. of John Dean-J.P., D. L. Cards and Carms.; H.S. Cards Drake of Stokestown, co Wexford. 1897; Lt. Col. late 51st Regt.

William Lewes (1878-1952), J.P., D.L. co = i. Daisy Franzeska Wylie, younger Carm.; H.S. Cardiganshire 1915; Capt. daughter of John Wylie of Westcliffe Carmarthen R.G. A; Col. Home Guard. Hall, Hythe, Kent and of Mrs. Coe, Blaendyffryn, Llandysul, co Card.
ii. Kathleen Leader

Lloyd of Bronwydd*

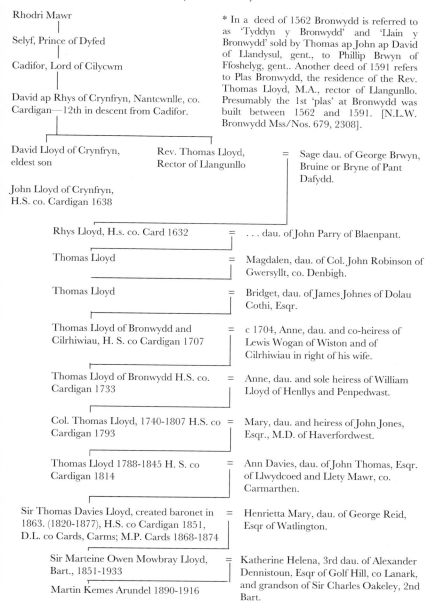

Rhodri Mawr
|
Selyf, Prince of Dyfed
|
Cadifor, Lord of Cilycwm
|
David ap Rhys of Crynfryn, Nantcwnlle, co.
Cardigan—12th in descent from Cadifor.

* In a deed of 1562 Bronwydd is referred to as 'Tyddyn y Bronwydd' and 'Llain y Bronwydd' sold by Thomas ap John ap David of Llandysul, gent., to Phillip Brwyn of Ffoshelyg, gent.. Another deed of 1591 refers to Plas Bronwydd, the residence of the Rev. Thomas Lloyd, M.A., rector of Llangunllo. Presumably the 1st 'plas' at Bronwydd was built between 1562 and 1591. [N.L.W. Bronwydd Mss/Nos. 679, 2308].

David Lloyd of Crynfryn,
eldest son

Rev. Thomas Lloyd,   =   Sage dau. of George Brwyn,
Rector of Llangunllo   Bruine or Bryne of Pant
                           Dafydd.

John Lloyd of Crynfryn,
H.S. co. Cardigan 1638

Rhys Lloyd, H.s. co. Card 1632   =   . . . dau. of John Parry of Blaenpant.

Thomas Lloyd   =   Magdalen, dau. of Col. John Robinson of Gwersyllt, co. Denbigh.

Thomas Lloyd   =   Bridget, dau. of James Johnes of Dolau Cothi, Esqr.

Thomas Lloyd of Bronwydd and Cilrhiwiau, H. S. co Cardigan 1707   =   c 1704, Anne, dau. and co-heiress of Lewis Wogan of Wiston and of Cilrhiwiau in right of his wife.

Thomas Lloyd of Bronwydd H.S. co. Cardigan 1733   =   Anne, dau. and sole heiress of William Lloyd of Henllys and Penpedwast.

Col. Thomas Lloyd, 1740-1807 H.S. co Cardigan 1793   =   Mary, dau. and heiress of John Jones, Esqr., M.D. of Haverfordwest.

Thomas Lloyd 1788-1845 H. S. co Cardigan 1814   =   Ann Davies, dau. of John Thomas, Esqr. of Llwydcoed and Llety Mawr, co. Carmarthen.

Sir Thomas Davies Lloyd, created baronet in 1863. (1820-1877), H.S. co Cardigan 1851, D.L. co Cards, Carms; M.P. Cards 1868-1874   =   Henrietta Mary, dau. of George Reid, Esqr of Watlington.

Sir Marteine Owen Mowbray Lloyd, Bart., 1851-1933   =   Katherine Helena, 3rd dau. of Alexander Dennistoun, Esqr of Golf Hill, co Lanark, and grandson of Sir Charles Oakeley, 2nd Bart.

Martin Kemes Arundel 1890-1916

Lloyd of Coedmore

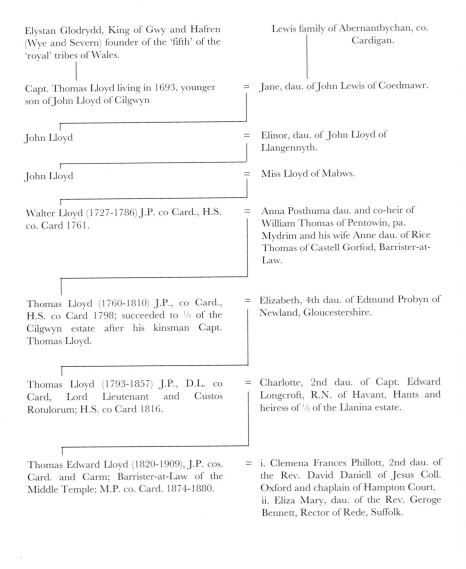

Elystan Glodrydd, King of Gwy and Hafren (Wye and Severn) founder of the 'fifth' of the 'royal' tribes of Wales.

Lewis family of Abernantbychan, co. Cardigan.

Capt. Thomas Lloyd living in 1693, younger son of John Lloyd of Cilgwyn   =   Jane, dau. of John Lewis of Coedmawr.

John Lloyd   =   Elinor, dau. of John Lloyd of Llangennyth.

John Lloyd   =   Miss Lloyd of Mabws.

Walter Lloyd (1727-1786) J.P. co Card., H.S. co. Card 1761.   =   Anna Posthuma dau. and co-heir of William Thomas of Pentowin, pa. Mydrim and his wife Anne dau. of Rice Thomas of Castell Gorfod, Barrister-at-Law.

Thomas Lloyd (1760-1810) J.P., co Card., H.S. co Card 1798; succeeded to ⅓ of the Cilgwyn estate after his kinsman Capt. Thomas Lloyd.   =   Elizabeth, 4th dau. of Edmund Probyn of Newland, Gloucestershire.

Thomas Lloyd (1793-1857) J.P., D.L. co Card, Lord Lieutenant and Custos Rotulorum; H.S. co Card 1816.   =   Charlotte, 2nd dau. of Capt. Edward Longcroft, R.N. of Havant, Hants and heiress of ½ of the Llanina estate.

Thomas Edward Lloyd (1820-1909), J.P. cos. Card. and Carm; Barrister-at-Law of the Middle Temple; M.P. co. Card. 1874-1880.   =   i. Clemena Frances Phillott, 2nd dau. of the Rev. David Daniell of Jesus Coll. Oxford and chaplain of Hampton Court.
ii. Eliza Mary, dau. of the Rev. Geroge Bennett, Rector of Rede, Suffolk.

Saunders Davies of Pentre

The family of Davies had resided for generations in Llandovery; one Evan Davies commanded a troop of cavalry under John, Duke of Marlborough.

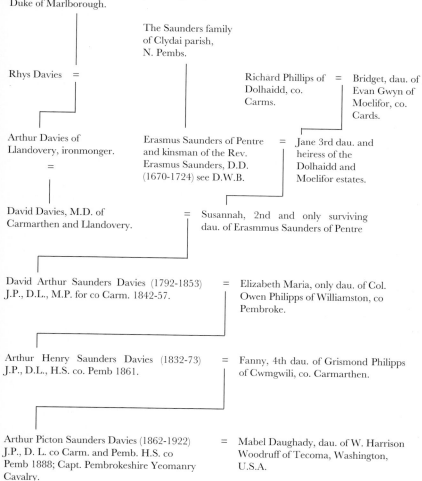

The Saunders family of Clydai parish, N. Pembs.

Rhys Davies =

Richard Phillips of = Bridget, dau. of
Dolhaidd, co.   Evan Gwyn of
Carms.   Moelifor, co.
    Cards.

Arthur Davies of Llandovery, ironmonger.

=

Erasmus Saunders of Pentre = Jane 3rd dau. and
and kinsman of the Rev.   heiress of the
Erasmus Saunders, D.D.   Dolhaidd and
(1670-1724) see D.W.B.   Moelifor estates.

David Davies, M.D. of Carmarthen and Llandovery.

= Susannah, 2nd and only surviving dau. of Erasmmus Saunders of Pentre

David Arthur Saunders Davies (1792-1853) J.P., D.L., M.P. for co Carm. 1842-57.

= Elizabeth Maria, only dau. of Col. Owen Philipps of Williamston, co Pembroke.

Arthur Henry Saunders Davies (1832-73) J.P., D.L., H.S. co. Pemb 1861.

= Fanny, 4th dau. of Grismond Philipps of Cwmgwili, co. Carmarthen.

Arthur Picton Saunders Davies (1862-1922) J.P., D. L. co Carm. and Pemb. H.S. co Pemb 1888; Capt. Pembrokeshire Yeomanry Cavalry.

= Mabel Daughady, dau. of W. Harrison Woodruff of Tecoma, Washington, U.S.A.

APPENDIX 2   Gentry Houses and Parishes c. 1700

Aberduar	— Llanybydder, Carms
Aberdwylan	— Cenarth, "
Abernantbychan	— Penbryn, Cards
Berllan	— Eglwyswrw, Pembs
Blaenbylan	— Llanfihangel Penbedw, Pembs
Blaencerdin	— Llandysul, Cards
Blaendyffryn	— Bangor Teifi, Cards
Blaenpant	— Llandugwydd, "
Blaenythan	— Llangeler, Carms
Bridell	— Llantood, Pembs
Bronhydden	— Penboyr, Carms
Bronwydd	— Llangunllo, Cards
Bwlch Bychan	— Llanwenog, "
Bwlch Cynon	— L:landysilio, "
Bwlch Mawr	— Llanwenog "
Camnant	— Llandysul, "
Cardigan Priory	— St. Mary's Cardigan
Castell Hywel	— Llandysul, Cards
Castell Malgwyn	— Maenordeifi, Pembs
Cilast	— Maenordeifi, Pembs
Cilbronne	— Llangoedmor, Cards
Cilgwyn	— Llandyfriog, "
Cilgynfydd	— Llangeler, Carms
Cilrhiwe	— Llanfihangel Penbedw, Pembs
Cilwendeg	— Llanfihangel Penbedw, Pembs
Cilyblaidd	— Pencarreg, Carms
Clunfelin	— Cilrhedyn, E. Carms
Clyn Fyw	— Maenordeifi, Pembs
Coedmore	— Llangoedmor, "
Coedstre-isaf	— Llangeler, Carms
Court	— Eglwyswrw, Pembs
Crugbychan	— Ferwig, Cards
Crugmawr	— " "
Cryngae	— Penboyr, Carms
Cwmawen	— Llangrannog, Cards
Cwmcynon	— Llandysilio-gogo, Cards
Cwmeudwy	— Llandysul, Cards
Cwmgloyn	— Bayvil, Pembs
Cwmhyar	— Llandysul, Cards
Cwmtydy	— Llandysilio-gogo, Cards
Cwrt Newydd	— Llanwenog, "
Dinas Cerdin	— Llandysul, "
Dolau bach	— Llanwenog, "
Dolau Cletwr	— Llanwenog, "
Dolgrogws	— Llanfihangel-ar-Arth, Carms
Dolgwm	— Pencarreg, Carms
Dolhaidd-isaf	— Penboyr, Carms
Dolhaidd-uchaf	— " "
Dol Llannerch	— Clydai, Pembs
Dolwlph	— Llanwenog, Cards
Drefawr (Noyadd D)	— Llandugwydd, "
Dyffryn Llynod	— Llandysul, "
Faenor	— Maenordeifi, Pembs
Faerdref	— Llandysul, Cards
Faerdref Fach	— " "
Ffinnone bychan	— Maenordeifi, Pembs
Fforest	— Cilgerran, Pembs
Ffosesgob	— Llandysul, Cards
Ffoshelig	— " "
Ffynnonbedr	— Lampeter, Cards
Gallt-yr-Odyn	— Llandysul, "
Gelly-Dywell	— Cenarth, Carms
Gellyfraith	— Llandysul, Cards
Gellygatti	— Cenarth, Carms
Gernos	— Llangunllo, Cards
Gilfach	— Llangeler, Carms
Gilfach Wen	— Llandysul, Cards
Gilfachwith	— Bangor Teifi, "
Glanduad	— Meline, Pembs
Glanduan (-dovan)	— Cilgerran, "
Glandyweli	— Llanfihangel-ar-Arth, Carms
Goetre-isaf	— Penboyr, Carms
Goetre-uchaf	— Penboyr, "
Gorllwyn	— Penboyr, "
Gwernant	— Troedyraur, Cards
Gwern-y-Macwy	— Llanfihangel-ar-Arth, Carms
Henbant	— Llandysul, Cards
Henllys	— Nevern, Pembs
Lancych	— Clydai, Pembs
Llanborth	— Penbryn, Cards
Llanfechan	— Llanwenog, "
Lletherneuadd	— Llanfihangel-ar-Arth, Carms
Llwynbedw	— Llanfihangel Penbedw, Pembs
Llwyncadfor	— Llanfair Treflygen, Cards
Llwyndafydd	— Llandysilio-gogo, Cards
Llwynderw	— Llangeler, Carms
Llwyngrawis	— Llangoedmor, Cards
Llwyngwair	— Nevern, Pembs
Llwyn-y-fedw	— Llanybydder, Carms
Llysnewydd	— Llangeler, "
Maesycrugiau	— Llanllwni, "

Morfa Bychan — Llangrannog, Cards
Mountain Hall — Llangeler, Carms
Nant-du — Llangrannog, Cards
Pantcilgan — Llangeler, Carms
Pantdafydd — Llangunllo, Cards
Pantirion — St. Dogmaels, Pembs
Pantsaison — Monington, Pembs
Pantstreimon — Llandysul, Cards
Pant-y-betws — Betws Ifan, "
Pant-y-deri — Llanfair Nantgwyn, Pembs
Pant-yr-Lys — Llandugwydd, Cards
Pant-yr-Odyn — Troedyraur, "
Parc-y-prat — St. Dogmaels, Pembs
Penallt-y-Llyn — Clydai, "
Penbeili — Llangunllo, Cards
Penbryn — Penbryn, Cards
Penbuarth — Cenarth, Carms
Pengelly — Troedyraur, Cards
Pengwern — Cenarth, Carms
Penllwyn coch — Penboyr, "
Penrallt — Aberporth, Cards

Pentre — Maenordeifi, Pembs
Pentre Evan — Nevern, Pembs
Penwenallt — Llandugwydd, Cards
Pen-y-benglog — Meline, Pembs
Plas — Aberporth, Cards
Pontcynon — Melin, Pembs
Rhos-y-gilwen — Cilgerran, "
Rhyd-ar-benne — Llangeler, Carms
Rhyd-y-golomen — Llangrannog, Cards
Tredefed — Llantood, Pembs
Trefach — Llanfair Nantgwyn, Pembs
Trefigyn — Monington, Pembs
Tregamon — Nevern, "
Tregibby — Ferwig, Cards
Trewern — Nevern, Pembs
Troedyraur — Troedyraur, Cards
Troedyrhiw — Penbryn, "
Tywyn — Ferwig, "
Waun — Henllan, "
Waunifor — Llandysul. "
Wernfullbrook — Llandysilio-gogo, "

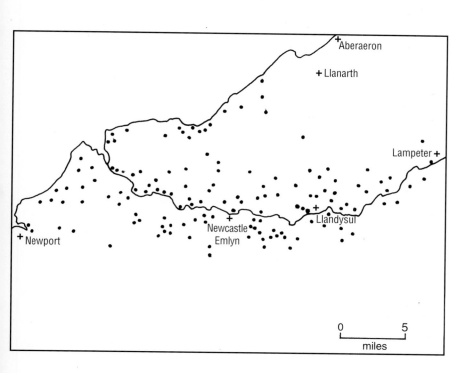

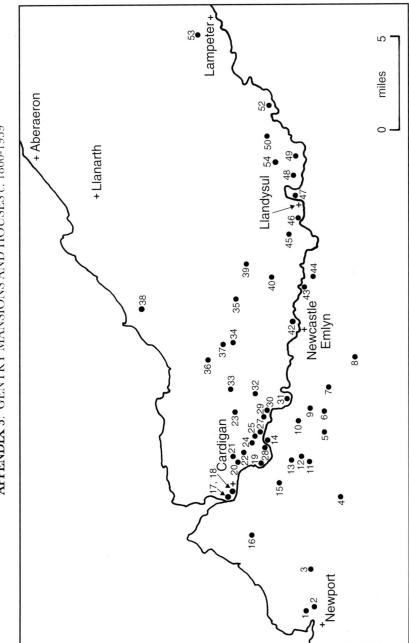

APPENDIX 3: GENTRY MANSIONS AND HOUSES c. 1800-1939

1 Berry Hill
2 Llwyngwair
3 Cwmgloyn
4 Pantyderi
5 Cilwendeg
6 Ffynone
7 Lancych
8 Glaspant
9 Clynfyw
10 Pentre
11 Cilrhiwe
12 Rhosygilwen
13 Glandovan
14 Castle Malgwyn
15 Bridell
16 Pantsaison
17 Castle Green
18 The Priory

19 Coedmore
20 Plas Llangoedmore
21 Treforgan
22 Cilbronne
23 Pantgwyn
24 Glanhelyg
25 Glanolmarch
26 Pencraig
27 Glanarberth
28 Penlan
29 Manereifed
30 Llwynduris
31 Stradmore
32 Blaenpant
33 Noyadd Trefawr
34 Troedyraur
35 Gwernant

36 Tŷ Llwyd
37 Glanmadeni
38 Pigeonsford
39 Gernos
40 Bronwydd
41 Aberceri
42 Cilgwyn
43 Dôl-haidd
44 Llysnewydd
45 Blaendyffryn
46 Gilfachwen
47 Dôl-Llan
48 Llanfair
49 Waunifor
50 Bwlchbychan
52 Highmead
53 Falcondale
54 Alltyrodyn

BIBLIOGRAPHY

A. Primary Sources

1. *Manuscripts*

(a) Society of Antiquaries Library, Burlington House, London. A. W. Gould: A History of the Society of Antiquaries (Ms. vol. 678).

(b) Cardiff Public Library
Ms 4.4669

(c) Dyfed Archives Service
Aberystwyth Record Office
BRA/11/Alltyrodyn; Shipping Records.
Carmarthen Record Office
Carmarthenshire Quarter Sessions Files, Order Books; Aberglasney, Beckingsale, Cawdor, Coedmore, Cwmgwili, Derwydd, Dynevor, Enclosure Awards and Maps, John Francis, Museum, Plas Llanstephan, Talardd, Trant, and Turnpike—deeds, documents and manuscripts.
Haverfordwest Record Office
Francis Green, F. Jones—Pembrokeshire Land Tax 1786, Lewis of Henllan, Pembrokeshire Quarter Sessions Order Books, Pentre, Robertson Williams, and Williams—deeds, documents and manuscripts.

(d) National Library of Wales, Aberystwyth
Additional and miscellaneous mss; Brawdy, Bronwydd, Cardiganshire Quarter Sessions Order Books, Cilgwyn, Clynfyw, Cwmgwili, Cwrtmawr, John Davies, Dolaucothi, T. I. Ellis, D. Roy Evans, Evans George, Falcondale, Great Sessions (Wales) Files, Highmead, Howell (Glaspant), Lancych, A. Lewis and Evans, Llanstephan, Llwynduris, Llwyngwair, Llysnewydd, Lucas, Morgan Richardson, Noyadd Trefawr, Ottley, Owen-Colby, Penally, Penboyr (co. Carm) Vestry Book 1748-80, Picton Castle, Plas Llangoedmore, Poyston, D. Pryse Williams, St David's Diocese, Ticehurst Wyatt (Gwernant), Trevecka Letters, Tŷ Llwyd (E. B. Wood, Journal), Sir John Williams, F.C. Winchester (Hove).

(e) Public Record Office
Crown Office Dedimus Dedimus Books 1738-63, 1763-1835; Hearth Tax Returns, Land Tax Returns

(f) Dr Williams Library, Gordon Square, London
John Evans List of Dissenting Ministers and Causes. Ms. 38.4.

(g) Private Collections
Llysnewydd Farm Accounts Book, Morgan Richardson Diary, R. Stedman Lewis Letters

2. *Printed*

(a) Anonymous, editorial and news items in newspapers and periodicals—
The Annual Register 1809, *Blackwood's Magazine* 1830, *The British Press* 1813, *The Cambrian Journal* 1850-60, *Cambrian Register* 1795, *Cardigan and Tivyside Advertiser*, *Carmarthen Journal*, *Church Times*, *Cymru Fydd*, *Yr Efangylydd*, *Y Genhinen*, *Gentleman's Magazine*, *Yr Haul*, *The Llanelly Telegraph*, *The London Magazine* or *The Gentleman's Monthly Intelligence*, *Seren Gomer*, *Sporting Magazine*, *Tarian y Gweithiwr*, *Y Traethodydd*, *The Welshman*, *Welsh Outlook*.

(b) Adam's: *Index Villaris or an Exact Register*, 1700.
Allestree, R.: *The Gentleman's Calling*, 1659.
Ancient Monuments: *Report of the Pembrokeshire Association for the Preservation of...*, 1907.
Asylum: *Joint Counties' Asylum (Carmarthen) Report*, 1886.

Barber, J. T.: *A Tour Throughout South Wales*, 1803.
Bateman, J.: *The Great Landowners of Great Britain and Ireland*, 1876.
Blome: *Brittania or Geographical Description of the Kingdoms of England, Scotland and Ireland...*, 1677.
Bowen, E.: *An Accurate Map...*, 1763.
Brown, J.: *An Estimate of the Manners and Principles of the Times*, 1757-58.

Carlisle, N.: *Endowed Grammar Schools in England and Wales*, 1818.
Cawdor, Lord: *Address to the Freeholders of the County of Pembroke*, 1829.
Celtic Researches on the Origins, Traditions and Languages of the Ancient Britons, 1804.
Chamberlayne, E.: *Anglia Notitiae*, 2nd ed., 1707.
Country Gentleman's Lawyer and Farmers' Complete Law Library..., 1810.
Cresset, J.: 'Of the Charterhouse'. A pamphlet,1662.

Davies, W.: *A General View of the Agriculture... of South Wales*, i, 1814.
Davis, D.: *Telyn Dewi*, 1824.
Doddridge, P.: *Memoirs...*, 1766.

Edwards, T. (Twm o'r Nant): *Gardd o Gerddi neu Gasgliad Caniadau*, 1790.
Ellis, T. F.: *Report upon the Borough of Adpar*, 1832.
Enumerators' Returns (Census): 1841, 1851, 1861, 1871.
Episcopate: *The Inexpediency, Folly and Sin of a Barbarian Episcopate in a Christian Principality*, 1858.

Fenton, R.: *A Historical Tour through Pembrokeshire*, 1811.
Friendly Societies: *Instructions for the Establishment of Friendly Societies with a Form of Rules and Tables...*, 1835.

Gambold, W.: *A Welsh Grammar...*, 1724.

Hansard: Parliamentary Debates.

Hassall, C.: *A General View of the Agriculture of the County of Carmarthen*, 1794.

Hassall, C.: *A General View of the Agriculture of the County of Pembroke*, 1794.

Hywel Dda: *Cyvreithiau Hywel dda . . . seu Leges Wallicae*, 1793.

Johnes, A. J.: *An Essay on the Causes of Dissent in the Principality of Wales*, 1832.

Jones, E.: *Musical and Poetical Relics of the Welsh Bards*, 1784.

Lewis, S.: *A Topographical History of Wales*, 2 vols., 1833.

Lhuyd, E.: *Archaeologia Brittania*, 1727.

Lloyd, T. and Rev. Turnor: *A General View of Agriculture in the County of Cardigan*, 1794.

Llwyd, D.: *Gwaith Prydyddawl y diweddar Barch. Dafydd Llwyd . . .*, 1785.

Meyrick, S. R.: *History and Antiquities of the County of Cardigan*, 1808.

Miller, J.: *The Origins and Distinctions of Rank and Society*, 1771.

Morgan, T.: *An Essay in Draining . . .*, 1849.

Morgan, T.: *An Essay on the Systems of Agriculture and the Rotation of Crops . . .*, 1852.

Morris, L.: *Plans of Harbours . . .*, 1748.

Oldfield, T. H. B.: *An Entire and Complete History of the Boroughs of Great Britain*, ii, 1794.

Owen, George: *Description of Pembrokeshire*, (ed.) H. Owen, 1908.

Paley, W.: *Reasons for Contentment*, 1781.

Phillips, Sir T.: *Wales, the language, social condition, moral character . . . in relation to education*, 1849.

Prichard, T. J. Ll.: *Welsh Minstrelsy*, 1824.

Pughe, W. O.: *A Dictionary of the Welsh Language*, 1832.

Rees, T.: *A Topographical . . . History of South Wales*, 1815.

Reports of Royal Commissions and Select Committees:

1834: *Report of the Commissioners into the administration of the Poor Law*.

1835: *. . . on Ecclesiastical Revenues in England and Wales*.

1844: *. . . on Commons' Inclosure*.

1844: *. . . for England and South Wales (Turnpike Trusts)*.

1847: *. . . of Inquiry into the State of Education in Wales*.

1853: *. . . Universities of Oxford and Cambridge*.

1864: *. . . on Public Schools*, 1864.

1874: *Returns of Owners of Land, 1873*, ii, Wales, 1875.

1881: *. . . On Higher Education in Wales*, 1.

1887: *. . . Tithes*.

1888: *. . . Markets and Tolls*.

1893-94: . . . *Agricultural Labourers in Wales*, 1893-94.
1894-95: . . . *on Land in Wales and Monmouthshire. Evidence.*
1896: . . . *on Land in Wales and Monmouthshire. Report.*
1907: . . . *Welsh Church (St Davids)*, 1907.

Saunders, E.: *A View of the State of Religion in the Diocese of St David's*, 1721.
Slater's Directory, 1868.
Smith, T.: *De Republica Anglorum*, 1582.
Singer, J.: *A New Map of Cardiganshire . . . gentleman's seats, etc, printed for
    J. Cary*, 1803.
Smith, A.: *Wealth of Nations*, 1776.
Statutes of the Realm.
Stephens, E. L.: *A Review of the National Advantages to be derived by the
    Improvement of Fishguard Harbour*, 1837.
Walters, J.: *An English and Welsh Dictionary*, 1815.
Webley-Parry, E.: *David Lloyd of Hafod Fach*, 1849.
Webley-Parry, E.: *An Epitome of Anglican Church History* [n.d.].
Williams, R.: *An Analysis of the Medicinal Waters of Llandrindod* [n.d.].
Woods and Forests: The Eleventh Report . . . Woods and Forests, 1792.

B. Secondary Sources

1. Books

Anon: *A Tour in Wales . . .*, 1806.
Ashdown, C. H.: *British Costume through Nineteen Centuries* [n.d.].
Aslet, C.: *The Last Country Houses*, 1982.

Baronets, Roll of the . . ., 1960.
Bowen, I.: *The Statutes of Wales*, 1908.
Bowen, I.: *The Great Enclosures of Common Lands in Wales*, 1914.
Briggs, A.: *The Age of Improvement*, 1979.
Burke, E.: *Selections from his Political Writings and Speeches* [n.d.].
Burke, J. B.: *A Visitation of the Seats of Arms of the Noblemen, Gentlemen . . .*, i, 1853.
Burke, J. B.: *Peerage, Baronetage and Knightage*, 1893.
Burke, J. B.: *Landed Gentry*, 1906.

Cannadine, D.: *The Decline and Fall of the British Aristocracy*, 1990.
Cannon, G.: *The Letters of Sir William Jones*, i, ii, 1969.
Carpenter, S. C.: *Church and People, 1789-1889*, 1933.
Carr, R.: *English Fox Hunting*, 1976.
Chadwick, O.: *The Victorian Church*, i, ii, 1971.
Clark, G. K.: *The Making of Victorian England*, 1962.

Clement, M.: *Correspondence and Minutes of the SPCK relating to Wales, 1699-1740*, 1952.

Colley, L.: *Britons Forging the Nation 1707-1837*, 1992.

Colvin, H. M.: *A Biographical Dictionary of British Architects, 1600 to 1840*, 1978.

Cragoe, M.: *An Anglican Aristocracy—the Moral Economy of the Landed Estate in Carmarthenshire, 1832-1895*, 1996.

Curl, J. S.: *A Celebration of Death . . . an Introduction to some of the Buildings, Monuments and Settings of Funerary Architecture in the Western European Tradition*, 1980.

Davies, D.: *The Ancient Celtic Church of Wales* [n.d.].

Davies, E.: *Hanes Plwyf Llangunllo*, 1906.

Davies, E. T.: *Religion and Society in Wales in the Nineteenth Century*, 1981.

Davies, J. H.: *The Morris Letters*, i, ii, 1905.

Davies, W. J.: *Hanes Plwyf Llandyssul*, 1896.

Davis, T.: *The Architecture of John Nash*, 1960.

Deane, P. and Cole, W. A.: *British Economic Growth*, 1967.

Ditchfield, P.: *The Old English Squire*, 1912.

Dictionary of Welsh Biography.

Dineley, T. (ed).: *Official Progress of the First Duke of Beaufort . . . Wales, 1684*, 1888.

Dobree, B. (ed).: *Letters of P. D. Stanhope, 4th Earl of Chesterfield*, iii, 1932.

Dodd, A. H.: *Studies in Stuart Wales*, 1952.

Dowell, S.: *Taxes in England* [n.d.].

Dunbabin, J. P. D.: *Rural Discontent in Nineteenth Century Britain*, 1974.

Eastlake, C. L.: *A History of the Gothic Revival in England*, 1872.

Edwards, O. M.: *Gwilym Marles (Cyfres y Fil)*, 1905.

Eliot, George: *Silas Marner*, [n.d.].

Ellis, A. J.: *Speeches and Letters by the late T. E. Ellis*, 1912.

Ellis, T. I.: *Cofiant Thomas Edward Ellis*, i, ii, 1944.

Emden, C. S.: *Selected Speeches on the Constitution*, ii, 1939.

Encyclopaedia Brittanica, 1937.

Evans, E. D.: *A History of Wales, 2, 1600-1815*, 1976.

Evans, E. J.: *The Contentious Tithe—The Tithe Problem and English Agriculture, 1750-1850*, 1976.

Evans, G. E.: *Lloyd Letters 1754-59*, 1908.

Evans, H.: *Cwm Eithin*, 1943.

Evans, H. Tobit: *Rebecca and her Daughters*, 1910.

Evans, J. G.: *Aros Mae*, 1971.

Evans, W. E.: *Dwy Farwnad Arobryn yn Eisteddfod Llandysil*, 1877.

Flenley, R.: *Calendar of the Register of the Council of the Marches of Wales, 1569-71*, 1916.

Foster, I. and Alcock, L. (eds): *Culture and Environment*, 1963.

Foster, J.: *Alumni Oxonienses, 1500-1714, 1715-1886*, 6 vols, 1888-1892.
Franklin, J.: *The Englishman's Country House and its Plan, 1835-1914*, 1981.
Fraser, D.: *The Evolution of the British Welfare State*, 1973.

Gash, N.: *Politics in the Age of Peel*, 1953.
Y Genhinen Eisteddfodol, Awst 1902.
Girouard, M.: *Life in the English Country House*, 1978.
Girouard, M.: *The Victorian Country House*, 1979.
Girouard, M.: *The Return to Camelot*, 1981.
Gleason, J.: *The Justice of the Peace in England 1558-1640*, 1969 ed.
Glynne, Sir S. R.: *The Older Welsh Churches, 1824-74*, 1903.

Hammond, J. L. and B.: *The Village Labourer*, 1912, 1966 ed.
Harford, J.S.: *The Life of Bishop Burgess*, 1841.
Hill, G.B.: *Memoirs of the Life of Bishop Burgess . . .*, 1900.
Hope, Deaconess E.: *Llangranog and the Pigeonsford Family*, 1934.
Horn, P.: *The Tithe War in Pembrokeshire*, 1982.
Hoskins, W. G. and Finberg, H. P. R.: *Devonshire Studies*, 1952.
Howell, D. W.: *Land and People in Nineteenth Century Wales*, 1976.
Howell, D. W.: *Patriarchs and Parasites, the Gentry of South West Wales in the Eighteenth Century*, 1986.
Hughes, G. H.: *Bywyd a Gwaith Iaco ap Dewi, 1648-1722*, 1953.

James, A. J. and Thomas, J. E.: *A History of the Parliamentary Representation of Wales, 1800-1979*, 1981.
James, J.: *Hanes Eglwys Annibynol Saron, Llangeler*, 1937.
James, J. R.: *Yr Amaethydd Cymreig*, 1869.
Jenkins, D.: *The Agricultural Community in South West Wales at the turn of the Twentieth Century*, 1971.
Jenkins, G. H.: *Literature, Religion and Society in Wales 1660-1730*, 1978.
Jenkins, G. H.: *The Foundations of Modern Wales 1642-1780*, 1987.
Jenkins, J. G.: *The Welsh Woollen Industry*, 1969.
Jenkins, P.: *The Making of a Ruling Class—the Glamorgan Gentry 1640-1790*, 1983.
Jenkins, R. T.: *Hanes Cymru yn y Bedwaredd Ganrif ar Bymtheg*, 1933.
John, A. H.: *The Industrial Developments of South Wales*, 1950.
Jones, B.: *Follies and Grottoes*, 1974.
Jones, D.: *The Welsh Church and Nationality*, [n.d.].
Jones, D. E.: *Hanes Plwyfi Llangeler and Penboyr*, 1899.
Jones, D. J. V.: *Before Rebecca*, 1973.
Jones, D. J. V.: *Crime, Protest, Community and Police in Nineteenth Century Britain*, 1982.
Jones, E. D.: *Gwaith Lewis Glyn Cothi*, 1953.
Jones, E. Pan: *Oes Gofion*, [n.d.].
Jones, Francis: *Historic Carmarthenshire Houses and their Families*, 1987.

Jones, I.G.: *The Dynamics of Politics in Nineteenth Century Wales*, 1971.
Jones, J.: *Crwth Dyffryn Cletwr*, 1848.
Jones, J. M. and Morgan, W.: *Y Tadau Methodistaidd*, i, 1895.
Jones, M. H.: *The Trevecka Letters*, 1932.
Jones, T. I. J.: *Acts of Parliament Concerning Wales 1714-1901*, 1959.
Jowitt, Earl (ed.): *Dictionary of English Law*, 1959.

Kelly, F. M. and Schwabe, R.: *A Short History of Costume and Armour, ii, 1485-1800*, 2nd ed. 1972.
Kerr, R.: *The Gentleman's Country House, or How to Plan English Residences from the Parsonage to the Palace*, 1864.

Lampson, G. L.: *Life in the Country*, 1948.
Laws, E.: *A History of Little England beyond Wales*, 1888.
Lees-Milne, J.: *Earls of Creation*, 1962.
Lewis, E. A.: *The Welsh Port Books 1550-1603*, 1927.
Lewis, Saunders: *A School of Welsh Augustans*, 1924.
Lewis, Saunders: *Meistri'r Canrifoedd*, (gol.) Geraint Gruffydd, 1972.
Linnard, W.: *Welsh Woods and Forests*, 1982.
Lloyd, J. E. (ed.): *History of Carmarthenshire*, ii, 1939.
Lloyd, Lady K.: *The Lords Marcher of Kemes*, 1930.
Lloyd, T.: *The Lost Houses of Wales*, 1986.

Macaulay, T. B.: *History of England*, i, 1861.
Malcolmson, R. W.: *Popular Recreations in Rural England, 1700-1850*, 1973.
Marshall, J. D.: *The Old Poor Law 1795-1834*, 1968.
Megarry, R. E.: *The Law of Real Property*, 2nd ed. 1955.
Mingay, G. E.: *English Landed Society*, 1963.
Mingay, G. E.: *The Gentry, the Rise and Fall of a Ruling Class*, 1976.
Mingay, G. E.: *The Agricultural Revolution—Changes in Agriculture 1650-1850*, 1977.
Mingay, G. E.: *Rural Life in Victorian England*, 1977.
Moir, E.: *The Justice of the Peace*, 1969.
Moore, D. (ed.): *Wales in the Eighteenth Century*, 1976.
Morgan, E.: *John Elias, Life and Letters*, 1973.
Morgan, K. O.: *Wales in British Politics*, 2nd ed., 1970.
Morgan, P.: *The Eighteenth Century Renaissance*, 1981.
Morgan Richardson, C.E.D.: *Henry Vaughan*, 1902.
Morley, J.: *The Life of Richard Cobden*, 1903 ed.
Morris, J. H. and Williams, L. J.: *The South Wales Coal Industry 1841-75*, 1955.
Munsche, P. B.: *Gentlemen and Poachers, The English Game Laws 1670-1831*, 1981.
Myvyrian Archaiology, 1801.

Namier, Sir L.: *The Structure of Politics at the Accession of George III*, i, 1929.
Namier, Sir L. and Brooke, J. (eds): *The House of Commons 1754-90*, 1964.

Needham, A.: *How to Study an Old Church*, 1944.
Nicholas, T.: *Annals and Antiquities . . . Wales*, 2vv, 1872.

Oman, C.: *Memories of Victorian Oxford*, 2nd ed., 1941.
Ottewill, D.: *The Edwardian Garden*, 1989.
Oxford, Victorian History of the Counties of England: Oxfordshire, 1954.
Owen, G. D.: *Ysgolion a Cholegau yr Annibynwyr*, 1939.
Owen, H.: *Additional Morris Letters*, 2vv, 1949.
Owen, H. (ed.): *Description of Pembrokeshire by George Owen of Henllys*, 1906.

Parry, T.: *Hanes Llenyddiaeth Gymraeg hyd 1900*, 1944.
Parry-Jones, D.: *Welsh Country Upbringing*, 2nd ed., 1949.
Perkin, H.: *The Origins of Modern English Society 1780-1888*, 1969.
Phillips, J. R.: *History of Cilgerran*, 1867.
Phillips, J. R.: *Memoirs of the Civil Wars in Wales . . .*, 2vv., 1874.
Phillips, G.: *Llofruddiaeth Shadrach Lewis*, 1986.
Phillips, J. R. S.: *The Justice of the Peace in Wales and Monmouthshire*, 1975.
Plumb, J. H.: *The First Four Georges*, 1956.
Plumb, J. H.: *Sir Robert Walpole*, 1956.
Plumb, J. H.: *England in the Eighteenth Century*, 1961.
Potter, H.: *A Historical Introduction to English Law*, 3rd ed., 1949.
Poynter, J. R.: *Society and Pauperism, English Ideas on Poor Relief 1795-1834*, 1969.

Rees, W.: *An Historical Atlas of Wales*, 1951.
Rees, W.: *The Union of England and Wales*, 1937.
Rhys, J. and Jones, D. B.: *The Welsh People*, 1906.
Richard, H.: *Letters and Essays on Wales*, 1884.
Roberts, D.: *Victorian Origins of the British Welfare State*, 1960.
Roberts, G. M.: *Y Pêr Ganiedydd*, ii, 1958.
Rudé, G.: *The Crowd in History*, 1964.
Ruffer, J. G.: *The Big Shots—Edwardian Shooting Parties*, 1978.

Scholes, P. A. (ed.): *The Oxford Companion to Music*, 1975.
Smiles, S.: *Self Help*, 1859.
Smith, P.: *Houses of the Welsh Countryside*, 1975.
Steegman, J.: *A Survey of Portraits in Welsh Houses, ii, South Wales*, 1962.
Stephenson, Sir E.: *Clerks to the Courts, 1760-1960*, 1961.
Stone, L. and J. C. F.: *An Open Elite? England 1540-1880*, 1986.
Stuart-Jones, E. H.: *The Last Invasion of Britain*, 1950.
Suggett, R.: *John Nash, Architect-Pensaer*, 1995.
Summerson, J.: *John Nash*, 1936.
Sutherland, L. S. and Mitchell, L. G. M. (eds): *The History of the University of Oxford, V. The Eighteenth Century*, 1986.
Sykes, B.: *Church and State in England in the Eighteenth Century*, 1934.

Thomas, Sir J. Lynn: *The Key of All Wales*, 1932.
Thomas, W.: *The Tithe Movement in Wales*, 1891.
Thompson, F. M. L.: *Landed Society in the Nineteenth Century*, 1963.
Trollope, A.: *The Vicar of Bullhampton*, [n.d.].
Turner, M.: *Enclosures in Britain 1750-1830*, 1984.

Vaughan, H. M.: *The South Wales Squires*, 1926.
Venn, J. and J. A.: *Alumni Cantabrigienses*, 1922.
Vincent, J. E.: *The Land Question in South Wales*, 1897.

Wagner, A.: *English Genealogy*, 1983.
Walford, E.: *County Families*, 1907.
Walpole, H.: *Letters*, vi, 1859 ed.
Watson, J. S.: *The Reign of George III*, 1960.
Webb, S. and B.: *The Parish and the County*, i, 1906.
Who's Who in Wales, 1920.
Williams, A. H.: *John Wesley in Wales 1759-90*, 1971.
Williams, B.: *The Whig Supremacy 1714-60*, 1937 re-ed. by C. H. Stuart, 1985.
Williams, Dd.: *The Rebecca Riots—A Study in Agrarian Discontent*, 1955.
Williams, Dd.: *Modern Wales*, 2nd ed., 1957.
Williams, G.: *Religion, Language and Nationality in Wales*, 1979.
Williams, G.A.: *The Search for Beulah Land*, 1980.
Williams, P.: *The Council in the Marches of Wales under Elizabeth I*, 1958.
Ward, W. R.: *The English Land Tax in the Eighteenth Century*, 1953.
Williams, W. R.: *The Parliamentary History of the Principality of Wales . . . 1545-1895*, 1895.
Williams-Jones, K.: *A Calendar of the Merionethshire Q.S. Rolls 1763-65 with a Critical and Historical Introduction*, 1967.
Willis, P.: *Charles Bridgeman and the English Landscape Garden*, 1977.
Wilson, C.: *England's Apprenticeship, 1603-1763*, 1965.
Wood, C.: *The Age of Chivalry*, 1970.
Wynne, Ellis: *Gweledigeutheu'r Bardd Cwsc 1703*, 1948 ed.

2. Articles

Anon: 'Atgofion am Athrofa Ffrwdfâl', *Y Tyst*, 30/11/1883.
   ” : 'The Obsequies of Squire Thomas', *Red Dragon*, May 1884.
   ” : 'Review of Emily Prichard "Cardigan Priory in the Olden Days"', *Arch. Camb.*, 1904.
   ” : 'Review of H. M. Vaughan: The South Wales Squires. The Welsh Outlook 1926', *Manchester Guardian*, 18/5/1926.
Baker-Jones, D. L.: 'Christian Sepulchral Monuments in and around Carmarthenshire', *Carm. Antiq.*, iv, 3, 4, 1963.

idem: 'Ffynone, Pembrokeshire—A Country House and its Occupants', *T.H.S.C.*, i, 1965.

idem: 'Notes on the Orielton Chancery Proceedings', *N.L.W.J.*, xv, 3, 4, 1968.

idem: 'The Carmarthen Eisteddfod of 1867', *Carms. Historian*, ix, 1972.

idem: 'Pantglas and the Jones Families', *ibid*, xii, 1975.

idem: 'C. E. D. Morgan Richardson', *Ceredigion*, iii, 2, 1977.

Bartrum, P. C.: 'Pedigrees of the Welsh Tribal Patriarchs', *N.L.W.J.*, xiii, 2, 1963.

Best, G. F. A.: 'Popular Protestantism in Victorian Britain,' in R. A. Robson (ed.), *Essays in Honour of G. Kitson Clark*, 1967.

Briggs, A.: 'Middle Class Consciousness in English Politics 1780-1846', *P. and P.*, ix, 1946.

Buck, A.: Dress as a Social Record, *Folk Life*, vol. 14, 1976.

Caröe, A. D. R.: Report on the Old Church of Maenordeifi, 31/8/1950.

Charles, B. G.: 'The Highmead Dairy 1778-97', *Ceredigion*, v. i, 1964.

Clay, C.: 'Marriage Inheritance and the Rise of Large Estates in England, 1600-1815', *Ec.H.R.*, x, 21, 1968.

Colyer, R. J.: 'The Edwinsford Estate in the Early Nineteenth Century', *B.B.C.S.*, xxvi, ii, 1975.

idem: 'A Landed Estate in Decline, 1800-1930', *Ceredigion*, ix, i, 1980.

idem: 'Aspects of Land Occupation in Nineteenth Century Cardiganshire,' *T.H.S.C.*, 1981.

idem: 'The Gentry and County in Nineteenth Century Cardiganshire,' *W.H.R.*, 10, 4, 1981.

idem: 'Crop Husbandry in Wales before the Onset of Mechanisation', *Folk Life*, 21, 1982-83.

Crawley, C. W.: 'Economic Change in England and Europe', *New Cambridge Modern History*, ix, 1965.

Davies, D. S.: 'Cardiganshire and the Inns of Court to 1850', *Camb. L.R.*, 1976.

Davies, G. G.: 'Addysg Elfennol yn Sir Aberteifi 1890-1902', *Ceredigion*, iv, 4, 1963.

Davies, J.: 'The Alltyrodyn Manuscripts', *J.W.B.S.*, July 1935.

Davies, J. Ll.: 'The Diary of a Cardiganshire Farmer', 1870-1900, *W.J.Ag.*, x, 1934.

Derfel, R. J.: 'Tai'r Gweithwyr', *Y Beirniad*, 4, 1862-63.

Ellis, E. Ll.: 'Some Aspects of the Early History of the University of Wales', *T.H.S.C.*, ii, 1967.

Evans, E. J.: 'Noddwyr y Beirdd yn Sir Benfro', *T.H.S.C.*, 1972-73.

Evans, G. E.: 'Carmarthenshire Schools', *T.Cms.Antiq.Soc.*, 16, 1921.

Evans, J.: 'The Cryngae Hounds', *ibid*, 23-24, 1932-33.

Evans, M. C. S.: 'Coedmore Forge, Llechryd' in *Carmarthenshire Studies* (eds), T. Barnes and N. Yates, 1974.

idem: 'Pioneers of Estate Mapping in Carmarthenshire', *Carms. Antiq.*, xxiii, 1977.

Evans, W. G.: 'The Aberdare Report and Cardiganshire', *Ceredigion*, ix, 3, 1982.

Glassey, L. J. K. and Landau, N.: 'The Commission of the Peace in the Eighteenth Century, A New Source', *B.I.H.R.*, xlv, 1972.

Green, F.: 'Pedigrees of South West Wales Families', *W.W.H.R.*, ii, 1913.
idem: 'Pembrokeshire Parsons', *ibid.*, vi, 1916.

Griffith, J.: 'Rees Jones 1797-1844', *Cymru*, vii, 1894.

Griffiths, G. M.: 'A Visitation of the Archdeaconry of Carmarthen 1710', *N.L.W.J.*, xxviii, 1974.

Habakkuk, H. J.: 'England' ch. 1 in *The European Nobility in the Eighteenth Century*, A. Goodwin (ed.), 1953.
idem: 'English Landownership 1680-1740', *Ec.H.R.*, x, i, 1940.

Howell, D. W.: 'The Agricultural Labourer in Nineteenth Century Wales', *W.H.R.*, 6, 3, 1973.
idem: 'The Impact of Railways on Agricultural Development in Nineteenth Century Wales', *W. H.R.*, 7, 1974.
idem: 'The Pembrokeshire Gentry in the Eighteenth Century' in *Carms. Studies* (eds) T. Barnes and N. Yates, 1974.
idem: 'Landlords and Estate Management in Wales' in *The Agrarian History of England and Wales*—vol. 5 part 2 (ed.) J. Thirsk, 1985.

Howells, B.: 'Social and Agrarian Change in Early Modern Cardiganshire', *Ceredigion*, vol. vii, nos, 3, 4, 1974-75.

Howells, J. M.: 'The Land Question', *Red Dragon*, v, 1854.

Howells, W.: 'The Library of Edward Richard, Ystrad Meurig', *Ceredigion*, ix, 3, 1982.

Hughes, E.: 'The Eighteenth Century Estate Agent' in H. A. Cronne, T. W. Moody and D. B. Quinn (eds), *Essays in British and Irish History*, 1949.

Huws, D.: 'Noyadd Trefawr Deeds and Documents', *NLWJ*, x, 4, 1962.

James, B. Ll.: 'The Great Landowners of Wales in 1873', *ibid.*, xiv, 3, 1966.

Jarman, A. O. H.: 'Cymru'n Rhan o Loegr 1485-1900' yn *Seiliau Hanesyddol Plaid Cymru*, (gol) *DML*, 1950.

Jenkins, G. H.: 'Bywiogrwydd Crefyddol a Llenyddol Dyffryn Teifi 1689-1740', *Ceredigion*, vol. viii, 1979.

Jenkins, J. G.: 'The Maritime Heritage of Some Southern Ceredigion Villages', *Ceredigion*, ix, 2, 1981.

Jenkins, P.: 'Jacobites and Freemasons in Eighteenth Century Wales', *WHR*, 9, 1979.

Jones, D. J. V.: 'The Second Rebecca Riots, A Study of Poaching on the River Wye', *Llafur*, vol. 2, no. 1, 1976.
idem: 'The Poacher, A Study in Victorian Crime and Protest', *Hist. Jnl*, 22, (4), 1979.

Jones, D. S.: 'Dyffryn Teifi', *Y Geninen*, 1901.

Jones, E. W.: 'The First Carmarthenshire Agricultural Society', *Carm. Antiq.*, vii, 1961.

Jones, F.: 'An Approach to Welsh Geneaology', *THSC*, 1948.

idem: 'Report on Welsh Mss in the College of Arms 1957', (unpublished typed copy in CRO).

idem: 'The Vaughans of Golden Grove', *THSC*, i, 1960.

idem: 'The Old Families of South West Wales', *Ceredigion*, iv, 1960.

idem: 'The Society of Sea Serjeants,' *THSC*, i, 1967.

idem: 'Walters of Perthgereint', *Ceredigion*, iv, x, 1969.

idem: 'The Sheriffs of the County of Pembroke 1541-1972', (ed.) D. Miles [n.d.].

idem: 'Lloyd of Cilciffeth', *Pembs. Hist.*, 4, 1972.

idem: 'Blaenbylan, Chronicle of a Minor Gentry House', *Ceredigion*, vii, 1974-75.

idem: 'The Old Families of Wales', in D. Moore (ed.), *Wales in the Eighteenth Century*, 1976.

idem: 'Lloyd of Gilfachwen, Cilgwyn and Coedmore', *Ceredigion*, viii, i, 1976.

idem: 'Bowen of Pentre Ifan and Llwyngwair', *Pembs. Hist.*, 6, 1979.

Jones, I. G.: 'The Liberation Society and Welsh Politics 1844 to 1865', *WHR*, vol. 1, 2, 1961.

Jones, I. G.: 'The Elections of 1865 and 1868 in Wales with special reference to Cardiganshire', *THSC*, i, 1964.

idem: 'Cardiganshire Politics in Mid-Nineteenth Century Cardiganshire', *Ceredigion*, v, i, 1964.

idem: 'Language and Community in Nineteenth Century Wales', in D. Smith (ed.), *A People and Proletariat*, 1980.

Jones, J. (Machynlleth): 'Hen Emynwr, Mr Thomas Jones, Rhiw Siôn, ger Emlyn', *Cenad Hedd*, 1888, viii, 86, t. 50.

Jones, J. Graham: 'Forming Plaid Cymru, Laying the Foundations', 1923-26, *N.L.W.J.*, xii, 4, 1982.

Jones, M. H.: 'The Letters of Arthur James Johnes', *NLWJ*, x, 1957-8, xiv, 2, 1965.

Jones, R. J. (Aberdâr): 'John Thomas, Pontsiaen, 1775-1836', *Cymru*, vi, 1893.

Jones, R. T.: 'Agweddau ar Ddiwylliant Ymneilltuwyr', *THSC*, ii, 1963.

idem: 'The Origins of the Disestablishment Campaign', *JHSChW*, 25, 1970.

Jones, W. R. O.: 'The Contribution of Welshmen to the Administration of India', *THSC*, ii, 1970.

Lewis. T. H.: 'The Justice of the Peace in Wales', *THSC*, 1943-44.

Lewis, W. J.: 'Labour in Mid Cardiganshire in the Early Nineteenth Century', *Ceredigion*, iv, 4, 1963.

Linnard, W.: 'Thomas Johnes of Hafod—Pioneer in Upland Afforestation in Wales', *Ceredigion*, iv, 3, 1970.

Lloyd, D. T.: 'Cymru yn Saesneg', *THSC*, ii, 1966.

Lloyd, T. A.: 'The Georgian Period in Welsh Building', *Arch. Camb.*, vol. cvi, 1957.

Machin, G. I. T.: 'Catholic Emancipation as an Issue in North Wales Politics 1825-29', *THSC*, 1962.

Meyler, L. J.: 'Wesley in Pembrokeshire', *Pr. Wes. H. Soc.*, xxi, 8, 1939.

Morgan, K. O.: 'Cardiganshire Politics, The Liberal Ascendancy, 1885-1923', *Ceredigion*, v, 1967.

Morris, G. M.: 'The Land Question', *Red Dragon*, v, 1884.

O'Gorman: 'Electoral Deference in "Unreformed" England, 1760-1832', *J.M.L.*, no 56, 1984.

Owen, J. D.: *The Pattern of Politics in Eighteenth Century England*, Hist. Assoc. Pamphlet 10, 1962.

Parry, J. G.: 'Terfysgoedd Ŷd yng Ngogledd Cymru', *Trans. Caerns. Hist. Socy.*, 2, 1978.

Plumb, J. H.: 'Nobility and Gentry in the Early Nineteenth Century', *History Today*, v, 1955.
    idem: 'The Noble Houses of Eighteenth Century England' in *Men and Places*, 1963.

Powell, J. M.: 'Tithe Surveys and Schedules', *NLWJ*, xv, 1, 1969.

Prest, W.: 'Legal Education of the Gentry at the Inns of Court 1560-1640', *P. and P.*, 38, 1967.

Price, C.: 'Portable Theatres in Wales, 1843-1914', *NLWJ*, ix, i, 1955.

Price, C.: 'Polite Life in Eighteenth Century Wales', *The Welsh Anvil*, v, 1953.

Raglan Lord: 'The Origin of Vernacular Architecture' in I. Ll. Foster and L. Alcock, *op. cit.*

Rees, E.: 'An Introductory Survey of Eighteenth Century Welsh Libraries', *J.W.B.S.*, x, 1966-71.

Rees, O. G.: 'Connop Thirlwall, Liberal Anglican', *J.H.S.Ch.W.*, 19, 1964.

Rees, R. D.: 'Electioneering Ideals Current in South Wales, 1790-1832', *W.H.R.*, 2, 3, 1965.

Richards, M.: 'Iscoed uwch Hirwern in 1651', *Ceredigion*, iv, 4, 1963.

Richards, T.: 'The Puritan Visitation of Jesus College', *T.H.S.C.*, 1922-23.

Roberts, D. H. E.: 'Noddi Beirdd yng Ngheredigion', *Ceredigion*, viii, 1, 1972.

Roberts, G.: 'Political Affairs from 1536 to 1900', in J. E. Lloyd (ed.), *op cit.*

Roberts, G. M.: 'Y Morafiaid yn Neheudir Cymru', *N.L.W.J.*, xx, 3, 1978.

Roberts, H. P.: 'Nonconformist Academies in Wales', *T.H.S.C.*, 1928-29.

Roberts, P. R.: 'The Decline of the Welsh Squires in the Eighteenth Century', *N.L.W.J.*, xiii, 2, 1963.
    idem: 'The Act of Union in Welsh History', *T.H.S.C.*, 1972-73.

Roderick, G. W. and Stevens, M. D.: 'The Influence of Welsh Culture on Scientific and Technical Education in Wales in the Nineteenth Century', *T.H.S.C.*, 1981.

Scourfield, E.: 'Rhai o Gyfrinfeydd Iforaidd ac Odyddol—Sir Gaerfyrddin yn y Bedwaredd Ganrif ar Bymtheg', *Carms. Antiq.*, vii, 1971.

Sherrington, E.: 'Welsh Nationalism, the French Revolution and the Influence of the French Right 1880-1930' in D. Smith (ed.): *A People of the French Right, Essays in the History of Wales, 1780-1980*, 1960.

Stone, L.: 'The Educational Revolution in England', *P. and P.*, 24, 1964.

idem: 'Social Mobility in England', *P. and P.*, 33, 1969.

Thomas, C.: 'Land Surveyors in Wales, 1750-1850, The Matthews Family', *B.B.C.S.*, 32, 1985.

Thomas, G. T.: 'A Short Study in Welsh Genealogy, the Lineage of Griffith Jones of Llanddowror', *Arch. Camb.*, 2, 1923.

Thomas, J.: 'Gyda'r Camera', *Cymru*, 1895.

Thomas, P. D.G.: 'Society, Government and Politics' in D. Moore, *op. cit.*, 1976.

Thorne, R. G.: 'Herbert Lloyd of Carmarthen', *T.H.S.C.*, 1977.

Tucker, G. M.: 'The Old Slate Industry of Pembrokeshire and other parts of South Wales,' *N.L.W.J.*, xxiii, 2, 1983.

Vaughan, H. M.: 'Some Letters of Thomas Johnes of Hafod, 1794-1807', *Y Cymmrodor*, xxxv, 1925.

Williams, G.: 'Gomer, Sylfaenydd ein Llenyddiaeth Gyfnodol', *T.H.S.C.*, 1982.

Williams, L. J. and Jones, D.: 'The Wages of Agricultural Labourers in the Nineteenth Century—the Evidence from Glamorgan', *B.B.C.S.*, 29, 1982.

Williams, M. I.: 'The Port of Aberdyfi in the Eighteenth Century', *N.L.W.J.*, xviii, 1, 1973.

Williams, W. O.: 'The Survival of the Welsh Language after the Union of England and Wales . . . 1536-1642', *W.H.R.*, 2, 1964.

idem: 'The Social Order in Tudor Wales', *T.H.S.C.*, 1967.

Williams-Davies, J.: 'Merched y Gerddi—A Seasonal Migration of Female Labour from Rural Cardiganshire', *Folk Life*, 15, 1977.

3. Dissertations

Bowen, G.: Traddodiad Llenyddol Deau Ceredigion, 1640-1850 (MA, Wales, 1943).

Davies, J. Hd.: The Social Structure and Economy of South West Wales in the late Nineteenth Century (MA, Wales, 1967).

Humphreys, T. M.: Rural Society in Montgomeryshire in the Eighteenth Century (PhD, Wales, 1982).

Jones, A. W.: Agriculture and the Rural Community of Glamorgan, *circa* 1830-1896 (PhD, Wales, 1980).

Martin, J.O.: The Landed Estate in Glamorgan 1660-1760 (PhD, Cambridge, 1978).

Thomas, S. R.: The Diocese of St Davids in the Eighteenth Century (MA, Wales, 1983).

4. Oral Sources

The late Miss D. Lewis Bowen, Boncath.
The late Alderman Mrs M. Brynmor Williams, BEM, Felindre.
The late W. Beynon Davies, Aberystwyth.
The late Mr Esau Evans, Felindre.
The late Capt. C. Fitzwilliams, JP, DL, Old Cilgwyn, Newcastle Emlyn.
Dr E. L. James, UCW, Aberystwyth.
Mr B. H. Jones, Penrhiw-llan, Llandysul.
The late Major Francis Jones, Wales Herald Extraordinary, Carmarthen.
Mr T. Lewis, Penrhiw-pâl, Newcastle Emlyn.
The late Mr W. Hill Morris, MA, Kidwelly.

INDEX

Index entries followed by 'n' denote information in chapter footnotes which supplements that given in the main text. Bibliographical references are not indexes.
Where given names are not shown in the text for individual members of gentry families, e.g. 'Brigstocke of Blaenpant', the page references to the family or estate should also be consulted.